T0319729

ECONOMIC THEORY AND POLICY IN CONTEXT

ECONOMISTS OF THE TWENTIETH CENTURY

General Editors: Mark Perlman, *University Professor of Economics, Emeritus, University of Pittsburgh* and Mark Blaug, *Professor Emeritus, University of London, Professor Emeritus, University of Buckingham and Visiting Professor, University of Exeter*

This innovative series comprises specially invited collections of articles and papers by economists whose work has made an important contribution to economics in the late twentieth century.

The proliferation of new journals and the ever-increasing number of new articles make it difficult for even the most assiduous economist to keep track of all the important recent advances. By focusing on those economists whose work is generally recognized to be at the forefront of the discipline, the series will be an essential reference point for the different specialisms included.

A list of published and future titles in this series is printed at the end of this volume.

Economic Theory and Policy in Context

The Selected Essays of R.D. Collison Black

R.D. Collison Black

Emeritus Professor of Economics,
Queens University, Belfast, UK

ECONOMISTS OF THE TWENTIETH CENTURY

Edward Elgar
Aldershot, UK • Brookfield, US

Published by
Edward Elgar Publishing Limited
Gower House
Croft Road
Aldershot
Hants GU11 3HR
UK

Edward Elgar Publishing Company
Old Post Road
Brookfield
Vermont 05036
US

British Library Cataloguing in Publication Data
Black, R.D. Collison
  Economic Theory and Policy in Context:
  Selected Essays of R.D. Collison Black. –
  (Economists of the Twentieth Century
  Series)
  I. Title II. Series
  333.01

Library of Congress Cataloguing in Publication Data
Black, R.D. Collison.
  Economic theory and policy in context : the selected essays of
R.D. Collison Black / R.D. Collison Black.
    p. cm. — (Economists of the twentieth century)
  Includes bibliographical references and index.
  1. Economics—History. 2. Jevons, William Stanley, 1835–1882.
3. Ireland—Economic conditions. I. Title. II. Series.
  HB75.B633 1995
  330'.09—dc20   95–7196
                                                                        CIP

ISBN 1 85898 123 9

Printed and bound in Great Britain by
Biddles Ltd, Guildford and King's Lynn

To

Rosemary and Terence

Contents

Acknowledgements

The publishers wish to thank the following who have kindly given permission for the use of copyright material.

Blackwell Publishers for articles: 'Jevons, Marshall and the Utilitarian Tradition', *Scottish Journal of Political Economy*, **37**(1), February 1990, 5–17; 'Parson Malthus, the General and the Captain', *Economic Journal*, **LXXVII**, March 1967, 59–74.

The British Academy for article: 'Ralph George Hawtrey 1879–1975' in *Proceedings of the British Academy*, **LXIII**, 1977, 363–97.

Duke University Press for article: 'W.S. Jevons and the Foundation of Modern Economics', *History of Political Economy*, **4**(2), Fall 1972, 364–78.

Hermathena for article: 'The Irish Dissenters and Nineteenth-Century Political Economy', *Hermathena: A Trinity College Dublin Review*, CXXXV, Winter 1983, 120–37.

JAI Press for article: 'Dr Kondratieff and Mr. Hyde Clarke' in *Research in the History of Economic Thought and Methodology*, **9**, 1992, 35–58.

Journal of the History of Economic Thought for article: 'Political Economy and the Irish', *History of Economics Society Bulletin*, **IV**(1), 1982, 33–47. Invited lecture given to the Annual Meeting of the History of Economics Society, Duke University, May 23–26, 1982.

Oxford University Press for article: Smith's Contribution in Historical Perspective' in *The Market and the State: Essays in Honour of Adam Smith*, (eds T. Wilson and A.S. Skinner), 1976, Oxford: Clarendon Press, 42–72.

Professor Ian Steedman and the University of Manchester for articles: 'Transitions in Political Economy, 1862–1882: I, Economic Analysis'; 'Transitions in Political Economy, 1862–1882: II, Economic Policy'.

Routledge for article: 'Jevons's Contribution to the Teaching of Political Economy in Manchester and London' in *The Market for Political Economy*, (eds A. Kadish and K. Tribe), 1993, London: Routledge, 162–83.

Introduction

This book is made up from a selection of the papers on economic subjects which I have written over a period of almost 50 years. Although concerned with different aspects of economic theory and policy, these papers obviously share one common thread – they are all essays in the history of ideas.

Perhaps to as large an extent as any economist of the twentieth century, and to a larger extent than most, I have concentrated in my research on the history of economic thought. How did that come about? Why have I thought, and do I continue to think, that such a concentration is worthwhile? Answers to these questions may provide readers with some clarification of the origins and purposes of the papers reprinted here, but cannot be given without an excursion into autobiography. Those who do not share the view that an understanding of an economist's work can be improved by a knowledge of his or her biography can omit the following section. Equally, those who enjoy reading good biographies and autobiographies are asked to bear in mind that what follows here has no pretension to be anything of the kind, but is simply an attempt to explain why I did the work which I have done in the history of economic ideas and why I thought it was worth doing.

II

The careers of academic economists are not normally particularly eventful, and mine has been no exception in that respect. Yet in one way it was, I think, exceptional: I began my undergraduate career in the Honours School of Economics and Political Science in the University of Dublin, Trinity College, in 1937 at the age of 15. Looking back, it seems to me that this was more foolish than admirable and I wonder that none of my teachers, at school or university, saw fit to say so; no doubt they thought that I would soon learn from my mistake.

My reasons for wanting to go up to University so early were simple. By 1937 it was clear that a second world war was inevitable and equally clear that its effects on the lives of young men, once it began, were likely to be large and unpredictable. Before all this happened I was anxious to experience something of life beyond the school classroom; but at my age about the only move which seemed to be possible, and possibly advantageous, was from school to university. There was nothing in the matriculation regulations of Trinity College in 1937 which stipulated the age at which a candidate would be allowed to enter the College, so long as he or she could satisfy the other requirements, which I did.

My original intention, formed at school, had been to read for a business-related degree, the degree of Bachelor of Commerce, as it was then called. I did take that degree, but the statutes of the University of Dublin then still required that any student enrolled in a 'professional School', such as medicine, engineering or commerce, must also qualify for the degree of Bachelor of Arts. Many of them met this requirement by taking a pass degree which involved reading a variety of courses in subjects often little related to their main interest, but in which the necessary standard for a pass was not onerous. The alternative, of reading an integrated course for honours in a subject cognate with that of one's 'professional School', although much more demanding, seemed also much more logical to me. So by that indirect route I came to the study of economics and by the time that I had earned my two primary degrees my interest in the discipline, particularly its theoretical side, had become much stronger, and my interest in business studies had waned considerably.

Although the four year undergraduate economics course which I followed from 1937 to 1941 was organized along the then normal lines of value and distribution, money, theories of the trade cycle and international trade, it was taught in such a way as to expose us more to Continental European than to Anglo-American sources. At the end of it, I was more familiar with the names and works of Cassel, Myrdal, Lindahl, Hayek and Ohlin than with those of Marshall, Pigou, Keynes or Taussig. I had completed all the course requirements, which included statistical methods and economic history – but not the history of economic thought.

In the meantime, the Second World War had indeed broken out as expected, but followed a highly unexpected course. With the fall of France in the summer of 1940 Irish neutrality became precarious and life in Dublin took on a curious, almost trance-like, quality. While growing shortages of imported food and fuel made their mark, in many respects things were little changed: Trinity College, like most of the city's institutions, continued its normal processes. Newspaper reports and comments were subject to censorship, but both the BBC and Lord Haw-Haw could be, and were, listened to by anyone with a radio, providing daily reminders of the harsh realities of the world outside. For many months it seemed that invasion must come, and come soon. I enrolled as a volunteer in the 'second line' or reserve of the Irish Army; we did our weekly drilling and training, and our summer camp, but the call-up which had seemed so imminent somehow never came. The trance remained unbroken until 1945, and I continued to live within it.

By the time when I graduated in the autumn of 1941 I had become sufficiently interested in economics to want to undertake further studies in it, and in the constricted circumstances of the time it seemed that this might be the best thing for me to do. Postgraduate courses by teaching and examination did not then exist in Dublin University, and so I was directly enrolled as a research student working towards the degree of PhD.

My choice of research topic arose out of our final year undergraduate course in international economics. For this the core text was Ohlin's *Interregional and International Trade*, and I had been struck by the references in it to the original contributions made to trade theory by Mountifort Longfield, 'an Irish economist of considerable originality' (Ohlin, 1933, p. 31). My curiosity about this author quickly led me to the knowledge that Longfield had been the first holder of the Whately Chair of Political Economy at Trinity College, Dublin, more than a century earlier. So when the opportunity arose to do postgraduate research, I looked into the question of whether there had been any full-length study of Longfield's economic work and found there had not. My supervisor, Professor G.A. Duncan, then himself the holder of the Whately Chair, agreed to my suggestion that I might undertake such a study for my thesis. So I began the task of enlarging my then sketchy knowledge of the history of economic thought by a detailed study of the works of the principal classical authors on value and distribution and international trade, the fields on which Longfield had published his lectures, comparing their analyses with his.

My thesis on 'The Economic Thought of Mountifort Longfield' was submitted in April 1943 and gained me my doctorate. In 1942–43 I taught my first course in elementary economics as a part-time tutor in Trinity College, Dublin. The idea of an academic career had strong appeal for me, but I saw no prospect then of gaining entry to it. I devoted myself to preparing for the open competition for places in the Administrative Grade of the Irish Civil Service, which I was by then qualified to enter, on age and other grounds. At this point chance again played a part. Professor Duncan was asked to take on a war-time post in the Ministry of Production in London; the Board of Trinity College were prepared to release him to do so, but only on condition that he could find a suitable deputy or deputies to carry out his teaching duties during his absence. The proposal which Professor Duncan made was that James Meenan, already an established Lecturer in University College, Dublin, should take on about one-third of those duties, while I carried out the remainder. I accepted my part in the scheme with a mixture of enthusiasm and trepidation and thus in October 1943 found myself quite unexpectedly employed as a full-time university teacher. It was almost a quantum leap from giving one lecture a week to providing courses in every one of the four years of the undergraduate curriculum, but it was excellent experience. A lot of learning on the job was needed and in that I had invaluable help and support from James Meenan, an able economist and a wise and genial gentleman whose friendship I was privileged to enjoy until his death in 1987.

With the ending of World War II Professor Duncan returned to Dublin in the summer of 1945, and my impressively titled post as 'Deputy for the Professor of Political Economy' came to an end. It had not afforded me much time for research, but my work on Longfield had led me to ask myself whether or not his successors in the Whately Chair had followed the original approach which he took on the analysis of value and distribution. Since during Whately's lifetime appointments to the Chair which he personally funded were made by examination for a period of five years there was a series of incumbents. Whately's further stipulation that they must publish at least one of their lectures each year, although not always rigidly enforced, had ensured that, with only one exception, some of each professor's ideas were in print. Trying to answer my question by searching out and reading their publications in the magnificent Library of Trinity College proved a source of real enjoyment and confirmed the taste which I had already acquired for this type of work. From it I developed the view that Longfield had inititated something of a tradition of a demand-oriented approach to the explanation of value, and I wrote this up in the form of an article. When I had typed it out on my father's ancient Remington I decided I might as well try sending it to a well-known journal first; it could at worst only be rejected. So I posted it off to *Economica* and was very pleasantly surprised to receive a letter from the editor, F.A. Hayek, saying that it had been accepted and would appear in the August, 1945 issue (Black, 1945a).

Meanwhile, in economics as in other disciplines, the end of the war had led to an increase in the number of university posts being advertised to be filled in

October 1945. I had no doubt now that I wanted to follow an academic career if I could, and so I spent much of the summer of that year answering advertisements for any likely post. Among them was a Lectureship in Economics in the Queen's University of Belfast, at which I decided to take a shot even though I realized it was likely to be filled by someone older and more experienced than myself. It was, but a few weeks later I received a letter from the Head of Department, H.O. Meredith, offering me a one-year appointment as Assistant Lecturer. For family reasons just at that time it suited me very well to stay on the island of Ireland, and I had no reservations about going to live in Northern Ireland, so I accepted gladly.

In many, perhaps most, of the 'red brick' provincial universities of the United Kingdom before 1939 the staff of the Economics Department consisted of 'a man and a boy', or in other words a professor and an assistant – often not even dignified with the title of Assistant Lecturer. Queen's, Belfast, was no exception to this rule but now the University had taken the bold decision to double the size of the department. H.O. Meredith, due to retire in 1943, had agreed to remain in post until the end of the war. In 1945 K.S. Isles, Professor of Economics in the University of Adelaide, was appointed as his successor; two newly created Lectureships were filled by Duncan Black and Tom Wilson, and I came in as 'the boy', the assistant.

Things were getting back to normal in the autumn of 1945, but only slowly, and when the academic year opened neither Keith Isles nor Tom Wilson had been released from their war-time duties. So the staff of the department was still just two – two people named Black, Duncan and myself. Between us we had to provide all the teaching for all the undergraduates taking economics courses, from first year arts students to fourth year honours finalists. For most of that academic year 'research' for me often assumed the very basic meaning of working up enough of some of the subjects I had never taught before to be able to give a respectable lecture on them the following day. A second paper I had finished on 'Economic Studies at Trinity College, Dublin' had been accepted for publication, but the other two which completed the series did not appear in print until 1947 and 1948 (Black, 1945b, 1947a, 1948).

In the summer of 1946 I was again scanning the advertisements for a job, testing whether I could achieve promotion to the Lectureship level. At Queen's, there were again vacancies, Duncan Black having moved to a Senior Lectureship at Glasgow and Tom Wilson to a Fellowship at University College, Oxford. My application for one of the Lectureships was successful and so, to cut a long story short, the one year which I had expected to spend in the Queen's University of Belfast stretched out to 40 – until I retired from my position as Professor of Economics and Head of Department in 1985.

My interest in Irish contributions to economic thought led soon after my appointment to a Lectureship in Queen's to an invitation to write the official history of the Statistical and Social Inquiry Society of Ireland which was to celebrate its centenary in 1947 (Black, 1947b). At the same time F.G. Hall was working on his history of the Bank of Ireland (Hall, 1949) and George O'Brien, the Professor of Economics in University College, Dublin, who had pioneered with his series of books on the economic history of Ireland in the 1920s, invited me when I came to Dublin in vacations to come to his house in Burlington Road to join with him and Fred Hall in discussing our work. Those were memorable evenings in which I learned a great deal, not all of which could have been found in libraries, for George O'Brien was not only a learned man but a brilliant conversationalist whose circle of acquaintances and friends included not just economists but most of the leading literary figures of the Ireland of his time.

These were years of expanding horizons and deepening knowledge for me. In the bleak mid-winter of 1946–47 I found my way for the first time to a conference of the Association of University Teachers of Economics in Oxford. On that occasion all the members could fit comfortably into the Junior Common Room at Wadham College, and I suddenly found myself able to meet and talk with people whose names I had previously known only from the title pages of their books. I listened with growing interest and admiration to D.H. Robertson giving 'A Survey of Recent Developments in Economics' and formed the opinion, which I have never seen cause to alter, that here was the most able, sane and wise economist of his generation.

I encountered Robertson again in the autumn of 1947, when the British Association for the Advancement of Science held its first post-war meeting in Dundee, and he was President of Section F, Economics and Statistics. In that capacity he chaired a meeting of the Section at which Duncan Black presented his first paper on his theory of committees and elections, which was to earn him an international reputation as one of the founding fathers of public choice theory. I had already had a glimpse of a first draft of that paper when Duncan expounded his ideas to me from the sixpenny school exercise book in which he had written it out. As he now presented the theory in more developed form, Dennis Robertson appeared to take little interest, looking for all the world like a turtle in one of Tenniel's illustrations to his beloved *Alice in Wonderland*, his chin sunk on his chest and the sun shining on his domed bald head. Yet after the paper, when the initial flow of questions from the audience faltered, Robertson looked up and said, 'I'm a child in these matters, but it does seem to me that the whole thing depends on the *order* in which the chairman puts the motions to the committee'. It was a point which Duncan Black admitted he had not taken into account at that stage of his work, but it appears in his classic *Theory of Committee and Elections* (Black, D., 1958, pp. 39–41). To be able to listen to a paper on a completely new subject, remote from one's own interests, and to grasp it so clearly as to be able to add to the analysis seemed to me to show intellectual acumen of a high order, and my admiration for Dennis Robertson increased.

By 1949 I felt that I had done as much as I wanted to do on the work of Irish economists and began to cast about for other research projects which might prove interesting and rewarding. In the early post-war years books like E.R. Walker's *From Economic Theory to Economic Policy* (1943) had aroused interest in the question of the ways in which theory and policy interacted. Discussing it with me one day my colleague Bruce (now Sir Bruce) Williams suggested that this was a question well suited to investigation by historical methods, and the more I thought and read about it the more it seemed to me that he was right.

I decided to do a pilot project in the area by looking at the inter-relations of theory and policy involved in the introduction of 'free trade' so-called between Britain and Ireland in the last quarter of the eighteenth century. The paper which resulted was very much a 'prentice effort' (Black, 1950), but it taught me a good deal about the range of sources involved in such work and the problems which arise in evaluating them.

Around this time Norman S. Buchanan came to Britain and Ireland as a Rockefeller Foundation consultant looking for suitable candidates to apply for Fellowships to study at United States universities. Encouraged by him I applied for and was awarded a Rockefeller Post-Doctoral Fellowship for 1950–51, to study at Princeton under the supervision of Professor Jacob Viner. Nowadays when jet aircraft have reduced the trans-Atlantic crossing time to six or seven hours and undergraduates who have *not* been to the United States are more the exception than the rule, it is difficult to realize that in 1950, with dollar shortages and exchange control, a visit to America was for most European academics a remote possibility. By 1949 I had managed a couple of holiday trips to France; to go to live and work in the United States for a year meant, quite literally, entering a new world.

In undergraduate days I had realized that the academic life could be a good one and through good fortune I had gained entry to it and enjoyed it. Yet I can see now as I look back that it was only at Princeton that I came to know academic life at its fullest. It was a rich mixture, stimulating and nourishing, a mixture of hard work and good debate, listening and learning, making new acquaintances, some of whom became old friends, sometimes good talk, into the small hours, sometimes good parties, good music ....

I had rooms in the Graduate College, then strictly an all-male institution referred to by its inmates (with some exaggeration) as 'the largest monastery on the East Coast', and every day I enjoyed the walk from there to the Firestone Library and spent most of my time exploring its splendid collections, although I also sat in on some graduate courses, notably Friedrich Lutz's microeconomics and Jacob Viner's international trade. I had read and been impressed by Viner's classic *Studies in the Theory of International Trade* (1937) as an undergraduate, and when I applied for a Rockefeller Fellowship I had submitted a scheme for extending my research into the relations of theory and policy in international trade to the case of America in the first half of the nineteenth century, and asked to be allowed to work under his supervision if possible.

Viner had agreed, provisionally, at least, to take me on as a student, but at our first meeting he made short work of my research proposal. American thought in the period I was proposing to study was, in his view, uninteresting – either a pale reflection of, or a reaction against, English classical doctrines. 'Why don't you work on the influence of classical political economy on Ireland in the nineteenth century?' he said. 'There's a good subject there.' I knew he was right, but suggested that the Rockefeller Foundation might not be too happy to have an Irishman whom they had brought to America to study American affairs turn around and start to work on Ireland instead. 'They'll agree if I tell them,' said Viner, and they did.

Thus it came about that I spent my year in the States laying the foundation for what became, almost nine years later, my book on *Economic Thought and the Irish Question 1817–1870* (Black, 1960) – with, I am proud to say, a foreword by Jacob Viner. Viner became unquestionably the greatest single influence on my work; I quickly recognized in him a man of the same calibre as Dennis Robertson – an outstanding economist but also a learned and wise man. His command of modern economics was backed up by a genuinely encyclopaedic knowledge of its history; it seemed impossible to mention any printed source in it which he had not read. If one raised a point which he thought worth exploring he would say, 'I'll see what I can find for you on that' and come back the next day with a handful of relevant references, culled from the vast card index which filled a series of filing cabinets in his study. As his writings, now much underestimated, make clear, Jacob Viner was a great scholar. To be apprenticed to one of the great is itself a great experience, and I was privileged to have it.

There were other valuable experiences in that year in America: the second half of it became a *Wanderjahr* because after a semester at Princeton, Viner sent me to discover what I could about my subject in other major American libraries which he knew well. So I went first to New York, to work in the Seligman Collection at Columbia, and in the New York Public Library; to Yale University to study in the Manuscripts Department of its library the letters of John Stuart Mill and Thomas Carlyle on Irish issues; to Chicago to work in the John Crerar and Newberry Libraries as well as in the University of Chicago Library; to Washington, DC to see what could be found in the riches of the Library of Congress; and finally to Harvard where H.S. Foxwell's second collection provided the core for one of the greatest Western libraries in the history of economic ideas, the Kress.

In the process I made contact with many more economists and historians, and received much help from them. I had many discussions with Joseph Dorfman and George Stigler, as well as the historian J. Bartlett Brebner, at Columbia. At Chicago my most frequent contact was with Earl J. Hamilton, but while there I also began a long-lasting working relationship with F.W. Fetter, of Northwestern University, who had a special interest in Irish monetary history. Another special highlight of my Chicago days was attending the closing sessions of Frank Knight's graduate course in history of economic thought; and from Harvard I took away a lasting kindly memory of Arthur H. Cole, a genial scholar for whom nothing that might help a student was ever too much trouble.

In September 1951 I sailed back to Ireland carrying these and other good memories, a suitcase or more full of notes and index cards, and a realization that if my research project was well launched it was also far from complete.

A year spent in some of the greatest libraries of the United States had amply confirmed Viner's good judgement in guiding me towards a study of the interaction of classical economic thought and economic policy in Ireland in the nineteenth century. That year had enabled me to deepen my knowledge of the main structure of the classical system and in the process to appreciate that it had many variants. It had enabled me also to widen my acquaintance with the less orthodox and less renowned economic writers of the period. Wherever in that literature the economists had used Ireland as an example – as Malthus, Ricardo, the Mills and McCulloch often did in various contexts – I had noted it and tried to follow it out. Similarly, when in parliamentary papers and reports and other commentaries on policies for Ireland I found politicians and other interested parties appealing to, or raging against, 'the principles of political economy', I had tried to discover what they really meant and whence their ideas came.

As a result, the main outlines of a picture of the relations between economic theories and policies for tackling Irish economic problems in what has often been called the 'classic' period of political economy had become clear in my head and I managed to get this outline picture written up in a form which appeared in *Oxford Economic Papers* (Black, 1953). However, I could not be content with outlines; what I wanted to do was to fill in the details as fully as possible, supporting them with proper documentation. My aim was to trace out, as fully as available sources allowed, the ways in which economic theory could be shown to have actually influenced economic policy, and *vice versa*. To accomplish this was a task which proved both fascinating and frustrating. It required not only the reading of all the reports of relevant parliamentary debates, Select Committees and Royal Commissions, but in addition detailed study of many newspapers and periodicals and of the numerous surviving manuscript sources in Dublin, London and elsewhere. The fascination lay in picking up and following the trails which could be found through this wilderness. For example, at one stage when I was working on the processes which led up to the drafting and final enactment of Gladstone's Irish Land Bill of 1870, I found it necessary to reconstruct Gladstone's movements and contacts day by day, sometimes even hour by hour, from October 1869 to February 1870, in order to be able to write five pages of my book to my own satisfaction (Black, 1960, pp. 63–7). The frustration lay partly in the fact that the trails sometimes faded out, but mainly in the fact that the process of reading and interpreting all this material was heavily time-consuming and research time was limited, so progress was inevitably slow.

I could, and sometimes did, sigh for those palmy days when I had been a full-time Research Fellow, but I was back to being a Lecturer now with the usual load of courses and examining. However, my contract allowed time for research, and it was just a matter of buckling down and using it to the best advantage. By 1958 I had a manuscript of my book completed; the fact that it was only finally published in 1960 was due to there being added to the delays normal with any book, a prolonged printer's strike in 1959.

Meanwhile I had managed to start another fairly large project, not itself involving research in the history of economic ideas, but attempting in one specific area to add to the then very limited supply of bibliographical tools available to those working in this field. In the course of my own study of the voluminous materials relating to ideas and policy in nineteenth century Ireland, I had become only too well aware of the scarcity of published bibliographies of such material. Some reputable sources there were, notably the *Catalogue of the Kress Library* (1940–57), Wagner's *Irish Economics, 1700–1783, a Bibliography with Notes* (1907) and Higgs's *Bibliography of Economics, 1751–1775* (1935). Good as they were (and remain), these by no means covered the whole field. Many major libraries had no published catalogues, and even their in-house catalogues often failed to list their entire holdings, or, when items had been bound up into volumes, listed each volume but only as 'Tracts: Economic, 1780–1840' or some such catchall title.

I had discussions about problems such as this with Frank Fetter when he visited Ireland in 1955 to look for material in connection with his book on *British Monetary Orthodoxy* (Fetter, 1965). He had been particularly impressed by the wealth of material in the Haliday Collection of pamphlets in the Royal Irish Academy, then almost wholly unknown to economists and historians outside Ireland, and encouraged me to look into the possibility of producing a union catalogue of economic pamphlets in Irish libraries. I took his advice and came up with a proposal which was approved for funding by the Rockefeller Foundation. This enabled me to employ a full-time research assistant for the period from September 1958 until March 1963, during which material for the catalogue was being assembled. My approach was to go with this assistant to libraries known to me to have pamphlet collections and try to assess their extent and relevance to the terms of reference I had set myself. Then I would leave the assistant to follow the guidelines I had set in cataloguing every pamphlet in every volume we decided met those terms, leaving duplicates and doubtfully relevant items to be weeded out in later reviews of the thousands of index cards which this process generated. From these in turn author and title indexes had to be compiled – a task which even a modest personal computer would make light today, but which then had to be done entirely by hand. Consequently the process of editing the material and seeing it through the press took as long as the process of collecting it. The final result was *A Catalogue of Pamphlets on Economic Subjects Published between 1750 and 1900 and now Housed in Irish Libraries*, which was published by Queen's University itself in 1969. Though not without the sort of imperfections commonly found in any bibliography compiled by a non-bibliographer, it has established itself alongside catalogues like those of Kress and Goldsmiths as a recognized information source in the field.

Towards the end of 1958 with my thought and policy book finished, although not published, and the Pamphlet Catalogue begun, I found myself again looking for a new direction for research. I had enjoyed the blending of theory and history which my attempt to trace the linkages of thought and policy involved, but having learned by experience just how long the period of production was for such work I was reluctant to commit myself to another monograph of that kind. My inclination was rather to look for something which needed doing in the area of economic analysis; as it happened one day in the Manuscripts Department of the National Library in Dublin the Librarian, Alf MacLochlainn, asked me if I would like to see the papers of John Elliot Cairnes, which had just been presented to the Library. I agreed with alacrity, for here there could be the makings of a good book on Cairnes.

At that time the Cairnes Papers had not been sorted, laid down or catalogued. Among the bundles my eye was caught by a small one which proved to contain six or seven letters from W.S. Jevons to Cairnes written in the years 1863 to 1874. As such, they belonged to a period in English economic thought in which I had hitherto taken no special interest, but on a first reading they did not seem to me to fit with the (then) accepted stereotype which cast Cairnes as the last of the classical economists and Jevons as the first of the neo-classicals. Here was an interesting hypothesis and obviously the first step in testing it had to be to find and read the replies which Cairnes clearly had sent to Jevons. I foresaw no problem about that: in the case of an economist so well-known, it seemed to me, his papers would already be available, in the best of order, in the Library of University College London, or the University of Manchester.

I was somewhat crestfallen when in due course replies to my enquiries revealed that neither at UCL nor at Manchester was there any trace of Jevons's papers. For the moment my search was halted, but fortunately the Manchester University

Librarian of the time, the late Moses Tyson, mentioned my enquiry to Dr Wolfe
Mays, of the Philosophy Department of the University, who was already engaged
on research into Jevons's contributions to logic. Dr Mays confirmed to me that
W.S. Jevons's daughter Harriet Winefrid, born in 1877, was still alive, provided
me with her address and encouraged me to write to her.

Miss Jevons replied promptly and helpfully to my letter, explaining that it was
her brother Professor H.S. Jevons who had held their father's papers, but that on
his death in 1955 his daughter, Rosamond Könekamp (née Jevons) had become their
custodian. Mrs Könekamp's response to my subsequent enquiry was far more
generous and helpful than I could reasonably have expected. Not only did she confirm
that a number of letters to Jevons from Cairnes were in her possession, but she
supplied me with meticulous copies of them. Hence I was enabled to complete my
study of the Jevons-Cairnes exchange of ideas and put it into the form of a paper
which I sent to Mrs Könekamp for her approval before submitting it for publication.
Along with her reply, which contained some valuable comments and criticisms of my
paper, she also enclosed a copy of a letter from Alfred Marshall to her grandfather.
This, she wrote, 'may be of no interest to you at all, but as Darwin and Cairnes
are mentioned in a footnote you might at any rate care to see it'.[1]

Far from being of no interest, this Marshall letter naturally aroused my curiosity
as to the full extent and importance of the correspondence between Jevons and other
economists of his time. Again through the kindness of Mrs Könekamp and Miss
Jevons, I was able to satisfy that curiosity by a visit to London in July 1959 during
which I met them both for the first time and was afterwards able to make a preliminary
inspection of all the papers they held.

It was immediately clear that there was a large quantity of Jevons's professional
papers and correspondence which had not been previously published and which
required collation and editing. My first intention was to make the correspondence
with economists the subject of further articles and subsequently to try to collate his
papers with Jevons's published works in a thorough study of the development of
his economic ideas, but further discussions with my colleague C.F. Carter (now
Sir Charles Carter), who was then Stanley Jevons Professor of Economics at the
University of Manchester, and Lord Robbins led to decisions that the Jevons Papers
should be deposited in the Library of the University of Manchester, and that the
Royal Economic Society should sponsor the publication of an edition of them, which
I was to prepare.

At the time I did not realize that this was a project which would involve an even
longer period of production than that required for my earlier study of the inter-
relations of economic thought and policy. Like many another editor, I underestimated
the length of time which it would take to carry out the work, and overestimated
the amount of time I would have available to do it. In the first instance, the edition
of the Jevons Papers was planned to appear in four volumes, two containing Jevons's
personal journal and papers, to be edited by Rosamond Könekamp, and two devoted
to his professional papers and correspondence as an economist, which I was to edit.

In the event, the edition appeared in seven volumes: the first, edited by Mrs
Könekamp and myself, was not published until 1972, and the remaining six, prepared
under my editorship, appeared between 1973 and 1981. It would be tedious to give

here a chronological account of all the vicissitudes through which the project passed in a 20-year period[2] but the main reasons why that proved to be the length of time it required deserve to be briefly summarized.

In the early stages the nature of the work made it almost inevitable that progress would be slow. Jevons did not normally make drafts of his papers or keep copies of letters he wrote to colleagues so a primary requirement was to look for missing manuscripts and to discover whether and where his correspondence with other economists survived. This involved a search process which seldom paid quick dividends and often none at all. Perhaps inevitably too, some important collections came to light long after the search for them had been given up as hopeless and this necessitated revision of the planned layout of the whole edition.

Unfortunately, ill health forced Mrs Könekamp to give up her work on editing the personal papers in 1968, when she had largely completed a valuable biographical introduction and the editing of Jevons's private journal. So the proportion of the edition which I had to complete was unexpectedly increased, although Mrs Könekamp continued to be an important source of information, advice and criticism throughout the whole undertaking.

These were some of the factors I had not foreseen which made the task of editing Jevons a longer one than I had expected, but there proved to be even more reasons why I had less time to devote to it than I expected. In 1962 I was appointed to the Chair of Economics at Queen's, in succession to Stanley Dennison. At the same time Jack Parkinson was appointed to the Chair of Applied Economics; and in a somewhat unusual move for the time the University also appointed the two of us Joint Heads of the Department of Economics – an arrangement which worked efficiently and comfortably until Jack moved to the University of Nottingham in 1968, when I became sole Head.

Inevitably these changes brought new and wider responsibilities for me. However well the arrangements for running the Department worked, they made daily demands on time, which were never negligible and sometimes total. I quickly learned that meetings which a Lecturer could occasionally miss with a clear conscience, a Head of Department could not. Apart from this, the holders of the Economics chairs were drawn into many activities in the community, more or less *ex officio*. Jack Parkinson and I became involved in the work of the Northern Ireland Chamber of Commerce, and in something of a campaign to improve the economic situation in the province – which led to the decision of the government to establish the Northern Ireland Economic Council.

The first stages of preparing the Jevons volumes were nearing completion when I received an invitation from William Fellner to teach at Yale University for the academic year 1964–65. Having lived and enjoyed the life of a graduate student at Princeton for a year in the 1950s, I was very pleased to live the life of a faculty member at Yale in the 1960s. Central to it was the opportunity to teach graduate and undergraduate students within the course structure of a leading American university, to sit in as a guest in other people's courses and to participate in a seminar programme which provided not only opportunities to hear about the research of other faculty members, but to hear and meet some of the many visiting speakers who came to the Economics Department and to the Cowles Foundation.

In addition, there were opportunities, both on and off campus, to renew old friendships and to make new ones, to share the good experience of living through four seasons in a Connecticut suburb with my wife and children, and travelling first around New England and later across the United States with them in vacation times. Martin Shubik, with whom I had found much in common when we were both living in the Graduate College at Princeton, was by 1964 installed in his chair at Yale, developing his work in game theory, and we had some stimulating discussions in that year on the possibilities of, and prospects for, mathematical-institutional economics.

On more than one occasion during that year I took the opportunity to make weekend visits to Princeton itself, particularly to make personal contact again with Jacob Viner – by then retired from teaching but certainly not from research – and it was good to find his sharpness of intellect and wit undulled. Attending the 1964 meetings of the American Economic Association in Chicago allowed me to make a valuable new professional contact, which was in due course to ripen into an old friendship, with William Jaffé who was then about to bring out the first volume of his monumental *Correspondence of Léon Walras and Related Papers*. With Mrs Könekamp's consent I was able to supply him with a copy of Walras's first letter to Jevons, the only one of which Walras had kept no draft;[3] but he was able to supply me, both then and in subsequent years of regular correspondence and occasional meetings, with the benefit of his unrivalled scholarship and experience as an editor of economists' papers. In editing Jevons's papers and correspondence I was in a sense following in Bill Jaffé's footsteps, and the help and encouragement which he gave me were of inestimable value.

In the years after my return to Belfast in 1965, my responsibilities inside and outside Queen's University did not diminish; in fact, they increased considerably. Within the University I served as Dean of the Faculty of Economics and Social Sciences from 1967 until 1970 and as a Pro-Vice-Chancellor from 1971 until 1975. These were not easy years in any university in Western Europe or the United States but in Queen's they were particularly difficult. It was no easy task to keep the University functioning as a place of learning open to all in a time of growing political unrest. Deans and Pro-Vice-Chancellors had a more than usually significant rôle to play in these years in supporting Arthur Vick, the Vice-Chancellor, whose courageous and level-headed impartiality provided them with exemplary leadership.

During this time I came to adopt, more by a process of adjustment, perhaps, than through any single conscious decision, what might be called a two-track approach to my research and writing. Work on the Jevons edition I came to regard as a medium to long-term project which I tried to keep moving forward while also undertaking short-term projects, some relating to and some independent of the Jevons work. In the circumstances in which I found myself in the late 1960s and early 1970s, it would have been difficult, if not impossible, to maintain this approach had it not been for the University policy of establishing posts of Research Assistant and Research Officer within departments to support academic research programmes.

Under this policy from 1966 onwards I was able to draw on the services of a member of research staff to assist by following up references and looking out material for me. My first two research assistants were, as is often the case with holders of such posts, birds of passage, but it was very fortunate for me that Jacqueline Bowen (later Mrs Jacqueline Wright) who joined the research staff of the department as an Assistant in 1969, remained on it, earning promotion first to Research Officer and later to Senior Research Officer, until 1985. Thus she was able to help me throughout the last 12 years of the Jevons project and became familiar with all its details and ramifications. I am glad to have a new opportunity here to express, and stress, my gratitude for all the hard work she did for me, without which the project must have taken much longer, if indeed it could have been accomplished at all.

During the 1970s my responsibilities outside the University were also growing. Not surprisingly, most of them arose from collaboration with colleagues to promote the study of the history of economic thought. In 1966 Donald Winch and I discussed the possibility of organizing a specialist conference on the subject and, encouraged by support from Lionel Robbins and a few others, decided to try the experiment once at least.

This conference, organized by Donald at the University of Sussex in January 1968, proved so successful that it became the first of an annual series which is still continuing. From it, other related activities developed in which I was glad to have some part – the publication, twice yearly, of a *History of Economic Thought Newsletter* and the organization (with the aid of grants from the Social Science Research Council and the Royal Economic Society) of a survey and listing of the surviving unpublished papers of British economists of the period 1750–1950 (Sturges, 1975).

During this same period, international contacts between economists sharing an interest in the history of their subject grew notably. For me, as, I think, for everyone who was involved in it, developing such contacts was interesting work which produced an unexpectedly wide range of rewards – which can be well illustrated by the case of my contacts with Craufurd Goodwin, of Duke University, whom I first met at the 1968 Sussex conference. In 1969, along with J.J. Spengler and Robert S. Smith, Craufurd launched the first specialist journal in our field, *History of Political Economy* (HOPE). Like Bob Coats and Donald Winch, I accepted his invitation to serve on the Advisory Board of the new journal and found it a stimulating experience over the next 18 years to act as referee for a wide selection from the many papers submitted.

Out of this there developed a related type of collaboration when Craufurd Goodwin, Bob Coats and myself organized an international conference in the summer of 1971 to commemorate the centenary of what had come to be known as 'the Marginal Revolution in Economics'. Since my own part in its organization was minor, I think I can say without seeming to boast that for me, and I think for all the other participants, this conference provided the ideal example of the sort of meeting which international academic cooperation ought to produce. Scholars from half a dozen different countries produced original papers which were calmly and constructively discussed – a process surely helped by the elegance and beauty of the place in which the meetings were held, the Villa Serbelloni at Bellagio on Lake Como.[4]

In addition to this my contact, which became a friendship, with Craufurd Goodwin enabled me to bring him to Belfast as a guest lecturer, and to visit Duke on more than one occasion to give seminars and to attend conferences.

Similarly fruitful contacts, which in time became friendships, developed for me in the 1970s in Italy and in Japan. In 1973 I had the privilege of lecturing in the University of Venice at the invitation of Umberto Meoli, and on several other occasions I took part in conferences at the University of Florence organized by Piero Barucci and Piero Roggi. All these visits arose as a result of earlier contacts made with these and other Italian academics when they came to our conferences on history of economic thought in England.

It was likewise through conferences organized first to commemorate the two hundred and fiftieth anniversary of Adam Smith's birth, at Kirkcaldy in 1973, and secondly to celebrate the bicentenary of the publication of the *Wealth of Nations*, at Glasgow in 1976, that I met Hiroshi Mizuta of Nagoya University, the leading Smith scholar in Japan. It was through him that I first became aware of much of the work being done in history of economic ideas in Japan, and subsequently I was able to be of some assistance to him in his work on Adam Smith's library, a part of which is housed in the Library of Queen's University Belfast.

Later, in 1977–78, Shoichiro Uemiya, Professor of Economics at Kobe University, came to Queen's University to spend that academic year with me pursuing his research into the work of Jevons. At that same time Professor Hideo Yamada of Hitotsubashi University was visiting University College Dublin and accepted my invitation to come to Queen's to deliver a public lecture. Once again, through continuing correspondence and exchanges of information, contacts ripened into friendships and I was happy to have the opportunity to lecture in each of their universities when I was awarded a Research Fellowship by the Japan Society for Promotion of Science which enabled me and my wife to spend six weeks there in the autumn of 1980. This was one of the most valuable experiences which my work has ever afforded me, allowing me to see something of the ancient culture and modern life of Japan, to appreciate by first hand experience the high importance which Japanese economists attach to the history of ideas, and to visit some of the leading universities whose libraries house collections of world importance in that field.

Not all of my responsibilities outside the University over this period were connected with the history of economic ideas, however. Others were concerned with the support and encouragement of training and research in the social sciences, in Ireland and elsewhere. In 1972 the Ford Foundation was receiving increasing numbers of applications to study the economic, social and political problems of both parts of Ireland, and its officers were uncertain as to how best to evaluate and coordinate them. As it happened, Craufurd Goodwin was then on secondment from Duke University working as a Program Officer with the Ford Foundation. He contacted me and later came to Belfast to discuss with me the possibility of establishing a coordinating committee on which the Foundation would delegate the task of administering an overall grant for social science research and training in Ireland for a period of three years in the first instance. I agreed to try to set up such a committee and made a series of brief visits to other universities and research institutes around Ireland to test the reactions of people concerned. As they were encouragingly positive, I invited them to a weekend conference in Belfast in January 1973 at which Craufurd Goodwin and another Europe-based Ford Program Officer, Alessandro Silj from Rome, outlined the Foundation's proposal. It was agreed to set up what came to be called the Committee for Social Science Research in Ireland, (CSSRI) to which the Ford Foundation made an initial grant of \$250 000.

I was appointed Chairman of the Committee and became much involved in its work until 1979 when I handed over to Professor Dermot McAleese of Trinity College Dublin. That work had special significance in Ireland in the 1970s: taught graduate courses in the social sciences were still in the early stages of development and young graduates interested in a career in a social science discipline could not always obtain the training which was desirable for them within Ireland. Others more experienced and keen to do independent research often found it very difficult to obtain the funds to finance a leave of absence or pay for some research assistance.

These were deficiencies which Ford Foundation officers had identified, and the Committee was charged by the Foundation with the task of trying to remedy them. In that I think it is fair to say that the Committee had considerable success although, by their very nature, the needs which it sought to meet could never be completely satisfied.

At first the Committee followed a policy of inviting applications for grants from suitably qualified people in the subject areas of economics, politics and sociology, allowing the distribution of grants to be determined by the number and quality of the applications. However, at a conference held by the Committee in Dublin in December 1974 to invite the views of other social scientists from Ireland and abroad, it was decided to devote a considerable proportion of the funds available to the Committee to the encouragement of research into the causes and results of the conflict which had begun in Northern Ireland in 1969. As a result of the conference decision, a conflict research programme was established in 1975, concentrating on two main approaches – attitude surveys and participant observer studies. Six such studies were undertaken and their results published; the programme was rounded off with what was its largest, and perhaps most successful, publication, John Whyte's monumental review (Whyte, 1990) of all the literature on the conflict published up to the end of 1989.[5]

Unfortunately it cannot be claimed that this research has yet had any great influence with politicians or others who could affect the conflict situation in Ireland. Nevertheless, I still think it was right for CSSRI to use some of its resources to make objectively observed facts accessible to those who may prefer them to the constant repetition of preconceived opinions, and I am glad to have played some part in bringing this about.

While for a decade such preoccupations often kept me away from my research in the history of economic ideas, I never allowed them to halt it entirely. Had I done so my work on the Jevons Papers might even now be uncompleted; as it was, the seventh and final volume did not appear until 1981, 22 years after I had begun my research on them. From discussions with Bill Jaffé about his *Correspondence of Léon Walras* I had long since realized that it is unwise for an editor ever to describe work of this kind as 'finished'. So I was not particularly surprised to find my research time for the next few years taken up by what might be called 'mopping-up operations'.

A striking example of this occurred within a year. In 1982, Margaret Schabas informed me of the existence of almost a hundred letters exchanged between W.S. Jevons and his younger brother T.E. Jevons which she had discovered in the archives of Seton Hall University, South Orange, New Jersey. During a visit to the United States to attend the History of Economics Society meetings in the summer of 1982 I was able to see these letters, and it was clear that many of them contained material which would have justified their inclusion in Volumes II–V of *Papers and Correspondence of William Stanley Jevons*. This was doubly disappointing, because the letters had been in the possession of T.E. Jevons's youngest son, Ferdinand Jevons, who had been alive and living on Long Island when I was at Yale in 1964–65. I had written to him then and asked if I might come to see any Jevons letters which he had. In reply he assured me – as he assured Mrs Könekamp also – that he had no letters written by his father or uncle. As Ferdinand Jevons was then 88 years of age he had perhaps forgotten the hundred or so letters gathering dust in his cellar. Be that as it may, I had to content myself with publishing a detailed listing of these letters in the Autumn 1982 issue of *History of Economic Thought Newsletter* and enlarging on it in an article (Black, 1982a, b) for the Jevons Centenary Issue of *The Manchester School* in December 1982, of which Michael Artis had invited me to be a guest editor.

When I took early retirement from my chair at Queen's University, Belfast, in 1985, it was my intention soon to draw a definite line under my studies on Jevons and his work and to strike out in a new direction by taking a fresh look at the work of the Irish philosopher-economists of the eighteenth century, notably Francis Hutcheson. Perhaps my previous experiences have made me fight shy of undertaking another project involving uncertain prospects of 'roundabout production', perhaps I have not been sufficiently strong-minded to decline the pleasant and interesting invitations which colleagues have extended to me to write papers on topics in which they think I have some expertise. In any event, I became involved for a time in a series of studies of the relation of utilitarian philosophy to nineteenth-century economics, and as yet my only excursion into the eighteenth century has been to produce a paper on 'Theories of Population before Malthus' for the session of the International Population Conference held in Florence in 1985 organized by Piero Roggi (Black, 1987). It may, I hope, yet happen that, to use a French expression, 'if God lends me life' my study of Irish economic ideas in the eighteenth century will at least be begun.

III

In the preceding section I have tried to put my own work in context, to show how I came to develop an interest in the history of economic ideas and why I chose the specific areas within that field in which I have sought to make a contribution. It remains to deal with the other question posed at the start of this Introduction, why have I thought, and continue to think, that this is a worthwhile field in which to work?

On the narrowest and most basic level, those who have read Section II will already know that there is an obvious answer – once I became interested in the field I found that I enjoyed working in it. All forms of research go well at some times and badly at others and it would be dishonest for me to deny that there have been times when working on the history of economic ideas has seemed to me 'flat, stale and unprofitable' but by and large it has never lost its attraction for me.

Wherein then does this attraction lie? To me, it lies in the opportunities which the subject affords for the use and development of scholarship. If asked what I understand by scholarship I repeat the definition given by my teacher, Jacob Viner: 'I mean by it nothing more than the pursuit of broad and exact knowledge of the history of the working of the human mind as revealed in written records' (Viner, 1950, p. 369). From my own experience I have proved the truth of his dictum that 'once the taste for it has been aroused, it gives a sense of largeness even to one's small quests, and a sense of fullness even to the small answers to problems large or small which it yields, a sense which can never in any other way be attained, for which no other source of human gratification can, to the addict, be a satisfying substitute, which gains instead of loses in quality and quantity and in pleasure-yielding capacity by being shared with others – and which, unlike golf, improves with age' (Viner, 1950, p. 375).

Yet scholarship, like most other things which give pleasure, is not a free good. Its real price, as I have already suggested, lies in the time which it demands and when the would-be scholar is also a teacher with many other calls on his time, that price is often ultimately paid by his family. So it was in my case; when I wrote the Preface to Volume I of the Jevons Papers just before Christmas 1970 (Black and Könekamp, 1972 p. xiv), I tried to express what I have always felt – my gratitude to my wife and children 'for accepting without complaint the many hours of silence and absence which the completion of this project has necessarily involved'. They have indeed willingly accepted too many such hours over the years before and since then, and whatever success my pursuit of scholarship may have had, no one has contributed more to it than they have, in the special ways which only an understanding family could.

Whatever satisfaction scholarship may give to those who practise it, that is not nowadays a sufficient justification for academic research and its publication. To what audience is it addressed and what value does it have for the members of that audience? In my case, I have addressed two audiences – first, an audience consisting of other students of the history of economic thought specifically, and second, a wider audience composed mainly but perhaps not entirely of economists who are not specialists in the history of their discipline. Insofar as my work has been concerned with what may be called 'tool-making' – the production of bibliographies and catalogues, such as my *Catalogue of Economic Pamphlets*, and editions of hitherto unpublished documents, such as the Jevons papers – it has been directed primarily towards the first audience. To the extent that these tools have been used, they have served their purpose in helping to generate further studies and fresh interpretations in the history of economics.

This latter is the category into which the major part of my work falls: using the available tools of primary and secondary sources along with the methods of scholarship to throw fresh light on the history of economic analysis, of economic policy, and of the inter-relations between the two. Here I would hope that some of my writing has perhaps reached not only the first but also the second of the audiences I have mentioned and proved of some value to both.

This second, wider audience obviously divides into a number of sub-groups. It consists not only of academic economists who are engaged in teaching and research in all the different branches of their subject, both theoretical and applied, but also of economists who are using their expertise in the public and private sectors of their national economies, or in international organizations. It may extend to include non-economists who, for a variety of reasons, have become involved in making, or commenting on, economic policy.

Clearly the extent to which people in these various groups might gain from a knowledge of the history of economic thought can itself vary widely. Some years ago I contended, and would still contend today, that 'in the foundation of economic policy at any level it is arguable that a knowledge of the history of economic thought and its links with past policy can be a valuable corrective to provincialism in time and space and serve to reduce the risk of repeating past mistakes which that involves' (Black, 1986, p. 13). This is particularly true for those involved in policy-making in and for developing countries, but it is not without relevance in more advanced economics also. In these countries debates on economic issues are conducted almost continuously. 'In these debates competing views of how the economic system operates, and should or should not be controlled, are strenuously presented, but there is no unanimity as to which is correct. In these circumstances an examination of the intellectual origins of our present understanding of economic affairs could ... contribute to a clearer appreciation of the nature of Economics as a discipline, its potentialities and limitations. Hence economists might in the end be in a better position both to put it to use themselves and to interpret critically the ways in which it is used by others' (Black, 1986, pp. ix–x).

Some economists who are engaged mainly in teaching and research in pure economic analysis may feel that comments such as this have no application to them; as scientists they can leave the history of their subject to antiquaries who enjoy such pastimes. I have never been convinced of the validity of the view which is implicit in this approach – that the history of a social science like economics is akin to that of an experimental science like chemistry – a record of progress from error to truth in which it can safely be taken that all that is of value in earlier work has been incorporated into the body of knowledge which constitutes the science in its present form. That there has been progress in economics, especially in economic theory, is undeniable, but it has been erratic, sometimes seeming more nearly circular than linear and by no means always resulting from the internal logic of theory alone.

So even for the pure theorist there may be an advantage in being at least acquainted with the history of economic analysis, if only to avoid the danger of repeating past mistakes, or, even worse, past successes. Such at least are the convictions I hold and which have led me to hope that in studying some facets of the history of economic theory and policy I may have produced something of use not only to my fellow-specialists but to economists generally.

IV

The papers reprinted in this book I have selected as being broadly representative of my work in each of the main areas in which I have tried to make a contribution. So I have grouped them into three parts, in the first of which I have collected together some essays concerned with the Irish economy and the Irish economists of the nineteenth century.

The first, 'Political Economy and the Irish', which gives its title to the group, is something of a 'broad brush' survey, giving an outline of the main features of the economy of nineteenth-century Ireland, and the reaction of economists from outside and inside Ireland to its problems. As such it represents to some extent a return to the ground which I covered in *Economic Thought and the Irish Question*, but extending the period covered – or rather, in this piece, sketched in – up to and beyond 1920 and giving particular attention to the solutions which the Irish themselves put forward and adopted.

The second paper, 'Economic Policy in Ireland and India in the time of J.S. Mill', comes under the head of what I have called 'mopping-up operations'. When I was working on the relations of economic thought and policy in Ireland, I was struck by the many comparisons with the Indian case in the literature; J.S. Mill in particular frequently cited parallels between the problems of Ireland and India. However, I could not make more than passing references to these points in my book without unbalancing the treatment of the main issues. So I set the material to one side for later work and, after finishing *Economic Thought and the Irish Question*, devoted most of one long vacation to working up the Indian material as fully as I could. The results were later presented in a paper read to the 1967 conference of the Economic History Society, of which this essay is a revised version.

The third and last paper in this part, 'The Irish dissenters and nineteenth century political economy' represents another 'return visit', in this case to my early work on Mountifort Longfield's ideas on value and distribution and their treatment by his successors in the Whately Chair of Political Economy in the University of Dublin. Written and first presented as one of a series of lectures organized to commemorate the 150th anniversary of the founding of that chair in 1832, it reviews my 1945 interpretation of the work of this group of Irish dissenters in the light of developments in the treatment of value and distribution theory in the history of economic thought over the 37 years since I first published it.

Part III is devoted to a series of essays on the economic work of W.S. Jevons, all arising directly or indirectly from my work on the Jevons Papers. Numbers 8 and 9, 'Transitions in Political Economy', were originally the Manchester Special lectures for 1982, two invited lectures given before the University of Manchester to commemorate the centenary of Jevons's death. As they have not been published previously I have taken the opportunity to revise them substantially in the light of recent research on Jevons, by others and by myself. Their overall form and purpose remains unaltered – to present a general survey of the work of Jevons on both economic analysis and economic policy within the context of the idea that his work should be regarded as transitional in character, retaining many features of classical political economy as well as introducing many features of neo-classical economics.

The essays numbered 10 and 11 are in a sense also a pair, although first published more than 20 years apart. Number 10, 'W.S. Jevons and the Foundation of Modern Economics' is the paper which I read at the Bellagio conference on the Marginal Revolution in 1972. In it I stressed that the attributes which Jevons brought to political economy were those of a trained scientist and logician and that this helps to explain the approach which he adopted in *The Theory of Political Economy*, seeking 'to establish the core of [the] subject as a science of economising behaviour'.

While this essay thus deals with Jevons's contribution to the transformation of classical political economy into neo-classical economic science, Number 11, 'Jevons's Contribution to the Teaching of Political Economy in Manchester and London' appeared first in a volume dealing with the institutionalization of economics as an autonomous discipline and was designed as a case study in this process. It shows that in this respect also Jevons was something of a transitional figure – more of an academic than most of his predecessors, but less of one than many of his successors. Yet here again the significance of Jevons's early training in experimental science comes out, influencing him towards research to an extent which set an example for other university economists.

The last essay in Part III, No. 12, 'Jevons, Marshall and the Utilitarian Tradition', was contributed to the Marshall Centenary issue of the *Scottish Journal of Political Economy* at the invitation of its guest editor, Professor D.P. O'Brien, and highlights another important, but very different, side of Jevons's intellectual equipment. In the early stages of my study of Jevons's economic work I came to recognize the significance of Bentham's utilitarianism for it. In the latter half of the 1980s I became interested in the part which utilitarianism, Benthamite or otherwise, played in the thinking of economists throughout the nineteenth century. In this paper I brought these two points together in a comparison of the philosophical backgrounds of Marshall and Jevons, showing how each in his own way blended the old utilitarianism with the new evolutionism.

Part III differs from the other Parts of this book in that it is not linked to any of the long-term projects in which I have tended to get myself involved. I have always been interested in economists as people, and supported Bill Jaffé's view that the understanding of an economist's work can be illuminated by a knowledge of that person's life. Part II then contains a selection of essays about individual economists, some famous and some neglected, but which look at their work from a variety of angles.

The first essay in this group, Number 4, 'Smith's Contribution in Historical Perspective' is the least biographical of the set. Written for the Glasgow University conference convened to mark the bicentenary of the publication of the *Wealth of Nations*, it gave me an opportunity to work with the concept of historical perspective, which I have always considered important but under-utilized in the history of economic ideas, to bring out the widely differing ways in which Smith and his *Wealth of Nations* have been seen by different generations over those two centuries.

Number 5, 'Parson Malthus, the General and the Captain' deals briefly with the lives, and more at length with the works of Major-General Sir William Sleeman and Captain W.R.A. Pettman, R.N., two colourful characters who in the course of active careers found time to write and publish critiques of classical political economy. During the 1950s and 1960s the question, to what extent, if any, Malthus was a forerunner of Keynes was much debated. It was this debate which provided me with an opportunity to put the writings of these two 'neglected economists' into perspective by comparison with the work of Malthus on under-consumption.

Number 6, 'Doctor Kondratieff and Mr Hyde Clarke' is another essay in much the same vein, but here perhaps the life of the man takes pride of place over the work. Hyde Clarke's anticipation of Kondratieff's concept of long waves in economic activity was a brilliantly perceptive insight which he did not really develop very far, possibly through scientific caution, but more probably because in a long life he found so many other interesting things to do.

The final essay in this Part, Number 7, 'Ralph George Hawtrey 1879–1975' returns to the mainstream, being a straightforward biographical memoir of an economist who in my student days was as famous as Keynes for his work on money and the trade cycle. This rather overshadowed the work which he had done in other branches of economics, and in moral philosophy. In this Memoir, prepared for the British Academy, I tried to bring these out as part of what I hope is a balanced assessment of Hawtrey's work, and to do justice to his qualities of character as a person as much as to his qualities of intellect as an economist.

R.D. Collison Black

Notes

1. R. Könekamp to R.D.C. Black, 17 May 1959. (Ms letter in the author's possession.) The letter from Marshall to Jevons, dated '4 Feb. 1875' is reproduced as Letter 416 in Black, 1977b.
2. Further details are given in the Preface to Black and Könekamp 1972 and Black 1977a, as well as in Black 1988.
3. This letter was included as an Addendum to Volume III of Jaffé, 1965, p. 445.
4. The papers were subsequently published in a special issue of *HOPE*, **4**(2), 1972 and afterwards in book form – Black, Coats and Goodwin, 1973a.
5. For further details see 'The CSSRI Research Programme', Appendix A, Whyte, 1990, pp. 261–6.
   John Whyte, sometime Reader in Political Science in Queen's University, Belfast, and from 1984 Professor of Political Science in University College, Dublin, was a member of CSSRI from its inception and Convener of its sub-committee coordinating the conflict research programme. Sadly, he died in 1990 shortly after completing this book.

References

Black, Duncan (1958), *The Theory of Committees and Elections*, Cambridge (England): Cambridge University Press.

Black, R.D. Collison (1945a), 'Trinity College, Dublin and the Theory of Value, 1832–1863', *Economica*, **12**(47), 140–8.

____ (1945b), 'A Select Bibliography of Economic Writings by members of Trinity College, Dublin', *Hermathena*, 66, 55–68.

____ (1947a), *The Statistical and Social Inquiry Society of Ireland, Centenary Volume 1847–1947 with a History of the Society*, Dublin: Eason & Son Ltd.

____ (1947b), 'Economic Studies at Trinity College, Dublin – I', *Hermathena*, 70, 65–80.

____ (1948), 'Economic Studies at Trinity College, Dublin – II', *Hermathena*, 71, 52–63.

____ (1950), 'Theory and Policy in Anglo-Irish Trade Relations, 1775–1800', *Journal of the Statistical and Social Inquiry Society of Ireland*, **18**(3), 1–13.

____ (1953), 'The Classical Economists and the Irish Problem', *Oxford Economic Papers*, New Series, 5(1), 26–40.

____ (1960), *Economic Thought and the Irish Question 1817–1870*, Cambridge (England): Cambridge University Press.

____ (1969), *A Catalogue of Pamphlets on Economic Subjects published between 1750 and 1900 and now housed in Irish libraries*, Belfast: The Queen's University.

____ (1972) (with Rosamond Könekamp), *Papers and Correspondence of William Stanley Jevons*, Vol. I, Biography and Personal Journal, London: Macmillan in association with the Royal Economic Society.

____ (1973a) (with A.W. Coats and Craufurd D. Goodwin (eds)), *The Marginal Revolution in Economics*, Durham NC: Duke University Press.

____ (1973b), *Papers and Correspondence of William Stanley Jevons*, Vol. II, Correspondence 1850–1862, London: Macmillan in association with the Royal Economic Society.

____ (1977a), *Papers and Correspondence of William Stanley Jevons*, Vol. III, Correspondence 1863–1872, London: Macmillan in association with the Royal Economic Society.

____ (1977b), *Papers and Correspondence of William Stanley Jevons*, Vol. IV, Correspondence 1873–1878, London: Macmillan in association with the Royal Economic Society.

____ (1977c), *Papers and Correspondence of William Stanley Jevons*, Vol. V, Correspondence 1879–1882, London: Macmillan in association with the Royal Economic Society.

____ (1977d), *Papers and Correspondence of William Stanley Jevons*, Vol. VI, Lectures on Political Economy 1875–1876, London: Macmillan in association with the Royal Economic Society.

____ (1981), *Papers and Correspondence of William Stanley Jevons*, Vol. VII, Papers on Political Economy, London: Macmillan in association with the Royal Economic Society.

____ (1982a), 'W.S. Jevons's Correspondence with T.E. Jevons', *History of Economic Thought Newsletter*, 29, 1–11.

____ (1982b), 'The Papers and Correspondence of W.S. Jevons: A Supplementary Note', *The Manchester School*, **50**(4), 417–28.

____ (ed.) (1986), *Ideas in Economics*, London: The Macmillan Press Ltd.

____ (1987), 'Le teorie della popolazione prima di Malthus in Inghilterra e in Irlanda' in G. Gioli (ed.), *Le teorie della popolazione prima di Malthus*, Milan: Franco Angeli, pp. 47–69.

____ (1988), 'Editing the Papers of W.S. Jevons', in D.E. Moggridge (ed.) *Editing Modern Economists*, New York: AMS Press, Inc., pp. 19–42.

Fetter, Frank W. (1965), *Development of British Monetary Orthodoxy, 1797–1875*, Cambridge, Mass.: Harvard University Press.

Hall, Frederick G. (1949), *The Bank of Ireland 1783–1946*, Oxford: Basil Blackwell.

Higgs, Henry (1935), *Bibliography of Economics, 1751–1775*, Cambridge (England): Cambridge University Press.

Jaffé, William (1965), *Correspondence of Léon Walras and Related Papers*, Vols. I–III, Amsterdam: North-Holland Publishing Company.

Kress Library of Business and Economics, *Catalogue Through 1776*: 1940; *Supplement*: 1955; *Catalogue 1777–1817*: 1957; *1818–1848*: 1964; Boston, Mass: Baker Library, Harvard Graduate School of Business Administration.

Ohlin, Bertil (1933), *Interregional and International Trade*, Cambridge, Mass.: Harvard University Press.

Sturges, R. Paul (1975), *Economists' Papers 1750–1950. A Guide to Archive and other Manuscript Sources for the History of British and Irish Economic Thought*, London: The Macmillan Press Ltd.

Viner, Jacob (1937), *Studies in the Theory of International Trade*, New York and London: Harper and Brothers.

Viner, Jacob (1950), 'A Modest Proposal for Some Stress on Scholarship in Graduate Training'. Address before the Graduate Convocation, Brown University, June 3, 1950. Reprinted (from *Brown University Papers*, 24) in *The Long View and the Short* (Glencoe, Illinois: Free Press, 1958), pp.369–84.

Wagner, Henry R. (1907), *Irish Economics 1700–1783, a Bibliography with Notes*, London: privately printed, Dryden Press.

Walker, E. Ronald (1943), *From Economic Theory to Economic Policy*, Chicago: University of Chicago Press.

Whyte, John H. (1990), *Interpreting Northern Ireland*, Oxford: Clarendon Press.

PART ONE

POLITICAL ECONOMY
AND THE IRISH

[1]

INVITED LECTURE – HES ANNUAL MEETING
Duke University, May 23-26, 1982

POLITICAL ECONOMY AND THE IRISH

R. D. Collison Black
Queen's University of Belfast

I

According to Professor J. K. Galbraith "all races have produced notable economists with the exception of the Irish who can doubtless protest their devotion to higher arts" (Galbraith (1977) p. 13). More to the point than such a protest might be the comment of one modern Irish historian that "Ireland suffered severely from the consequences of the touching faith of educated opinion . . . in the power of abstract economic theory" (Lee (1973) p. 22). In other words if asked what have the Irish done for political economy? the Irish could well reply, what has political economy done for the Irish?

The purpose of this paper is to look at both these questions and attempt an answer to them, for the period from 1800 to 1920. This, the period of legislative union between Britain and Ireland, also corresponds broadly to the period when the mainstream of economic thought can be said to have been dominated by English classical and neoclassical ideas. Throughout the whole of this period the 'Irish question' was a persistent issue in British politics and public discussion. When it is considered how many other issues were forcing themselves on public attention over that century and more, the persistence of the Irish question is remarkable and proof in itself that the question was no simple single-dimensional one. It did indeed have political, religious and social dimensions, but undoubtedly it also had a very important economic dimension. As Jacob Viner put it, "the 'Irish problem' had many facets, but for the economist it was primarily the problem of Irish poverty" (Viner (1960) p. v). Throughout most of the nineteenth century the majority of the Irish were not only poor, but obtrusively so. Since political economy was concerned with the production and distribution of wealth there were few political economists who did not feel themselves called on at some time to explain why Ireland appeared to produce so little wealth and distribute it so unevenly, and to suggest appropriate remedies. It is necessary to begin from an outline of their subject matter – the Irish economy and its problems – even though no more than a sketch of its main features can be given here.

At the beginning of the nineteenth century, Ireland had come through a period of considerable economic expansion, both in agriculture and industry; yet by the middle of the century its industry had declined substantially and its agriculture had passed through a protracted crisis which culminated in something approaching collapse during the years of the Great Famine from 1846 to 1849. In the broadest terms, this reversal of fortunes can be explained in terms of a rapid growth of population unaccompanied by a corresponding growth in the means to support and employ it.

33

In manufacturing technological change which was so favourable to economic growth in England had almost precisely opposite effects for Ireland, for
the new technology placed a premium on supplies of coal and iron, neither of
which were to be found in quantity anywhere in Ireland. This, combined with
later reductions in transport costs through the development of railroads and
steamships, made it impossible for Irish industries to compete effectively with
their British counterparts except in a few well-known cases of comparative
advantage such as brewing, distilling and linen.

So the burden of supporting a population which increased from under five
millions in 1791 to over eight millions in 1841 fell mainly on agriculture, from
which 66 percent of all families obtained their living at the latter date (*Census of
Ireland*, 1841, p. xviii). Up to 1846 agriculture contrived to carry the burden
although with increasing difficulty in many areas. The output of agriculture increased, but the standard of living of many of those employed in it declined.
This was the result of a complex of relationships between the markets for
agricultural produce, the conditions of cultivation and land tenure, and the
growing pressure of population.

In the early years of the nineteenth century high prices for grain crops led to
a considerable expansion of tillage, which was labour-intensive. With a rapidly
growing population farmers could obtain cheap labour by providing labourers
with small patches of land from which a crop of potatoes, adequate to feed them
and their families, could be raised. Landlords and their agents did not oppose
such sub-division and fragmentation of holdings, for it enabled the labour force
to subsist on the land without reducing the area available for the cultivation of
profitable rent-yielding grain crops.

It was by this means that agriculture carried the growing population, but it
was a process which ensured that few of the benefits of agricultural expansion
filtered down to those at the bottom of the social scale – the cottier labourers.
The slump in the price of wheat and other crops after the end of the Napoleonic
Wars removed one of the essential props from this ramshackle system. "The
more prosperous farmers had the capacity to meet the new circumstances,
albeit with a tightening of the belt: but for many small farmers there was really
no further economy that they could make, and accordingly they either fell
heavily into debt or else lost their hold on the land. The cottier and labourer
encountered a growing reluctance on the part of farmers and landlords to permit
subsistence plots to encroach on profitable land." (Ó Tuathaigh (1972) pp. 135-6).

In this situation a growing proportion of the agricultural population came to
depend on the potato as their essential means of subsistence. Partial failures of
the potato crop in 1817 and 1821 gave grave indications of what a total failure
might involve and when the potato blight came in 1845 to produce just such a
failure in 1846 the long crisis of Irish agriculture was quickly converted into a
catastrophe, the details of which we need not review here. (But cf. Edwards and
Williams (1956).)

After the years of actual famine the government of Lord John Russell took
the view that one of the main requirements for the recovery of the Irish economy was to put new and improving proprietors in place of the old shiftless and

inefficient landlords, many of whom the famine had driven into bankruptcy by burdening them with heavily increased poor rates at a time when they could not collect most of their rents. The government solved this problem by passing the Encumbered Estates Act, 1849 which provided for the speedy sale and transfer of such properties through a special court (one of whose judges, incidentally, was Mountifort Longfield). Little beyond poor relief was offered to the small tenants and labourers, but they proceeded to solve their own problem by means of voluntary emigration. Emigration had been increasing in Ireland before the Famine, but the subsequent scale of the movement was unprecedented; more than 1.1 million people left Ireland, mostly for America, between 1851 and 1860.

Inevitably it was the cottiers and small tenants who were hardest hit by the Famine and later formed the bulk of the emigrants. For those who remained on the Irish land, mostly the more substantial farmers, conditions undoubtedly improved considerably from about 1850 until 1880. Price movements in those years favoured a further shift from grain crops to livestock, and Irish farmers were quick to respond to them. As a result agriculture became reasonably profitable, but afforded relatively little demand for labour or pressure for improved efficiency.

The profitability of agriculture was endangered in the early eighteen-sixties and again in the late eighteen-seventies when the value of agricultural output declined. In these depression years tenants fell into arrears with their rent and so came under threat of eviction from their holdings. Actual evictions were few in number but landlord-tenant relations became embittered and demands for land reform which would give the tenants "fixity of tenure" and "fair rents" became widespread.

Since nothing of the kind existed or seemed to be required in English land law, the British parliament, still heavily influenced by landed interests at this period, was reluctant to grant any such demands but in 1870 Gladstone's first Land Act became law. "In 1870 . . . Gladstone believed, for a time, that he had solved the Irish agrarian problem" (Magnus (1954) p. 203) but his Act gave only a very limited measure of tenant compensation and its limitations were exposed by the onset of agricultural depression in and after 1875. In the years 1877-9 particularly the effects of foreign competition were made worse by the recurrence of bad harvests of potatoes and oats, and the value of Irish tillage produce fell by £14 millions between 1876 and 1879 (Lee (1973) p. 65).

From 1879 onwards the farmers met this new threat to their standard of living in a new way — not by quiet emigration but by noisy agitation. In 1879 the Irish National Land League was formed to campaign for "the land of Ireland for the people of Ireland"; its short-term objective was the protection of tenants against eviction and rent increases and its long-term objective to convert them into owners of their own land. It was the Land League which invented the technique of "boycotting" and as a result of the pressure it was able to exert by this means in Ireland and in Westminster through the Irish Members of Parliament, a series of further Land Acts was passed between 1881 and 1903, initially conceding the principle of tenant security with rents fixed by law, and ultimately that of peasant proprietorship.

Modern writers do not see the solution of the land question as having the key importance in Irish economic development which contemporaries assigned to it (cf. Solow (1971), Lyons (1971)). Certainly the revolution in ownership brought about no revolution in agricultural methods and the growth performance of agriculture remained weak. Nor was the record of development in other sectors much different. Development there was but it was patchy and insufficient to provide even the reduced population with employment at reasonable income levels. Manufacturing industry continued to be confined to the north-eastern part of the country, and especially Belfast. In that city the growth of ship-building and engineering caused an increase of population from 100,000 in 1850 to 400,000 in 1914 and gave it a considerable similarity to the industrial cities of the north of England. Elsewhere in Ireland there was nothing comparable; Dublin and Cork grew little and remained cities in which commerce and the professions mattered more than industry.

The reasons for this are by no means obvious. Lack of natural resources is one possible explanation – but the iron and steel and coal which fed the foundries and shipyards of Belfast were all imported, and could have been equally well imported into Dublin or Cork. Lack of capital was another explanation to which contemporaries attached great weight – but recent research does not support their view. Bank deposits in Ireland rose from £16 million in 1859 to £60 million in 1913 and there was considerable investment also in central and local government bonds. In other words, the Irish investor was not without funds, but generally he was not prepared to risk them in Irish business ventures (Lee (1973) pp. 11-12). This in itself would suggest that there may be more substance in a third explanation which has been less often emphasized – lack of local entrepreneurial ability.

Whatever the reason, the effect of the localisation of manufacturing industry in the north-east was to accentuate the differences which already existed between Ulster and the other three provinces of Ireland. To the religious differences between the Protestant majority in Ulster and the Catholic majority in the rest of the country were added differences in economic interest and outlook; the former were more and more concerned with the problems of industries which required imported raw materials and export markets, and so tended to favour the union with Great Britain and her free trade policy, while the latter were more interested in 'the land for the people,' national independence and protection for the home market.

II

Such then was the material which political economists had to work on in the Irish case in the nineteenth century. Let us now consider how it was perceived and handled by two major schools of economic thought of the time – the English classical economists on the one hand and Marx-Engels on the other.

Turning to the classical economists, the first general point which can be made is that they considered economic development in Ireland to be not only desirable, but practicable. In terms of the Ricardian model, they did not see Ireland as having reached the stationary state; it was rather a case of stagnation or arrested development which could be cured by appropriate policy. As to what the limits of appropriate policy might be, it should be remembered that all the classical economists took the existence of the Act of Union for granted and did not consider any modification of it either possible or necessary; hence they viewed the improvement of the Irish economy entirely within a free trade context. The possibilities of achieving it by protection, manipulation of exchange rates or fiscal variations were therefore excluded from debate.

Within these limitations, the classical economists, up to the time of John Stuart Mill, presented a generally agreed diagnosis of Ireland's ills and a consistent set of proposals for their treatment. The diagnosis rested essentially on those propositions about the relation of population to capital which were basic to the analysis of wages and profits from the time of Adam Smith onwards. In the light of these it seemed clear that in Ireland the increase of population had outstripped the growth of capital, and this accounted for low wages and the intense competition for occupation of land. Hence it followed readily that the first condition for any economic developoment in a genuine sense was an alteration in the ratio of population to capital, whether by an increase of capital, a reduction of population or some well-timed combination of these two.

With agriculture as the source of livelihood for the vast majority of the population, it was here that the adjustment would have to start; most economists considered that a more efficient and productive agriculture could only be secured through replacement of Ireland's cottier system with capitalist leasehold tenancy on the English model – involving an increased investment of capital and the removal of population to allow consolidation of small farms into larger units. For the – inevitably considerable – population thus displaced from the land what were the possible alternative sources of real income and employment? To this the economists' answer was that some, perhaps a majority, might find employment on the land as wage-paid labourers, earning more than they might previously have been able to grub out from their patches of potato ground. The remainder must either be absorbed into non-agricultural employment promoted by private or public investment, or encouraged to emigrate.

On the whole, the economists were disposed to favour state investment in public works only to the extent necessary to create the basic infrastructure required by private enterprise. Incentives to private investment, in turn, were not commonly thought of as going much beyond ensuring 'security' through a stable political climate. Since this could only have a substantial effect in the long term, with pre-Famine rates of population growth it followed that a quite considerable amount of emigration might be required in the short-run if the programme were to be effective.

On the whole, this was a consistent and positive programme, based on a reasoned appraisal of the position in terms of the political economy of the time. To carry it into proper effect would have required a concerted series of measures; this "package" as a whole was never within the realm of practical politics, although some of its separate ingredients were. Yet even if the obstacles to carrying the whole programme out had been removed it is far from certain that it would have produced the desired result. The economists generally seem to have over-estimated the amount of employment which a capitalist agriculture in Ireland would give and to have under-estimated the problems of finding non-agricultural employment or emigration outlets for the remainder of the working population. Above all, they overlooked the strength of the Irish tenants belief in their right to the occupation of the soil, which made them deeply reluctant to accept the status of wage labourers as a substitute.

In fact, as John Stuart Mill forcefully pointed out (Mill (1868) p. 8), much of this development programme was based on the premiss, explicit or implicit, that English conditions provided a norm towards which Ireland should be adjusted as far and as fast as possible. Mill himself did much to change this attitude by his powerful advocacy of peasant proprietorship as a system which he contended would be more acceptable socially in Ireland and no less productive economically.

Mill originally proposed a limited scheme for the resettlement of Irish cottiers on waste lands, of which they were to become the owners after reclaiming the land, as early as 1846-7 and this proposal was subsequently incorporated into his *Principles of Political Economy.* At this time only one other economist, W. T. Thornton, was prepared to advocate peasant proprietorship; although he and Mill were colleagues in the East India Company, they seem to have reached their conclusions on this subject independently (Martin (1976) p. 301).

Twenty years later, during the agitation and debates preceding the passing of Gladstone's Land Act of 1870, Mill was the most respected independent advocate of the case for Irish land reform and occupying ownership; but by then almost every other economist, including the very orthodox J. E. Cairnes was also prepared to concede that in the circumstances of Ireland interference with the workings of the market, to the extent at least of fixing rents and tenures, was permissible.

III

Conventional wisdom suggests the existence of a great gulf between the orthodoxy of the classical economists and the radicalism of Marx and Engels. So a comparison of the approaches of these two schools to the Irish question might be expected to reveal striking contrasts between them. To some extent this is indeed the case, but the similarities between the two approaches are sometimes equally striking and perhaps more interesting, particularly when it is borne in mind that the main classical views of Irish problems were framed before the Famine, while the Marx-Engels diagnosis relates to post-Famine Ireland.

Although the collected writings of Marx and Engels on Ireland fill a substantial volume (Marx-Engels (1971)) they do not represent a comprehensive or systematic treatment of the Irish question; since many of them took the form of newspaper articles they are often more concerned with immediate issues than with general principles. Nevertheless it is possible to build up from these writings an adequate picture of Marx and Engels's application of their tools of analysis to the problems of Ireland. Irish affairs were envisaged by Marx and Engels essentially in terms of the materialist interpretation of history and in a world revolutionary context. Such an approach is, if nothing else, a refreshing change from the well-worn channels of English and Irish nineteenth century debate.

The most substantial treatment which Marx gave to Irish problems is to be found in Volume I of *Capital,* where Marx uses Ireland as an example of the General Law of Capitalist Accumulation (Marx (1887; 1958) Chap. XXV, Section 5f).

In this Marx gives a perceptive account of developments in Ireland from 1849 to 1869, showing how a decrease in total produce had been accompanied by an increase in surplus produce as 'scattered means of production' were transformed into capital through the reduction of the smallest holdings and their consolidation into larger farms. Thus, in his view, the effect of famine and emigration might have been to reduce the population of Ireland in absolute terms, but not to eliminate relative over-population. While the money wages of agricultural labourers might have increased, Marx argued that price rises ensured that real wages had actually fallen − and produced some decidedly inadequate statistics to prove his point.[1]

Marx's interpretation of post-Famine Ireland was therefore a model of an agrarian economy in which the growth of large-scale livestock farming produced increased profits and rents, but forced the reserve army of surplus agricultural labourers either to emigrate or find employment in poor conditions in the town, while those who remained employed on the land obtained lower real wages. He himself described this as "a process which might serve the orthodox economists supremely well for the support of their dogma that poverty is the outcome of absolute overpopulation, and that equilibrium can be re-established by depopulation" (Marx (1887; 1958) pp. 703-4). Marx's disagreement with this conclusion can be deduced from what has already been said, but the affinity between his approach and the Ricardian-style model which so many of the classical commentators used is none the less evident and noteworthy. Marx, always a faithful disciple of Ricardo, on another occasion pointed out that Ricardo had not seen the rent surplus as the "right" of landlords and had seen a clear distinction between the shares of rent, profits and wages. In Ireland pressure of demand for land might enable the landlord to absorb the small tenant's profits and even part of his wage, but there was no sanction in Ricardian theory for this. "Thus, from the very point of view of modern English political economists, it is not the usurping English landlord but the Irish tenants and labourers who have the only right in the soil of their native country." (Marx-Engels (1971) p. 75).

It was precisely considerations of this kind which were leading orthodox or, if one prefers the phrase, *bourgeois* economists like J. S. Mill and Cairnes towards the end of the eighteen-sixties to think in terms of legislative interference with rent contracts and recognition of tenants' rights. Marx and Engels naturally did not envisage matters as developing along such lines and indeed greatly under-estimated the significance of the tenant-right movement and the Land Acts.[2] As Paul Sweezy once wrote, "Marx, recognising and making full

---

[1] Marx quoted only the absolute unweighted prices for provisions and clothing at one Irish workhouse in 1849 and 1869 and argued from this that the price of wage-goods had doubled over the period, while money wages had risen only 60%. Marx (1887 : 1958) p. 706.

[2] On the passing of the first Land Act Marx wrote to Engels "thus the mountain Gladstone has successfully given birth to his Irish mouse" − letter of 17 February 1870, quoted in Steele (1974) p. 350, n. 74.

allowance for the profound transformation effected by the industrial revolution, took as his model an economy based on modern machine industry" (Sweezy (1968) p. 115). In Ireland, however, the industrial revolution had not happened and in Ireland, as elsewhere, Marx and Engels failed to recognise the special relationship of the cultivator to the soil which caused the Irish tenant to believe that he as well as the landlord possessed property rights in it (Mitrany (1961), Chap. 9; Black (1960) pp. 24-5; Solow (1981) p. 301). What was to be expected according to their view was a continuance of the trend towards large-scale agriculture and the eviction of small tenants and cottiers, leading on to a revolution aided and promoted by those who had emigrated to America. In later years, when the flow of cheap food imports from America was producing depression in Irish agriculture and leading to the activities of the Land League, Engels predicted that "The upshot will and must be that it will force upon us the nationalisation of the land and its cultivation by co-operative societies under national control" (Marx-Engels (1971) p. 434).

To Marx and Engels, the most important question was how the revolution which they foresaw in Ireland could be promoted and turned to the advantage of the proletariat, not only in Ireland but elsewhere. At first, in 1867, Marx thought that the process should start by the English workers agitating for self-government for Ireland, accompanied by an agrarian revolution and followed by protective tariffs for Irish manufactures against English competition. By 1869 he had decided that the English working class had no interest in the Irish question and that therefore the reverse process of using the Irish national movement to promote an eventual worker's revolution in England was likely to be more successful (Mansergh (1975) pp. 109-121). However logically this prediction may have followed from Marx's theory of history and of revolution it was one which was not to be borne out by the course of events.

On an overall view, the similarity between the classical and the Marxian approaches to the Irish question again emerges strikingly. It is true that in content the two were widely and obviously different, but in form they are notably similar so far as Ireland is concerned. I have said above that the classical economists had a consistent and positive program, based on a reasoned appraisal of the position in terms of their political economy. The same could equally well be said of Marx and Engels – but they were open to the same criticism. Their program, however consistent in itself, ignored not only many of the facts of the situation but also most of the aspirations of the Irish people.

According to the editor of their Irish papers and manuscripts, L. I. Golman, Marx and Engels "arrived scientifically at the conception of a worker's alliance with the working peasants and of the peasants' involvement in the socialist reconstruction of society under the guidance of the proletariat . . .. They created an essentially new conception of Irish history based on the analytical method of historical materialism." (Marx-Engels (1971) pp. 23-6). Unfortunately this conception of Irish history involves not so much ignoring the facts of Irish history as misconstruing them. In the process Marx and Engels were led to treat like grains of sand some features of the Irish question which have proved to be immovable rocks.

It is natural for those who think in terms of the materialist interpretation of history to treat such things as nationality and religion as of secondary importance, merely superficial manifestations of underlying economic reality. This approach and its corollary, the concept of class warfare between bourgeoisie and proletariat as the only ultimately significant conflict, led Marx constantly to over-simplify and under-estimate what history has shown to be vital factors in the Irish situation – factors of which Engels sometimes showed more appreciation.

Given his general approach to the whole question of religion, it is perhaps scarcely to be expected that Marx should have appreciated the subtle complexities of religious divisions in Ireland. The point, however, is not so much that Marx did not appreciate these often tedious tangles as that he considered that he had no need to try. It was this approach which led him to write at the time when the disestablishment of the Church of Ireland was under consideration: –

"Once the Irish Church is dead, the Protestant Irish tenants in the province of Ulster will unite with the Catholic tenants in the three other provinces of Ireland and join their movement, whereas up to the present landlordism has been able to exploit this religious hostility" (Marx-Engels (1971) p. 160). Now it is undeniable that in Ireland religious differences have often been exploited for economic ends, but to assume that the removal of the privileges of the Anglican Church, to which the majority of the Protestants in Ulster did not belong, would remove the fear and suspicion built up over generations between them and their Catholic neighbours was simply naive and irrelevant.

Contemporary leaders of the Irish national movement, such as Parnell and Michael Davitt (the founder and organiser of the Irish National Land League), would not have disagreed with Marx when he asserted that "the land question was inseparable from the national question." They saw the settlement of the land question as only a stepping-stone to national independence. Yet when self-government for Ireland was ultimately achieved it was not accompanied by any move towards that extinction of private property which Marx considered to be its inevitable concomitant.

Here, to my mind, we reach the heart of the matter. The plain fact is that the conception "of a worker's alliance with the working peasants and of the peasant's involvement in the socialist reconstruction of society under the guidance of the proletariat" is one which possessed no real meaning or appeal for either the rural peasants or the urban workers of Ireland in the nineteenth century. Michael Davitt might advocate the nationalisation of the land, but for the vast majority of the tenants who supported the Land League "the land of Ireland for the people of Ireland" meant that they should become the owners of the land which they cultivated, and the guidance of the proletariat would have been no more acceptable to them than the guidance of the landlord.

So far as the urban workers were concerned, some might share the nationalist aspirations of the peasants, but many had not even that much in common with them. Certainly few of the workers of Belfast would have been prepared to see their jobs threatened by protective tariffs imposed to create employment for workers in the cities and towns of southern Ireland, towards whom they felt more antipathy than affinity. The stubborn insistence of the Irish on clinging to cultural identities and groupings which transcend the boundaries of class has always made the Marxian system a poor instrument for interpreting the Irish question.

IV

The preceding two sections have dealt with the question "What did political economy do for Ireland?" both as regards the main orthodox and the main radical schools of nineteenth century thought. We have now to deal with the other side of the coin − "what did the Irish do for political economy?" To begin with, let us rephrase that question somewhat more precisely. The nineteenth century could be said to be the great formative period of economic science; did Irish economists make any significant or characteristic contribution to its formation? As long ago as 1945 I put forward the view that a noteworthy group of them − the holders of the Whately chair at Trinity College, Dublin from 1832 to 1863 − did (Black (1945)). That view has lately been the subject of some criticism (Moss (1976) pp. 23-4; Hollander (1977) p. 236) but time does not permit me to enter on a detailed discussion of these criticisms here. What I would maintain is this − that if one accepts the distinction made by Sir John Hicks between 'classical political economy' as concerned with a flow of wealth and 'catallactics' as concerned with the study of exchanges (Hicks (1976) pp. 210-214) then the Irish contribution to the development of the subject in the mid-nineteenth century was essentially in the area of catallactics. More particularly, it still seems to me that there were no true Ricardians in Ireland before J. E. Cairnes.

In one sense this is not surprising for Whately, the founder of the first Professorship of Political Economy in Ireland, was also the originator of the term 'catallactics.' In another sense it is surprising when the problem of the size and distribution of the flow of wealth was so much to the fore in Ireland that Irish economists were not more disposed to use the classical model which had been already widely used by others as an engine for the analysis of Irish problems. Some weight must certainly be attached to the influence of Whately, who is known to have taken an active interest in the way in which political economy was taught from the chair he founded, but this cannot outweigh the plain fact that men like Mountifort Longfield and Isaac Butt were original thinkers of some stature, not afraid to strike out a line of their own when teaching economic principles. On the other hand when it came to the consideration of Irish economic problems they were too well acquainted with the realities and details of the situation to try to force them on to the Procrustean bed of the classical model.

This same interest in Irish social and economic problems has been advanced as a reason for the contribution which a later generation of Irish economists made to the development of the historical method in political economy (Koot (1975) p. 312). It is a well-known point that during the methodological controversy of the eighteen-seventies which marked the transition from classical to neo-classical economics there were those who saw the future of the discipline as lying not in the adoption of the quasi-mathematical analytics of Jevons and Walras but in the complete replacement of deductive analysis by historical and institutional studies. It is a less well-known point that the two leading advocates of this approach who wrote in English, John Kells Ingram and T. E. Cliffe Leslie, were both Irishmen. Hence, paradoxically enough, when much of the rest of the

42

world of economists was developing a growing interest in the catallactic approach Irish economists were moving away from that type of theory towards inductive and comparative methods.

Undoubtedly knowledge of the differences between institutions such as land tenure in England and Ireland and the inappropriateness of trying to apply English models to Irish cases did play some part in this, notably for Cliffe Leslie. Yet both he and his contemporary, Ingram, derived their ideas also from other sources outside Ireland. The post which Leslie held at Queen's College, Belfast, was a Chair of Jurisprudence and Political Economy and he was a trained lawyer. It was during his studies at the Middle Temple in London that he came under the influence of Sir Henry Maine, the great advocate of the historical approach to jurisprudence and Leslie later extended this to political economy. For Ingram Irish social questions, such as poor law reform were also important, but the prime influence on the development of his economic thought was Auguste Comte, of whose Positivist philosophy he was a devoted follower. Although nowadays the analytical achievements of the early Whately professors may be more highly esteemed than the methodological contributions of Leslie and Ingram, these latter did enjoy international reputations in their own lifetimes and their cosmopolitan connections were probably not without influence in that respect.

Of all these Irish economists it could be said that their ideas were in some respect heterodox; nevertheless their contributions were to the mainstream of economic thought, and they themselves were accepted members of the academic establishment in their own country. But what of the radicals? Surely Ireland of all places must have bred a few of that kind? If by radical is meant socialist, the answer is that it bred remarkably few of them in the nineteenth century. The only noteworthy example is William Thompson of Glandore, County Cork, "one of the idle classes" as he described himself. Thompson was recognised by Anton Menger and Foxwell as one of the Ricardian Socialists and his writings on surplus value and the exploitation of labour have been regarded as foreshadowing some of the work of Marx, which indeed includes several references to Thompson (Pankhurst (1954) pp. 216-224).

It should surprise no one to learn that Thompson as a socialist landowner came close to being a unique figure in nineteenth century Ireland, but even among other classes socialism had virtually no support.

Yet it does not follow from this that there was no radical political economy in Ireland. The middle of the century saw the beginnings of what John Stuart Mill called "the revolt of mere nationality" – and mere nationality developed its own brand of radical political economy. It was never given a full, and fully reasoned, statement by any Irish writer of the time but its appearance as a distinct set of ideas can be traced to about 1845 when the leadership of the national movement was passing from Daniel O'Connell and his Loyal National Repeal Association to Thomas Davis and the Young Irelanders. I have attempted a fairly detailed account of its main features elsewhere (Black (1971)); consequently here I need only reiterate that its essential ideas could be reduced to two – land reform and protection. Land reform, at first a demand for fixity of tenure for all cultivators, was transmuted after about 1870 into a demand for peasant proprietorship. Nationalisation of the land was indeed advocated by Michael Davitt, as we have already noted (above, p. 10), but in this respect he was almost as exceptional a figure as William Thompson had been in the earlier years of the century. The demand for peasant proprietorship − "the land of Ireland for the people of Ireland" − was primarily political and social in content but the economic argument advanced in its favour was that it would enable a greater number of people to be supported on the land and need not be less productive than large-scale farming, as J. S. Mill had shown.

Development of other sources of employment outside agriculture was nevertheless a strong feature of nationalist political economy, and to create this reliance was primarily placed on protection. Here nationalist thinking was often both naive and ambivalent; it was frequently assumed that protection would allow the growth of 'vast manufactures' of unspecified type without regard to the problems of technology, power sources and investment. Yet the same writers were apt to condemn the evils of the factory system and reluctant to see it destroy the purity of the Irish way of life. Similarly they generally failed to offer any solution to the problem created by the fact that while protection might guarantee the home market to native industry it could also damage those export-oriented industries which already existed, mainly in Ulster. At the end of the nineteenth and the beginning of the twentieth century this came to be of growing importance as one of the factors which divided north and south on the Home Rule issue.

V

Referring back to the two questions posed at the beginning of this paper, I would suggest that the answer to the first is simple, definite, and not the one given by Professor Galbraith. Irishmen did make contributions to the development of political economy in the nineteenth century, and contributions which would bear comparison with those from any other country. To the second question the answer is less simple and less clear. Political economists of all schools attempted to do much for Ireland and no doubt in every case those efforts were well meant; whether they were well directed is another matter.

On the one hand, both the classical and Marxian schools brought to bear upon the Irish problem their different but equally impressive analytical systems and used them to reason through to logical conclusions on which they based policy programs, sometimes broadly indicated, sometimes worked out in great detail. Yet these programs had, in the circumstances of the time, little chance of ever being carried out in full, and equally little prospect of producing results which would have satisfied the Irish people if they had been. (cf. Ó Tuathaigh (1972) p. 145).

On the other hand, the analysis and prescriptions put forward by what may be called the 'national economists' tended to be strong where the classical and Marxian analyses were weak, but weak in the areas where they were sound. The nationalist approach gave all due weight to the character and aspirations of the majority of Irish people − particularly to the special character of their attitudes towards the land. As aginst this the romantic bias of the early nationalists in particular led them to disdain economic analysis and to consider economic facts as capable of manipulation at will. Hence they failed to think out the implications and interrelations of their proposals or to face and make clear the fact that they might involve difficult choices – for example between a large population with a low standard of living and a small population with a higher standard.

While the classical economic analysis of Ireland's problems favoured free trade, reliance on the market mechanism and a contract system, the nationalist alternative favoured a status system, protection and the preservation of social stability. The former offered the prescription which was most likely to appeal to the industrial and commercial interests of Dublin and Belfast, along with the large farmers of the eastern counties; the latter offered a prescription with more appeal to the small farmers and tenants of the south and west. The third alternative – the Marxian prescription – had little appeal to any but the smallest minority.

Eventually political forces ensured that the nationalist alternative was the one adopted, first by the British parliament enacting the means to peasant proprietorship and later by the independent Irish government which nationalism had brought into existence enacting protection to home industries.

It may be too much to say, as has been suggested, that the nationalist insistence on protectionism "formed an insurmountable obstacle to any compromise between Protestant Ulster and the South" (Strauss (1951) p. 280) but it certainly did nothing to reduce the divisions between those two parts of the country. Apart from this, it can be said that the effect of adopting the economic philosophy favoured by the nationalists was to make Ireland an economy in which security took priority over progress. Of recent years, some observers who had noticed this have argued that if in Ireland economic development was sacrificed for the sake of national identity, this was a choice which the Irish were entitled to make.[3]

Now the intellectual validity of this proposition is beyond question; what is questionable is whether the Irish ever consciously made the choice. It would probably be nearer to historical truth, although less flattering to Irish sensibilities, to say that the majority of them either ignored the existence of the choice, or what is almost the same thing, persuaded themselves that it was possible to have both economic development and a securely conservative and nationalist society. Certainly nationalist writers rarely, if ever, made the choice clear; only too often was it suggested that national independence must bring prosperity to all.

In the years just after the Famine the majority of the Irish people might have been willing to accept a low standard of living if they had been also guaranteed security to live on the land in which they had been born. But in the century that followed the Irish were no more exempt from "the revolution of rising expectations" than any other people and they had the example of the higher standards achieved by emigrant relatives and friends to set the standard for them. Thus while the desired security was obtained through the alteration of policies and

---

[3]"If the Irish sacrificed economic progress on the altar of Irish nationalism, who can say it was the wrong choice?" – Solow (1971) p. 204.

"The Irish . . . were blamed for failing to achieve materialist and rationalist goals in which they were only marginally interested" – Hutchinson (1970) p. 529.

institutions, the fruits of economic progress were also sought – and to some extent obtained.

How was it possible in this way to evade the hard choice and gain both security and a rising standard of living? The key was found in a feature of the Irish economy which the Irish have always deplored – persistent emigration. In the eighteen-fifties and after "the Irish farmer behaved as a rational economic man, and, after the wave of famine evictions ebbed, it was he, not the landlord, who drove his children and the labourers off the land" (Lee (1973) p. 10). So it continued for the rest of the nineteenth century, and after. During most of that time it was comparatively easy for Irishmen to transfer their labour to Britain or America, so that a proportion of the population remaining in Ireland were able to maintain themselves in secure niches at acceptable standards of living. Those for whom there were no such niches and who were not content to accept lower standards had to find opportunities in other countries. By this means the Irish reluctance to accept change and surrender traditional values was reconciled with the equally real Irish desire to enjoy the fruits of economic progress.

If this interpretation is accepted, it follows that the nationalist solution to the economic aspects of the Irish question was not really any more satisfactory *in economic terms* than the classical solution might have been, or perhaps the Marxist solution either. The advantage which it had over both was simply that it was feasible. By combining a mediocre economic policy with maintenance of the social and political norms which were acceptable to the majority of the people it succeeded ultimately in producing an adjustment which enabled one historian to write in 1951:

"What used to be called "The Irish Question" has suffered the inevitable eclipse of all problems which have held the centre of the public stage for a long time. The hatreds and enthusiasms of the previous generation appear quaint and faintly ridiculous when their causes have disappeared, and nothing is less interesting than the attempt to rake up the embers of old controversies." (Strauss (1951) p. v).

Unfortunately the assumption that the causes of the Irish Question had disappeared was too facile. The potential for conflict still lay in the differences of culture among the Irish, so that twenty years later they had succeeded in raking the embers of old controversies into fresh and searing flames and thrusting the Irish Question back into the centre of British politics. That unhappy story lies outside the scope of this paper, but perhaps the account of how every major school of economic thought in the nineteenth century failed in various degrees to come up with a successful answer to the Irish Question may suffice to show that it was, and is, a problem with more dimensions than the merely economic.

REFERENCES

BLACK, R. D. Collison (1945) "Trinity College, Dublin, and the Theory of Value, 1832-1863," *Economica*, Vol. XII, No. 47, pp. 140-8.

BLACK, R. D. Collison (1960) *Economic Thought and the Irish Question, 1817-1870*, London, Cambridge University Press.

BLACK, R. D. Collison (1972) "The Irish Experience in Relation to the Theory and Policy of Economic Development" *in Economic Development in the Long Run*, ed. A. J. Youngson, pp. 192-210. London, Allen and Unwin.

EDWARDS, R. D. and WILLIAMS, T. D. (1956) *The Great Famine: Studies in Irish History 1845-52*, Dublin, Browne and Nolan.

GALBRAITH, J. K. (1977) *The Age of Uncertainty*, London, Andre Deutsch.

HICKS, J. R. (1976) " 'Revolutions' in economics;; *in Method and Appraisal in Economics*, ed. S. J. Latsis, pp. 207-18. Cambridge (England), Cambridge University Press.

HOLLANDER, S. (1977) "The Reception of Ricardian Economics," *Oxford Economic Papers*, Vol. 29, No. 2, pp. 221-57.

HUTCHINSON, B. (1970) "On the Study of Non-Economic Factors in Irish Economic Development," *Economic and Social Review*, Vol. 1, No. 4, pp. 509-530.

KOOT, G. M. (1975) "T. E. Cliffe Leslie, Irish Social Reform, and the Origins of the English Historical School of Economics," *History of Political Economy*, Vol. 7, No. 3, pp. 312-36.

LEE, J. J. (1973) *The Modernisation of Irish Society, 1848-1918*, Dublin, Gill and Macmillan.

LYONS, F. S. L. (1971) *Ireland since the Famine*, London, Weidenfeld and Nicolson.

MAGNUS, P. (1954) *Gladstone: A Biography*, London, John Murray.

MANSERGH, N. (1975) *The Irish Question, 1840-1921*, 3rd edition, London, Allen and Unwin.

MARTIN, D. E. (1976) "The rehabilitation of the peasant proprietor in nineteenth century economic thought: a comment," *History of Political Economy*, Vol. 8, No. 2, pp. 297-302.

MARX, K. (1887 : 1958) *Capital*, Volume I. Translated from the third German edition by S. Moore and E. Aveling and edited by F. Engels, London, 1887; reprinted Moscow, Foreign Languages Publishing House, 1958.

MARX, K. and ENGELS, F. (1971) *Ireland and the Irish Question*, London, Lawrence and Wishart.

MITRANY, D. (1961) *Marx against the Peasant*, New York, Collier Books.

MOSS, L. S. (1976) *Mountifort Longfield: Ireland's First Professor of Political Economy*, Ottawa, Illinois, Green Hill Publishers.

Ó TUATHAIGH, G. (1972) *Ireland before the Famine 1798-1848*, Dublin, Gill and Macmillan.

PANKHURST, R. K. P. (1954) *William Thompson (1775-1833)*, London, Watts and Co.

Report of the Commissioners appointed to take the Census of Ireland for the year 1841 (Dublin, 1843).

SOLOW, Barbara L. (1971) *The Land Question and the Irish Economy, 1870-1903*, Cambridge, Mass., Harvard University Press.

SOLOW, Barbara L. (1981) "A New Look at the Irish Land Question," *Economic and Social Review*, Vol. 12, No. 4 (July 1981) pp. 301-314.

STEELE, E. D. (1974) *Irish Land and British Politics, 1865-1870*, London and Cambridge, Cambridge University Press.

STRAUSS, E. (1951) *Irish Nationalism and British Democracy*, London, Methuen and Co. Ltd.

SWEEZY, P. M. (1968) "Karl Marx and the Industrial Revolution" *in Events, Ideology and Economic Theory*, ed. R. V. Eagly, Detroit, Wayne State University Press.

VINER, J. (1960) Foreword to Black (1960), pp. v-viii.

[2]

Reprinted from THE ECONOMIC HISTORY REVIEW
Second Series, Vol. XXI, No. 2, 1968
PRINTED IN ENGLAND BY THE BROADWATER PRESS LTD, WELWYN GARDEN CITY

Economic Policy in Ireland and India in the Time of J. S. Mill[1]

By R. D. COLLISON BLACK

I

"THOSE Englishmen who know something of India, are even now those who understand Ireland best," wrote John Stuart Mill in 1868.[2] "Persons who know both countries, have remarked many points of resemblance between the Irish and the Hindoo character; there certainly are many between the agricultural economy of Ireland and that of India." To Mill it appeared that England's government of India was comparatively more successful than her government of Ireland; and this he attributed to the fact that those who were responsible for the government of India had succeeded in "shaking off insular prejudices, and governing another country according to its wants, and not according to common English habits and notions", whereas for Ireland this had never been done. "What was not too bad for us, must be good enough for Ireland, or if not, Ireland or the nature of things was alone in fault."

The purpose of this article is to compare some of the main aspects of economic policy in Ireland and India in Mill's day, and to consider whether, as he believed, the paternal government of India was more successful than the semi-representative government of Ireland in its handling of the problems involved.

Such a comparison may have interest not only for the history of events but also for the history of ideas. Was the apparatus of economic thought which the policy-makers used in India and in Ireland essentially the same and did they apply it in the same way? Or did the obvious differences in customs, language, and many other factors make the Anglo-Indian official less willing to apply the "principles of [English] political economy" than his counterpart concerned with Irish problems? Was he perhaps more willing, and at the same time better able, to pursue an active policy of intervention where economic matters were concerned? Before proceeding to a comparison of policies and their results, it is necessary to look a little more closely at the term used above—"in Mill's day". John Stuart Mill entered the service of the East India Company in 1823, and died just half a century later. Does this half-century constitute a historical period in any true sense for Ireland, for India, for the development of economic ideas?

It is in this latter context that the period is perhaps a most meaningful one, for Mill's adult life did correspond almost exactly with the period of dominance of that Ricardian political economy in which his father had schooled him so thoroughly. Likewise in Ireland, these fifty years form a significant era, running from the emergence of "the Irish difficulty" in inescapable form during the distress of

---

[1] This article is based upon a paper read at the Economic History Society's Conference in Belfast in April 1967.
[2] Mill, *England and Ireland* (1868), p. 22. Wherever the name Mill is used by itself in this article, it is to be understood to refer to John Stuart Mill.

the years after Waterloo to the first real attempt to dispose of it by Gladstone's land legislation.[1]

It is in regard to India that the period has perhaps least distinctive quality, certainly if it be strictly interpreted in calendar terms. Yet, as Dr Thomas R. Metcalf has recently shown, it was in the years after the end of the Napoleonic Wars that the new spirit of liberalism and reform began to spread from Britain to India, while "the post-Mutiny decade was, in fact, with the possible exception of Curzon's Viceroyalty, the last great creative era for the British in India. From the 1870's onward they were concerned almost exclusively with the simple day-to-day operation of the administrative machinery."[2]

If it be accepted then that, considered broadly, "the time of John Stuart Mill" constitutes a valid historical period, we may turn our attention to those problems with which economic policy had to grapple in Ireland and India during that period.

At first sight, Ireland and India might seem to afford more grounds for contrast than comparison: but in the nineteenth century the similarity, remarked by Mill, between the economies of the two countries was quite considerable. In each, a growing population strained the resources of a backward agriculture, which was yet the only source of employment for the vast majority. Consequently, those charged with the government of both countries faced similar problems in regard to economic policy, arising eventually from the extreme poverty of the great mass of the people.

It hardly needs to be emphasized that the policy-makers of that day did not see the problem of economic development as involving them in a concerted effort to raise levels of real income, as would their counterparts today. Nevertheless, in India certainly its British governors realized their responsibility for the welfare of the people, and recognized its economic dimension.[3] In the case of Ireland there was not the same conviction that responsibility for the material welfare of the people rested, even partially, on the government; but certainly after 1829 it became clear that the problems which government faced in Ireland were not merely political and religious but economic also. They could not be solved by coercion alone, and conciliation must have its economic side.

To deal comprehensively with every aspect of economic policy as it developed in Ireland and India in the nineteenth century would require at least a volume, rather than a paper. Hence discussion must here be confined to two salient aspects of policy, important in both countries at the time and of interest for the light which examination of them may throw on the questions raised at the outset— these are land tenure and public works.

II

Land tenure forms the natural starting-point in a survey of economic policy in Ireland and India, for in the nineteenth century the dependence of the great

---

[1] For a fuller development of this point, see R. D. Collison Black, *Economic Thought and the Irish Question, 1817–1870* (Cambridge, 1960), pp. 2–3.

[2] T. R. Metcalf, *The Aftermath of Revolt, India 1857–1870* (Princeton, 1965), p. ix.

[3] "The welfare of the people of India is our primary object. If we are not here for their good, we ought not to be here at all," wrote its Viceroy, Lord Mayo, in 1870.—W. W. Hunter, *Life of the Earl of Mayo* (1875), II, 276.

majority of the population of both countries on agriculture made the ownership and cultivation of land the central economic issues in them.

It is unnecessary here to enter into a detailed account of the tenure systems of the two countries and the successive phases of land legislation in each of them during our period.[1] The approach used here will be to examine the attitudes of policy-makers to the institutions of land tenure, stressing the economic philosophy which conditioned those attitudes. We may begin from the fundamental and familiar concept of the contrast between custom and status on the one hand and contract on the other. The native land systems of both Ireland and India included considerable elements of status defined only by custom, and therefore by no means precisely defined. But "the British mind found incomprehensible a society based on unwritten custom and on government by personal discretion; and it knew of only one sure method of marking off public from private rights—the introduction of a system of legality".[2]

The replacement of native systems of law by British ones occurred at widely different periods in Ireland and India, and by the beginning of the nineteenth century Irish land law, outside Ulster at least, was ostensibly the same as English, although recollections among the people of an older and different system had by no means disappeared. Whatever the ostensible similarities, by the end of the Napoleonic Wars subdivision, sub-letting, tenancies-at-will, and absentee land-lords had produced a situation in Ireland which was patently different from that in England, and the depression of the post-war years made it clear that changes in the land system were the key to economic improvement.

At this time the prevailing attitude towards landed property among British policy-makers was what may be called "the Whig view". According to this, the system of land law which held out the best prospect of social stability and economic progress was one in which substantial landlords gave long leases of medium to large farms to improving tenants—not surprisingly, just that system which existed in England. Considered from this viewpoint, the solution of the land problem in Ireland lay in overhaul, rather than radical reform, of the existing system. It must cease to be a caricature of the English mode of land tenure and become instead its counterpart. This was a view which naturally found favour in the British parliaments of the day, and led to the passage of such legislation as the Sub-letting Act of 1826. Its essential aim was to replace the rabble of small subsistence tenants with capitalist farmers who would employ the people as wage labourers, and if necessary also to replace insolvent and improvident landlords by solvent and improving ones. Other legislative monuments to this view are the Incumbered Estates Act of 1849 and Deasy's Act of 1860, which laid down that "the relation of landlord and tenant shall be deemed to be founded on the express or implied contract of the parties, and not upon tenure or service."[3]

The problem of replacing the native system of land tenure arose in India not only at a later period than in Ireland but also under very different circumstances, since the greater part of the public revenues of India had been derived from land

---

[1] For such accounts see E. Hooker, *Re-adjustments of Agricultural Tenure in Ireland* (Chapel Hill, 1938); B. H. Baden-Powell, *Land Systems of British India*, 3 vols. (Oxford, 1892); E. Stokes, *The English Utilitarians and India* (Oxford, 1959), ch. II, 'Political Economy and the Land Revenue'.

[2] Stokes, op. cit. p. 82.   [3] 23 & 24 Vict. C.154.

taxes under the Mogul Empire. The same Whig view of the proper form which landed-property relations should take can be seen to emerge, notably in the famous Permanent Settlement of Bengal, carried through by Cornwallis in 1793.

Under the Moguls the land revenue had been collected from the *ryots*, or cultivators, through a class of *zemindars*, a term literally meaning "landholder". Whether the *zemindars* were or were not proprietors or landlords in the English sense was a matter of dispute amongst the Company's officials in Bengal, but the view of Sir John Shore, who held the *zemindars* to be proprietors subject only to the payment of a customary revenue to the government, prevailed. Shore thought that the company should determine the amount of revenue to be demanded from the *zemindars* for a period of years, leaving open the possibility of revision after the land had been more thoroughly surveyed. Cornwallis, however, believed that a permanent settlement of the revenue demand would provide the *zemindars* with a powerful incentive to improvement, and succeeded in obtaining the approval of the directors for his proposal to make the settlement arrived at in 1790 for ten years a perpetual one.[1]

The scathing judgement passed on this measure by James Mill in his *History of British India* is well known:

> There was an opportunity in India, to which the history of the world presents not a parallel. Next, after the sovereign, the immediate cultivators had, by far, the greatest portion of interest in the soil: For the rights (such as they were) of the *zemindars*, a complete compensation might have easily been made: The generous resolution was adopted of sacrificing to the improvement of the country, the proprietary rights of the sovereign: The motives to improvement which property gives, and of which the power was so justly appreciated, might have been bestowed upon those . . . from whom alone, in every country, the principal improvements in agriculture must be derived, the immediate cultivators of the soil: And a measure, worthy to be ranked among the noblest that ever were taken for the improvement of any country, might have helped to compensate the people of India, for the miseries of that misgovernment which they had so long endured—But the legislators were English aristocrats; and aristocratical prejudices prevailed.[2]

This view of the Bengal settlement was adopted without reservation by John Stuart Mill. In his *Principles of Political Economy* he quoted his father's comment with approval and characterized the measure as a total failure. Its promoters, he contended, "flattered themselves that they had created, throughout the Bengal provinces, English landlords, and it proved that they had only created Irish ones".[3] Ten years later, in his classic defence of the East India Company's rule, the *Memorandum on the Improvements in the Administration of India during the Last Thirty Years*, Mill made the same point even more strongly:

> Justice to the subsequent Governments of India requires it to be understood that in the most fertile and valuable portion of the Indian territory, they inherited from their predecessors an agrarian system, consisting of great landlords and cottier tenants, forming as close a parallel as the difference between Europe and Asia will

---

[1] Cf. G. W. Forrest, *Selections from the State Papers of the Governors-General of India : Lord Cornwallis* (Oxford, 1926), II, 72–126.

[2] James Mill, *History of British India*, ed. H. H. Wilson (1848), v, 491–2.

[3] Mill, *Principles of Political Economy* (1848), bk II, ch. IX, § 4.

admit, to the condition of Munster and Connaught; and that the Government has had, during the last sixty years, no more power of correcting the evils of this system, than the government of the mother country had, during the same period, of remedying the evils of a similar system in Ireland.[1]

The vehemence with which both James and John Stuart Mill attacked the Permanent Settlement of Bengal appears somewhat surprising if one takes the conventional view of classical political economy and its presumed association with *laissez-faire*. On this basis, one would expect a classical economist to support measures which encouraged the establishment of improving landlords and gave them a strong motive to profit by leasing their properties—and many nineteenth-century economists did take just this attitude.

The Mills' support of small proprietors and direct relations between these and the state can only be understood when it is recognized that they placed their own radical gloss on Ricardian rent theory, and hence departed fundamentally from what has here been called "the Whig view".[2] That the Ricardian theory could lead to highly radical doctrines as to the ownership of land and the taxation of its revenues is a familiar truth, but most people associate such doctrines with Henry George and not with the Utilitarians themselves. The great stress which Bentham laid on "security" and the danger of tampering with existing property relations prevented anything more extreme than John Stuart Mill's proposal for a tax on land-value increments from emerging in the English context, but the situation was quite different in relation to India, and somewhat different in relation to Ireland.

As Stokes has shown,[3] belief in the Ricardian view of rent as a pure surplus, and therefore an especially eligible source of public revenue, led the Mills to wish to avoid establishing any class of proprietors or quasi-proprietors intermediate between the state and the cultivator in India. This led them, again somewhat contrary to what might be expected, to take the side of some of the old school of Indian administrators, notably Sir Thomas Munro, who had developed the *ryotwar* system of land-revenue settlement in Madras in the early years of the nineteenth century.[4] This system involved making individual settlements of land tax directly with the individual cultivators, and for varying terms.

Munro's original *ryotwari* settlements were an attempt to discover and record the traditional rights of cultivators, but in Regulation VII of 1822 the influence of Ricardian doctrine was manifest in the attempt to define the "net produce" as the criterion for the revenue demand. While this regulation provided for comprehensive investigation of existing proprietary rights, it did not settle them on any particular class, in an attempt to avoid a repetition of the problems created by the *zemindari* settlements. In the years that followed, the Indian administration included those who favoured direct dealings with cultivators and those who were willing to maintain "superior tenures", but there seems little reason to question the judgement of an experienced Indian civil servant of the time, Sir George Campbell, who afterwards recounted how "the battle between the offi-

---

[1] P. 5; Parl. Papers, 1857–8 (75), xliii.

[2] This has been very fully and clearly shown by Stokes (op. cit.).   [3] Ibid. p. 91.

[4] For an account of the ideas and policy of Munro and his associates see T. H. Beaglehole, *Thomas Munro and the Development of Administrative Policy in Madras, 1792–1818* (Cambridge, 1966).

cers who supported the claims of the aristocracy and those who took the more popular view raged with intensity in the course of the settlement . . . neither one nor the other entirely prevailed: but it is not to be denied that the party which looked with disfavour on aristocratic claims had eventually more support of authority than the other".[1] Further evidence of the continuance of this state of affairs is provided by the history of the annexation of Oudh in 1856. In this colourful but ill-governed kingdom, much power had been exercised by local chieftains, known as *talukdars*, whose position in matters of land tenure was closely analogous to that of the *zemindars* in Bengal. Significantly enough, the first orders given to the British settlement officers were to deal with the village communities and to place on the *talukdars* the onus of proving their right to superior tenures.

While the land settlements effected in India after 1822 were certainly not without their defects and their critics, to John Stuart Mill they appeared as enlightened and praiseworthy as the Bengal settlement was regrettable. Under them, he argued in 1858, "the agricultural population either have, or will shortly have, the benefits of tenures and rights perfectly defined, and secured, and moderate rents fixed for a sufficient term to afford, in full strength, the natural incentives to improvement."[2] This was certainly more than could be said for the agricultural population of Ireland at the same date.

The passage of some thirty-five years had made clear the failure of the attempts to solve the Irish land problem along strict contract lines. From about 1830 onwards, the desire of the occupiers for security of tenure—essentially as described by Mill for India in the quotation above—gradually developed into a well-organized political demand. During the winter of 1846-7, Mill had himself published proposals which, though much milder in character than those which he and his father had advocated for India, still displayed the Radical basis of his thought. Mill's scheme involved the acquisition of waste lands by the state and the settlement of cottiers on it with fixity of tenure: interference with the institution of landed property other than waste was not contemplated, but Mill hoped that if his scheme was implemented capitalist farming in the rest of Ireland would become a practical proposition.[3]

Mill's influence on policy-making for Ireland was negligible compared to his influence in Indian affairs, and all attempts to secure statutory recognition of the tenant's rights, even to compensation for improvements, were defeated. Yet the unique opportunity, afforded by the Famine and its consequences, to sweep away both poor tenants and bad landlords did not bring the orthodox policy any nearer to success. In the late 1860's the strength of the Irish demand for fixity of tenure grew and was supported vigorously by Mill among others.[4] The demand was not conceded by Gladstone in his Land Act of 1870, but this did sanction compensation to tenants for disturbance as well as improvements. Hence the view that the position of the tenant must be defined and protected by law rather than left to

[1] G. Campbell, 'The Tenure of Land in India', in Cobden Club, *Systems of Land Tenure* (1870), p. 184. Campbell's statement referred primarily to the settlement in the North-West provinces.

[2] Mill, *Memorandum on the Improvements in the Administration of India during the Last Thirty Years* (1858), p. 7 (see p. 325, n. 1 above).

[3] Mill, *Principles of Political Economy*, 1st edn (1848), I, 381-400.

[4] Notably in his *England and Ireland* (quoted above, p. 321). For a fuller account of the interactions of thought and policy on Irish land at this period see Black, op. cit. pp. 51-71.

individual bargain and contract at length came to be a part of official policy for Ireland. On the other hand, over this same period in India the tide of affairs was running somewhat in the opposite direction.

The mutiny created a sharp change in the ideas of British administrators about land tenures in India. It was in the north-west provinces and in Oudh that the mutiny gained most ground, and there were many who attributed this to the way in which the status of the old native aristocracy had been undermined by the land settlements; numerous accounts were given of the way in which the people had reverted to their old allegiance to the *talukdars* and *zemindars*. It appears to have been this view of events which influenced Lord Canning, the Governor-General, to undo what had been done towards a land settlement in Oudh by the somewhat sweeping procedure of confiscating the entire property of the *talukdars*, and offering to restore it to them in full if they would submit and give their full allegiance to the Crown. Thus it was hoped to regain the support of the native leaders, and those who favoured their pretensions afterwards argued that the re-grant of their possessions gave absolute control of the land to the *talukdars* and abolished all subordinate rights.

The question of the relative rights of *talukdars* and *ryots* in Oudh arose at a time when the status of the cultivators in Bengal was also under examination. Their position, which had been left so vague under the Permanent Settlement, was attempted to be regulated by the famous Act X of 1859; its main provision conferred the right of continued tenancy at a "fair rent" on every *ryot* who had been in occupation of his holding for twelve years or more, excepting those who held under the terms of written leases. When the question of what constituted a fair rent came to be determined in the courts, the Chief Justice, Sir Barnes Peacock, decided that it must be regarded as the highest rent which could be obtained in open competition. This would have nullified the effect of the Act, which was intended to protect the customary position of the *ryot*, but when the matter was referred to the High Court, Peacock's decision was reversed.[1]

Hence the rights of the cultivators in Bengal were protected, but in the ensuing decade the conflict between those who advocated, broadly, the *ryotwari* and the *zemindari* systems of land tenure broke out in other parts of India—notably in Oudh and even in the Punjab. When new settlements were being made in these provinces in the 1860's the settlement commissioners were unfavourably disposed towards the *ryots'* claims, but in each case the Governor-General, Sir John Lawrence, whose long experience had accustomed him to land settlements with the cultivators, intervened to protect their interests,[2] and in 1868 gained support from Mill and Sir Henry Maine for his defence of the Punjab tenants.[3]

By this time, the appointment of Lord Mayo to succeed Sir John Lawrence as Viceroy had been announced. Since he was a Tory landowner who, as Irish Chief Secretary, had always stopped short of introducing legislation conferring any real security of tenure in that country, Mayo's appointment certainly seemed well calculated to advance the interests of the "aristocratic party" in India. Mill "dreaded to think" what would happen as a result of it,[4] but in fact Mayo's term

[1] Metcalf, op. cit. p. 184; Bosworth Smith, *Life of Lord Lawrence* (1883), II, 549–51.   [2] Ibid. II, 556–8.
[3] Mill to Henry Maine, 1 Jan. 1869, in H. S. R. Elliot, *Letters of John Stuart Mill* (1910), II, 169–72.
[4] Mill to Sir Charles Dilke, 9 Feb. 1869, in ibid. p. 188.

of office brought no significant weakening of the cultivators' position.[1] As Campbell shrewdly pointed out, it was his birth and circumstances which had made Mayo a Tory, but outside of Ireland he could follow his natural bent towards radicalism; "what really made him a power in India was his hearty sympathy for the people."[2]

Nevertheless, there can be no doubt that between 1857 and 1873 there was in India, as Mill said, "a reaction towards landlordism of the present English type, at the very time when in England opinion is, though slowly, beginning to turn the contrary way".[3] Thus in matters of land tenure, developments in India and Ireland over this period ran in opposite directions, policy in Ireland moving towards greater recognition and protection of the tenant, while in India the attempt to record and preserve the status of the tenant gave way to a policy more favourable to the rights and interests of superior landholders. Yet it would be wrong to represent the trends in the two countries as equal and opposite—a movement from contract to status in one, as against a movement from status to contract in the other—there was nothing so complete and general in either case; and it would be fair to say that if at the end of the period the position of the Irish tenant had been strengthened, but not greatly, the position of the Indian tenant had been undermined, but not greatly. In law, the Indian *ryot* generally enjoyed much greater security than the Irish tenant. Even in Oudh, where the aristocratic approach had been most fully accepted, the *talukdars* had promised privileges to their tenants which Irish landlords, outside Ulster, were most unwilling to concede, while in Bengal the bias of the Permanent Settlement towards the *zemindars* had largely been redressed by Act X of 1859. The fact that it was possible to have such a law, which specifically confined rents within "fair" limits, in India in 1859 is significant when it is remembered that in 1869 even Gladstone could not bring himself to contemplate the possibility of a legal restraint on rents in Ireland.[4]

These contrasts were not lost on Mill's contemporaries, and the supporters of the Irish tenant cause made frequent use of such comparisons with India in the attempt to press their claims. This is particularly noticeable during the 1860's, the very period when Indian authorities felt that matters were retrograding so far as the *ryot* was concerned. So in 1866, when the limited concessions which John Strachey had extracted from the *talukdars* in Oudh were announced, William Malcolmson, one of the few successful industrialists in the south of Ireland and a strong believer in tenant-right, at once wrote to the Chief Secretary,[5] saying that "this which to the Government of India seems fair and just ... is what we ask you as representing the legislating element of the present Government in this country to originate and carry out in the next session of Parliament."[6] Irishmen often looked enviously at the ease with which land legislation was carried out in India, while in Ireland years of agitation could not produce similar

---

[1] Only one important piece of land legislation was passed in India during Mayo's viceroyalty, the Punjab Land Revenue Act, XXXIII of 1871, which was in the nature of a consolidating Act and did not undermine the legislation of 1868.—Fitzjames Stephen, 'Legislation under Lord Mayo', in Hunter, op. cit. II, 211.

[2] G. Campbell, *Memoirs of my Indian Career* (1893), II, 205, and cf. Metcalf, op. cit. p. 201.

[3] Mill to Henry Maine, 1 Jan. 1869, in Elliot, op. cit. II, 169.

[4] Cf. J. Morley, *Life of Gladstone* (1903), II, 291.

[5] By coincidence, this was Lord Naas, who afterwards, as the Earl of Mayo, became Viceroy of India.

[6] Malcolmson to Naas, 9 Oct. 1866 (Mayo Papers, National Library of Ireland).

reforms. Isaac Butt saw clearly enough the reason for it: "And this is not done in the case of Ireland, just because we have the fiction of an identity with England. The owner of the soil is a 'landlord' not a '*zemindar*'—the occupier is a 'tenant', and not a '*ryot*'. I believe in my conscience, that if we had Irish or Gaelic names to express the relation, if the owner were a '*corbe*' and the occupier a '*kerne*', an English Parliament would not for one session tolerate the continuance of the wrong. Our misfortune is that English phrases are applied to relations that bear no resemblance to the things which the words describe in the English tongue."[1]

Butt's argument here closely corroborates the views of Mill, and there can be no doubt that the administrators of India, whose own interests were not involved in the question, were prepared to do much more to regulate the concerns of Indian landlords and tenants equitably than English ministries, appointed from a Parliament still dominated by landlords, would or could do on the same score for Ireland. In Mill's day the Indian *ryot* certainly received more consideration from his government than did the Irish tenant; but it does not follow from this that, as Mill believed, India was, in these matters, "governed according to its wants, and not according to English habits and notions". There is ground for the argument that while the theory of property applied at this time in India was more generous and democratic than that applied in Ireland, it was nonetheless alien to Indian ideas and circumstances in many cases. "Land throughout India is generally private property," wrote Mill unquestioningly,[2] and where private property did not exist, the settlement officers created it. But thus to establish private property in land was by no means an unmixed blessing for those concerned, whether the property was conferred on the *zemindar* or the *ryot*. In many districts where the cultivators held under landlords at a customary rent, the settlements were made when the population was small, and the landlords were glad to find and keep tenants. Later, when population increase began, competition for land swept away custom, and the *ryots* became subject to rackrents and eviction like the Irish cottiers of an earlier date. Just as in Ireland, it proved necessary to strengthen the legislation passed before 1873 in order to provide fixity of tenure at a fair rent.[3]

Even where the state did secure to the *ryot* a property in the soil, it did not always improve his lot, for once that property became valuable it could be mortgaged, and most *ryots* became indebted to usurers sooner or later. Here the introduction of Western economic ideas was certainly baneful. Measures which to Bentham and his followers seemed desirable advances, such as the free sale and transfer of land, abolition of the usury laws, and a civil code of law facilitating the recovery of debts, when transplanted into India often worked together not to protect but to destroy the small cultivator.[4] On the other hand, this illustrates

---

[1] I. Butt, *The Irish People and the Irish Land* (1867), pp. 267–8. For other comparisons of the land question in Ireland and India at this time, see *The Irish Land Question, by Indo-Hibernicus* (1868); *Ireland and Western India: a Parallel*, reprinted from *The Times of India*, Jan. 1868 (both these advocate the application of the Bombay thirty-year settlement system to Ireland); Speech of Thomas Hughes, M.P. for Lambeth, to his constituents (Jan. 1868); *Spectator*, 22 Feb. 1868. (These latter advocate a permanent settlement in Ireland "like that of Bengal", apparently in the belief that the Bengal settlement gave fixity of rents and tenures.)

[2] Mill, *East India: Tenure of Land*, P.P. 1857 (112—Sess. 2), xxix.

[3] Cf. T. Morison, *The Economic Transition in India* (1911), pp. 56–69.

[4] Cf. E. J. Thompson and G. T. Garratt, *Rise and Fulfilment of British Rule in India* (1934), pp. 428–9.

the fact that Indian experience did not always form a good precedent for Ireland, for when, at a later period, Irish tenants acquired a chargeable property in their holdings through the Land Purchase Acts, no special problem of rural indebtedness was created. During the early years of land purchase there was some increase of money-lending in Ireland, but generally "the new tenant purchasers appear to have shown extreme circumspection in borrowing upon the security of their holdings."[1]

III

Experience in Ireland and India in the nineteenth century clearly showed that a sound and acceptable system of land tenure is a necessary condition of economic development, but it is equally clear that it is not a sufficient one. The problems of landownership often seemed, in Ireland in any event, to occupy public attention to the exclusion of any consideration of improving the agriculture which might take place on the land. Yet in both countries the state of agriculture was such as to make the need for policies to improve it both pressing and obvious.

One cause of backward agriculture which operated both in Ireland and India was undercapitalization, and the obvious means of tackling it was by government loans on favourable terms to proprietors and cultivators. An Act for providing such assistance to Irish proprietors was passed in 1847; it allowed them to borrow on favourable terms for such purposes as fencing and drainage. The scheme was an immediate success, and subsequent Acts not only increased the funds available but extended the purposes for which they could be borrowed to include construction of many types of farm buildings.[2] These Land Improvement Acts were amongst the most successful economic measures applied to Ireland in the nineteenth century; from his own experience Lord Mayo had formed a high opinion of their value and, when he was appointed Viceroy of India one of his first ideas was to introduce a similar system into that country.[3]

In fact, as Mayo subsequently discovered, a very similar system had been in operation in India almost since the Bengal settlement of 1793. The government made advances, known as *takavi*, to *zemindars* or *ryots*, according to the nature of the land settlement. These advances were made not only for substantial improvements, such as the Irish Acts envisaged, but also for smaller requirements, such as the purchase of seed and cattle. It was common practice for the government, after years of scarcity or famine, to assist the cultivators by forgoing part of the land revenue demand and making advances of *takavi*. Mayo felt "satisfied that the principle may receive a wider development than has hitherto been given to it",[4] but this was not actually accomplished until ten years after his death, by the Land Improvement Act of 1883 and the Agriculturists' Loans Act of 1884.[5]

Improvements in cultivation were certainly of fundamental importance for both the Irish and Indian economies, but development could not come about

[1] *Report of the Departmental Committee on Agricultural Credit in Ireland*, p. 57, P.P. 1914 (Cmd. 7375), xiii, 57; cf. Section III of this report, *passim*.
[2] Cf. *Report from the Committee appointed by the Treasury to examine the Constitution and Duties of the Board of Works, Ireland*, P.P. 1878 (C. 2060), xxiii, pp. xxiii, xxiv.
[3] Cf. his correspondence with Richard Griffith, of the Irish Board of Works, on this subject, 30 and 31 Oct. 1868 (Mayo Papers, N.L.I.).
[4] Hunter, op. cit. II, 322.   [5] Baden-Powell, op. cit. I, 698; Thompson and Garratt, op. cit. p. 530.

through this means alone. At the opening of the period here being examined both countries lacked much of the equipment necessary for an organized exchange economy—such as roads, bridges, canals, and similar public works. Mill himself pointed out that in backward countries it was not to be expected that these things would be executed by private enterprise: "In many parts of the world, the people can do nothing for themselves which requires large means and combined action; all such things are left undone, unless done by the state. In these cases, the mode in which the government can most surely demonstrate the sincerity with which it intends the greatest good of its subjects is by doing the things which are made incumbent on it by the helplessness of the public, in such a manner as shall tend not to increase and perpetuate, but to correct that helplessness."[1] This passage might be said to strike the keynote for public works activity in "underdeveloped" countries during Mill's time; he certainly had India in mind when he wrote it, and he would have applied it to Ireland also, though he and his contemporaries would probably have added a rider to the effect that "the helplessness of the public" was not, or should not be allowed to be, as great in Ireland as in India.

In conformity with this view of the proper functions of the state, the governments of India and Ireland during the mid-nineteenth century both developed Public Works Departments, which came to be of considerable importance, although in neither case were they established for quite the reasons which economic theory alone would suggest. In Ireland, a Board of Works was established in 1831, partly in order to consolidate work which had previously been the responsibility of a number of bodies of dubious efficiency, but partly also in hopes of forestalling demands for the establishment of a poor law. In addition to taking over the functions of such bodies as the Directors of Ireland Navigation, the Board administered a new fund of £550,000 for making loans and grants in aid of public works: from 1842 onwards, it was also responsible for drainage operations and fisheries.[2]

Up to 1850 public works in India were the responsibility of a variety of authorities, civil and military, and the Indian administration was frequently criticized for its passive attitude on the subject. A new system, involving the formation of a separate public works department in each presidency as well as one in the central government of India, was introduced during Dalhousie's reforming administration in 1854.[3] It might seem surprising that the pressure for this came from Sir Charles Wood, then President of the Board of Control, for during his period as Chancellor of the Exchequer Wood had displayed himself as timid and parsimonious in the matter of relief and public works for Ireland.[4] Wood had undergone no change of heart on the subject of *laissez-faire*—he had simply come under heavy pressure from John Bright and the Manchester men, who were anxious to see India improved both as a market and as a source of raw materials for cotton manufacturers. The Manchester merchants did not share Mill's satisfaction with the East India Company's administration and alleged that Indian

---

[1] Mill, *Principles of Political Economy*, bk v, ch. xi, § 16.
[2] Cf. *Report ... Constitution and Duties of the Board of Works, Ireland*, P.P. 1878 (C. 2060).
[3] W. Lee-Warner, *Life of the Marquis of Dalhousie* (1904), ii, 182–5.
[4] Black, op. cit. pp. 115, 116, 196–7.

backwardness in cotton production "lay wholly in the maladministration of the Indian government, in its land tax, which had destroyed the security of property and checked cultivation, and in its almost incredible neglect of indispensable public works".[1] It was in consequence of this pressure that from 1854 onwards public works activity in India was considerably increased.[2]

There were two major branches of such activity which contemporary authorities believed could contribute specially to economic development in India and Ireland. These were the construction of railways and improvement of the soil, which in India generally implied irrigation, in Ireland drainage. Railways seemed likely to be especially valuable, providing much employment during their construction, opening up new markets, lowering the cost of raw materials, and, in India especially, diminishing the risk of local famine. But while the usefulness of railways in either country was rarely questioned, there was much controversy as to the proper forms of construction, finance, and management.

At first the official attitude towards railway-building in Ireland was one of complete *laissez-faire*; but when in 1836 only six miles of railway had been built by private enterprise, the Melbourne government set up a commission "to inquire and report upon the most advantageous lines of railways in Ireland". This commission, presided over by the energetic Under-Secretary for Ireland, Thomas Drummond, recommended that unless a group of capitalists ready to build a unified railway network could be found, the task should be undertaken by the state.[3] This proposal was never implemented and a later plan for executing lines under commissioners appointed by Parliament, with the aid of private capital raised under a guarantee of 4 per cent interest, came to nothing because of the fall of the Whig ministry in 1841. The ensuing Tory government left matters to private enterprise, but progress was slow. In 1845 there were still only 70 miles of railway open, and the famine, combined with the collapse of the railway mania in England, created further difficulties. A number of companies sought and obtained assistance from the Treasury, and in later years, while the construction and management remained in private hands, financial assistance from the state continued to be necessary for Irish railways. By 1865 the total of government advances to Irish railways had reached £2,364,000, and high charges did not prevent the companies from making low profits—partly because of limited traffic, but also because the existence of numerous separate companies produced high overheads and inefficient operation.[4]

A priori, it might seem more probable that the East India Company should have undertaken the construction and operation of railways in nineteenth-century India than that the British government should do so in nineteenth-century Ireland. Apart from the greater "helplessness of the people", the political and military importance of railways in India was obviously great, while it was generally (although wrongly) anticipated that they would attract little passenger traffic compared to freight. In spite of this, from the outset both the court

---

[1] *The Times*, 15 and 28 Nov. and 17 Dec. 1850, as quoted in A. Redford, *Manchester Merchants and Foreign Trade* (Manchester, 1934), I, 225.

[2] R. J. Moore, *Sir Charles Wood's Indian Policy* (Manchester, 1965), pp. 124–50.

[3] *Second Report from the Railway Commissioners, Ireland*, P.P. 1837/8 (145), xxxv, 94–5.

[4] *Report of the Royal Commission on Railways*, P.P. 1867 (3844), xxxviii, Sections 50 and 79.

of directors in London and officials in India herself generally favoured railways built and operated "by means of private enterprise and capital". This was in line with the views of commercial and financial circles in Britain, in which, as has been shown already, the Indian administration was held in low esteem for its record on public works. Yet British investors were not willing to risk their capital without some form of government backing: consequently the first Indian trunk lines were built by private enterprise, but with a government guarantee of interest of $4\frac{1}{2}$ or 5 per cent.[1]

This hybrid system, which Prof. Daniel Thorner has aptly called "private enterprise at public risk",[2] proved costly to the Indian government, and Wood, in his period at the India Office, resolutely refused to extend guarantees beyond those first sanctioned.[3] Experience in the 1860's showed that without guarantees private capital was not forthcoming; Wood was not prepared to see the lines undertaken by the state, but this step was taken in 1870. Mayo, the Irish land-owner who was Viceroy at the time, was a believer both in state railways and in narrow-gauge lines, which he thought could be most cheaply constructed. Hence most of the railways constructed in India after 1870 were narrow gauge, but this system which for a time served a useful purpose in Ireland proved less suited to the needs of India with her greater distances, and the mixture of gauges made it a costly economy. State railways thus provided no clearer solution to India's transport problem than privately owned lines, and in 1880 the policy of construction by private companies aided by a guarantee was revived.[4]

Land drainage in Ireland and irrigation in India both held promise of considerable economic improvement, but a promise which could not be realized without either co-operation among landholders or action by the state. For want of such communal action, little had been done in either country at the beginning of the period considered here. The East India Company devoted little of its resources to irrigation, but again Dalhousie's regime brought a change. Irrigation was developed along with other public works, and the famous Ganges Canal was opened in 1854. The cotton interests at home were not unaware of the benefits which irrigation and inland navigation might bring not only to India but to Lancashire, and in the Indian administration there were enthusiasts for irrigation such as Sir Arthur Cotton.[5]

Such enthusiasts were not slow to point out that while railways could open markets, and perhaps transport food in time of famine, irrigation alone could promise an actual and continuing increase of produce. To them, it was a source of bewilderment and frustration that irrigation received so little attention by comparison with railways. In fact, the reasons were mainly financial: up to the time of the mutiny, and after, the Indian government could not raise loans for public works, and many of the schemes sanctioned in Dalhousie's time had to be held up for lack of funds. In 1860 the government yielded to pressure to apply the guarantee system to capital raised for private irrigation schemes—reluctantly,

---

[1] L. H. Jenks, *Migration of British Capital to 1875* (New York, 1927), p. 213; D. Thorner, *Investment in Empire* (Philadelphia, 1950), p. 173.
[2] Ibid. p. 168.   [3] Moore, op. cit. p. 136.
[4] J. N. Sahni, *Indian Railways: One Hundred Years* (New Delhi, 1953), p. 24.
[5] Chief Engineer of Madras, whose *Public Works in India* was published in 1854. Cf. E. Hope, *General Sir Arthur Cotton, his Life and Work* (1900).

because the state was the ultimate landowner in India, and irrigation affected the land revenue. In any event the scheme was not a financial success: the government had to subsidize the first and largest company, the Madras Irrigation Company, to the extent of £1·2 million during the first eighteen years of its life.[1] There was at this time a tendency to judge essentially social investment projects by the strict criteria of private profit: on such a basis they were bound to be found wanting. It was not until Sir John Lawrence sought and obtained permission for the Indian government to raise loans, that irrigation works could be extensively developed. Lawrence appointed Richard Strachey, a noted military engineer, Superintendent of Irrigation; under his influence, public irrigation works were pressed forward with such vigour in the ensuing years that some authorities began to urge that the programme be slowed down, lest undue strain be placed on India's economy and public finances.[2]

The drainage and reclamation of land in Ireland seemed to many nineteenth-century authors to offer possibilities of improvement as great as did irrigation in India. Here too the same controversies about the appropriate sphere of public and private enterprise arose; but there was nothing in Irish experience to parallel the debate about the relative merits of railways and irrigation in India. No similar conflict arose between land drainage and railway-building in Ireland, largely because of differing financial arrangements.

In 1823 the Select Committee on the Employment of the Poor in Ireland drew attention to the fact that the need for special Acts to authorize each scheme was a great handicap to drainage in Ireland and advocated a general drainage Act.[3] No effective Act was passed until 1842, when the Board of Works was extended to include a Drainage Commission. Anyone desirous of draining lands might then apply to the Commission to have the proposed works surveyed, and if two-thirds of the proprietors affected consented to the scheme, they could then appeal to the commissioners to carry it out. On completion, the commissioners would charge the properties thus improved for the repayment of the sums advanced to carry out the drainage.

Little advantage was taken of this system until it was considerably simplified, in 1847, to encourage drainage as famine-relief work. For some years after this, state-aided drainage progressed rapidly, only to come to a virtual stop in 1853 after a number of proprietors had protested that the costs incurred by the Board of Works in carrying out drainage schemes far exceeded their original estimates and were out of proportion to the benefits obtainable.[4]

The question of legislation to aid drainage was not raised again until 1862–3, when a sequence of wet seasons underlined the need both for land improvement and for employment to relieve distress. Under the new code of drainage Acts then introduced, the state stood ready to provide loans to assist drainage, but no longer took responsibility for carrying out the works. Mill was critical of this legislation because the advances were to be made not to the cultivators but to the proprietors so "that the entire benefit of the improvement may accrue to their

[1] Moore, op. cit. pp. 144–5; *Report . . . on East India Public Works*, P.P. 1878/9 (312), ix.
[2] Cf. W. T. Thornton, *Indian Public Works* (1875), p. 121; A. K. Connell, *The Economic Revolution of India and the Public Works Policy* (1883), p. 12.
[3] *Report . . . Employment of the Poor in Ireland*, P.P. 1824 (561), vi, 11.
[4] Cf. *Report of Select Committee of the House of Lords on Drainage of Lands (Ireland)*, P.P. 1852/3 (10), xxvi.

rents".[1] On the whole, however, the measure was welcomed at the time as tending to discourage that tendency, which English observers often noted in Irish
landowners, "to look to the state for everything" and replace it with a wholesome
self-reliance.

The growth of this policy of attempting to wean Ireland from reliance on
public enterprise is clearly noticeable towards the end of the period here covered,
and it contrasts somewhat with the trend in India which was, on the whole, not
towards any contraction of the field of state activity in the second half of the
nineteenth century.

IV

The survey of economic policy in Ireland and India given above is manifestly
incomplete, but on the basis of it what conclusions can be reached about the
questions posed at the beginning of this article? Was the paternal government
of India more successful than the semi-representative government of Ireland in
its handling of economic problems, as Mill thought? Was it more successful in
governing the people "according to their wants", less hidebound in its interpretation of the principles of political economy?

There seems to be no compelling evidence that the answer to any of these
questions should be "Yes": the cautious investigator might mark Mill's conten-
tions with the old Scots judgement "not proven".

On the question of land tenure, fundamental to both economies, it might seem
that the record in India was better than in Ireland: many Irishmen of the time
would have agreed with Mill on this point. Certainly the men who ruled India
did, over much of her territory, attempt to ascertain the rights of the cultivators
and give them virtual fixity of tenure: but it is questionable whether the cultivators understood property rights in the same sense as their rulers, and they
certainly often found them a mixed blessing. Not only did possession of a mort-
gageable property often tempt the cultivator into debt, but also the revenue
demand was frequently fixed at so high a level as to give him no opportunity or
incentive for improvement.

On the question of adherence to *laissez-faire*, this was certainly less strict on
matters of land policy than in the Irish case: but, as has been indicated above,
there were variations in this respect over the period, and towards the end of it
some tendency to revert to market criteria is evident. So far as departure from
orthodoxy is concerned, it can be said that the Indian administration in this field
was certainly less influenced by the Whig orthodoxy, but what was substituted
for it was the Radical, or Utilitarian, orthodoxy.

In the matter of public works there would seem to be even less to choose between the outcome in India and that in Ireland. The East India Company, by
the very nature of its structure and function, was ill equipped to provide the
territory which it ruled with social overhead capital. When there was departure
from *laissez-faire* orthodoxy in this respect, it was not on grounds of principle but
of expediency, the result of pressure from (of all places!) the Manchester school.
The replacement of the company by the Crown after 1858 made some difference,

[1] Mill, *England and Ireland*, p. 43. For a similar complaint that railways and irrigation in many parts
of India brought benefits only to the *zemindars* or *talukdars* cf. Thornton, op. cit. pp. 183–4.

but at best one of degree. On the matter of public versus private enterprise for railways and other major works, the policy-makers of both India and Ireland showed a rather similar record of vacillation and uncertainty.

No doubt the differences of language and climate, if nothing else, served to prevent those who made policy in and for India from too readily assuming that her circumstances and needs coincided with those of England, while those who made policy for Ireland did often accept that "what was not too bad for us, must be good enough for Ireland". Yet it does not follow from this that India's rulers were any freer than Ireland's from one set of "common English notions"—the doctrines of classical political economy. Those doctrines centred around the concept of rational individuals operating in a contract economy—if not as a realized fact, at least as a desirable norm. Perhaps the most striking conclusion which emerges from this study is the extent to which theorists and policy-makers thought within this framework without questioning its general applicability. Mill himself deserves credit for his attempt to escape the strait-jacket of Benthamism, and his recognition of custom as a force in economic life alongside competition: but the attempt was never a complete success and had little influence on his contemporaries. It might have been better for both India and Ireland if the historical and comparative approach of thinkers like Sir Henry Maine had been developed earlier and gained more influence in English thought. It might have been better too if policy-makers in each economy had been more interested in examining the facts of what went on in the other and less inclined always to regard English conditions as the norm.

All this, it may be said, was typical of the complacency of the mid-Victorian era; but does it follow that we know better now? Perhaps the lessons of Mill's time may serve as a reminder to economists today, at once more confident of the scientific character of their discipline and more involved in policy-making for underdeveloped areas than ever before, not to forget the relativity of much of economic theory and the value of the historical and comparative approach.

Queen's University, Belfast

[3]

The Irish dissenters
and nineteenth-century political
economy

by R. D. Collison Black

I

To be a dissenter, according to the dictionaries, is to refuse to accept established doctrine; which implies in turn the existence of an orthodoxy of some sort.

According to the view of the history of economic ideas which prevailed some forty years ago, such an orthodoxy had indeed existed in political economy throughout the first seventy years of the nineteenth century. Its sources and character were well known and could be briefly summed up. It derived initially from Adam Smith's *Wealth of nations,* had absorbed as one of its essentials the doctrine of Malthus's *Essay on population,* received its definitive theoretical statement in Ricardo's *Principles of political economy* and had been finally rounded out and re-stated by John Stuart Mill in his *Principles* in 1848 — a re-statement which remained unchallenged until the appearance of Jevons's *Theory of political economy* in 1871.

The core of the classical orthodoxy which had been built up in this way was a cost of production theory of value, in which labour was seen as the major element of real cost and as in some sense the 'best' measure of value. Only Ricardo had sought (vainly) to establish an invariable measure of value and to make labour the sole source of value.

This cost theory of value in turn formed the foundation for a theory of production and distribution dominated by the law of diminishing returns and the Malthusian theory of population. In this the 'Ricardian' theory of rent was the best known and best regarded feature; the wage fund theory and the complementary theory of profits as a return (falling through time) mainly on circulating capital tended to be treated as crude aberrations long superseded by the superior techniques of neo-classical price theory.[1]

That nineteenth century economic literature encompassed a far greater variety and richness than is conveyed in this stereotype began to be recognised after the publication of Seligman's famous articles 'On some neglected British economists'.[2] It was not until

120

The Irish dissenters

some thirty years later that detailed research results began to be published on the work of the many authors to whom Seligman had first drawn attention; notable among these was Professor Marian Bowley's *Nassau Senior and classical economics* which put forward what was to become an influential view, that the economists of the first half of the nineteenth century could in fact be divided into four groups — 'the French school, particularly Say and his immediate followers; the Ricardians; the group which we may call the English dissenters, which includes economists as far apart in time as Lauderdale and Macleod, and the German theorists from Hufeland to von Mangoldt'.[3]

While naturally giving most attention to the work of Senior, Professor Bowley included among the [English!] Dissenters both Mountifort Longfield and Isaac Butt, the first and second holders of the Whately Professorship. Her suggestion that 'in Ireland . . . Longfield bid fair to set up a distinctive school of economists'[4] was one which I followed up in an article published in 1945,[5] contending that Longfield did really found such a local school, which included not only Butt but other early occupants of the Whately chair such as J. A. Lawson and W. Neilson Hancock. These then were the first group of Irish dissenters who in Schumpeter's 'Review of the Troops'[6] were ranked not with the Ricardians, but with 'The Men who wrote above their Time'.

Such was what one might call the topography of the relationship between the Irish Dissenters and mainstream English classical political economy as it had been mapped out when Schumpeter wrote. However Mark Blaug's well-known comment remains true — 'there is a mutual interaction between past and present economic thinking for, whether we set it down in so many words or not the history of economic thought is being rewritten every generation'.[7] The history of economic thought has indeed been re-written several times since Schumpeter, and in different versions the place of the early Whately professors, as dissenters or otherwise has been variously re-assessed. It is these re-assessments and their validity or otherwise that I wish mainly to discuss here.

II

The first major re-assessment of classical economic thought after that given in Schumpeter's *History of economic analysis* came with the appearance in 1951 of the first volume of Sraffa's superb edition of *The works and correspondence of David Ricardo*. It would be fair to say

R. D. Collison Black

that the interpretation of Ricardo's system which Sraffa gave in his introduction to the first volume of the edition, the *Principles of political economy and taxation,* came to dominate thinking on that subject for the ensuing thirty years. Indeed it is in one of the most recent works on Ricardian theory that one of the most concise statements of the interpretation of that theory which Sraffa promoted is to be found:—

Ricardo's thesis of the long-run tendency of the economy towards a stationary state situation is based on a set of crucial assumptions — diminishing returns in agriculture, reinvestment of profits and a theory of distribution in which the income of the capitalist class represents a residual. This set of assumptions implies a strict connection between the rate of profit and the rate of capital accumulation. It is thus necessary, for a theory which aims at proving the validity of that thesis, to solve the problem of the unambiguous determination of the profit rate and to show how diminishing returns affect its behaviour through time. These problems found a straightforward solution within Ricardo's primitive agricultural model of the *Essay on Profits.* [1815] It was in the attempt to escape the limitations of this model that Ricardo felt, in the *Principles* the need for a developed theory of value.[8]

Ricardo's convoluted thinking on labour as the measure and source of value was thus displayed in a new and much more sympathetic light by Sraffa's argument that it was crucial for the Ricardian analysis of distribution to 'find a measure of value which would be invariant to changes in the division of the product; for if a rise or fall of wages by itself brought about a change in the magnitude of the social product, it would be hard to determine accurately the effect on profits'.[9]

It was out of this Sraffa interpretation of Ricardo that there developed the view that 'there were, broadly speaking, two quite distinct and rival traditions in nineteenth-century economic thought as to the order and mode of determination of phenomena of exchange and income distribution'.[10]

One of these deriving from Adam Smith treated the value of any commodity as being determined as the sum of the various expenses or costs involved in its production; these expenses depending upon the necessary payments for land, capital and labour and upon the various amounts of these needed to produce the commodity in question. Determination of these necessary payments was viewed in a general supply-and-demand framework . . .

This line of thought is seen as running from Smith through Malthus to 'the Senior-Longfield group' and so on to John Stuart Mill and ultimately Marshall.

The Irish dissenters

The second main line of tradition also derived from Smith, even if in a quasi-Hegelian manner from certain doctrines or propositions of Smith inverted (and hence transmuted) by Ricardo. First, Smith's peculiar theory of value ... was refashioned by Ricardo so as to make conditions of production, and in particular quantities of labour expended in production, the basic determinant alike in capitalist and pre-capitalist society. In doing so he rejected the Adding-up-components Theory, and by implication rejected the possibility of treating the sphere of exchange relations as an 'isolated system', and anchored the explanations of these exchange-relations firmly in conditions and circumstances of production. Secondly, whatever his reason may have been for regarding distribution as the central problem, his instinct in doing so was undoubtedly right, and his mode of treating distribution was crucial. He saw this had to be explained in terms peculiar to itself and not as an outcome of general supply-demand exchange-relations, as Smith had treated it.[11]

According to this view J. S. Mill was not, whatever he himself may have said, a developer of the Ricardian tradition. That development was the work of Marx; thereafter it lived on only in the underworld of heresies, not to re-emerge finally and fully until the publication in 1960 of Sraffa's *Production of commodities by commodities* and the subsequent growth of 'neo-Ricardian' theory.

This 'two traditions' view of the history of economic thought has never won general acceptance, even among those who were ready to agree with Sraffa's interpretation of the Ricardian 'corn model'. Most such commentators would nevertheless have drawn a very clear distinction between what Baumol once termed 'the magnificent dynamics' of the classical school and the equilibrium theories of the neo-classical writers.

Of recent years, however, we have seen the emergence of another interpretation of classical political economy which harks back to Marshall's view of the essential continuity of the earlier classical and the later neo-classical approaches to questions of value and distribution. According to this interpretation, whose main exponent is Professor Samuel Hollander of Toronto, 'the economics of Ricardo and J. S. Mill in fact comprises in its essentials an exchange system fully consistent with the marginalist elaborations. In particular, their cost-price analysis is pre-eminently an analysis of the allocation of scarce resources, proceeding in terms of general equilibrium with allowance for final demand, and the interdependence of factor and commodity markets. . . . The demand side, the functional relation between cost and output, and the supply and demand determination of wages and profits, far from being "radical departures" from

123

R. D. Collison Black

Ricardianism, are central to that doctrine without which neither the cost theory of price nor the inverse wage-profit relation can be understood'.[12]

I am not called upon here to discuss the merits of these two contrasting approaches to the assessment of Ricardo and to the writing of the subsequent history of classical and neo-classical economic thought,[13] but only to deal with the re-assessments of the place of the Irish dissenting economists in that history which result from them. In each case that re-assessment is substantial, and substantially different.

III

To begin with the Sraffa approach, under this the notion of dissent from Ricardian ideas is preserved, but for very different reasons from those given by Schumpeter. From being among 'the men who wrote above their time' writers like Longfield are demoted (along with Senior) to form part of 'the reaction against Ricardo' by Maurice Dobb who, having assisted Sraffa in editing Ricardo's *Works and correspondence,* may be taken as perhaps the most authoritative expositor of this approach.[14] According to Dobb, Longfield's 'concern if not preoccupation, with the emerging "Labour question" is clear' from the form of his analysis of wages and profits. Having given rather more prominence to some of the rather naively sanctimonious corollaries which Longfield (perhaps for the benefit of Archbishop Whately) drew from this than to the analysis itself, Dobb comments: 'The laws of production and distribution, apparently, are not merely made of iron but are of divine origin'.[15]

Looked at from this point of view, the dissenters become the orthodox — 'harmony theorists' defending the *status quo* or, in other words, the lackeys of the capitalists. As it had been put earlier by Ronald Meek, 'it was the *dangerous* character of Ricardo's doctrines, rather than what they believed to be their falsity, with which they were primarily concerned'.[16]

On the other hand, Dobb does credit Longfield with having developed 'a "marginal efficiency" notion of profit' and describes his treatment of intensities of demand as 'certainly a foretaste of a Jevonian Law of Diminishing Utility'. Indeed one of Dobb's comments on Longfield's *Lectures on political economy* is that 'it is evident that we have here quite a number of preliminary sketches for economic theory at the end of the century' — a comment which of course is not inconsistent with the criticisms quoted above.

The Irish dissenters

The new interpretation of Ricardo given by Hollander leads to a treatment of the work of Longfield and his followers which comes near to being the simple inverse of that given by the followers of Sraffa. From being part of the reaction against Ricardo they now appear as dedicated Ricardians — but in the process inevitably their originality as theorists of value and distribution disappears. For Hollander says of Ricardo,

While, of course, his main interests lay in long-run price determination, his economics required and, implicitly at least, hinged upon the operation of the competitive mechanism involving demand-supply analysis. His rejection of demand-supply theory did not apply to the particular version elaborated by Longfield, and Longfield himself appreciated Ricardo's objections to the 'indefinite' and 'vague' expression, 'proportion between the demand and supply' as unhelpful in the prediction of market price.[17]

Now Hollander does admit that 'there can be little doubt that Ricardo failed to appreciate the conception of marginal utility'.[18] If then, as Dobb said, Longfield gave his readers 'a foretaste of a Jevonian Law of Diminishing Utility' there would still seem to be an important difference between his treatment of price determination and that of Ricardo. However, as against this view Hollander can invoke the authority of Professor Laurence Moss who in his book on Longfield has categorized him as merely a supply-and-demand theorist, though one whose ideas of demand derived from Malthus rather than Ricardo.[19]

On the other hand Moss contends that 'Longfield's *Lectures on political economy* does contain something approximating a complete non-Ricardian theory of income distribution and not simply a series of modifications of the Ricardian analysis',[20] whereas Hollander takes the view that 'much of the discussion of the *Lectures* is unmistakably "Ricardian" . . . on the whole Longfield retained a Ricardian structure throughout'.[21]

IV

Now, the broad title given to this series of lectures is 'Economists and the Irish economy . . .' and it may be noted that these re-assessments in the history of classical economic thought raise questions with regard to both. The 'two traditions' approach, associated with the names of Sraffa and Dobb puts the Irish dissenters into the category, if not of 'hired prizefighters', certainly of harmony theorists and defenders of the *status quo*. But this must presumably refer

125

R. D. Collison Black

to the status quo in Ireland and hence it raises the whole issue of the attitude of the early Whately professors to conditions in Ireland generally and to the distribution of income and wealth in particular.

As against this, the 'new interpretation' of Ricardo associated mainly with the name of Hollander does more to call into question the position of the early Whately professors *as economists* — in relation to their contemporaries and their place in the history of economic ideas. It suggests that the application of the term 'dissenter' to them may be misleading, for they were not so much dissenting from the Ricardian orthodoxy as following in it and perhaps developing it to some small extent. It may be convenient to deal with this latter contention first, since it follows on somewhat more directly from my discussion of the various assessments of classical economic theory earlier in this lecture.

The question we have to deal with is essentially whether writers like Longfield were or were not Ricardians. The fact that it is possible for able and scholarly commentators such as Professors Hollander and Moss, in addition to the late Mr Dobb, to return diametrically opposite answers to this question arises from the fact that they employ different criteria to determine what constitutes the essence of a Ricardian.

For Sraffa, Dobb and their followers, as we have already seen, the key feature of the Ricardian system is that in it distribution was explained in terms peculiar to itself and not as an outcome of general supply-and-demand exchange relations. On this criterion an economist like Longfield could definitely not be classed as a Ricardian, for his analysis of distribution is characterised by statements such as 'it is evident that the wages of labour, like the exchangeable value of every thing else, must depend upon the relation between the supply and the demand'.[22] Consequently followers of the 'dual development' approach to nineteenth century economic thought must inevitably see a sharp break between Ricardo and the dissenters, just as Professor Bowley originally did although not for quite the same reasons.

On the other hand, for Hollander the essential distinguishing feature of Ricardo's work is what he calls 'the fundamental theorem on distribution' — 'the entire Ricardian scheme is designed to relate the rate of return on capital to the "value" of per capita wages (Ricardian real wages) — which in effect amounts to the proportion of the work-day devoted to the production of wages — and variations in the rate of return to (inverse) variations in the real wage rate'.[23] He contends that this theorem displays an impressive resilience in

126

The Irish dissenters

nineteenth century economic thought and states his 'primary conclusion that the Ricardian theorem on distribution — the inverse
wage-profit relationship — left a firm and positive impression on
the work of a number of authors normally regarded as "dissenters"
par excellence' — including Longfield.[24]

In contrast to this Moss (as Hollander himself has noted) adopts
a version of the Ricardian system 'running in terms of the agricultural model of distribution in a growth context' and treating the
role of the measure of value as basis for the inverse wage-profit
relationship as only a secondary feature of the structure.[25] Arising
from this Moss finds that 'the major area of disagreement between
Longfield and Ricardo has to do with the question of the determination of profit and wages';[26] not surprisingly he considers Longfield's marginal productivity theory of profits and productivity
theory of wages to amount to a fundamentally non-Ricardian theory
of distribution.

As between these two very different interpretations of the essence
of Ricardo, it seems to me that one focuses primarily on the structure
of Ricardian theory, the other on the content. There can be no
doubt that Longfield had a very clear grasp of the structure of
Ricardian theory — he recognised the reasons for Ricardo's search
for an invariable measure of value and was able to present the idea
of the inverse wage-profit theorem in a manner which led Torrens
to withdraw his objections to it.[27]

Now if this particular feature of Ricardo's system is to be seen as
the essential one, some of the traces of Ricardian ideas which, as I
have always pointed out, are to be found all through Longfield's
Lectures on Political Economy will assume enhanced significance. Longfield did devote one whole lecture (Lecture VIII) to examining
what profits are, 'and how their amount is to be calculated'. By
assuming all advances of capital to be made in the form of wages
and for the same length of time 'it will follow, that the rate of profit
depends upon the proportion in which the value of any commodity
is divided between the labourer and the capitalist'.[28] This is indeed
a Ricardian way of measuring profits, but when it comes to 'the
investigation of the laws which determine their actual amount'
Longfield's treatment of this question involves a polite but total
refutation of Ricardo's ideas.

Admitting that 'some of the most distinguished writers have
adopted the theory, first, I believe, proposed and explained by the
late Sir Edward West, which considers profits to be almost entirely
regulated by the fertility of the last and worst soil that is brought

R. D. Collison Black

under cultivation', Longfield declared that 'the theory is an ingenious one, and I should feel much pleasure in assenting to it, and it is with corresponding regret that I have come to the very contrary conclusion, namely, that the decreasing fertility of the soil has scarcely any direct effect upon the rate of profits . . .'.[29]

In the Ricardian system rent is a surplus resulting from the 'indestructible powers of the soil'; of the remainder of the produce the share which goes to the labourer is determined by the cost of his subsistence, and the residue forms the profits of the capitalist. Hence it follows 'that in all countries, and all times, profits depend on the quantity of labour requisite to provide necessaries for the labourers on that land or with that capital which yields no rent'.[30]

In Longfield's system, on the other hand, rent is a surplus indeed, but one which could arise from land scarcity without differences in fertility; profits are determined by the marginal productivity of capital, and the residue is divided among the labourers in accordance with their specific productivity. 'Naturally, therefore, Longfield reaches very different conclusions from Ricardo on the question of how economic progress affects the division of the social product. Superficially his conclusions seem identical with those of the Ricardians, for like them he also predicts a rise in rents, a fall in profits and a rise in wages — but the fall in profits is to be the outcome of increased accumulations of capital, and the rise in wages, of increased productiveness of labour. Longfield enlarges on the favourable social consequences of a low rate of profits, and concludes that in the course of progress the circumstances affecting the state of the labourer will alter "in a manner favourable to his condition". Optimism is substituted for Ricardian pessimism.'[31]

Professor Hollander himself admits that Longfield 'fails to state precisely how his own theory [of profits] was related to the preceding defence of the Ricardian inverse profit-wage relationship' but nevertheless asserts with emphasis that '*it seems clear enough that he envisaged the latter as a valid framework for a satisfactory theory*'.[32] No evidence is adduced to support this assertion, but even if it is accepted at its face value the fact remains that Longfield clearly did not find the Ricardian theory of profits, and the resulting view of the relation between profits and wages in the course of economic growth, satisfactory.

If one accepts, as I am disposed to do, Dr Terry Peach's view of Ricardo's central object of analysis as having been 'specifically to isolate and "illustrate" what he believed to be the only serious basis for a permanent reduction in profitability in the course of capital

The Irish dissenters

accumulation — worsening conditions of production on the land',[33] then it is not possible to regard Longfield as anything but non-Ricardian in his analysis of distribution. But what of his analysis of value? We have already seen that Longfield's treatment of the returns to factors of production as determined by the supply of and demand for them prevents him from being regarded as a follower of Ricardo by the members of what I have called the 'dual development' school. On the other hand if one accepts Professor Hollander's view that 'Ricardian economics . . . comprises in its essentials an exchange system fully consistent with the marginalist elaborations'[34] and sets it alongside Professor Moss's view that 'Longfield developed a supply and demand explanation of market price',[35] it would seem that his value analysis added little to what Malthus and Ricardo had already done.

Is it then to be seen as no more than a minor improvement in supply-and-demand analysis, already well understood and accepted by Ricardo, instead of the major departure from his '93% labour theory of value' which it was formerly thought to be?

This is really a combination of two questions; the first is, to what extent was Longfield's analysis of market price an improvement on whatever may have been done by Ricardo in this field. The second, perhaps more fundamental, is, was that analysis merely a supply and demand one, or did it also contain elements of utility theory?

On the first point, there has recently been more than one attempt to reinterpret Ricardo's supply and demand analysis and to show it to have been more complete and consistent, particularly on the question of price-quantity relationships, than has hitherto been recognised. These attempts have served to bring out what one of the reinterpreters has described as the 'formidable interpretative problems engendered by the absence of any systematic treatment of the theory of price in Ricardo's *Principles*'.[36] Consequently the view put forward by commentators such as Rankin and Hollander — that Ricardo held essentially the same ideas about the relations of price and quantity demanded as had been stated by Malthus — has to be inferred mainly from widely separated passages in his pamphlets, letters and speeches.[37]

On the other hand, as Professor Moss has rightly said, 'it was Longfield (and not Ricardo) who made the concept of a demand schedule an integral part of his theory of price'. Nothing in the recent writing on Ricardo's treatment of supply and demand seems to warrant any revision of Moss's judgement that 'Longfield must be credited with having developed one of the earliest and most

129

R. D. Collison Black

complete supply-and-demand explanations of market price in British economic thought'.[38]

The second question is the more controversial one. Professor Moss is critical of the idea that Longfield can be regarded as a precursor of the marginal utility approach — an idea which I presented in my 1945 article and which others have also put forward. It seems to me that this is another instance where the answer depends on the criteria adopted — in this case the criteria which make a writer into a utility theorist. If that description is to be confined to those who have given an explicit statement of the principle of diminishing marginal utility it cannot be applied to Longfield, but if the description is extended to include those whose writings make clear their understanding of the principle then it would be my judgement that Longfield would properly come under it. I still would contend that important elements of utility analysis are to be found in Longfield's value theory, which is thus more than a mere supply-and-demand treatment of the problem.

Moss does concede that Longfield 'was quite willing to admit that utility does influence price, but only in the same way as cost of production, that is, *indirectly*. Cost influences market price by way of supply and utility by way of demand because, in Longfield's words, it is to utility that the "demand is to be entirely attributed". But in another place he was quick to warn that the effect utility has on actually determining the market price is "not so easily calculated", and on the basis of this remark we may be confident that Longfield did not intend to connect the "intensity of demand" with a measure of utility'.[39]

This does seem to me to make as little as possible out of what Longfield says about utility and consumer behaviour. Has *any* utility theorist ever tried to show that utility influences price other than 'by way of demand'? Apart from that I do not really see why Longfield's statement that the effect utility has in determining price is not easily calculated ensures confidence that he did not intend to connect intensity of demand with a measure of utility. To my mind the essential point about Longfield's treatment of intensity of demand is that he relates it not merely to market demand but to the demand of the individual consumer.[40]

It seems to me that Professor Bowley's reading of this passage is much more careful and therefore much closer to the truth than that of Professor Moss:

130

The Irish dissenters

Longfield's exposition of diminishing degrees of intensity of demand provides an explanation of the downward slope of an individual's demand curve, as well as of the market demand curve. It has already been noticed that his degrees of intensity of demand coincide with Dupuit's 'maximum sacrifice' used by him as the measure of utility and the reflection of diminishing marginal utility. Longfield did not take the final step of showing the relation of the concept of intensity of demand to the concept of utility, although he had said that demand 'was to be entirely attributed' to utility. It seems to me then that Longfield introduced the degrees of intensity of demand as a way round the difficulty of discovering the effect of utility on price because although he, like so many others, observed the phenomenon of diminishing utility, he was unable to draw conclusions from it in a way which demonstrated the precise influence of utility on exchange value.[41]

If the matter is seen in this way, Longfield's failure to take the final step explicitly does not seem to me adequate ground for denying that he was a precursor of the marginal utility approach. And the grounds for claiming him as such seem to be strengthened by Moss's own statement that 'Longfield came closer than any of his contemporaries to stating what is now commonly referred to as the "first-order condition" in the theory of consumer choice—that a consumer will vary his purchases of several commodities in such a way that the proportions between their respective marginal utilities and prices will all be equal to one another'.[42] Taking all the evidence into consideration then, it seems to me that even if Longfield did not state the law of diminishing marginal utility explicitly and precisely, it is still reasonable to classify him as a 'utility' or 'subjective value' theorist, and that to treat his theory as no more than a supply and demand one is to give it an unduly narrow interpretation.

V

Finally, we come to consider the view that the Irish dissenters, in line with their English counterparts, were harmony theorists and defenders of the status quo whose opposition to Ricardian distribution theory was partly, if not mainly, founded in a desire to play down those conflicts between classes which it so starkly highlighted. Now one would scarcely expect the early occupants of the Whately Chair to have been radicals, appointed as they were by an Archbishop of the then established Church of Ireland to lecture on political economy in a college whose students were mainly drawn

R. D. Collison Black

from the ascendancy class and whose revenues derived from extensive landholdings. Nor indeed were they, although Mr Antoin Murphy elsewhere in this volume (pp. 13-24)[43] has drawn together interesting evidence of the proceedings of the Board at the time of the first elections to the Chair which indicates that Longfield was looked at askance by some of the Senior Fellows because of his supposed radical opinions. On the other hand his successor Isaac Butt at the time of his election in 1836 was well known for his high Tory views, views far removed from those he was later to express as leader of the Irish Home Rule party.[44]

Viewed objectively against the background of these facts, the Irish dissenters appear neither as radicals nor as defenders of the status quo but rather as concerned reformers. On some aspects of social and economic policy, notably that of trades unions and combinations, their position was undoubtedly a conservative one.

'Let the labourer be taught to know', declared Longfield, 'and the proof is simple and easy to be understood by all, that the wages of his labour cannot be determined by the wishes of his employer, that they are even as independent of the decrees of the legislature as they are of his own will, and that they are ultimately entirely dependent upon the prudence or improvidence, the industry or idleness, of the labouring classes themselves.'[45]

Professor Hollander has recently suggested that these comments may have been intended as a reply to the radical socialism of Thomas Hodgskin; 'the tone of Longfield's remarks here and his general emphasis upon the rule of law and the limited potential of union activity suggest that he may have been familiar with Hodgskin's writings.'[46] That is possible, but it seems to me much more likely that Longfield's remarks were directed against the Dublin trades unions whose notoriously violent tendencies at that period had earned the condemnation of Daniel O'Connell among others.

It is also Professor Hollander's contention that Longfield provides an instance of one of the dissenters using Ricardian doctrine to counter radical arguments rather than rejecting them because of their radical implications—a neat reversal of the reading of the historical record given by such commentators as Sraffa and Dobb.[47] Again, the significance to be attached to this depends on one's view of the importance of the traces of Ricardian doctrine to be found in Longfield's writings. To my mind it was Longfield's departures from Ricardo's theory of distribution—his reversal of the place of profits and wages in the sharing of the total product and his productivity analysis of their determination—which enabled him to

The Irish dissenters

take an optimistic view of the progress of capitalist society and the prospects for labour within it.

However the significant point in this context is not the degree of importance to be attached to the Ricardian elements in Longfield's economic theory. Rather it is the undoubted fact that Longfield gave clear and frequent indication that he was no uncritical defender of the existing order. As Professor Hollander has rightly noted, 'the matter of "undesirable" distribution was placed squarely within the domain of the economist' by Longfield.[48] The position which he took on this question is a specially interesting one. On the one hand in his *Four lectures on Poor Laws*[49] he supported the stern principle, developed by Nassau Senior, of giving aid to the able-bodied only on a basis of 'less eligibility'. On the other he asserted that '*every individual is entitled to the means of support from that society which is determined to compel him to obey its laws*'.[50]

The basis for this assertion was that 'society is nothing but a combination of individuals for the common good. Can they with justice (I speak not of compassion now) say, we have divided the land and property of the country among us in a manner that we have found by experience is well calculated to promote our interests, but you have got no share in this distribution, and we do not want your labour, therefore you must starve.' The able-bodied therefore might as of right demand and receive subsistence from the society which demanded their allegiance—but nothing more.

It was always Longfield's view that others less fortunate—'the blind, the insane, the crippled poor' and the aged—in whose case the granting of assistance could involve no risk of encouraging idleness and improvidence should be generously aided by the state. Even in 1834 he was prepared to advocate 'a small pension as a superannuation allowance, to every labourer of sixty years of age'[51] and when in 1872 he came to consider 'The limits of state interference with the distribution of wealth' he 'set out a programme of redistribution of wealth and social investment which anticipates most features of the modern welfare state'.[52]

In this remarkable paper there are interesting anticipations of Keynes in references to 'the average strength of the disposition to accumulate' which Longfield argued to be 'greater than is necessary, and can bear reduction without loss to the public'.[53] Similarly his 1834 discussion of the right to subsistence finds echoes today in current discussions of the 'right to food' which often make reference to Rawls's *Theory of justice*.[54] One criticism which can be made of Longfield, particularly in relation to his 1834 *Four lectures on the Poor*

R. D. Collison Black

Laws is that he did assume that the able-bodied would normally find no difficulty in obtaining employment through the workings of the labour market—an assumption which was scarcely borne out by the facts in Ireland at that time. It was left to the young Tory barrister who succeeded him, Isaac Butt, to point this out and draw attention to the limitations of an economic theory based on full employment assumptions.

'It appears to me,' he wrote in an unobtrusive footnote, 'that in all the arguments which attempt to prove, as a general proposition, the injury of protective duties, it is assumed that the industry of a country must always be fully employed'.[55] Recognising the restricted validity of this assumption, particularly in pre-famime Ireland, he was prepared to swim against the full tide of orthodox economic opinion and state the case for protection to home industry as a means of increasing employment. The argument by which Butt supported his case is still worth hearing almost a century and a half later:

Enough for us now to state the general principle, that if there be in our own land a state of society in which men are willing to work, and cannot find the opportunity of exchanging their labour for bread, and if the community in which this occurs have resources enough at its command, by the best and most carefully contrived combination of all its skill and power to find bread for all its people, there ought to be an effort made to bring about that result. To this end, if it can be obtained, there is no taxation that might be necessary to accomplish it that ought not cheerfully to be borne—there is no sacrifice from those who own the revenue of the country, too great to demand. In the progress of society, the masses of the people ought surely to have their share. . . These principles and these reasonings may fall strange upon the ear of some present. Be assured, the time is coming when they shall not be so.[56]

Such are some of the writings of the Irish dissenters on the economic situation in their time. They are not, in my judgement, the words of Ricardians but assuredly they are equally not the words of harmony theorists, Pollyannas, or the running dogs of the capitalist class.

VI

The development of economic thought in the nineteenth century was a complex process with many facets—about which we have learned much as a result of the scholarly studies carried out during

The Irish dissenters

the last forty years. Inevitably attempts must be made to elucidate the complexity by imposing patterns on it. One such is the 'dual development' thesis, promoted mostly by economists of the Cambridge school since Sraffa, another what may be called the 'general equilibrium' approach of which Hollander is the leading exponent.

According to the first the Irish economists who held the Whately Chair in its early days are to be seen as part of the reaction against Ricardo, forerunners of neoclassical or marginalist economics indeed but tarnished by all the unhappy features which the term 'neoclassical' implies in modern Cambridge thinking. According to the second they become not part of the reaction against Ricardo but of a resilient Ricardian tradition involved in 'the sharing of a common heritage or "central core", which amounts largely to allocation theory and the mechanisms of demand-supply analysis'.[57]

With what may well be regarded as typical Irish stubbornness I have chosen to dissent from both these interpretations; but I hope that I may be judged to have given adequate reasons for my continuing belief that the early Whately professors can be correctly seen as constituting something like a school of their own which had its own original thread to weave into the pattern of nineteenth century economic thought, as regards both theory and policy.

Notes

1. These views are perhaps to be found most clearly and forcefully stated in Edwin Cannan, *A history of theories of production and distribution in English political economy from 1776 to 1848* (London, 1893) and *A review of economic theory* (London, 1929). But cf. also F. H. Knight, 'The Ricardian theory of production and distribution' in *Canadian Journal of Economics and Political Science*, i, (1935), pp 3-25 and 171-96.

2. E.R.A. Seligman, 'On some neglected British economists, I and II' in *Economic Journal*, XIII (1903), pp 335-63 and 511-35.

3. Marian Bowley, *Nassau Senior and classical economics* (London, 1937), p. 67.

4. ibid., p. 109.

5. R.D. Collison Black, 'Trinity College, Dublin, and the theory of value, 1832-1863' in *Economica*, N.S., xii (August 1945), pp 140-8.

6. J.A. Schumpeter, *History of economic analysis* (London, 1954), Part III, ch.4.

7. Mark Blaug, *Economic theory in retrospect* (3rd ed., London, 1978), p. vii.

8. G.A. Caravale and D.A. Tosato, *Ricardo and the theory of value, distribution and growth* (London, 1980), p. 4.

9. Piero Sraffa, Introduction to Vol i of *Works and correspondence of David Ricardo* (10 vols, Cambridge, 1951-73), pp xiviii-ix.

10. M.H. Dobb, *Theories of value and distribution since Adam Smith* (Cambridge, 1973), p. 112.

11. ibid., p. 115.

R. D. Collison Black

12. Samuel Hollander, 'On the substantive identity of the Ricardian and neo-classical conceptions of economic organization: the French connection in British classicism' in *Canadian Journal of Economics*, xv, no. 4 (November 1982), pp 586-612 (pp 590-91).

13. Nevertheless I may be allowed to comment that I do not find either wholly convincing. I would agree with the recently expressed view of Dr T. Peach—'Ricardo's words and intentions have all too often been strained and distorted so that he might be bracketed with "Neoclassical" economists, "Marxist" economists or "Sraffian" economists.'—Terry Peach, *A re-interpretation of David Ricardo's writings on value and distribution* (Unpublished thesis for the degree of D. Phil, University of Oxford, Trinity Term, 1982), p. 241.

14. Dobb, *Theories of value and distribution*, pp 107 et seq.

15. ibid., p. 108.

16. R.L. Meek, *Studies in the labour theory of value* (London, 1956), pp 124-5.

17. Samuel Hollander, *The economics of David Ricardo* (London, 1979), p. 671 (hereafter cited as *E.D.R.*).

18. ibid., p. 277.

19. L.S. Moss, *Mountifort Longfield, Ireland's first professor of political economy* (Ottawa, Illinois, 1976), pp 33 et seq.

20. ibid., p. 97.

21. Samuel Hollander, 'The reception of Richardian economics' in *Oxford Economic Papers*, xxix, no. 2 (July 1977), pp 222-57 (pp 232-3).

22. Mountifort Longfield, *Lectures on political economy, delivered in Trinity and Michaelmas Terms, 1833* (Dublin, 1834), p. 209 (hereafter cited as *L.P.E.*).

23. Hollander, *E.D.R.*, p.7.

24. Hollander, 'Reception of Ricardian economics' in *O.E.P.*, xxix (1977), p. 224.

25. Cf. Samuel Hollander, 'Review of Moss, *Mountifort Longfield*' in *Canadian Journal of Economics*, xi (1978), pp 378-80 (379). In a review of Hollander's *E.D.R.*, Moss has argued that the 'consensus view' of Ricardian theory is that which 'insists that the truly unique or novel element in Ricardo's theorizing was his "agricultural theory of profit" ' (L.S. Moss, 'Professor Hollander and Ricardian economics', *Eastern Economic Journal*, 5, (Dec. 1979) p. 503). Cf. also Hollander, 'Professor Hollander and Ricardian economics: a reply to Professor Moss', *Eastern Economic Journal*, 8 (July 1982), pp 237-41 and Moss, 'Reply to Hollander', *ibid*, pp 243-5.

26. Moss, *Mountifort Longfield*, p. 97.

27. Hollander, 'Reception of Ricardian economics' pp 234-5; Lionel Robbins, *Robert Torrens and the evolution of classical economics* (London, 1958), pp 55-7. Professor Hollander has rightly stressed the influence of Longfield on Torrens, which was not noted in my Introduction to the 1971 reprint of Longfield's economic writings (see below, note 31). On this point see also Moss, 'Professor Hollander and Ricardian economics', *Eastern Economic Journal* 5 (Dec. 1979), p. 505.

28. Longfield, *L.P.E.*, pp 171, 179.

29. ibid., p. 183.

30. Ricardo, *Works and correspondence* (ed. P. Sraffa), i, 126.

31. R.D. Collison Black (ed.) *The economic writings of Mountifort Longfield* (with introduction and bibliography, New York, 1971), p. 16.

32. Hollander, 'Reception of Ricardian economics', p. 235.

33. Peach, *A re-interpretation of David Ricardo's writings. . .*, p. 235.

34. Hollander, 'The French connection in British classicism' in *C.J.E.* xv no. 4 (November 1982), p. 590.

35. Moss, *Mountifort Longfield. . .*, p. 30.

The Irish dissenters

36. S.C. Rankin, 'Supply and demand in Ricardian price theory: a re-interpretation' in *Oxford Economic Papers*, xxxii, no. 2 (July 1980), pp 241-62 (p. 244).

37. Rankin, op. cit., pp 244-54 and Hollander, *E.D.R.*, pp 273-80. On this point cf. also G.J. Stigler's review of Hollander, *E.D.R.* in *Journal of Economic Literature*, xix (March 1981), p. 101.

38. Moss, op. cit., pp. 34, 38.

39. ibid., p. 40.

40. Longfield, *L.P.E.*, p. 115.

41. Marian Bowley, *Studies in the history of economic theory before 1870* (London 1973), pp 152-3.

42. Moss, *Mountifort Longfield*, p. 41.

43. Antoin Murphy, 'Mountifort Longfield's appointment to the chair of political economy in Trinity College, Dublin, *Hermathena* CXXXV , pp. 13-24.

44. Cf. Terence De Vere White, *The road of excess* (Dublin 1945).

45. Longfield, *L.P.E.*, p. 19.

46. Samuel Hollander, 'The post-Ricardian dissension: a case study in economics and ideology' in *Oxford Economic Papers*, xxxii, no. 3 (September 1980), pp 370-410 (p. 395).

47. ibid., p. 403.

48. ibid., p. 405.

49. Mountifort Longfield, *Four lectures on Poor Laws*, delivered in Trinity Term, 1834 (Dublin, 1834).

50. ibid., p. 19. Italics in original.

51. ibid., p. 33.

52. Black, *Economic writings of Mountifort Longfield*, p. 25.

53. Mountifort Longfield, 'The limits of state interference with the distribution of wealth, in applying taxation to the assistance of the public' in *Journal of the Statistical and Social Inquiry Society of Ireland*, part xiii (1872), pp 105-114. (Reprinted in Black, *Economic Writings of Mountifort Longfield*).

54. N.J. Faramelli, *World hunger, ethics and the right to eat* (Rome, 1982) pp 7, 8, 13. I am indebted to my son, Mr T.R.W. Black, for drawing my attention to this and other references on the *right to food*.

55. Isaac Butt, *Protection to home industry. Some cases of its advantages considered. The substance of two lectures delivered before the University of Dublin, in Michaelmas term, 1840* (Dublin, 1846), p. 133.

56. ibid., p. 63.

57. Hollander, *E.D.R.*, pp 683-4.

PART TWO

IN AND OUT OF
THE MAINSTREAM

2

Smith's Contribution in Historical Perspective

BY R. D. COLLISON BLACK*

THE brief which has been given to me in the title of this paper might well be handled by giving my estimate of what exactly Smith's contribution was and then viewing it from the perspective of the present time. But in reflecting on my theme I have come to the conclusion that the very nature of historical perspective makes it difficult to be categorical about the nature of Smith's contribution. For we are all familiar with the illusions which perspective generates. As one writer on the phenomenon has said, 'Most people have observed that objects diminish in size as they recede farther from the eye, that parallel lines appear to converge, that in general the appearance of objects differs from the reality.'[1] Now just as the size and shape of objects appears to change in visual perspective as the position of the observer changes, so in historical perspective the significance of an event or an idea changes as it is seen from different points of time. So rather than add my own contemporary assessment of Adam Smith's work to the not inconsiderable number of such estimates which have already been offered in this bicentenary period, I have decided that it might be a more useful and valid interpretation of my brief to review the various ways in which it has been evaluated at various points in history, and to compare those earlier estimates with those presently being made.

In the hope of making my treatment of the theme both manageable and relevant I have limited it in a number of ways which it may be useful to make clear at the outset. First of all, I shall confine myself to Smith's contribution to the development of

* Professor of Economics in The Queen's University, Belfast.
[1] *Encyclopaedia Americana* (New York, Americana Corp., 1965), art. 'Perspective', vol. xxi, 632.

political economy—partly because it is only this aspect of his total contribution.to knowledge that I am at all qualified to discuss, but also because it is the bicentenary of the *Wealth of Nations* which we are now celebrating.

In considering how perspectives on that great work have changed in the course of history, I shall limit myself to three points in time —1826, the golden jubilee of its publication, 1876, the centenary and 1926, the sesquicentenary. I shall not confine myself strictly to works written in those years with commemorative intent, but such writings will form the bulk of the material here surveyed and where I go beyond them it will be to look at works of these periods in which the authors did specifically indicate their view of Smith's system of political economy.

Not all writings commemorating the *Wealth of Nations* are included in this paper, for unfortunately I have not been able to discover copies of a number of the commemorative pieces published overseas; my survey is therefore largely devoted to Anglo-American writings and I do not claim that even when thus limited it is exhaustive. A further obvious and important omission is any reference to the treatment of Smith's political economy given by Karl Marx. Marx did not write anything directly commemorating the *Wealth of Nations*, but he did leave ample material for assessing his view of Smith's economic ideas. This, however, would provide the basis for a paper in itself and I have decided that it is better to omit the topic from this one than to treat it inadequately.

The contribution which Smith made in the *Wealth of Nations* can be said to have two major aspects—analysis and policy—and I shall examine how each of these was viewed at the three different periods considered. It should be pointed out, however, that while it is convenient and even perhaps essential to make that distinction now, it is one which commentators on Smith did not begin to make clearly until the centenary of the *Wealth of Nations* was approaching.

I

Half a century after the publication of the *Wealth of Nations* there appears to have been no thought of commemorating that anniversary of its publication; but that does not imply that its influence on the development of economic analysis at that time was small. Just as Keynes's *General Theory* remains today a work of continuing significance on which other authors are building by a process of action and reaction, so was the *Wealth of Nations* in or about 1826 a work of continuing significance.

The position has been very clearly stated by Lord Robbins:

> There is a vast extent of analysis and prescription which the genera-
> tion of Malthus and Ricardo more or less take for granted, the essential
> work having been done by Hume and Smith; and a great deal of what
> they do themselves is to be regarded, not as a series of propositions
> thought out in a void, but rather as an attempt to correct or improve
> propositions and explanations which are already to be found in the
> *Wealth of Nations*.[2]

In fact it is noticeable that the generation of Malthus and Ricardo, while always respecting the authority of Smith, were much more willing than later generations to point out what they considered to be mistakes in Smith and to offer corrections.[3] The *Wealth of Nations* was to them not so much a classical monument to be inspected as a structure to be extended and improved where necessary.

As to what was the most controversial feature of the structure in the view of this generation, an examination of the literature leaves no doubt that it was Smith's treatment of labour, especially in relation to the theories of value and distribution. Ricardo, re-reading Smith in the course of preparing his own *Principles* in 1816, found 'many opinions to question, all I believe founded on his original error respecting value'.[4] Ten years later the view of value and of labour in relation to it which Ricardo himself had put forward had served to split English economists into two camps. On the one side were those—a majority in influence if not in numbers—who accepted the Ricardian theory either in whole or in part. To them Smith's cost of production theory of value was

[2] Robbins, *Robert Torrens and the Evolution of Classical Economics* (London, MacMillan 1958), 233.

[3] Perhaps the best known example of this approach is contained in the Preface to Ricardo's *Principles*: 'The writer, in combating received opinions, has found it necessary to advert more particularly to those passages in the writings of Adam Smith from which he sees reason to differ; but he hopes it will not, on that account, be suspected that he does not, in common with all those who acknowledge the importance of the science of Political Economy, participate in the admiration which the profound work of this celebrated author so justly excites.'

[4] Ricardo to James Mill, 2 December 1816—*Works and Correspondence*, ed. Sraffa (Cambridge University Press), vii, 100.

essentially 'a more superficial approach' than Ricardo's attempt at
a pure labour theory. Of this group the most influential perhaps
was J. R. McCulloch, to whom it appeared in 1827 that:

> I might advantageously employ myself in the publication of a new
> edition of the Wealth of Nations, subjoining such short notes to the
> text, as might serve to point out the changes that have taken place since
> the work was finally revised by the author . . . and . . . such more
> lengthened notes as might appear necessary to make the reader aware
> of the fallacy of the principles which Dr. Smith has sometimes advocated,
> and to furnish him with a brief, but distinct, account of the principal
> discoveries and improvements that have been made in the science. . . .[5]

Now Professor O'Brien has made clear that McCulloch's treatment of value proceeded on two levels and that while in his
'scientific' theory he departed considerably from Ricardo's example,
particularly on the question of the invariable measure, in more
popular expositions he remained always an uncomprising advocate
of a straightforward labour quantity theory.[6] Although some of the
significant modifications of his 'scientific' theory appeared in the
1838 as compared with the 1828 version of his edition of the *Wealth
of Nations*, these were well concealed in the Notes[7] and to contemporary readers in general it must have appeared that McCulloch
was replacing Smith's 'erroneous' cost of production theory with
the 'superior insights' of Ricardo's labour theory. Certainly they
were firmly informed by the editor that 'in consequence of the
incorrectness of the opinions entertained by Dr. Smith, on two
such important and fundamental points as the value of commodities and the nature and causes of rent, many of the principles
which pervade other parts of his work are necessarily vitiated and
unsound. This is particularly the case where he investigates the
circumstances which determine the rate of wages and the rate of
profit.'[8]

Influential as such statements may have been, the opposite view
was not without its advocates. Thus the anonymous author of *The*

[5] J. R. McCulloch (ed.), *An Inquiry into the Nature and Causes of the Wealth of Nations, by Adam Smith LL.D. With a Life of the Author, an Introductory Discourse, Notes, and Supplemental Dissertations.* (Edinburgh, A. Black and W. Tait, 1828), Preface, I. ix.

[6] D. P. O'Brien, *J. R. McCulloch, a Study in Classical Economics* (London, Allen and Unwin, 1970), 126–46.

[7] Cf. 1838 ed., 436, and O'Brien, op. cit. 143.

[8] McCulloch, op. cit., (1828 ed.), I, lxxvi.

46   *Smith's Contribution in Historical Perspective*

Opinions of the late Mr. Ricardo and of Adam Smith, on some of the leading doctrines of Political Economy, stated and compared,[9] while concluding that the systems of the two economists on the subject of value were not contradictory, went on to say:

> We must, however, own we prefer the view which A. Smith takes of the subject, as it is more comfortable to general experience, and serves to explain things under all the variations to which they are liable; whereas Mr. Ricardo's view seems designed to show how things should be under given circumstances rather than how they are in reality found to exist.[10]

This view must have commended itself to many readers of Smith and Ricardo at this period; but if the *Pamphleteer* articles came into the hands of Samuel Bailey he must have found the author's assertion that 'Value, as explained by Mr. Ricardo, is *relative* value, and as explained by A. Smith, *positive* or absolute value'[11] a curious one. For Bailey, whose critique of Ricardo rested on the proposition that 'value denotes merely a relation' set out from Smith's definition that the value of a good 'expresses the power of purchasing other goods, which the possession of that object conveys'[12] and claimed the authority of Smith for his relativist approach.

If we accept the view which has recently been put forward by Professor Bowley that Smith 'was not concerned primarily with physical inputs as the basis either of value or its measurement'[13] we may be inclined to think that Bailey and his followers were better interpreters of Smith than the Ricardians, but it was the Ricardian interpretation which became dominant. And perhaps the reason for this can be found in McCulloch's view that Smith's treatment of the relation of labour to value vitiated his account of the determinants of wages and profits. For as Professor Winch has said 'the questions which concerned Smith's successors were not merely more urgent, but more politically divisive as between the still dominant land-owning classes and the new commercial and industrial classes', and it was natural therefore that they should

---

[9] *The Pamphleteer*, 23 (1824), 518–26, 24 (1824), 508.
[10] *Pamphleteer*, 23, 525.   [11] Ibid. 523.
[12] Cf. R. M. Rauner, *Samuel Bailey and the Classical Theory of Value* (London, G. Bell & Sons Ltd., for L.S.E., 1961), 7.
[13] M. Bowley, *Studies in the History of Economic Theory before 1870* (London, MacMillan, 1973), 116.

favour an approach which gave to distribution, and particularly the question of the relative shares of wage earners and profit receivers, a more central place than Smith had done.[14] For this, as Ricardo had realized, a theory of value such as Smith had used was not an appropriate foundation.

On the side of policy, the general impression left by the historical evidence is that by 1826 not only economists but a great many other influential public men were prepared to give assent and support to the system of natural liberty and the consequent doctrine of free trade set out by Adam Smith. Baring in 1820 had presented to an approving House of Commons the famous Merchants' Petition prepared by Thomas Tooke, one result of which was the establishment in 1821 of the Political Economy Club 'to support the principles of Free Trade'. By 1826 Parliament had begun the work of dismantling the Navigation Acts and other parts of the mercantile system, and of reducing protective tariffs. This was largely due to the influence of Huskisson, than whom 'Smith had no disciple more true to his doctrines in the sphere of statesmanship'.[15]

Nevertheless, free trade was still far from having triumphed, either in the sphere of doctrine or of legislation. In the eighteentwenties probably even those economists who were firmest in their support of free trade principles would still have agreed with Smith's oft-quoted dictum that 'To expect, indeed that the freedom of trade should ever be entirely restored in Great Britain is as absurd as to expect that an Oceana or Utopia should ever be established in it.'[16] We may remind ourselves that when, in 1822, Ricardo wrote of a free trade in corn it was to say 'that is not, under our circumstances, the course which I should recommend.'[17] Instead he proposed a countervailing duty of 10 shillings per quarter to offset the 'peculiar burdens' on land. For similar reasons, McCulloch, who has been seen as an influential propagandist for free trade in the years 1825–30,[18] was not in favour of

[14] Cf. D. N. Winch, Introduction to the Everyman edition of Ricardo's *Principles of Political Economy* (London, Dent, 1973), ix.

[15] A. Brady, *William Huskisson and Liberal Reform* (2nd ed., London, Cass, 1967), 168.   [16] *Wealth of Nations*, Book IV, Chap. II.

[17] D. Ricardo, On Protection to Agriculture (1822) Section VI, § 19; *Works and Correspondence*, ed. Sraffa, vol. iv, 243. And see also Ricardo to McCulloch, March 1821, op. cit., vol. viii, 355–60.

[18] Cf. L. Brown, *The Board of Trade and the Free Trade Movement, 1830–42* (Oxford, Clarendon Press, 1958), 18.

the complete removal of agricultural protection.[19] And even those, like Torrens in his early days, who were prepared to urge the abolition of the Corn Laws, did not extend their arguments to advocate a general free trade.[20]

Such caution may have been due in part to a recognition of the limits of what was politically feasible, although no one would now dispute the reality and importance of the *caveats* which many classical economists entered, on purely analytical grounds, against the free trade case. Thus when Huskisson and Ricardo served together on the Commons Committee on the Agriculture of the United Kingdom in 1821 they found themselves in complete agreement—yet the Committee's Report, which Huskisson wrote, endorsed the 'universally acknowledged' principles of free trade without recommending a free trade in corn, in order to 'spare vested interests' and 'deal tenderly with those obstacles to improvement which the long existence of a vicious and artificial system too often creates'.[21]

There was probably a great deal of truth in Greville's comment about Huskisson—'all the ablest men in the country coincide with him, and . . . the mass of the community are persuaded that his plans are mischievous to the last degree'.[22] Certainly both the tactical situation in Parliament and social conditions in the country as a whole did not favour pressing ahead too rapidly with far reaching reforms of trade policy in the later eighteen-twenties. Nevertheless the movement gained momentum in the next decade, with the appointment of Poulett Thomson as Vice-President of the Board of Trade in 1830; and as it did so, some of the reservations in the field of ideas were swept away also. So J. L. Mallet could write in his diary in 1834:

All the economists of my time and Ricardo at the head of them, held that the landlords were entitled to protection in respect of tithes, land tax and all direct charges on land. 'Mais nous avons changé tout cela.' As the times become more radical and the landlords and agricultural interests lose ground, the economists shift their quarters.[23]

[19] O'Brien, *J. R. McCulloch*, 225.   [20] Cf. Robbins, *Robert Torrens*, 185.
[21] B. Semmel, *The Rise of Free Trade Imperialism* (Cambridge, Cambridge University Press, 1970), 137.
[22] *The Greville Memoirs*, 1814–60 (ed. Lytton Strachey and Roger Fulford) (London, MacMillan, 1938), vol. ii, 47. The entry is for 18 September 1830.
[23] From the diary of J. L. Mallet, 3 July 1834. *Proceedings of the Political Economy Club*, vol. vi (London, MacMillan, 1921), 262.

II

The centenary of the *Wealth of Nations* was duly celebrated with banquets, speeches, and articles in Britain, America, and on the Continent of Europe;[24] and half a century had produced no small difference in the way in which Smith's contribution was viewed. The distinction between its analytical and practical aspects was now consciously and deliberately made[25] and since, in Britain at least, it was the latter which tended to receive most attention in the discussions of 1876 it may be appropriate to reverse the order of the preceding section and take the policy side first.

The principal celebration of the centenary in Britain was the dinner given by the Political Economy Club on 31 May 1876, the proceedings of which were fully reported and made the subject of comment by a number of newspapers and reviews.[26] With Gladstone in the chair, Robert Lowe as the first speaker and the French Minister of Finance, Léon Say (grandson of J. B. Say) as second speaker it was, as Jevons said, 'true that the statesmen had it mostly their own way, and . . . the company appeared to care little what mere literary economists thought about Adam Smith'.[27]

The note which Lowe chose to strike was a confident one—so confident as now to appear complacent, but nevertheless fairly typical of the attitude of British public men of the day. After a somewhat facile and condescending survey of Smith's work in the course of which he declared that where Smith failed· it was 'mainly because he had not sufficient confidence in the truth of the doctrines which he laid down', Lowe went on to deal with the question before the meeting—'What are the more important results which have followed from the publication of the *Wealth of Nations* . . . and in what principal directions do the doctrines of

---

[24] Cf. note 26 below, and *The Adam Smith Centennial to commemorate the hundredth anniversary of the publication of the Wealth of Nations* (New York, 1876); E. Nasse, 'Das hundertjährige Jubiläum der Schrift von Adam Smith über den Reichtum der Nationen' *Preussen Jahrbuch*, 38 (1876), 384–400 (Berlin, G. Reimer). K. T. von Inama-Sternegg, *Adam Smith und die Bedeutung seines Wealth of Nations für die Moderne Nationalökonomie* (Innsbruck, 1876).

[25] Notably by Walter Bagehot in his essay 'Adam Smith and our Modern Economy', *Economic Studies* (Longmans Green, London, 1879), 125–30.

[26] *Political Economy Club. Revised Report of the Proceedings at the Dinner of 31 May 1876, held in celebration of the Hundredth Year of the Publication of the 'Wealth of Nations'.* (London, Longmans Green, Reader and Dyer, 1876).

[27] W. S. Jevons, 'The Future of Political Economy', *Fortnightly Review*, vol. xx (1876), 617–31.

that book still remain to be applied?' His audience can scarcely
have been surprised to hear him single out the achievement of free
trade as the most important consequence of the work of 'this simple
Glasgow Professor'. Quoting Smith's cynical comment about the
prospects of free trade in Britain,[28] Lowe exclaimed 'He under-
estimated his own strength; Free Trade has found its way'.[29] But
the corollary of this glowing account of the way in which the nineteenth century had learned and acted upon the lessons of Smith
was a less encouraging view of the future of political economy—
'I cannot help thinking that we must look rather to the negative
than to the positive side, at least at present. . . . The controversies
that we now have in Political Economy, although they offer a
capital exercise for the logical faculties, are not the same thrilling
importance as those of earlier days; the great work has been done.'[30]

This view that the mission of Political Economy, as Smith had
presented it, had been accomplished, or soon would be, was
echoed by several of the newspapers which commented on the
occasion. 'It is perhaps true', *The Times* leader declared, 'that Free
Trade has established itself more as a fact than a doctrine; but
when the first position is firmly occupied the second must follow,
and the time is not distant when the supremacy of Adam Smith's
teaching shall surpass his largest hopes.'[31] What had seemed
tentatively possible in 1826 was glorious reality in 1876, and ideas
which had seemed sound but admitted of modifications and
exceptions then had been raised to the status of incontrovertible
truths half a century later.

George Warde Norman, the only survivor of the original
members of 1821 to attend the Political Economy Club's centenary
dinner, stated the position as he saw it unequivocally—'it seems to
me that the real doctrines of Political Economy as they were first
taught by Adam Smith . . . remain unimpeached; that they have
never been successfully attacked; that they are in fact unattackable;
that they are true now and will be true to all time'—and William
Newmarch took Lowe's point about the future of political economy
a stage further by predicting that 'there will be what may be called
a large negative development of Political Economy tending to
produce an important and beneficial effect; and that is, such a

[28] Cf. above, p. 47 and note 16.
[29] *Political Economy Club. Revised Report of the Proceedings . . .*, 11, 19, 21.
[30] Ibid. 20, 21.   [31] *The Times*, 1 June 1876.

R. D. Collison Black

development of Political Economy as will reduce the functions of government within a smaller and smaller compass'. Only W. E. Forster ventured to declare himself 'strongly of the contrary opinion, that we cannot undertake the *laissez-faire* principle in the present condition of our politics or of parties in Parliament, or in the general condition of the country'.[32]

This then was economic policy as the politicians of 1876 saw it; and had it not been for the hint dropped by Forster it would have been hard to realise, from the report of the Adam Smith centenary dinner that the 'mere literary economists' in the person of John Elliott Cairnes, had declared six years earlier that Political Economy 'has nothing to do with *laissez-faire* any more than with communism'.[33] Yet among the economists of the day there were many who shared Lowe's despondent view about the future of their subject in its second century, without sharing his optimistic idea of the reasons for it. For whatever men like Lowe and Norman might say there were, as Professor T. W. Hutchison has said,[34] unsettled questions in political economy in the eighteen-seventies on the three fronts of policy, theory, and method.

Political economy, said Bagehot at this time, 'lies rather dead in the public mind. Not only does it not excite the same interest as formerly, but there is not exactly the same confidence in it. Younger men either do not study it, or do not feel that it comes home to them, and that it matches with their most living ideas.'[35] Such lack of interest, bordering on hostility seems to have been a result of the tendency, which Lowe exemplified and which Cairnes opposed, to associate political economy with the doctrines of *laissez-faire* and free trade and to gloss over the social problems which urban industrialism had produced. If such policy issues were the basis for the disenchantment of the general public with political economy, the doubts and disillusionment expressed by the economists themselves arose also out of problems of theory and method.

It was the very fact that the principles of political economy—

---

[32] *Political Economy Club. Revised Report of the Proceedings . . .*, 26, 38, 50.

[33] J. E. Cairnes, 'Political Economy and Laissez Faire' in *Essays in Political Economy, Theoretical and Applied* (London, MacMillan, 1873), 255.

[34] T. W. Hutchison, *A Review of Economic Doctrines 1870–1929* (Oxford, Clarendon Press, 1953), 5–22.

[35] W. Bagehot, *Economic Studies* (1879, 2nd ed. Longman's Green, 1888), 3–4.

principles laid down by Smith, modified by Ricardo and restated by J. S. Mill—seemed 'perfectly unattackable' to men like Norman and Lowe which was so galling to economists of the younger generation like Cliffe Leslie and Jevons. In their view if political economy was to have a future as well as a past it must be freed from what Jevons had called 'the noxious influence of authority'.[36] Now I am disposed to think that this was a point which Jevons exaggerated, and that his opposition to J. S. Mill particularly has in turn been exaggerated by others;[37] but a study of the presentation of political economy to undergraduates at this period does produce a strong impression of a stagnant subject.[38] Nor does there seem any reason to question the view that this was the result of the way in which John Stuart Mill had in 1848 given fresh life and authority to Ricardian analysis set within a Smithian comparative framework.[39] Hence the very success of those revisions of Smith's analytical system which the Ricardians had felt to be necessary half a century after the publication of the *Wealth of Nations* was in turn the source of that stagnation and dogmatism which were tending to bring political economy into disrepute at the time of the centenary.

The way in which economists of the historical stamp of Cliffe Leslie on the one hand and of the mathematical stamp of Jevons on the other, reacted to this state of affairs with proposals for the reform and reconstruction of their discipline is a familiar story which need not concern us here; what is relevant is the way in which they viewed Smith's century-old contribution.

In fact, comparatively little of what was written at the time of the centenary dealt with the *Wealth of Nations* directly, the economists generally preferring to use the occasion to discuss their

[36] W. S. Jevons, *Theory of Political Economy* (London, MacMillan, 1871), 265–7.

[37] Cf. R. D. C. Black, 'W. S. Jevons and the Foundation of Modern Economics', in Black, Coats, and Goodwin (eds.), *The Marginal Revolution in Economics* (Durham, N.C., Duke University Press, 1973), 99–103; N. B. de Marchi, 'The Noxious Influence of Authority; a Correction of Jevons' Charge', *Journal of Law and Economics*, vol. xvi (1973), 179–89.

[38] See, for example, W. P. Emerton, *Palaestra Oxoniensis; Questions and Exercises in Political Economy, with references to Adam Smith, Ricardo . . . and others. Adapted to the Oxford Pass and Honour and the Cambridge Ordinary B.A. Examinations*. (Oxford, Thornton, 1879).

[39] Cf. S. Hollander, 'Ricardianism, J. S. Mill and the Neo-Classical Challenge' (Toronto, 1973). In this working paper, Hollander sets out to challenge Schumpeter's contention that J. S. Mill was not really a Ricardian economist.

R. D. Collison Black 53

current pre-occupations; but serious consideration was given to Smith's theoretical work by both Cliffe Leslie and Walter Bagehot, while Jevons dealt with it more incidentally.

Cliffe Leslie's treatment of 'The Political Economy of Adam Smith'[40] was perhaps the most subtle of the three, and the one which is most interesting today because of its parallels with modern studies. Attacking the crude stereotype put forward by Robert Lowe of Adam Smith as the founder of a political economy which is 'a body of necessary and universal truth, founded on invariable laws of nature, and deduced from the constitution of the human mind', Cliffe Leslie stressed that the *Wealth of Nations* must be interpreted as a part of Smith's whole system of moral philosophy. Leslie indeed was exceptional amongst economists of his time in showing both familiarity with, and respect for, the *Theory of Moral Sentiments*. After a scholarly account of the origins of the doctrine of natural law and its place in Smith's philosophical system Leslie went on to argue that 'there ran thus through the political economy of both Adam Smith and the Physiocrats, though much more extensively and systematically in the former, a combination of the experience philosophy, of inductive investigation, with *a priori* speculation derived from the Nature hypothesis'. Hence, he contended, 'Adam Smith has been preserved by the inductive method which he combined with *a priori* deduction from enormous fallacies into which the school of Ricardo has since been betrayed by their method of pure deduction'.[41]

Coming from a leading exponent of the historical method, such conclusions are hardly surprising, and it was entirely consistent with the historical approach that Leslie should argue that Smith's theories were influenced by the early phase of industrial development in which he lived and hence could not be accepted and applied without modification a century later. All this is very much what we would expect but it leads on to a little-noticed conclusion which seems to have fresh relevance in the world of 1976:

Although 'the obvious and simple system of natural liberty' is the foundation of Smith's whole system, though he regarded it as the law of the beneficent Author of Nature, it turns out that he applied it

[40] *Fortnightly Review*, N.S. vol. viii (November, 1870), 549–63. Reprinted in *Essays in Political and Moral Philosophy* (Dublin, Hodges, Foster, and Figgis, 1879), 148–66.   [41] Leslie, *Essays*, 160–61 and 163.

only to one-half of mankind . . . He seems to have been perfectly content—though it involves an inconsistency which is fatal to his whole theory—with the existing restraints on the energies of women; and the only effort on the part of a woman to better her own condition which he has in view is 'to become the mistress of a family'.[42]

So far as I am aware, none of the redoubtable women economists of the nineteenth century made this point[43] and there is a certain piquancy in Adam Smith, the eighteenth century bachelor, being berated by Cliffe Leslie, the nineteenth century bachelor, for his neglect of women's rights.

Jevons was the foremost of the economists who used the centenary not for a detailed study of Smith's contribution, but for a review of the current state and prospects of economic thought. In the course of that review he insisted that the historical method so much favoured by Leslie while it might supplement abstract analysis could never replace it. So again it is hardly surprising to find that when Jevons came to refer directly to Smith's method he declared it 'very wise of Adam Smith to attempt no subdivision, but to expound his mathematical theory (for I hold that his reasoning was really mathematical in nature) in conjunction with concrete applications and historical illustrations'.[44] Thus Jevons and Leslie, writing in the same decade, contrived to see the analytical and historical parts of Smith's work in almost precisely inverse order of importance, but both were equally prepared to exempt Smith from the harsh criticism which they directed against Ricardo and his followers.

On other aspects of Smith's system, Jevons's views have to be pieced together from scattered references, mainly in his posthumous *Principles of Economics*. There he dealt specifically with the paradox of value (to which there is only incidental reference in his *Theory of Political Economy*) and made the point that in the famous 'water and diamonds' passage Smith was using the term utility in its ordinary connotation of usefulness and not in the sense of desirability—a point which has also been stressed by modern commentators.[45] Jevons had high praise for the 'exquisite

[42] Leslie, *Essays*, 166.

[43] Cf. Dorothy. Lampen Thomson, *Adam Smith's Daughters* (New York, Exposition Press, 1973).

[44] Jevons, 'The Future of Political Economy', *Principles*, 200–1.

[45] Cf. Hollander, 'The Role of Utility and Demand in *The Wealth of Nations*', *Essays on Adam Smith*, Part II, 315.

chapters' on division of labour in the *Wealth of Nations*, but con-
demned the distinction between productive and unproductive
labour as 'quite untenable' on the ground that 'all labour is
directed to the production of utility'.[46]

An economist who in 1871 had stated 'the somewhat novel
opinion, that *value depends entirely upon utility*'[47] could hardly
have taken any other view, but the limited extent to which Jevons's
ideas had penetrated English economic thinking in 1876 is demonstrated by Bagehot in the most closely argued of the several pieces
he wrote on Smith, 'Adam Smith and our Modern Economy'.[48]
In this Bagehot suggested that:

if we look at *The Wealth of Nations* as if it were a book of modern
Political Economy, we should ask four questions about it.

(1) What, by its teaching, is the cause which makes one thing
     exchange for more or less of other things?
(2) What are the laws under which that cause acts in producing
     these things?—the full reply to which gives the laws of population
     and growth of capital.
(3) If it turns out (as of course it does) that these things are pro-
     duced by the co-operation of many people, what settles the
     share of each of those people in those things, or in their proceeds?
     The answer to this question gives what are called the laws of
     distribution.
(4) If this co-operation costs something (as of course it does), like
     all other co-operations, who is to pay that cost, and how is it to
     be levied? The reply to this inquiry is the theory of taxation.[49]

Bagehot in fact attempted to answer only the first of these
questions. In the course of forty pages on the subject he referred
once to Jevons's definition of a market, but not at all to utility
concepts or their absence in Smith's theory. Bagehot's final
conclusion was that:

although . . . Adam Smith had the merit of teaching the world that the
exchangeable value of commodities is proportioned to the cost of their
production, his analysis of that cost was so very defective as to throw
that part of Political Economy into great confusion for many years,
and as quite to prevent his teaching being used as an authority upon
it now.[50]

In this final point at least Bagehot concurred with Cliffe Leslie

[46] Jevons, *Principles*, 87.   [47] Id., *Theory of Political Economy* (1871), 2.
[48] Essay III in his *Economic Studies* (1879).
[49] Bagehot, *Economic Studies*, 131.   [50] Ibid. 169.

and Jevons. The fifty years which had seen the policy message of the *Wealth of Nations* converted from a desideratum into an accepted truth and an accomplished fact had also seen Smith's economic analysis converted from the foundation of current thinking to a set of ideas which, while they might command more respect than those of Ricardo, were generally admitted to belong to a past age. If there was as yet no unanimity as to what the foundation of a new political economy might be there was equally no doubt that it could no longer be the Smithian system.

III

Between the centenary of the *Wealth of Nations* and its sesquicentenary the perspective in which it was viewed underwent another change—in fact almost a reversal, reminiscent of one of those drawings of hollow squares which when stared at for a time seem to turn inside out. For while the economists of 1878 had lost faith in classical theory without having found what to put in its place, the economists of 1926 were for the most part secure in their acceptance of the neo-classical doctrines as developed by Marshall and supported by the great weight of his authority. On the side of policy, however, the certainties of 1876 had completely dissolved and there was no agreement as to what should be put in their place.

Perhaps for this very reason, the academic economists, who had rather played second fiddle to the politicians and public men at the centenary celebrations, were mainly to the fore in both Britain and America when the time came to celebrate the 150th anniversary in 1926. Indeed the occasion attracted little notice from the wider public, perhaps not surprisingly.

In Britain, the London School of Economics marked the occasion with a series of lectures given by members of its staff, as did the University of Chicago on the other side of the Atlantic.[51] From

[51] The full series of L.S.E. lectures comprised—Edwin Cannan on 'Adam Smith as an Economist'; Morris Ginsberg on 'Adam Smith's Ethical Theory'; T. E. Gregory on 'Adam Smith's relation to Currency Theory'; H. J. Laski on 'Adam Smith's relation to Political Thought'; Hugh Dalton on 'Adam Smith's relation to Public Finance'; F. W. Hirst on 'Adam Smith and English Fiscal Policy', and James Bonar 'The Tables Turned—A Lecture and Dialogue on Adam Smith and the Classical Economists'. Bonar's lecture was separately published in pamphlet form (London, 1926). The Chicago lectures, by J. M. Clark, Paul H. Douglas, Jacob Hollander, Glenn R. Morrow, Melchior Palyi, and Jacob Viner were published under the title *Adam Smith 1776–1926* (Chicago, Chicago University Press, 1928).

the point of view of economic theory the most important lectures in these two series were Edwin Cannan's 'Adam Smith as an Economist'[52] and Paul H. Douglas's 'Smith's Theory of Value and Distribution'.[53]

Cannan, who thirty years before had discovered and published the notes of Smith's 1763 Lectures on Justice and twenty-two years previously had published what has remained until now the standard edition of the *Wealth of Nations*, was then perhaps uniquely qualified to pronounce on his topic. Yet for an established authority the estimate which he gave of his subject's contribution to economic thought was remarkably low—remarkably though perhaps not surprisingly to those who are familiar with what Jacob Viner shrewdly characterised as Cannan's 'Tom Tulliver' approach to classical economics.[54]

According to Cannan, 'Very little of Adam Smith's scheme of economics has been left standing by subsequent inquirers. No one now holds his theory of value, his account of capital is seen to be hopelessly confused, and his theory of distribution is explained as an ill-assorted union between his own theory of prices and the physiocrats' fanciful Economic Table.' He was equally scathing with regard to Smith's classification of incomes and theory of taxation but did credit him with accomplishing 'three great things'.[55]

These turn out to be—first, the substitution of the idea of real income or produce for the accumulation of gold and silver as the end of economic activity; second, the development of the idea that 'wealth per head' is the significant variable rather than 'wealth in the aggregate, whatever that may be'; and third, the development of the idea that regard for one's own interest may be, in economic affairs, 'a laudable principle of action' which does not damage others under a system of free competition.

Cannan's list of Smith's positive contributions as an economist was thus not only short, but such as to suggest that Smith's power

[52] *Economica*, vol. vi (1926), 123–34.

[53] In *Adam Smith 1776–1926*, 77–115.

[54] Its sharpest critic, he is also one of the most complete of the posthumous conquests of the classical school, although his attachment to it reminds one of George Eliot's Tom Tulliver, who, it may be remembered, was 'very fond of birds, that is of throwing stones at them'—Viner, Review of E. Cannan, *A Review of Economic Theory* (London, King, 1929) *Economica*, vol. x (1930), 74–84.

[55] *Economica*, vol. vi (1926), 123.

of analysis was not much more than rudimentary. Paul Douglas's account of 'Smith's Theory of Value and Distribution' was considerably more sympathetic and indeed presented what until recently could be considered the standard interpretation of the theoretical core of the *Wealth of Nations*. Even so, Douglas began by asserting that:

the contributions of Adam Smith to the theory of value and distribution were not great, and in commemorating the publication of the *Wealth of Nations* it might seem to be the path of wisdom to pass these topics by in discreet silence and to reserve discussion instead for those subjects, such as the division of labour, where his realistic talents enabled him to appear at a better advantage.[56]

It is unnecessary to rehearse the details of Douglas's well known account of Smith's theory of value, with its emphasis on the rejection of utility by Smith and elucidation of the labour-embodied and labour-commanded theories. On the subject of distribution, Douglas agreed with Cannan that Smith 'interested himself primarily in the question of profits per cent., wages per head and rent per acre' and tended to view his ideas very much in this 'functional distribution' or 'factor pricing' context.

In this perhaps lies the clue to the low estimate which the economists of 1926 gave of Smith's theoretical work. For however true it may be that an embryonic notion of general equilibrium can be traced in Smith's account of competitive market mechanisms, no one would contend that his treatment of the determination of individual market price is other than sketchy. Given that neoclassical partial equilibrium analysis placed its main emphasis in that quarter, and that in America particularly Austrian influences had tended to undermine the Marshallian attachment to real cost ideas, it is only natural that from this perspective the Smithian contribution to the analysis of the market economy could be written down as 'not great'.

On the side of policy, however, Smith's performance earned an equally low mark from Cannan. According to him, 'Smith was wrong in supposing that the desire for individual gain would pull the industrial chariot safely along in the absence of harness.' He argued that this 'vitiated Smith's doctrine' and explained the failure of free trade in the international sphere, where no framework of legal regulation existed as compared to its relative success

[56] *Adam Smith 1776–1926*, 77.

in the internal sphere, where there was such a framework. Thus Smith 'failed to see that self-interest had been put in the shafts and harnessed by law and order, products of collective wisdom', in Cannan's opinion, but nevertheless this 'detracts little from the value of his exposition that it was a very good horse'.[57]

It was left to Jacob Viner to show in his famous paper 'Adam Smith and Laissez Faire' that 'the absence of harness' had never been one of Smith's assumptions. After a pentrating survey of the place of the system of natural liberty in both the *Theory of Moral Sentiments* and the *Wealth of Nations* which he modestly claimed to be 'familiar matter' Viner went on to say:

> What is not so familiar, however, is the extent to which Smith acknowledged exceptions to the doctrine of a natural harmony in the economic order even when left to take its natural course. Smith himself never brought these together; but if this is done, they make a surprisingly comprehensive list and they demonstrate beyond dispute the existence of a wide divergence between the perfectly harmonious, completely beneficient natural order of the *Theory of Moral Sentiments* and the partial and limited harmony in the economic order of the *Wealth of Nations*.[58]

Having proved his point by an impressive assembly of instances from Smith's own writings, Viner concluded:

> Adam Smith was not a doctrinaire advocate of laissez-faire. He saw a wide and elastic range of activity for government, and he was prepared to extend it even farther if government, by improving its standards of competence, honesty and public spirit, showed itself entitled to wider responsibilities.[59]

Viner provided an important correction of the stereotyped picture of Adam Smith as the high priest of non-intervention with free enterprise. Yet he certainly did not deny the significance of that 'strong presumption against government activity beyond its fundamental duties of protection against foreign foes and maintenance of justice' from which Smith started, nor would he have denied the immense practical influence of the stereotype which had grown from it. It was, however, precisely this practical influence which was finally fading at this time.

'We do not dance even yet to a new tune', wrote Keynes in another 1926 publication, *The End of Laissez-faire*. 'But a change

[57] *Economica*, vol. vi (1926), 134.   [58] *Adam Smith 1776–1926*, 134.
[59] Ibid. 154.

is in the air. We hear but indistinctly what were once the clearest and most distinguishable voices which have ever instructed political mankind. The orchestra of diverse instruments, the chorus of articulate sound, is receding at last into the distance.'[60]

Keynes's assertion that 'It is *not* a correct deduction from the principles of economics that enlightened self-interest always operates in the public interest' was not essentially different from what Cairnes had said on the same subject in 1870.[61] The real difference which the intervening years had made to the economists' approach is shown by the fact that Cairnes went on to say that 'as a practical rule, I hold *laissez-faire* to be incomparably the safer guide' whereas Keynes urged that the chief task of economists was to distinguish afresh the *Agenda* of government from the *Non-Agenda* but 'without Bentham's prior presumption that inter-ference is . . . "generally needless" and "generally pernicious" '.

Keynes in *The End of Laissez-faire* had succeeded in capturing the spirit of the times with his customary felicity. No one in 1926, the year of the General Strike, would have dared to assert the beneficence of free trade, external or internal, with the confident dogmatism of Robert Lowe fifty years earlier, but many had still to learn that there was no way back to the comfortable certainties of the era before 1914. Many others who appreciated this fact had no idea of what could or should be put in place of those certainties. They 'did not dance even yet to a new tune', but when Keynes went on, in the closing sections of his essay, to reflect on 'possible improvements in the technique of modern capitalism by the agency of collective action' he showed that he had already sketched out the main elements of the tune to which so many were to dance in years to come.[62]

IV

The half-century between 1926 and 1976 has probably seen more and greater changes in both the method and content of economic

[60] J. M. Keynes, *The End of Laissez-Faire, Collected Writings* (London, MacMillan, for the R.E.S., 1972), vol. ix, 272.

[61] Ibid. 288; and cf. Cairnes, 'Political Economy and Laissez-Faire', *Essays in Political Economy*, 250–1.

[62] For a fuller account of the problems of economic policy in this period, and of the work of Keynes—then without the widespread influence on public affairs which it later gained—see D. N. Winch, *Economics and Policy* (London, Hodder and Stoughton, 1969), Part II.

analysis than did the whole century and a half which went before—
and these changes reflect, in part at least, equally great changes in
the circumstances of economic life. So it is hardly surprising that
Smith's contribution should be seen today in a new perspective;
what is surprising is that economists today should be finding more
of value in that contribution than did their predecessors of fifty
and even a hundred years ago. But there can be no denying that
such is the case, for the evidence is abundant—in the other papers
presented at this conference, in the volume of essays published in
conjunction with the bicentenary edition of Smith's works, and in
the numerous other works on and relating to Smith which have
appeared in recent years.

What is the reason for this remarkable revival and extension of
interest in Smith's ideas? It can, I think, be at least partly explained by the very nature of the change in perspective which has
occurred; for the standpoint from which the majority of economists
today are accustomed to view Smith's contribution is that of the
economics of growth and development. Seen from there, it
naturally appears more sensible and significant than when it is
viewed from the angle of a static theory of value and distribution
of the neo-classical type.

The striking point which emerges here is how very recently the
position from which we are now accustomed to judge Smith's
contribution has been reached. It was really only after the appearance of Professor Hla Myint's pioneer article on 'The Welfare
Significance of Productive Labour' in the *Review of Economic
Studies* in 1943 and his *Theories of Welfare Economics* in 1948 that
economists generally began to see Adam Smith in this light. The
lack of emphasis on growth in the thinking of 1926 can perhaps be
explained in terms of the dominance of the neo-classical approach
at that time; but the same emphasis is also notably lacking in
earlier appraisals of Smith. Bagehot in 1876 had noted:

in this very science of Political Economy, the first writers endeavoured
to deal in a single science with all the causes . . . which, as they would
have said 'made nations rich or poor' . . . But considered in this simple
and practical way, the science of Political Economy becomes useless,
because of its immense extent.[63]

Slight and dismissive as it is, this is the only direct reference to the

[63] Bagehot, 'The Preliminary of Political Economy', *Economic Studies*,
98–9.

treatment of economic growth in classical work which I have been able to find in the literature of 1876. Nor does the theme of growth figure prominently in 1826, although this may be because the writers of that day were still too much 'inside' the Smithian approach to select out this element for comment.

By no means all of what has recently been written about Smith's economics is concerned with its growth aspects, however. There have been significant re-interpretations of the utility aspects of his theory of value, and notable re-assessments of what can perhaps only be described as aspects of his political economy—the treatment of public goods in the *Wealth of Nations*, for example, and more broadly the relations between the views of the individual in society which Smith took in the *Wealth of Nations* and in the *Theory of Moral Sentiments*, now seen afresh as two parts of one system.[64]

Some of this represents a very valuable effort to set Smith's work properly into the context of eighteenth century ideas, events, and institutions; but some of it can also be seen as symptomatic of another shift in viewpoint, producing another new perspective on Smith's contribution. Many economists today are disenchanted about the prospects and results of economic growth, and many are likewise dubious or defensive about the long-vaunted idea of economics as a science, positive and value free. It is little wonder that such authors can find fresh interest in a system of thought which placed economic problems firmly in the context of ethics and jurisprudence and which was informed throughout by a concept of justice. This may well prove to be the aspect of Smith's ideas which the next generation of economists will see as vital.

Each period, indeed, has tended and will tend to see Smith's contribution in its own way and to evaluate it accordingly. Certainly also each one has tended and will tend to see the treatment of those problems and theories in which it has most interest as constituting the most significant part of Smith's work. There is a good deal of truth in Jacob Viner's typically astringent comment

---

[64] e.g. M. Bowley, *Studies in the History of Economic Theory before 1870* (London, MacMillan, 1973), especially Parts III and IV; S. Hollander, *The Economics of Adam Smith* (Toronto, University of Toronto Press, 1973), G. J. Stigler, 'Smith's Travels on the Ship of State', A. Peacock, 'The Treatment of the Principles of Public Finance in *The Wealth of Nations*', in *Essays on Adam Smith*, 237–46, 553–67. E. G. West, 'Adam Smith's Economics of Politics', *Carleton Economic Papers* (forthcoming in *History of Political Economy*, vol. viii, 1976).

that 'traces of every conceivable sort of doctrine can be found in that most catholic book, and an economist must have peculiar theories indeed who cannot quote from *The Wealth of Nations* to support his special purposes'.[65]

Is this the only reason why successive generations have continued to find something of value in Smith's contribution, from whatever angle it is viewed? Is this why the *Wealth of Nations* continues to form 'part of an extended present'?[66] Surely there is more to it than this. I am inclined to think that the perennial appeal of the *Wealth of Nations* rests not only on the wealth of ideas which it contains, even though it may be that 'there is scarcely any economic truth now known of which he [Smith] did not get some glimpse'.[67] Something also must be credited to Smith's realism and understanding of his fellow-men—in fact, to his possession of those virtues of humanity and self-command on which he placed so high a value.[68] In the words which Edmund Burke used to Smith himself in commenting on the TMS:

A theory like yours founded on the nature of man, which is always the same, will last, when those that are founded on his opinions, which are always changing, will and must be forgotten.[69]

COMMENT

by D. P. O'Brien*

Professor Black has given us an excellent survey, with characteristic lucidity and scholarship, of the changing historical perspective on Adam Smith. This is a tremendously important theme with implications for the entire history of economic thought. What I would like to do, very briefly, is to enlarge a little upon this theme

[65] Viner, op. cit. 126.

[66] K. E. Boulding, 'After Samuelson, who needs Adam Smith?', *History of Political Economy* vol. vii, No. 2 (Fall, 1971), 231.

[67] Marshall, *Principles of Economics*, App. B, §3 (9th ed., London, MacMillan, for the R.E.S.) vol. i, 757.

[68] Cf. D. D. Raphael, 'The Impartial Spectator' *Essays on Adam Smith*, Part I, 89.

[69] Letter 38, addressed to Adam Smith, dated 10 September, 1759. Quoted in C. R. Fay, *The World of Adam Smith* (Cambridge, Heffer, 1960), 9.

* University of Durham.

by indicating some of the specific ways in which perspective changes.

Firstly and most obviously the subject matter of economics, the central focus of the attention of economists at any particular time, is a changing thing. It is not I think profitable, particularly at this time, to discuss whether what is involved in a change of focus is a Khunian 'paradigm shift'. But every economist with any know-ledge of the wider literature of economics will recognize the truth of this assertion. Historians of economic thought themselves have to be trained as economists primarily rather than as historians and so the changes of focus of the subject Economics affect their training, their mental conditioning, and hence their view of their subject. A striking instance of this, in relation to Adam Smith, is the way in which economists rediscovered economic growth after World War II and it became an important part of the literature. Professor Myint had already shown that Adam Smith's great work was about economic growth;[1] but his important message, well formulated though it was, might have fallen on much less recep-tive ears but for the change of focus which the subject itself had experienced.

Secondly, as a subset of changes in the subject, are changes in technique. No one can doubt that what has occurred during the last fifteen years has been a major change in the technique of economists and in the standards of mathematical familiarity (if not elegance) which they are required to reach. Virtually all economists now have a reading knowledge of mathematics (and what might be loosely called a 'reproductive knowledge') even if their manipu-lative skills are not of a particularly high order. This in turn has influenced the treatment which has been accorded to the history of economics. Sometimes the influence has not always been a happy one. But the formalization of Smith's growth model by Thweatt and (especially) Barkhai[2] has certainly been influential as have some of the mathematical models of Ricardo.[3] Of course some

[1] H. Myint, 'The Classical View of the Economic Problem', *Economica* N.S. Vol. 13 (1946), 119–30.

[2] W. O. Thweatt, 'A Diagrammatic Presentation of Adam Smith's Growth Model', *Social Research* vol. 24 (1957), 227–30; H. Barkai, 'A Formal Outline of a Smithian Growth Model', *Quarterly Journal of Economics* vol. 88 (1969), 396–414.

[3] L. Pasinetti, 'A Mathematical Formulation of the Ricardian System', *Review of Economic Studies* vol. 27 (1960), 78–98; H. Brems, 'An Attempt at a

corrective to the perspective given by this formalisation is required —and Professor Spengler's contribution here is particularly noteworthy.[4] But even if corrective is required the change in the focus of historians of economic thought is undeniable.

Thirdly, and it is gratifying to be able to record this, research in the history of economic thought has itself produced changes of focus and made certain views no longer tenable. Decent scholarly work in the history of economic thought does have the great advantage of cutting the feet from underneath the caricatures of the subject which are used for propagandist purposes. The caricaturists are really of two kinds. There are those who caricature so as to exalt their theoretical system—Marx, Bohm-Bawerk, and Keynes come into this category—and those who caricature for the easy purposes of reader appeal. Recent work on Poverty and the Industrial Revolution comes into this category. Of course the propagandists and the caricaturists are not necessarily deterred from their efforts by the existence of scholarly work in the history of economic thought. There is, after all, the income from the public library market to consider. But at least their impact is very considerably lessened by the existence of a body of literature which does, I think fairly and objectively, evaluate the history of economic thought. But the very process of the development of this literature produces changes of focus. The gap between the view of Ricardo advanced by J. H. Hollander[5] in the early years of this century and the now widely accepted view stemming in particular from the work of Professors Stigler[6] and Blaug,[7] is enormous. (Incidentally it is, I believe, a tribute to Ricardo that it took better economists to make better sense of him.) Scholarly work has also changed our view of Adam Smith. Perhaps the outstanding contribution of the last generation of scholars was that by Jacob Viner.[8] In recent times there has been a most important contribution

Rigorous Restatement of Ricardo's Long-Run Equilibrium' *Canadian Journal of Economics* vol. 26 (1960), 74–86.

[4] J. J. Spengler, 'Adam Smith's Theory of Economic Growth' Parts I–II *Southern Economic Journal* vol. 25 (1959), 397–415; vol. 26 (1959), 1–12.

[5] J. H. Hollander, *David Ricardo. A Centenary Estimate* (Baltimore 1910).

[6] G. J. Stigler, 'The Ricardian Theory of Value and Distribution' *Journal of Political Economy* vol. 60 (1952), 187–207.

[7] M. Blaug, *Ricardian Economics* (New Haven 1958).

[8] J. Viner, 'Adam Smith and Laisser Faire', *Journal of Political Economy* vol. 35 (1927), 198–232 reprinted in *The Long View and the Short* (Glencoe, Illinois, 1958).

from Warren Samuels[9] and most recently of all we have had Professor Hollander's weighty book.[10] These contributions to Smith scholarship help to correct not only the deliberate caricaturists but also the *simpliste* representation of Smith which the radical right like Robert Lowe, to whom Professor Black referred, often purveys. It also helps to correct the views advanced by those with very *subtle* minds, who over-simplify for a particular public occasion, like George Warde Norman who was also quoted. It also offers some check on Smith's 'good press' which stems in part from Viner's well known remark that it is a strange economist who cannot find support for his views in the *Wealth of Nations*.

Fourthly, there are in fact two distinct sources of writings in the history of economic thought. On the one hand there are books which are designedly written as works in the history of economic thought—and these, as Schumpeter[11] and Viner[12] showed, can themselves be great books. On the other hand there is a less obvious but certainly no less important source—criticism. For it is a fact that, for a certain kind of creative mind, criticism of previous work is itself a method of working. Schumpeter has pointed to this in the case of Marx;[13] but it is even more true of Ricardo. Another, and perhaps less obvious, example is that of Irving Fisher. The owners of these creative minds may, as in the case of Ricardo, become the leaders in their subject. If this occurs they influence the development of the history of economic thought in two ways. On the one hand their personal prestige causes other writers to take note of their evaluation of previous economists; this works quickly, and indeed in the case of Ricardo it worked very quickly indeed. Ricardo's evaluation of Adam Smith, especially on the subject of value, rent, and colonies was greatly influential though I would argue that we must not over-rate the extent to which McCulloch, in particular, regarded Smith's work as 'vitiated' even in the 1820's. For the Ricardian analyses are treated by McCulloch in his Notes to the *Wealth of Nations* as essentially *glosses* on the fundamental *basis* provided by Smith. The other method by which

[9] W. Samuels, *The Classical Theory of Economic Policy* (Cleveland, Ohio, 1966).

[10] S. Hollander, *The Economics of Adam Smith* (London 1973).

[11] J. A. Schumpeter, *History of Economic Analysis* (New York 1954).

[12] J. Viner, *Studies in the Theory of International Trade* (London 1937).

[13] Schumpeter, *History*, 390. See also the same author's *Ten Great Economists* (London 1952), 26.

the owners of critically creative minds exercise their influence is slower but it is still effective. It is the influence exercised by these economists upon courses which train future economists and thus future historians of economic thought.

Finally there are what might be termed 'raids' by those who are not primarily (or even secondarily) historians of economic thought but economists with high (and admired) levels of technique, into the history of economic thought. Sometimes these are futile and fatuous. But occasionally the whole history of economic thought approach may be lastingly changed. Two instances which come to mind are Baumol's treatment of Classical Dynamics,[14] and Kaldor's treatment of Classical Distribution.[15]

For all these reasons, history of economic thought does not offer a fixed and unchanging view of the work of Smith or of other previous economists. To put the changes of view in perspective however, let it be said at once that total obsolescence does not affect the best work of any particular generation of historians of economic thought. Despite the harsh things which are said about Cannan, especially his 1926 contribution to which Professor Black referred, historians of economic thought can gain a great deal of illumination—sometimes indeed, even exhilaration—from a book more than three quarters of a century old; Cannan's *Production and Distribution*.[16] Indeed, until 1976, it was Cannan's edition of the *Wealth of Nations* which was exclusively used by every serious scholar. But there is a big gap between Cannan and J. H. Hollander. So although the highpoints remain the perspective does change: and it is this very fact which helps to make history of economic thought a living, continuing, and perennially fascinating subject.

COMMENT

by Donald Winch*

I find myself so much in sympathy with Professor Black's choice of theme, and his priorities in dealing with it, that were I to follow

---

[14] W. J. Baumol, *Economic Dynamics* (2nd edition New York 1959), chapter 2.

[15] N. Kaldor, *Essays on Value and Distribution* (London 1960).

[16] E. Cannan, *A History of the Theories of Production and Distribution in English Political Economy from 1776 to 1848* (London 1893).

* University of Sussex.

strictly in his footsteps it would only be to add a footnote here and there. Thus it occurred to me that I might expand a little on his treatment of the divergent appeals made to Smith's authority, especially during the formative period of what we now call classical political economy. I could, for example, draw attention to the appeals made by Malthus and Sismondi in their attempts to mount an opposition to various aspects of Ricardian orthodoxy. But this would entail showing why, in spite of the obvious fact that Smith remained an alternative authority, the heterodox claimants to his mantle were so signally unsuccessful in establishing their case, regardless of whether it was based on an accurate assessment of Smith's own methods and conclusions. Attention would thereby be shifted towards Ricardo and away from the *Wealth of Nations*, with the added risk of endorsing an already too prevalent view of Smith among economists, namely that he is best interpreted as some kind of muddled progenitor of an enterprise that only achieved clarity and fruition in the work of Ricardo, John Stuart Mill, and Marx.

If we are interested in establishing a less proleptic perspective on Smith, it may be helpful to entertain a quite different view of what occurred during the crucial transitional period marked out, say, by the publication of the fifth edition of the *Wealth of Nations* in 1789 and Ricardo's death in 1823. For it was during this period, in the aftermath of the French Revolution, and as a result of a series of problems connected with the Napoleonic Wars—rising food prices, growing population, fears of monetary disorder, heavy taxation, and increased public debt—that it became acceptable to conduct serious discussion of economic issues in a manner and form that was quite different from the example set by Smith. Ricardo's *Principles* epitomized the new style to followers and opponents alike, but perhaps he was only its most extreme practitioner rather than its originator; his opponents may have had more in common with him than with the father figure to whom they occasionally turned for authority.

Some years ago now, Professor Alec Macfie drew our attention to various discontinuities between the Scottish and English traditions of economic thought, partly by emphasizing those changes taking place during this period which centre on the Benthamite version of utilitarianism.[1] Can one go further and suggest that there

[1] A. L. Macfie, 'The Scottish Tradition in Economic Thought', in *The*

are no obvious candidates—Scottish, French, or English—for the role of economic successor to the author of the *Wealth of Nations*? For one reason or another, Say, Sismondi, and Lauderdale do not seem capable of filling the bill, while Millar and Dugald Stewart have some of the qualifications for doing so, but only if one is prepared to overlook their lack of any sustained interest in political economy.

Or take the case of Malthus—English true, but no Benthamite. In spite of what Keynes might say about the methodological differences between Ricardo and Malthus, it was Malthus himself who, in his first *Essay on Population* published in 1798, introduced a quasi-mathematical approach to one of the questions that was later to become a central matter of concern to classical political economy. It may also be revealing to consider Edmund Burke, whose political and economic affinities with Smith have been the subject of several learned accounts. Burke had little in common with later generations of political economists, but neither can he be said to have spoken Smith's philosophical language when he made his intemperate defence of economic liberty in *Thoughts and Details on Scarcity*, a pamphlet written only five years after Smith's death. In their different ways, of course, Malthus and Burke are both classic post- (or counter-) revolutionary authors, but this does not license us to minimize the extent of the changes that took place not long after Smith had passed from the scene—changes which gave a new kind of urgency to certain public issues, and encouraged a narrower and more dogmatic application of the tools of reason to economic argument.

The relevance to our present deliberations of what I am trying to suggest in these tentative remarks may become clearer if I pose two more, intentionally provocative, questions. If there was a major change of emphasis and a narrowing in the scope of the science of political economy soon after Smith's death, can economists assume quite so confidently, as they appear to be doing this bicentennial year, that they are his rightful, if not sole, heirs? If, according to modern taste, Ricardo is more of an economists' economist than Smith, are today's economists the most natural celebrants of the *Wealth of Nations*? It may be significant that in 1876 even the politician Sir Robert Lowe had to Ricardianise

Individual in Society: Papers on Adam Smith (Allen and Unwin, London, 1967).

Smith in order to praise him—a tactic criticized by Thorold Rogers and (as Professor Black has indicated) Cliffe Leslie, both of whom wished to claim Smith as a relevant ancestor for their own brand of historical and inductive economics. I mention this point without wishing to endorse the view that it is any more valid to depict Smith as the founder of historical economics. From my point of view, this may only be yet another attempt to impose nineteenth century perspectives on what remains, quintessentially, a work of the eighteenth century.

Let me complete this irreverent train of thought by returning to an earlier assessment of Smith, one which clearly belongs to Scotland and to the eighteenth century. Three years after Smith's death, Dugald Stewart wrote what is still one of the most authoritative accounts of Smith's life and writings, though it is consonant with my earlier point that he later found it necessary to explain that he had been unduly influenced in writing it by the conservative mood created by the French Revolution. Stewart may also have been answering a sneer published in *The Times* in 1790 to the effect that Smith had 'converted the chair of Moral Philosophy into a professorship of trade and finance'—a fact which was crudely attributed to Smith's residence in Glasgow, 'a great commercial town'—when he set out to show the connection between Smith's 'system of commercial politics, and those speculations of his earlier years, in which he aimed more professedly at the advancement of human improvement and happiness'. For as Stewart concluded, rather primly: 'It is this view of Political Economy that can alone render it interesting to the moralist, and can dignify calculations of profit and loss in the eye of the philosopher' (Stewart, IV. 12). Stewart's corrective is still relevant if it reminds us that the *Wealth of Nations* was successful not simply as a work on 'trade and finance', but as the most striking attempt to sustain a peculiarly Scottish line of philosophical and historical inquiry into one of the most important emerging features of civilized society, namely the spreading network of commercial relationships, with all its consequences for the questions examined by traditional moral and political discourse. In this respect the *Wealth of Nations* can be said to mark the triumphant culmination of an eighteenth century enterprise, as much as the beginning of nineteenth and twentieth century economics. It can certainly do no harm to check hubris by reminding economists that, apart from his additions and corrections to later editions of the *Wealth of Nations*, after 1776 Smith published no further work on political economy— not even a single reply to his critics, few though they were. On the other hand, he did return to the *Theory of Moral Sentiments*, and we know that, given time, his next task was to have been the completion of his 'account of the general principles of law and government' (TMS VII. iv. 37).

Let me close with a related observation, which can most tactfully be introduced by rephrasing the comment by Jevons on the 1876 festivities cited by Professor Black. Jevons said that 'the statesmen mostly had it their own way, and the company appeared to care little what mere literary economists thought about Adam Smith'. Since Professors Black, O'Brien, and myself are, so to speak, the only accredited antiquarians billed to speak at this conference— leaving aside the 'proper' historians who spoke at the first session —it occurred· to me, perhaps a little ungraciously, that we might echo Jevons by replacing 'statesmen' by 'economists', and 'literary economists' by 'historians of economic thought'. However, in view of Professor O'Brien's persuasive argument to the effect that we mere historians have a valuable corrective part to play, I concluded that my comment might be thought to embody an awkward mixture of presumption and undue pessimism. Nevertheless, I am a little less optimistic than Professor O'Brien appears to be in thinking that Gresham's Law operates very effectively in these matters to ensure that good scholarship drives out bad propaganda and caricature.

The record of shifting perspectives outlined by Professor Black ought to be sobering to any economist about to embark on yet another modern reconstruction of Smith's position on this or that sub-division of modern economics, particularly if he is anxious to present it as an interpretation of what Smith 'really meant'. Economists have not always been the most reliable or consistent interpreters of their own past, and their whiggish habits have perhaps done more damage to Smith than many later figures in the pantheon. The history of Smith scholarship and the history of economists' views on Smith have frequently lived entirely separate lives. Professor Black's remarks on Edwin Cannan are a good illustration of this state of affairs. For here was one of the leading Smith scholars of his generation, who, when he wrote on Smith as an economist, was guilty of being both perfunctory and patronizing.

Consider also the Chicago sesquicentennial volume. Paul Douglas's attempt to show how much Smith's theory of value 'almost inevitably gave rise' to theories of exploitation may have been interesting to economists at the time, but there is no doubt in my mind as to which of those essays has best stood the test of fifty years of discussion, namely Jacob Viner's scholarly contribution on 'Adam Smith and Laissez Faire'.[2] As an ex-Viner pupil—a privilege I share with Professor Black—I may be guilty of personal bias here, though I believe the judgement could be supported by the more objective evidence provided by the number of citations of the Viner article in the new volume of celebratory *Essays on Adam Smith*. Ideally, of course, we all ought to be more like Viner—as good as economists as we aspire to be as scholars. While this may be a counsel of perfection, one thing on which we can agree is that when we have all had our say this year, at this conference and elsewhere, the most important monument to the bicentenary of the *Wealth of Nations* will be that constructed so patiently by the scholars who have worked on the Glasgow edition of Smith's complete works. This alone should silence ungrateful thoughts by holding out the prospect of uniting what have all too often been disparate enterprises.

[2] Jacob Viner, 'Adam Smith and Laisser Faire' in *Adam Smith 1776–1926: Lectures to Commemorate the Sesqui-Centennial of the Publication of the Wealth of Nations* (Chicago, 1928, Kelley, New York, 1966).

[5]

PARSON MALTHUS, THE GENERAL AND THE CAPTAIN[1]

I

MORE than thirty years have passed since Keynes first eulogised Malthus for his views on the " Principle of Effective Demand "; [2] during those years research in the history of economic thought has made clear that Keynes's well-known dictum that (on the question of effective demand) " Ricardo conquered England as completely as the Holy Inquisition conquered Spain "[3] was something of an exaggeration. We have become familiar with the idea that there was an " anti-Ricardian tradition " on this question in (and, somehow, even before!) Ricardo's own day; we are acquainted with some of those who helped to form it, although even now there does not exist a complete bibliography of those writers who attacked Say's Law during the classical period, much less a complete account of their work.

It can therefore reasonably be said that the full extent and quality of " anti-Ricardian " writings on effective demand has never been firmly established; but more than this, there seems to be no general agreement about what those opponents of Say's Law who have received attention were trying to establish, and more particularly whether all of them were trying to argue the same case.

Attention was initially centred on Malthus, whom Keynes presented as, in his *Principles*, concerned to deal primarily with those same questions of income and employment which preoccupied Keynes himself. For example, Keynes specifically stated that " the whole problem of the balance between Saving and Investment had been posed in the *Preface* to the book ".[4] For some time after Keynes wrote this view commanded acceptance, but within the last ten years it has been subjected to increasing criticism, until now the question " Was Malthus an anticipator of Keynes? " seems to have received almost every possible answer. " It is our view that the similarities are more apparent than real," writes Dr. Corry; " la Théorie Générale contient d'avantage encore de Malthus que Keynes ne la pensé," asserts Professor Lambert[5]—and, as the latter admits, almost every shade of opinion in

---

[1] An earlier version of this paper was presented to the Faculty Seminar of the Department of Economics, Yale University, in December 1964. I am indebted to Professors James Tobin and R. G. Bodkin for helpful comment and criticism at this stage, and also to Mr. D. P. O'Brien for subsequent comments.

[2] Keynes: *Essays in Biography* (London, 1933; second edition reprint, 1961, p. 103).

[3] Keynes, *General Theory of Employment, Interest and Money* (London, 1936), p. 32.

[4] *Essays in Biography*, p. 122.

[5] Corry, *Money, Saving and Investment in English Economics, 1800–1850* (London, 1962), p. 126. Lambert, " Malthus et Keynes, Nouvel Examen de la Parenté Profonde des deux Œuvres," *Revue d'Économie Politique*, Vol. 72, No. 6 (November–December 1962), p. 783.

between these extremes can be found in the surprisingly extensive literature on the question.[1]

That Malthus was the central figure of the anti-Ricardian school of thought on effective demand is not in doubt, but almost everything else about his ideas would seem to be. Not surprisingly, the position about lesser figures is equally uncertain—most of them have been labelled as forerunners or disciples of Malthus, but sometimes they have been put into different categories. Lauderdale is perhaps the most notable case in point: Dr. Paglin and Professor Lambert would link him firmly with Malthus, while Messrs. Gordon and Jilek wish to separate and present him as the more " Keynesian " of the two.[2]

In the light of all this it seems worthwhile to attempt to survey the two questions: (1) Was Malthus, as the key figure of the anti-Ricardians, attempting to deal with the same problem as Keynes, and with similar tools? (2) Did other anti-Ricardians follow him in this, or use different approaches?

Perhaps the basic reason for regarding Malthus as a forerunner of Keynes is that both were attacking an orthodoxy; but the orthodoxy which Keynes chose to call classical was in fact neo-classical and if, as research in the history of thought over the past twenty years or so has tended to show, the classical mode of thinking was more fundamentally distinct from the neo-classical than was thought in the inter-war years, then this reason is not a very strong one. Keynes found fault with the Marshallian mode of thought in which he had been trained: Malthus found fault with the Smithian mode of thought in which he had been trained: does it not seem improbable that their thinking would coincide?

In essence, the Malthusian under-consumption doctrine starts from the position that a decision to save-and-invest more increases the funds devoted to the maintenance of productive labour, and so leads to the production of

---

[1] The principal items in the literature make a lengthy list:

S. Hollander, " Malthus and Keynes: A Note," Economic Journal, June 1962, pp. 355–9.
Paul Lambert, " The Law of Markets prior to J. B. Say and the Say–Malthus Debate," *International Economic Papers*, No. 6, pp. 7–22 (trans. from *Revue d'économie politique*, 1952).
Robert G. Link, *English Theories of Economic Fluctuations 1815–1848* (New York, 1959).
J. J. O'Leary, " Malthus and Keynes," *Journal of Political Economy*, December 1942.
——, " Malthus' General Theory of Employment and the Post-Napoleonic Depressions," *Journal of Economic History*, November 1943.
M. Paglin, *Malthus and Lauderdale: The Anti-Ricardian Tradition* (New York, 1961).
Omar Pancoast, " Malthus versus Ricardo," *Political Science Quarterly*, March 1943.
André Paquet, *Le Conflit historique entre la loi des débouches et la principe de la demande effective* (Paris, 1953).
T. Sowell, " The General Glut Controversy Reconsidered," *Oxford Economic Papers*, November 1963, pp. 193–203.
Harold G. Vatter, " The Malthusian Model of Income Determination and its Contemporary Relevance," *Canadian Journal of Economics*, Vol. 25 (1959), pp. 60–4.

[2] Paglin, *Malthus and Lauderdale: the anti-Ricardian Tradition* (New York, 1961). B. J. Gordon and T. S. Jilek: " Malthus, Keynes et l'apport de Lauderdale," *Revue d'Économie Politique*, Vol. 75, No. 1 (January 1965): pp. 110–21. P. Lambert, " Lauderdale, Malthus and Keynes," *Annals of Public and Co-operative Economy*, XXXVII, No. 1 (January 1966), pp. 3–23.

" an increased quantity of commodities "; but the demand of the labourers will be insufficient to provide a market for all the commodities produced at prices which will cover their costs of production, and the capitalists and landlords have " agreed to be parsimonious." Unless a body of unproductive consumers exists, then the commodities cannot be sold " without such a fall of price as would probably sink their value below that of the outlay."[1]

According to Malthus, " a country is always liable to an increase in the quantity of the funds for the maintenance of labour faster than the increase of population " and ". . . whenever this occurs, there may be an universal glut of commodities."[2]   Now this in Ricardo's analysis would imply merely a fall of profits, relative to wages, and when profits are sufficiently low, accumulation will cease; but this is the long-run phenomenon of the stationary state.   In the short-run Ricardo could see no reason why the *investment* demand of capitalists and landlords should not be sufficient to take up the difference between total output and consumption.   Malthus specifically answers this point, using the normal classical assumption that investment means the employment of productive labour: he describes it as " a very serious error " to suppose " that accumulation ensures demand; or that the consumption of the labourers employed by those whose object is to save, will create such an effectual demand for commodities as to encourage a continued increase of produce."[3]

What Malthus seems always to envisage is that increased saving-and-investment must be devoted to the production of the same narrow range of commodities, primarily wage goods: a " glut " of these is the consequence, with their prices falling while wages remain rigid downwards: the capitalists command over labour is thereby reduced, and unemployment ensues.   This possibility was specifically recognised by Ricardo, when he wrote:

> " If every man were to forego the use of luxuries and be intent only on accumulation a quantity of necessaries might be produced for which there could not be any immediate consumption.   Of commodities so limited in number, there might undoubtedly be an universal glut; and consequently there might neither be demand for an additional quantity of such commodities, nor profits on the employment of more capital. If men ceased to consume, they would cease to produce."

On this Ricardo commented: " this admission does not impugn the general principle," but Malthus retorted, " it appears to me most completely to impugn the general principle "—and here surely was the crux of the difference between them.[4]

Put in this way, it seems clear that while Malthus was interpreting the

[1] Malthus, *Principles of Political Economy* (2nd edn., London, 1836), p. 315.
[2] *Ibid.*, p. 320.
[3] *Ibid.*, p. 322.
[4] Ricardo, *Principles of Political Economy* (ed. Sraffa), Chapter XXI, p. 293; Malthus, *op. cit.*. p. 319.

classical model differently from Ricardo, there was little in his thinking which could be regarded as specifically " Keynesian." Yet it does not seem right to conclude, as some recent commentators have done, that Malthus was not concerned with the same problem as Keynes at all. This is the view put forward by Professor Sowell, who claims that " the question to which Malthus addressed himself was not the clearing of the market at a given time, but the maintenance of the on-going process of economic growth " and goes on to say—" Malthus did not claim that consumption would be insufficient for production, but that each would be insufficient for full employment of an increasing population under the conditions assumed." [1] It is very difficult to reconcile assertions such as these with the plain words of Malthus—such words as " if production be in a great excess above consumption, the motive to accumulate and produce must cease from the want of an effectual demand in those who have the principal means of purchasing." [2]

Even more difficult to reconcile with the repeated statements of Malthus is the categorical assertion of Messrs. Gordon and Jilek: " La préoccupation centrale de Malthus est donc de maximiser le taux de l'épargne." [3] Malthus wrote: "... if the conversion of revenue into capital pushed beyond a certain point must, by diminishing the effectual demand for produce, throw the labouring classes out of employment, it is obvious that the adoption of parsimonious habits beyond a certain point, may be accompanied by the most distressing effects at first, and by a marked depression of wealth and population afterwards." [4] These do not seem like the words of an economist whose " central preoccupation " is to maximise the rate of saving, and this is not the only passage in which Malthus warned of the danger of carrying parsimony to excess. [5]

We seem to be in danger of reaching a position where Malthus can be " all things to all men." This can only partly be attributed to that lack of clarity and precision in his writings which has sometimes been remarked: it is mainly due to the remarkable breadth of the inquiry which Malthus undertook in his famous chapter " On the Progress of Wealth." He undertook to examine this comparatively, considering both what would now be called " advanced " and " under-developed " countries, and going into all the factors which may prevent an economy from utilising its productive powers to the maximum at any stage. Hence growth, fluctuation and stagnation are all embraced within it. As Dr. Paglin has said: " It is with the conditions that make for the optimum progress of wealth—that is, with the conditions which make for a growing national income, which utilizes fully the labour and capital resources of the country—that Malthus was concerned." [6] It is certainly true that Malthus *was* concerned with the determinants of

[1] Sowell, " The General Glut Controversy re-considered," *loc. cit.*, pp. 198–9.
[2] Malthus, *op. cit.*, p. 7.
[3] Gordon and Jilek, *loc. cit.*, p. 120.   [4] Malthus, *Principles*, p. 326.
[5] E.g., *Principles*, pp. 417–18.   [6] Paglin, *op. cit.*, p. 123.

economic development over time, but it does not therefore follow that he was *not* concerned with the factors governing the level of employment and income at any point in time.   Yet seeing this latter issue as part of the wider problem of " the progress of wealth " and tackling it with the aid of an analytical apparatus of a two-sector, one-year production period form, deriving directly from Adam Smith, it is hardly surprising that Malthus came up with a treatment of it which sometimes resembles, but is certainly not identical with, the modern type of income analysis developed by Keynes.

If the view of what Malthus was saying advanced above be accepted as correct, it is clear that this is not the same as what Keynes described as " the primary evil," " a propensity to save in conditions of full employment more than the equivalent of the capital which is required."[1]   In this connection, there has been much debate as to whether Malthus recognised the possibility of divergences between *plans* to save and *plans* to invest, as distinct from the realised identity of savings and investment.   The fact is that Malthus normally seems to identify savings and investment, without making any clear distinction between *ex ante* and *ex post* senses, and he did commit himself to the frequently quoted phrase " no political economist of the present day can by saving mean mere hoarding."[2]   On the other hand, there are one or two passages in his *Principles* where he can be interpreted as referring to savings which can find no outlet in investment.[3]   In spite of these, Professor Lambert, the staunchest defender of the " Keynesian " view of Malthus, has admitted that the attempt, made by Paglin, to read a distinction between *ex ante* and *ex post* savings and investment into Malthus's *Principles* " does not accord with the whole body of the text.   We must repeat that this is one of Malthus's weak points."[4]

It is particularly noteworthy that in this same article Lambert goes on to say:

> " Keynes himself explained that a certain defect in Hobson did not prevent the latter from anticipating his own theory.   Now what was this defect?   It was his " exaggerated insistence on the fact that underconsumption leads to overinvestment in the sense of disadvantageous investment " (*General Theory*, p. 370), which needlessly implies an error in forecasting by the entrepreneurs.   The remark can be applied word for word to Malthus (and, as we have seen, to Lauderdale as well.)"[4]

Now Keynes was in fact much more critical of Hobson than of Malthus: he did indeed point out " Hobson's mistake, namely, his supposing that it is a case of excessive saving causing the *actual* accumulation of capital in excess of what is required," but never specifically attributed the same " mistake " to Malthus.

[1] Keynes, *General Theory*, p. 368.
[2] Malthus, *Principles*, (2nd ed.), p. 38.
[3] Notably pp. 323–4 and 420.
[4] "Lauderdale, Malthus and Keynes," *loc. cit.*, p. 18.

Yet it is quite true, as Lambert has argued, that what can be said of Hobson can be applied word for word to Malthus. The implication of this, however, is not that both men were involved in the same mistake, which did not prevent them from anticipating Keynes's theory of employment; it is that they were going beyond the problem of full employment to what Professor Domar has described as " perhaps a deeper problem "—that of capital stock adjustment in the process of growth. Discussing the relation between Keynes and Hobson, Domar writes:

> " Keynes analyzed what happens when savings (of the preceding period) are not invested. The answer was—unemployment, but the statement of the problem in this form might easily give the erroneous impression that if savings were invested, full employment would be assured. Hobson, on the other hand, went a step further and stated the problem in this form: suppose savings are invested—will the new plants be able to dispose of their products? Such a statement was not at all, as Keynes thought, a mistake." [1]

In Malthus's day the new plants would have been farms or " manufactories " employing productive labour, but, allowing for this, Domar's comment seems as well applicable to Malthus as to Hobson. If this is accepted it follows that the answer to the first question posed at the beginning of this paper must be that Malthus was not really tackling the same problem as Keynes or using the same tools.

We come then to the second question, did other anti-Ricardians follow him in this? The answer would seem to be that most of those who turned their attention to the effective demand problem produced analyses similar to those of Malthus and Hobson, stressing the dangers of too much saving-and-investment for the stability of the economy. This is certainly true of those who, like Malthus, worked within the framework of Adam Smith's productive labour approach. However, it is less true of those, comparatively few in number, whose thought was not set in this mould. The best-known figure in this small group is certainly Lauderdale, who specifically rejected the distinction of productive and unproductive labour and developed the concept of capital as supplanting labour. On the whole, the evidence for the view that Lauderdale and Malthus were similar in their approach to the problem of saving and investment seems stronger than the case for holding that the former recognised a distinction between *ex ante* saving and investment while the latter did not; but on the question of effective demand there was also a component present in Lauderdale's analysis which was absent from that of Malthus, as Paglin has clearly explained:

> " Sixteen years before the appearance of Malthus's *Principles*, Lauderdale focused attention on the highly variable nature of aggregate demand and showed that it was fundamentally tied to individual

[1] E. D. Domar, " Expansion and Employment," *American Economic Review*, Vol. XXXVII, No. 1 (March 1947), p. 52.

decisions to spend or save, and to government fiscal decisions to create budgetary surpluses or deficits.   Malthus continued this line of thought but without Lauderdale's strategic emphasis on debt policy and taxation." [1]

In terms of the elementary analysis of income and employment as it is presented to-day, effective demand or total expenditure is made up of three elements, consumption expenditure, investment expenditure and government expenditure or $E = C + I + G$.   Malthus concentrated on C and I and movements between them, whereas Lauderdale also brought in and examined the G element; this, rather than any differences of emphasis on the possibilities of hoarding, is surely the main distinction between the two authors.

These same differences can be found recurring in the works of later writers in the same tradition, of whom there were not a few—for Keynes's statement that from the time of Malthus " theories of under-consumption hibernated until the appearance in 1889 of *The Physiology of Industry* by J. A. Hobson and A. F. Mummery" [2] is certainly only correct in the most literal sense.   Throughout those seventy years there were authors who kept the doctrine of under-consumption alive, if not exactly flourishing.   To illustrate the continuance of the two approaches distinguished above, the remainder of this paper will be devoted to an examination of the writings of two such almost forgotten " anti-Ricardians "—Major-General Sir William Sleeman and Captain W. R. A. Pettman, R.N. [3]

II

Sleeman's work is a good example of the persistence of the " over-accumulation " approach of the Malthus type, although developed independently and under completely different circumstances.   To put his writings in their proper perspective it is necessary first to say something of the man and his career.   Sleeman was one of the more distinguished, and distinctive, figures in that remarkable body of men who served the East India Company in the nineteenth century.   In 1808, at the age of twenty, he entered the Bengal Army as a cadet, and transferred to the Political Service in 1819.   His career in India lasted forty-six years, and culminated in his being appointed Resident of Lucknow, but he is best remembered for his success in eliminating the Thugs, a sect whose religion required the strangulation and robbery of travellers.   Sleeman was given chief responsibility for tracking down the Thugs in 1826 and carried on his campaign against them for some twelve years.   The first full-length biography of Sleeman, published

[1] Paglin, Introduction to Lauderdale's *Inquiry into the Nature and Origin of Public Wealth* (New York, 1962), p. xii.   On the relation of Lauderdale and Malthus, see references cited above, note 2, p. 60.

[2] Keynes, *op. cit.*, p. 364.

[3] The present writer first drew attention to the work of Sleeman and Pettman in his *Economic Thought and the Irish Question, 1817–1870* (Cambridge, 1960), pp. 162–4.

as recently as 1961,[1] reveals him as a heroic soldier and a tireless administrator.

It might reasonably be concluded that the duties which Sleeman carried out would leave him with little time or energy for intellectual pursuits: yet it was during the course of his Thug campaign in 1829 that he published a substantial economic treatise, entitled *On Taxes; or Public Revenue, the Ultimate Incidence of their Payment, their Disbursement and the seats of their Consumption.* The book, which commences with a critique of the theories of the Physiocrats and Adam Smith, concludes with an " Outline of a New System of Political Economy." Sleeman followed it in 1837 with an *Analysis and Review of the Peculiar Doctrines of the Ricardo, or New, School of Political Economy.*[2] According to his own statement, this had been intended to form part of the larger work *On Taxes* " which the pressure of heavy official duties obliged me to suspend in 1828, and which I have never since had, and in all probability never again shall have, leisure to resume."[3]

In the *Analysis and Review* Sleeman declares his object to be " to bring men back to the study of Dr. Smith's great work," and he follows many of Smith's definitions. Yet the nature of his criticism of Ricardo and the character of his " New System " make it very clear that his true master was Malthus—so much so that it is surprising to find that Sleeman never attended the East India Company's college at Haileybury, where Malthus was Professor of Modern History and Political Economy from 1805.

The feature of Ricardian analysis which Sleeman singled out for criticism was the proposition that " profits depend on wages." He argued that there were classes other than capitalists and landlords to whom a rise of wages could be passed on, so that it need not follow that " as wages rise, profits fall " and asserted that the fall of profits in the advance of society must be attributed to the Smithian " accumulation of stock " and not to the Ricardian " resort to inferior soils."

Ricardo's view of the causes of the fall of profits rested on his belief that " in proportion to the increase of capital will be the increase in the demand for labour,"[4] and Sleeman's objection to it sprang from the same grounds as Malthus's—a belief that capital accumulation could be excessive and lead to stagnation and unemployment. This emerges clearly from his " New System," in which he starts from the concept of the gross produce of society as a " great reservoir " which is drained by four classes, wage earners, profit earners, rent receivers and " those who demand a portion in fulfilment of a

---

    [1] *The Yellow Scarf*, by Lt-General Sir Francis Tuker (London, 1961). Sir Francis Tuker refers to the writing of the *Analysis and Review*, but does not mention the earlier *On Taxes*; nor does he discuss Sleeman's economic ideas at all.

    [2] This was published under Sleeman's own name at the Mission Press in Serampore. *On Taxes* had appeared under the pseudonym " An Officer in the Military and Civil Service of the Honourable East Indian Company " and was published in London.

    [3] *Analysis and Review*, Preface, p. ii.

    [4] Ricardo, *Principles* (ed. Sraffa), p. 95.

claim secured directly or indirectly upon the *labour* of the first, the *stock* of the second, or the funds of the third."

" The desire to drain from this great reservoir may exist in any one of these four great classes, without the means, or beyond the extent of the means of gratification; but the desire without the means is inoperative; to effect the drain, the desire and the means must be united. But the means may exist without the desire, and the means without the desire are no less important than the desire without the means."

"... If the four classes into which I have supposed the society to be divided, drain periodically what the great reservoir periodically receives from the funds and instruments of supply, the annual reproduction goes on; and the claims secured directly or indirectly upon the funds and instruments continue to be fulfilled: because those who have secured them continue to take in fulfilment that which they are able to supply; but if these classes will not take what this great reservoir receives and owes to their collective claims, the annual supply must in time cease, through the medium of glut and stagnation. If men come to a resolution to limit their material enjoyments to the absolute necessaries of life, they must necessarily cease to drain from this great reservoir any of its luxuries ... etc.; and all the instruments employed in producing, preparing and distributing them, must, through the medium of stagnation and glut, cease to find employment, and consequently cease to have or convey any independent claim upon the annual returns of those employed in the production of the absolute necessaries of life ...

" The case I have supposed may, no doubt, be very properly considered as an extreme one; but a general disposition to save and accumulate, with a view to profit, must of necessity tend to produce it in any society ... It is said, that there is no occasion to drain this reservoir of any thing with a view to enjoyment, beyond the simple necessaries of life, because all that is over and above these necessaries, may be employed as *capital*, with a view to profit. But it is admitted that these things must be drawn out from the great mass of floating capital for some purpose or another, otherwise they must be left to stagnate, to the injury or ruin of those who cannot dispose of them. In this admission of Dr. Smith, everybody agrees: Mr. Ricardo, M. Say, Mr. Mill, and Mr. McCulloch, who *demonstrate* the *impossibility* of a glut and stagnation; Mr. Malthus and M. de Sismondi, who *prove* not only its *possibility*, but its *actual existence*. If we admit that these things must be drained from the mass of floating capital, in order to give employment; and argue, that they need not be drained with a view to enjoyment, because there will be always a sufficient inducement to drain them for employment, as capital, with a view to profit, we suppose that they can always be reinvested in funds and instruments for ever capable of finding employment, at an undiminished rate of profit."

" But this is great folly. It is extremely absurd to suppose that if men had no disposition to enjoy any thing more than the absolute necessaries of life, they will always have a sufficient motive to drain the other things which the genius and industry of man supply, in the assurance of being able to make a profit by their employment as capital.

To say, that if not drawn for enjoyment, they *may* be drawn for invest-ment in funds and instruments, is nothing more than to say that the means *may* be made the end; and, that a society of men may become a society of children! " [1]

All this is strongly reminiscent of Malthus, even in the choice of examples and phrases; but there is one assumption in it much stronger than any made by Malthus—savers and investors are said to expect an undiminished rate of profit whatever the amount of accumulation and investment. If this were so, clearly the rate of return could quickly be driven below the minimum acceptable to lenders, and if this did not increase their propensity to consume a stagnation of a truly Keynesian kind would ensue. Some idea of this seems to have been in Sleeman's mind, for he repeatedly expressed a preference for public works of all kinds, undertaken without a profit motive, as against investments governed by the profit motive: such works can provide em-ployment without " encumbrances of claims." Here again, however, he is not really moving outside the Malthusian framework, for Malthus similarly advocated public works which might increase consumption but not the sup-ply of commodities.

In fact, these passages are inconsistent with others in Sleeman's *On Taxes*, where the effects of falling profits and falling interest rates are discussed. Yet Sleeman nowhere considers how lower profits and interest rates might affect the volume of investment or savings. At a later stage he again argues:

> " Let us suppose that all the members of a highly civilized and luxurious society were at once to become parsimonious: and to send back all at once upon the mass of capital, seeking profitable employ-ment, all that they and their ancestors had set aside for enjoyment: would it not be extremely absurd to suppose that the whole would find profitable employment—that the whole would find borrowers willing to incur a claim upon themselves, to the amount of profits undiminished, while assured that the laws would rigorously enforce the claims so secured? " [2]

To this Ricardo might have answered—It would indeed be extremely absurd, but who has ever made such a supposition? On my assumptions, in such a case wages will rise, profits will fall, accumulation will be checked and consumption increased: so there will be no glut. To make out his case Sleeman would have required to show some reason why capitalists do not use their profits in increased consumption if investment is unprofitable, but, like Malthus, he simply assumes that everything above subsistence they will seek to save and invest. He does make a reference to hoarding when dis-cussing the quantity theory of money and the concept of velocity of cir-culation, but does not really seem to envisage the possibility of a speculative

---

[1] [Sleeman], *On Taxes*, pp. 147, 151, 154.
[2] *Ibid.*, pp. 340–1.

demand for money.[1]   There is a later passage which seems to contain the idea of plans to save going unrealised:

> " But we *may not* be able to add to capital, even as a particular term, what we save and retrench from our expenditure for enjoyment; and if we cannot, we diminish instead of increasing the aggregate amount of employment by such savings." [2]

Unfortunately, Sleeman's proof of this point rests on the obvious idea that luxury consumer goods already produced could not be converted to productive uses.   Any classical economist would have admitted this as a case of " particular over-production," and Sleeman does not argue that the savings would not lead ultimately to demand for investment goods.

Hence Sleeman's argument turns out to be essentially the same as that of Malthus—not that planned saving might exceed planned investment but that actual saving-and-investment might be overdone and create capacity greater than could be utilised.   This may be a respectable thesis in certain circumstances, but the time of Malthus and Sleeman was, as Blaug has said, " a particularly inappropriate time in history to decry oversaving," and this was as true for Sleeman's India as for Malthus's England—indeed, much more so.

One cannot but feel that to the Indian case the Ricardian model, which made capital the scarce and labour the unlimited factor in most circumstances, was more appropriate than the Malthusian one, which tended to reverse these roles.   But in Sleeman's approach one can detect some of those Physiocratic elements to which R. L. Meek has drawn attention in the work of Malthus, Sismondi and Chalmers.[3]   The landed proprietor is seen as the distributor of the agricultural surplus, and his consumption as necessary to give the labourers an " independent claim " on it; but, as Meek points out, the Physiocrats would always have enjoined investment as much as expenditure, provided it were made in agricultural improvements.

The problem of over-saving, which to Malthus was but one of a variety of factors bearing on the progress of wealth, became almost an exclusive preoccupation with Sleeman.   In view of the extent of his knowledge of India, this leaves one with the feeling of an opportunity missed—on such questions as the means of overcoming " indolence," and the effects on economic progress of different methods of division of landed property, with which Malthus dealt at length, Sleeman has nothing to say, although his observation of Indian life might have been expected to bring these problems to his attention.

---

[1] *On Taxes*, p. 242.

[2] *Ibid.*, p. 314.

[3] Meek, " Physiocracy and the Early Theories of Under-Consumption," *Economics of Physiocracy* (London, 1962), pp. 313–44.

III

If Sleeman's work follows closely on the lines of Malthus, that of Pettman may serve as an equally good example of what has been described above as the " fiscal " approach.   Like Sleeman—and their better-known contemporary Torrens—Pettman possessed the unusual combination of qualities which produced a serving officer and an economic analyst of some ability. Pettman's career is less well documented than Sleeman's, and presumably less colourful.   Only presumably, for to attain the rank of Captain in the British Navy in the early 1820s, he must have seen active service during the Napoleonic Wars; but his name does not figure in any of the naval biographies or histories of the time.   As an economist, Pettman's claim to distinction rests on two works, *An Essay on Political Economy*, published in two parts in 1828, and the *Resources of the United Kingdom* (1830).[1]   Both are very much policy-oriented, devoted to the question of finding remedies for the distresses of the post-Napoleonic War period.

Perhaps the best characterisation of Pettman's economic ideas is the one which he himself gave: " It may perhaps be said that he has rung the changes on the positive and incalculable advantages that nations ever have derived and ever must derive, from the full, uninterrupted and persevering employment of the working classes and from the beneficial tendency of paying them good money wages." [2]

In both his books Pettman's main emphasis falls on the necessity of maintaining aggregate expenditure, and the importance of the Government's fiscal policy and debt management is stressed in a manner strongly reminiscent of Lauderdale.   On a superficial reading of much of his work, one might conclude that Pettman was not going beyond what Hutchison calls " the simple massive idea " that " economic activity in an exchange economy is in response to an effective or ' effectual ' demand, and that a deficiency thereof may reduce the level of activity and national wealth below what it advantageously might be." [3]

On closer inspection, Pettman's analysis proves to contain more than this: he recommends a free-trade policy combined with an inconvertible paper currency, so that the increase of expenditure necessary to generate full employment may not be prematurely checked by an outflow of gold:

> " While bankers are liable to be called upon to pay their deposits
> and their paper in gold, they cannot in safety accommodate the public
> with advances when specie is leaving the country.   The trading com-
> munity are, therefore, at such times involved in losses and difficulties:

---

[1] W. R. A. Pettman, *An Essay on Political Economy: shewing in what way Fluctuations in the Price of Corn may be prevented....*   Part I (London, 1828).

—— *An Essay on Political Economy: shewing the means by which the Distresses of the Labouring Poor may be relieved.*   Part II (London, 1828).

—— *Resources of the United Kingdom* (London, 1830).

[2] Pettman, *Resources of the United Kingdom*, Preface, p. vi.

[3] Hutchison, *A Review of Economic Doctrines, 1870–1929* (Oxford, 1953), p. 346.

and their inability to obtain a medium from bankers, sufficient to supply their wants, obliges them to curtail their expenditure, and to discharge many of their workmen, and lower the rate of wages; and many are obliged to dispose of their commodities at prices below the cost of production, to enable them to meet the exigencies of the moment. A great reduction in the aggregate of expenditure is by such means produced, which, by diminishing the consumption and the demand for foreign consumable articles, brings back the exchanges in favour of England, and causes an accumulation of deposits in the coffers of banks, which, by producing a rise in the funds, reduces the rate of interest, and thereby lessens the income and expenditure of those who derive their income from money lent.

" Here we see the causes of the fluctuations in the rate of exchanges and in prices, and also the cause of the alternate periods of prosperity and distress, which the trading community has experienced since the resumption of cash payments."

This is strongly reminiscent of the work of Thomas Attwood, with which Pettman may quite possibly have been familiar.[1] One difference between Attwood and Pettman is that the latter was more frank and uncompromising in his recognition of the incompatability of his proposals with the gold standard. Of more importance is the fact that Attwood's proposals relied mainly on monetary policy, whereas Pettman advocated a blend of monetary and fiscal policy based on an understanding of expenditure flows more " Keynesian " in character than anything which can be found in Malthus:

" Money is to a nation what blood is to the body. The state is the heart from whence it is diffused, and to which it is continually returning. If blood accumulates in the head or the heart, health is impaired and life endangered; but by bleeding the patient a return of circulation is produced, and health is restored. It is the same with respect to money: if it accumulate in banks, or be hoarded by individuals, the prosperity of the nation is checked, its wealth decreases, and distress ensues. By means of loans, and a government expenditure, it is brought again into circulation; all classes acquire it in turn, and it is brought back to the Exchequer by taxation. By such a process a return of prosperity is produced—the wealth and resources of the nation increased, and all classes made prosperous."[2]

This is only one of several direct references to interruption of expenditure flows which can be found in Pettman's writings. His suggested offset is equally clearly stated and " modern " in tone: he advocates public works financed by borrowing—not by taxes, as Malthus had suggested[3]—and explains fully the " multiplier " effects of such expenditure:

" The community at large, however, are benefited by the public money being expended in building palaces, improving harbours, cutting

[1] Cf. Link, *English Theories of Economic Fluctuations 1815–1848* (New York, 1959), pp. 8–35.
[2] Pettman, *Resources of the United Kingdom*, p. 107.
[3] Malthus, *Principles* (2nd edition), p. 429.

canals, making roads, improving and cultivating waste lands, and in building and repairing shipping, and, in short, on any public works that find employment for the labouring classes, and thereby create in them an ability to purchase and consume the commodities produced by each other; inasmuch as all such works are carried on by the labour of men, who, were it not for their being so employed, would not be able to sell their labour; and who expend the sums they receive in payment for their labour, in the purchase of articles of various sorts, produced and made by the skill, ingenuity, and labour of others; and the interest of the money expended on such works is repaid *with interest* by an increase in the revenue, derived from the duties levied on the commodities consumed by the numerous individuals, through whose hands the money so expended circulates. In fact, money so expended is like seed sown in the ground—it produces more; it causes an increased number of wealthy people, and thereby creates an increase of incomes, of expenditure, and an increase of ability in all classes to buy and consume, which produces an increase of revenue, exceeding in amount the sum paid by the state as interest for the use of it; while, at the same time, it enables others to increase their capitals and their expenditure, by which the resources of the state are also much increased."[1]

To those who object to increasing public debt because of the burden involved, Pettman answers strikingly, " The burden of debt is much less to be feared than the burden of idleness: but a debt that produces incomes, and an expenditure that finds employment for millions of the population, who, but for such expenditure, would not be able to sell their labour, is not a burden, but a capital."

This puts one in mind of those naïve pamphleteers who regarded the national debt as a " a mine of gold"; but Pettman recognises plainly enough that a nation's resources cannot " be increased or decreased by its contracting debts, or by paying off debts contracted with its own members, unless by such a process it can augment the supply of products."[2] Unfortunately, he was not always clear about the different effects of an expenditure financed by borrowing and one financed by taxation, as the following passage shows:

" Whenever *there are a number of poor unemployed and the rate of interest low*, money does not so circulate as to produce a general benefit to the community at large. Government ought therefore on such occasions to borrow, because by doing so, it would cause a rise of interest, which, by increasing the incomes of money-lenders, would enable them to increase their expenditure; which, combined with the increased expenditure of the government, would create an increase of income and of expenditure in all other classes, and cause such an increase of consumption of taxable commodities as would produce a much greater increase in the amount of the revenue than would pay the interest of the money borrowed.

[1] Pettman, *Essay on Political Economy*, Part II, pp. 104–5.
[2] *Ibid.*, p. 74; *Resources of the United Kingdom*, p. 191.

" When all the poor are employed, and well paid for their labour, and when labour is in great demand, all classes of the people are prosperous: when such a state of things exists, there can be no excess of labourers. If then, at such a time, the state requires additional supplies, it requires an increased supply of labourers, and these it cannot obtain unless it takes them from those who have the benefit of their labour. And to do this, *direct taxes* should be imposed on *all classes* of the community in proportion to their incomes, and upon all articles of luxury, which taxes would oblige the public to reduce their expenditure in the purchase of labour, and enable the state to obtain it. Hence, whenever the poor are in full employ, the wants of the state should be supplied by direct taxes on incomes; but such taxes, and indeed all taxes that are imposed when labourers are in great demand, and wages *high*, are burdens. It being only when the poor are unemployed, and when wages are so low as to deprive the great mass of the population of the ability to purchase and consume the necessaries of life, that taxation and an increase in the government expenditure produces a benefit."

This somewhat ambiguous reasoning rests on an invalid distinction between indirect and direct taxes: according to Pettman " the one produces a rise in prices and an increase in the amounts of circulating property, and the other merely causes a division of property."[1] Had Pettman not become involved in this confusion, his reasoning about the relevance of deficit financing in depression and direct taxation in periods of full employment would have been unexceptionable.

IV

To sum up: under-consumption doctrines did not suffer total eclipse between the time of Malthus and Hobson, but were kept alive by a series of writers, of whom Sleeman and Pettman are able representatives. The one may be regarded as continuing the tradition of Malthus, with its emphasis on the distinction between productive and unproductive labour and all that that implies, the other as stressing the fiscal policy aspect in a manner more reminiscent of Lauderdale—although there is no evidence of any direct influence of Lauderdale on Pettman as there certainly is of Malthus on Sleeman.

Sleeman was certainly using a very similar analytical apparatus to that of Malthus—one which, it has been argued here, cannot really be regarded as " Keynesian " in any strict sense. Pettman's approach might be considered as more nearly meriting that adjective, but again the anticipation of Keynes is far from complete. The works of the General and the Captain in fact afford further justification for Paglin's judgment:

" The Lauderdale–Malthus theory of effective demand could not be put into a neat formula because the technical concept of a consumption function was lacking. Thus a basically sound approach to income and

---

[1] Pettman, *Essay on Political Economy*, Part II, pp. 111–12, and 84.

employment became the happy hunting ground of economically untrained pamphleteers while the sophisticated economists clung to Say's
Law." [1]

Sleeman and Pettman were well above the level of pamphleteers, and for
men who were economically untrained, they achieved a remarkably high
analytical standard. Nevertheless, their work again illustrates a basic
reason for the failure of the anti-Ricardian tradition—as gifted amateurs they
failed to achieve the logical consistency which the sophisticated economists
did; their work combines brilliant insights with undeniable errors. Hence
they must be ranked with those " who, following their intuitions, have preferred to see the truth obscurely and imperfectly rather than to maintain
error, reached indeed with clearness and consistency and by easy logic, but
on hypotheses inappropriate to the facts." [2] But if Malthus and Hobson
deserve a place in the history of economic ideas for doing this, Sleeman and
Pettman deserve to figure with them there.

R. D. Collison Black

Queens University, Belfast.

---

[1] Paglin, *Malthus and Lauderdale*, p. 159.
[2] Keyens, *General Theory*, p. 371.

[6]
DR. KONDRATIEFF AND
MR. HYDE CLARKE

R.D. Collison Black

If you can avoid calling me Doctor I shall be glad, for I find that people are indisposed to treat me as a practical man if I am a colonel or a Doctor.

—Hyde Clarke
(quoted in Jevons, 1977, p. 296).

I

In the recent years of international economic disturbance and depression there has been a considerable increase of interest in the phenomenon of "long waves" in economic activity, just as there was during the world economic depression of the thirties.[1] The original suggestion of the existence of such a phenomenon is usually attributed to the Russian economist N.D. Kondratieff (1892-1931),

---

Research in the History of Economic Thought and Methodology, Volume 9, pages 35-58.
Copyright © 1992 by JAI Press Inc.
All rights of reproduction in any form reserved.
ISBN: 1-55938-428-X

and through the work of Schumpeter the long wave hypothesis has come to be widely known as the "Kondratieff cycle."

In some of the current writing on the subject it has been suggested that Kondratieff may have had anticipators in the two Dutch socialists, S. de Wolff and Jacob van Gelderen, and the Russian Marxist Alexander Helphand who wrote under the pseudonym "Parvus" (Van Duijn, 1983, pp. 60-63). In a postscript to his well-known 1926 article Kondratieff himself acknowledged the work of the first two of these writers, but stated that while he had arrived at the long wave hypothesis in 1919-1921, he had not seen de Wolff's writings until 1926 and had not read van Gelderen's—which appeared only in Dutch—at all.

De Wolff and van Gelderen were fairly close contemporaries of Kondratieff and their writings predated his by only a few years, while Helphand's earliest work on crises and cycles appeared in 1901. Considering that Kondratieff's observations covered only 140 years, or approximately two-and-a-half long cycles, it would seem unlikely that there could have been any earlier anticipations of his hypothesis; yet those with an interest in the history of trade cycle theories could find tucked away in a footnote in Schumpeter's *History of Economic Analysis* a reference to one Hyde Clarke who "had a ten year cycle, and *in addition a longer period of about 54 years*, a striking anticipation of the major cycles or spans of later days, especially of Kondratieff's long waves" (Schumpeter, 1954, p. 743). More recently, J.J. van Duijn in a chapter on "The Discovery of the Long Wave" has credited "Dr. Hyde Clarke" (sic!) with making "the first reference to a possible long wave in economic activity" (van Duijn, 1983, p. 59).

In fact the name of Hyde Clarke has figured in footnotes to various contributions to the history of economic thought for the past half-century or more. It occurs in the review of various theories given by Wesley Mitchell in the first chapters of *Business Cycles* (Mitchell, 1930, pp. 10-11) and also receives mention in Link's *English Theories of Economic Fluctuations* (Link, 1959, p. 205) and Leland H. Jenks' *The Migration of British Capital to 1875* (Jenks, 1963, p. 153). At an earlier period, W.S. Jevons in his article on "Commercial Crises and Sun-Spots," first published in *Nature* in 1878, gave an extended and favourable notice of the views of "Dr. Hyde Clarke" on the periodicity of crises.[2] This was probably the source of another reference to Hyde Clarke by the French economist A.M. de Foville in an article which dealt in some detail with the work of Jevons and Juglar (de Foville, 1879, p. 191). Certainly Schumpeter stated that he knew Hyde Clarke's writings "only from Jevons' report."

With the current revival of interest in the concept of long waves in economic life, it would seem to be worthwhile to rescue one of the people who first articulated it from the obscurity of footnotes and to attempt at least to provide some more details of his life and work. Who then was Hyde Clarke and to what extent did his writings anticipate the work of Kondratieff and others who have taken up the long wave theory?

II

During his own lifetime Hyde Clarke was sufficiently well know to receive mention in works of reference such as *Men and Women of the Time* (Moon, 1891, pp. 194-5) and *Celebrities of the Century* (Sanders, 1887, pp. 256-7) and on his death there were obituary notices of him in *The Times* (Mar. 7, 1895, p. 10b.) and the *Annual Register* (*The Annual Register*, 1895, p. 164)[3], as well as in journals such as *Nature* (51, 468) and *The Engineer* (79, 217). From these sources a picture can be built up of a long, varied and colourful career, but not all its details can now be filled in or adequately verified.

Hyde Clarke was born in London in 1815[4] and appears to have been a precocious youth. Details of his education are lacking, but he evidently took up engineering at an early age. According to the writer of the obituary in *The Engineer*, Clarke's first engineering work was done in Spain and Portugal during the Wars of Succession, while he was "attached to the Duke of Saldanha." There was a detachment of Royal Engineers among the British troops which went to assist the Spanish constitutionalist forces against the Carlists between 1835 and 1839, but Hyde Clarke's name does not appear in the Royal Engineers Lists for this period.[5]

If Hyde Clarke was with the forces of the Duke of Saldanha, this would place him in Portugal; Saldanha's military campaign there ended in May 1834 but until 1837 he remained an important figure in the government formed after the war by Queen Maria II. So the writer of *The Times* obituary of Hyde Clarke may have been nearer the mark in describing him as "employed in diplomatic missions" in Spain and Portugal at this time. The variant offered by *The Annual*

Register (1895, p. 164), which states that Hyde Clarke "fought with the British legion in the Portuguese and Spanish Wars of Succession, 1830-31," seems obviously unreliable if only because of the fact that this legion was not formed until 1834 (Ridley, 1970, pp. 196-8).

Whatever the young Hyde Clarke may or may not have done in the Iberian peninsula there seems to be no doubt that in 1836 he was back in England, where he became involved in plans for the building of a railway from Lancaster via the West Cumberland coast to Carlisle and thence to Glasgow via Nithsdale. Although I have not been able to discover anything precise about how and where Hyde Clarke received his engineering training, he seems to have made the engineering of dams and embankments one of his specialities. Although never actually a Member of the Institution of Civil Engineers, he later took part in discussions on these subjects at several meetings of the Institution (Clarke, 1847a, 1878-79) and among his many publications was one entitled *Engineering of Holland: On the Construction of Dykes* (cf. Henderson, 1992b). Presumably on the basis of his knowledge in this field, Hyde Clarke proposed a bold plan to build an embankment across Morecambe Bay, designed not only to carry the railway but at the same time to provide the capital for it from the proceeds of the sale of land reclaimed from the Bay. Although this scheme gained the support of no less a railway engineer than George Stephenson, it was not carried into effect for a variety of local reasons. While the project fell through as a trunk route, the railway was nevertheless completed by several companies, the Nithsdale section becoming the Glasgow and South Western Railway and subsequently part of the Midland Anglo-Scottish route (Clarke, 1884b).

Through this Morecambe Bay project Hyde Clarke became acquainted with John Rooke, since recognised as one of the neglected economists of this period (Seligman, 1903, pp. 511-14). Of Rooke, Clarke afterwards wrote: "Many of his writings are wild, but contain striking and original thoughts. In 1836 he came in contact with me and some of his writings passed under my hand." On more than one occasion Hyde Clarke asserted that Lonsdale, the author of a six-volume work of reference entitled *The Worthies of Cumberland*, had represented Rooke therein as the originator of the scheme for a west coast railway as being Clarke's employer, "but it was directly the reverse" (Clarke to Jevons, August 31, 1878; Black, 1977, Vol. IV, 275-6). In fact, while Lonsdale did mention both Rooke and Clarke, he did not portray their relationship in this way.[6]

From 1836 until 1849, Hyde Clarke appears to have been engaged not so much in the actual construction of railways as in financial operations and journalism connected with the growth of the English railway system. There are indications that he had significant connections in the London financial community at this period. The author of *The Times* obituary followed the writer of the biography in *Men and Women of the Time* in stating that "in 1836 Hyde Clarke founded the London and County Bank." The claim is a considerable one, for after an initial period of difficulty the London and County had by the end of the nineteenth century become one of the largest branch banking concerns in the south of England. If the twenty-one-year-old Hyde Clarke had indeed founded, or even helped to found, such a bank it would presumably have provided him with ample remuneration and occupation for the rest of his life; but no evidence which supports the claim can now be discovered.[7] Nevertheless, it is clear from his correspondence and other writings that Hyde Clarke was known to the London bankers of the 1830s and 1840s and had contact with such men as James Wilson, J.W. Gilbart, Thomas Tooke and Thomas Joplin (Black, 1977, Vol. IV, p. 275). Like them, his attention was drawn to the fluctuations of the price level and the "commercial panics" of 1839 and 1847 and it is from this period that his most original economic writings date.

The promotion of railways continued to occupy a large place in Hyde Clarke's concerns at this time of his life and in 1844 he founded a periodical called the *Railway Register* which he edited until 1847, writing extensively in it on railway management and finance. His interest extended to the promotion of railways in India which, like many others at the time, he considered could make a major contribution to the economic development of the sub-continent (Clarke, 1847c; Ambirajan, 1978, p. 250).

Hyde Clarke concerned himself with Indian development to a considerable extent in the decade from 1849 to 1859. In 1849 he was associated with Francis Whishaw, another railway engineer who was also Secretary of the Royal Society of Arts from 1843 to 1845, in producing a report for the East India Company on the practicability of a telegraph system for the country; he advocated a chain of telegraphs linking Calcutta with Simla, Darjeeling and other hill settlements (Clarke, 1881, pp. 544-5). It was in the development of these parts of Northern India that he was especially interested: at one time he was honorary agent for Darjeeling in London and in 1857 he was concerned with the flotation of a Northern Bengal Railway Company, pressing for the extension of railways to hill stations such as Simla.[8] Yet these activities did not absorb the whole of Hyde Clarke's energies; in the intervening years he found time to produce *A Grammar of the English Tongue* in 1853, *A New and Comprehensive Dictionary of the English Language* in 1855—which went through many subsequent editions—as well as several pamphlets on *The Statistics of Fire Assurance* between 1853 and 1986 (cf. Henderson, 1992b).

According to his own account, from 1859 to 1866 Hyde Clarke lived and worked in "the East," mainly apparently in Turkey, where he acted as Commissioner of Works for the province of Smyrna and as "Cotton Councillor" during the period when attempts were being made to develop cotton exports to Lancashire from the Ottoman Empire in place of American supplies (Henderson, 1934, pp. 46-7). Typically, again Hyde Clarke found time to add other activities to these official duties. He used his years in the Middle East to extend his knowledge of languages and began to develop the interests in comparative philology and anthropology which occupied him for much of the rest of his life.

For almost thirty years following his return to England in 1866 until his death in 1895, Hyde Clarke seems to have lived a busy life in London not only writing extensively on these subjects but concerning himself with many financial and public activities. In 1868 he founded the Council of Foreign Bondholders and, according to *The Times*, "in the commercial world his services were frequently in requisition as an expert in the ways of States which borrow, but forget to repay their loans" (March 7, 1895, p. 10b). Clarke was also Treasurer of the Newspaper Press Fund, a charitable organisation for journalists which still exists today, and it is on record that one of those who helped him in raising funds for it was Charles Dickens.[9]

In addition, Hyde Clarke played an active part in a number of the learned societies of Victorian London. He had a substantial influence on the organisation of the Royal Society of Arts; already in 1857 he had proposed to its Council that "a special section should be formed for India, another for Australia, one for English America, and so on." He renewed this proposal in 1868 and an Indian Section was then established, followed by an African section in 1874—"again, largely due to the zeal of Hyde Clarke" (Hudson and Luckhurst, 1954, pp. 344-5).

That zeal was also exerted on behalf of the London (later Royal) Statistical Society on the Council of which Hyde Clarke served at various time from 1868 until his death. As with the Royal Society of Arts, he seems to have played an active part in attempts to alter the organisation of the society. In November 1885, Hyde Clarke proposed that the Statistical Society should hold periodical Economic meetings, a development which had the support of the newly appointed Professor of Political Economy at Cambridge, Alfred Marshall. Hyde Clarke's motion was in fact passed but against such opposition from other members that Foxwell pronounced it "rather a Pyrrhic victory." In consequence, Clarke's proposal was not implemented and Foxwell and others turned their attention to the establishment of a separate Economic Society (Coats, 1968, pp. 351-3).[10]

Hyde Clarke also contributed a number of papers to the proceedings of the London Statistical Society. Like many contributions of the period, they could only be described as statistical in the sense that they contained statistical material to illustrate the social or political problems with which the author was concerned. Papers such as "On the Debts of Sovereign and Quasi-Sovereign States, owing to Foreign Countries" (Clarke, 1878) or "On a Form of Savings Banks among the Christians of Asia Minor" (Clarke, 1865), reflect the range and character of Hyde Clarke's later interests, although his contributions to the discussions on other papers sometimes reveal a continuing interest in the economic problems on which he had written in earlier years.

His membership of the Ethnological Society of London and the Anthropological Institute provide further indications of the direction of Hyde Clarke's intellectual concerns in later life. For these and for the Royal Historical Society he wrote numerous papers on philology and the origins of languages and races—interests which led him into the related fields of archaeology and ancient history. The period after 1870 witnessed the rediscovery of the monuments and inscriptions of the Hittites, the ancient inhabitants of Turkey and northern Syria. Hyde Clarke is said by some contemporary sources to have been the first to identify the Hittite inscriptions of Khita and Hamah, but his theories as to their possible origin did not find favour with other experts on the archaeology of the Middle East (Wright, 1884, pp. 129-31). Indeed in this area of study the comment of *The Times* obituarist seems to accord with the judgement of history—"while his views on many subjects were undoubtedly original, most of his

generalisations failed to commend themselves as sound to really
scientific philologists."

III

Hyde Clarke's long life of varied activity makes him difficult to
characterise: an engineer who filled a variety of administrative posts
at home and abroad, he seems like many Victorians to have combined
enormous energy with wide intellectual curiosity. It was in the period
from 1838 to 1848 that Hyde Clarke did most of his writing on
economic problems and in these years produced his most original
ideas. Not surprisingly, the starting point for his thinking on
economic matters was his involvement as an engineer and journalist
in the rapid growth of the English railway system. In that respect,
it could be argued, he was evolving in a way which was not
uncommon, and certainly not unfruitful, at this period. The
development of railways and public works in the nineteenth century
led a number of engineers—and some scientists with engineering
training—in Britain, France, Germany and the United States to look
at the economic problems involved. The works of Lardner, Dupuit,
Minard, Launhardt and Ellet broke important new ground and their
significance is now well recognised in the history of economic thought
(Ekelund and Hébert, 1975 part IV). Most of this work belonged to
the area of what would now be called pricing and allocation theory
or the related field of welfare economics. Hyde Clarke's writings, on
the other hand, fall into the area now called macroeconomics. He
was conerned essentially with two problems—understanding in real
as well as in financial terms the process of investment in railways,
then taking place in Britain on an unprecedented scale, and tracing
and explaining the cyclical phenomena which he detected in
economic life.

Concerns such as these, as Professor Henderson (1992a) has noted
lay outside the mainstream of classical political economy. Indeed,
in the mid-nineteenth century most economists had little if any grasp
of the concept of economic cycles. Perhaps the most striking feature
of Hyde Clarke's thought is not merely that he at this time recognised
the existence of such cycles, but that, as Schumpeter noted, he
"recognised a muliplicity of cycles that run their course
simultaneously" (Schumpeter, 1954, p. 743). Hyde Clarke himself

explained how this recognition came about, in a passage which shows him already much involved in observing the workings of the economy at the age of 17 or 18:

> I begun in 1832 and 1833, when I saw the dawn of a period of these speculations, which from a close acquaintance with the history of the mania of 1823, 1824 and 1825, I was induced to look upon as a recurrence of the same phenomena. I therefore gave a particular attention to the events of the railway mania of 1835, and [formed] a conviction that the true nature of that epoch was connected with periodical laws. While entertaining these views my attention was directed to the general elementary laws which govern periodical or cyclal [sic] action, and I wrote a paper on the subject in Herapath's *Railway Magazine* in 1838. At this time it was my impression that the period of speculation was a period of ten years, but I was led also to look for a period of thirteen or fourteen years as half a period of twenty-seven or twenty-eight years, and for a period of seven or eight years as the quarter revolution, and I vainly endeavoured to obtain information on these points from scientific friends, or to collect corroborative facts. In the course of these inquiries I looked at the astronomical periods and the meterological theories, without finding anything at all available for my purposes" (Clarke, 1847b, p. 3).

Hyde Clarke did not give an exact reference for the article which he here claims to have written and its identification presents something of a problem. There is an article in two parts by Hyde Clarke in Vol IV of Herapath's *Railway Magazine*, entitled "On the Political Economy and Capital of Joint-Stock Banks" but as Professor Henderson says, "in that article, there is only the most general commentary on periodic or cyclical events" and its content "is hardly an explanation of the "general elementary laws which govern periodical or cyclar action" (Henderson, 1992a). However, in his letter of August 31, 1878 to Jevons, Hyde Clarke wrote: "There was a paper on Cycles in Herapath's Journal about 1837 or 1838, which contains an hypothesis for a selfworking variable cycle, but it has no reference to the cycle of crises." Now this description exactly fits an anomymous article which appeared in Volume V of Herapath's *Railway Magazine* in October 1838, entitled "On the Mathematical Law of the Cycle." This curious article runs to no more than two-and-a-half quarto pages and contains no actual mathematics. Its starting point is "Babbage's discovery, that after a certain extent the formulae of equations ceased to operate, but that new formulae were required"; the author's claim is that this "instead of being a mere exception in one particular branch of science... is a universal law of nature" (Clarke, 1838, p. 378).

After the fashion of his day, the writer does not give any specific reference to indicate the part of Babbage's work to which he was referring—it may well have been *Examples of the Solutions of Functional Equations*, published in 1820 (cf. Dubbey, 1978). In any event, it is clear from the context that what the author had in mind was certain properties of abstract periodic functions which may be duplicated in natural phenomena. As instances he quotes irregularities in the procession of the equinoxes, and eccentricities in the variation of the magnetic needle, while "in mechanics there is every presumption that after a certain number of revolutions of a machine the ratio of those movements is changed, and something of this may certainly be perceived in watches. It is perceptible in a watch going very irregularly, that the ratio of its movement will change as if by starts.... In statistics this cyclar action decidedly prevails, and although we cannot point out any more prominent instances, yet there is sufficient of these examples to authorize the presumption that in other instances it equally exists" (Clarke, 1838, p. 379).

Essentially all that the article was saying was that certain types of equation might define series which would display damped cyclical movements, that similar cycles could be traced in a variety of natural phenomena and that further reseach might lead to the establishment of a general law explaining their form (Kendall, 1948, p. 402; Dubbey, 1978, pp. 51, 87). Interest in such "cyclar action" was in fact quite widespread at this period; astronomers, for example, were interested in how it might affect the accuracy of chronometers used for navigational purposes (Bennett, 1980). To modern specialists it may appear strange that a contribution of this kind should appear in a railway journal, but the explanation of this may lie in the fact that its full title was *The Railway Magazine and Annals of Science* and its editor John Herapath was, according to Hyde Clarke himself, "a zealous physical mathematician." Forty years later he recounted to Jevons how Herapath "more than once talked with me of cosmical cycles, down to 1844, but he had no idea of any period affecting production, and exhibiting itself in economical results" (Black, 1977, Vol. IV, p. 276).

It is noteworthy that in his letter to Jevons of August 31, 1878, Hyde Clarke did not claim the authorship of the 1838 *Railway*

Magazine article, but as many of the articles in that periodical were anonymous it seems reasonable to suggest that this was the same piece as the one to which he laid claim in *Physical Economy* in 1847.

From that pamphlet, which bore the subtitle "a Preliminary Inquiry into the Physical Laws governing the Periods of Famines and Panics," it is evident that Hyde Clarke, like Jevons a generation later, had become fascinated with the idea of periodicity in nature and its possible influence on the affairs of men. In it he not only developed the idea of cyclical fluctuations in natural phenomena with a considerable volume of supporting evidence but sought to emphasise the relation of such fluctuations to economic activity:

> While political economy restricts itself principally to the moral laws which influence society, it seems advisable that the influence of physical laws and operations upon mankind should for their better study, be formed also into a distinct science. This would include the laws of life (vital statistics) those which regulate famines and pestilence, and the operations of physical phenomena as affecting mankind and society. Such a science might usefully be called physical economy" (Clarke, 1847b, p. 1).

From an initial and somewhat sketchy outline of the course of prices and economic activity since 1815, Hyde Clarke argued that "this outline is enough to show the close connection of abundant food, active enterprise and speculation, and of scarce food, panic and political disturbance. It is sufficient also to suggest that there is some definite period which governs the occurrence of these phenomena." Recalling his earlier preoccupation with the ten-year period, Hyde Clarke explained that "the present famine" (in Ireland) had led him "to look for a larger period" and directed his thoughts "to the famine so strongly felt during the French Revolution," fifty-four years earlier.

One of Hyde Clarke's closest friends at this time, as he later explained to Jevons, was James Thomas Hackett, "a very fair mathematician and astronomical computer, who had been Secretary of the London Astrological Society and whose inner craze was astrology and consequently periodicity" (Black, 1977, Vol. IV, p. 275). It was Hackett who pointed out to Hyde Clarke that the idea of a 54-year cycle was central to the work of George Mackenzie, a Scottish climatologist who in 1818 had published *The System of the Weather of the British Isles*—a system in which he placed so much confidence that in 1829 he was prepared to publish a *Manual of the Weather for the year MDCCCXXX* giving forecasts for each month a year in advance.

Mackenzie's system was based on a weather register which he had kept since 1802; his records led him to the idea that the wind was "the foremost element" in the weather and that its movements followed a regular pattern. Over a period of 14 years he believed that he had established that there were (in the part of Scotland where he made his observations) on average 135 days of east wind and 216 days of west wind annually. When the number of days of east wind in a year was greater than 135 he termed this an "excess" or a year of "Solar east winds" and similarly if the number fell below 135 this would be in his terminology a "deficiency" of easterly winds or a year of "Lunar east winds." "Having in this manner found the excesses and deficiencies of the east and west winds for 14 years, he began to compare them together, and was surprised to find that they followed one another in a regular progression, the excesses and deficiences of both winds arranging themselves in groups.... Now it is a very remarkable fact that by following out these progressions the series returns into itself in 54 years, forming a perfect cycle" (Brewster, 1818, p. 86).

It may well be asked how Mackenzie arrived at this result on the basis of only 14 years of observations; he seems simply to have observed that the terms in the "regular progression" of the winds noted in his journal formed part of a series which would "return into itself" in 54 years, but in 1829 he claimed that "the observations of subsequent years which have been kept by the Register have exactly corresponded with the series of alternations of the Solar and Lunar winds made out at that time by induction—and it could not be otherwise" (Mackenzie, 1829, p. 27).

"From this time of discovering the primary cycle of the winds in 1817" Mackenzie went on to search for a relation between his weather cycle and movements in the price of wheat, using the Eton College records and Fleetwood's *Chronicon Preciosum* as quoted by Adam Smith. He claimed to have discovered in 1826 "the regular rotation of the cheap and dear prices of wheat in every 54 year period." His contention was that the 54-year cycle could be divided into two periods of 27 years each—"one of these is generally wet, windy and cloudy with generally high prices of corn; the other dry, less windy, and clear with generally low prices of corn" (Mackenzie, 1829, pp. 45, 49).

Although Hyde Clarkes's conclusion was that "the general prognostications of Mr Mackenzie as to prices have... certainly been borne out hitherto," he did not adopt either Mackenzie's figures or his theories. However, they do seem to have encouraged him to search through the available data—again primarily Fleetwood and the Eton College returns—for evidence supporting or contradicting his hypothesis of a 54 year periodicity. To his credit, it must be recorded that he did not try to force the data to fit, but frankly stated his conclusion that "the elements thus obtained, although in some points corresponding to 54 years, were far from answering determinately to a rigorous period of 54 years throughout, though there was sufficient conformity to justify the assumption that some general period regulated the critical years" (Clarke, 1847b, pp. 5, 6).

Hyde Clarke's measurement and dating of both decennial and longer cycles are examined in detail by James P. Henderson (1992a) and therefore need not be further discussed here, but we may particularly note that Professor Henderson finds that the dating of Kondratieff's main measures—prices, agricultural wages and interest rates—for his "First Cycle" closely matches Hyde Clarke's dates.

IV

Between 1838 and 1847 then, Hyde Clarke had moved from formulating a very broad hypothesis about cycles in natural phenomena to empirical investigations which had convinced him of the existence, among others, of a 54 year cycle in economic activity resulting from physical causes. But in 1846 Hyde Clarke had published another pamphlet, reprinting material which first appeared in Volume IV of the *Railway Register*, under the title *Theory of Investment in Railway Companies*. Now to modern economists who remember Schumpeter's words—"railroad developments in the forties, particularly in England, are a chief reason for dating the beginning of the second Kondratieff as we do" (i.e., in 1843) (Schumpeter, 1939, Vol. I, p. 304)—this title naturally suggest the interesting possibility that Hyde Clarke's intention was to present a theory of the influence of investment in railways on fluctuations in economic activity, but such was not the case.

In fact, Hyde Clarke's purpose in expounding a theory of railway investment was strictly practical and by no means disinterested. He was concerned to argue a case against those "panic mongers," as he called them, who were urging a restriction on the number of railway bills sanctioned by Parliament annually (Simmons, 1978, Vol. I, pp. 40-42), and therefore to show that the very large volume of railway investment then being pushed forward could be financed without damage to the national economy. In endeavouring to do so, Hyde Clarke did present a sound and interesting account of the real transfers of resources which lay behind the then unfamiliar facade of finance throught joint-stock company promotion. His main argument was that it could not "be said, with any degree of truth or seeming, that capital has been diverted from any of the great staples by the extensive progress of railway enterprise in the present year. Till this pressure takes place, till it makes itself felt, interference is surely needless" (Clarke, 1846, p. 9).

In real terms, Hyde Clarke suggested, the labor required for railway building need not be drawn from that employed in other industries, but could come partly from those unemployed in workhouses and partly from reductions in the labor force required in agriculture, where improvements had generated increases in productivity. "To extract this *dormant* labour, a small additional stimulus only would be required, which is to be obtained from the increasing surplus of agricultural produce yearly provided." Here an echo of Gibbon Wakefield's views can be detected, for Hyde Clarke suggested that to employ labor released from agriculture in manufactures "is dangerous, because it is only increasing production at a time when the foreign markets are overstocked." On the other hand, "employment in public works does not interfere with the markets, while it increases the fixed capital or working plant of the community and at the same time, enlarges the permanent resources of subsistence." And for this, "railways fulfil, in the most eminent degree, all the conditions required" (Clarke, 1846, p. 14).

Turning to the capital which would employ the labor, Hyde Clarke contended that much of the capital required for railways was merely a transfer and not a net new investment—as most notably in the case of land acquired against payment in railway shares. Where actual new investment was required Hyde Clarke, as might be expected, stressed the extent to which it came from the small savings of farmers and tradespeople, mobilised through the joint stock mechanism, and minimised or ignored the possibilities of speculative share purchases financed by short-term credit.

In all this, there was no mention of the cyclical theory which he must by then have largely formulated and was to publish a year later in *Physical Economy.* Yet the two were connected, though not by the mechanism which a twentieth-century economist would expect. Most economists nowadays would consider that if fluctuations in economic activity can be shown to be regularly generated by some exogenous cause, then it would be desirable to arrange, through government policy or otherwise, that other factors influencing the level of activity should do so in a counter-cyclical fashion. Writing in 1847, Hyde Clarke did not see the matter in that light; to him the only policy conclusion which seemed clear was that "if the mania for speculation be a periodical consequence of a regular series of events, it must be utterly futile to pass laws for its suppression and interference inconsistent with such fact can only have the effect of doing mischief" (Clarke, 1847b, p. 2; cf. Henderson, 1992a). So, far from the railways being major contributors to an investment cycle, they appear as being passively involved in a process which would have occurred even had they never existed.

This may give rise to the suspicion that Hyde Clarke was no more than a spokesman for the railway interests, inventing arguments to justify unlimited scope for their activities. That there is some substance in this is undeniable: Hyde Clarke was writing *ex parte* and did not attempt to conceal the fact. Yet this in itself does not mean that his writings can be treated as mere propaganda. The results which Hyde Clarke presented in *Physical Economy* could not have been reached without extended research and computation; better propaganda could have been produced with less effort. It would seem more reasonable simply to see Hyde Clarke as an engineer with a somewhat unusual cast of mind who on the one hand was led by his mathematical and scientific studies to a lasting interest in the phenomena of cycles and their possible economic implications and on the other, by his railway interests to attempt a pioneer account of the real processes which railway investment involved.

Writing in the boom conditions of 1846, the view which Hyde Clarke took of the effects of railway investment at the time was certainly unduly optimistic. While those effects have been a subject of some controversy among economic historians, few if any would now suggest that investment in railways did not contribute in some measure to the crisis of 1847. Nevertheless, writers like Gary Hawke have stressed that time lags in railway-investment outlays at this period ensured that much of it was contracyclical, while spending on maintenance was little affected by trade conditions (Hawke, 1970, pp. 363-73). So the results of modern research do afford some support for Hyde Clarke's defence of investment in railways.

V

In conclusion, we may return to the question posed at the beginning of this paper—how far can Hyde Clarke be properly regarded as a precursor of Kondratieff, and indeed of more recent long-wave theorists?

If we look first at this from the point of view of the perception and measurement of the cycle, it seems that there is a strong case for regarding Hyde Clarke as genuinely anticipating later presenters of the long-wave hypothesis. At a time when only a few thinkers outside the mainstream of contemporary political economy had even grasped the concept of a decennial cycle, Hyde Clarke made the intellectual leap involved in realising that this might only be part of a larger cycle. He followed this up with considerable empirical research as far as the distinctly sketchy data available to him would allow and succeeded in working out the basic chronology in a manner which later and more sophisticated research has not contradicted. This alone should have been enough to earn Hyde Clarke a more prominent place in the history of economic thought than he has so far been conceded.

On the more specific question of a comparison between the work of Hyde Clarke and that of Kondratieff, there is first of all a noticeable resemblance between their views on periodic movements in the economic and other spheres. In 1924 Kondratieff published a paper entitled "On the Notion of Economic Statics, Dynamics and Fluctuations," a section of which appeared in an English translation in the following year (Kondratieff, 1925).[11] Comparatively little attention has been paid to this article in the West, probably because of the very general terms in which the translated section was cast. In it he divided dynamic processes "into the evolutionary (or nonreversible) processes on the one hand, and the wave-like or fluctuating one the other.... By "wave-like" or "fluctuating" processes are meant processes of variation which are changing their direction in the course of time and are subject to repetition and reversion.... The conceptions of reversible and nonreversible processes, as well as those of statics and dynamics, belong, strictly speaking, to the domain of natural science in the narrower sense of the word, such as physics, chemistry and biology.... But if the necessary caution is exercised in making use of the conceptions in economics, there would appear to be no obstacles to their application in this field as well; and the use of the conceptions of reversible and nonreversible processes in economics may be looked upon as an application of a general idea to a specific class of cases. Attentive empirical, and especially statistical, analysis shows, further, that there exist both regular and irregular reversible processes. Regular processes in turn, may be either seasonal or cyclical. As to cycles, the processes may again be different"—which leads Kondratieff to the identification of the various types of cycles (Kondratieff, 1925, pp. 579-81).

All this casts light on the way in which Kondratieff thought about the problem of the long waves. Similarities with the mind-set which Hyde Clarke had displayed in his 1838 and 1847 writings are apparent. There is the same central concern with periodicity, with "wave-like fluctuations," the same recognition that these occur in the domains of both the natural and the social sciences, and the same realisation that in economic activity more than one cycle can be identified. Turning to the question of the causation of the cycle, we can again note a resemblance between the writings of Hyde Clarke and Kondratieff, in that both were distinctly cautious and reticent in what they wrote on this point.

Hyde Clarke came no closer to a definitive statement about it than his comment that "Mr. Mackenzie has alluded to the shifting or oscillation of the magnetic poles in connection with the periods of the weather, and my own impressions and observations go far to persuade me that the great causes of the phenomena manifested in the seasons and the harvests at present are referable to fluctuations in the electromagnetic condition of this globe" (Clarke, 1847b, p. 9).

In his paper "The Long Waves in Economic Life," which has become the version of his work most familiar to Western economists, Kondratieff rejected the idea that long waves "are conditioned by casual extra economic circumstances and events" but did not go beyond saying that "in asserting the existence of long waves and in denying that they arise out of random causes, we are also of the opinion that the long waves arise out of causes which are inherent in the essence of the capitalistic economy" (Kondratieff, 1935, 1944, pp. 41-2).

After penetrating beyond the caution and reticence which both authors displayed in formulating their hypotheses, a fundamental difference between them is apparent in that ultimately Hyde Clarke's explanation of the long cycle was exogenous, whereas Kondratieff's was endogenous. The essence of Hyde Clarke's concept of "Physical Economy" was that "the operation of physical phenomena as affecting mankind and society" must be taken into account by economists as well as "the moral laws which influence society" and which formed the subject matter of political economy as he knew it. As to the mechanisms by which physical phenomena affected economic activity, he never committed himself to any single and simple hypothesis and his thinking on this seemed to become more tentative in his later years.

Here Hyde Clarke's approach is in notable contrast to that of Jevons, whose belief in the truth of his sun-spot explanation of decennial crises seemed to grow ever stronger, and who to the end of his life was "sufficiently convinced of the truth of the theory though it may not be possible at present to meet every difficulty" (Black, 1977, Vol. V, p. 194). Hyde Clarke, on the other hand, was sceptical of the value of sun-spot research: "instead of assisting the economical investigation or the meteorological discussion, it had rather interfered with our obtaining clear results," he argued. This was because "in all these discussions with regard to sun-spots, periods had been laid out almost in some cases like minutes and seconds" (Clarke, 1884a, p. 66), while in a situation where so many disturbing factors were involved, such precision was not to be expected in cause and effect sequences.

In the papers which he presented to the British Association between 1884 and 1887 and which are fully discussed in Professor Henderson's article (1992a), Hyde Clarke made clear that, partly because of innovations affecting the relative prices and transport costs of industrial and agricultural products, the conditions of trade in the later nineteenth century were very different from those which had existed in its earlier years, and the growth of international exchange reduced the importance of fluctuations in the yield of single crops. Yet even apart from this, "it was the interference of the larger cycles...which would prevent them from predicting so readily as some persons thought what would be the incidents of agriculture and industry all over the world, or in any one region" (Clarke, 1884a, p. 67). So Hyde Clarke's belief that there were at least two cycle patterns observable in the price data led him to think that "it would always be beyond their power absolutely to predict what the result would be;" but all these reservations did not lead him to doubt that there was a long cycle in economic activity and that it had an exogenous, physical cause.

In the paper on "Major Economic Cycles" which he first read before the Economic Institute in Moscow in 1926, but of which an English translation was not available until 1984, Kondratieff "set forth briefly...a first attempt—a first hypothesis—to explain those cycles" (Kondratieff, 1984, p. 89). Central to this explanation was the idea "that the material basis for the long cycles is the wear and tear, replacement and increase in those basic capital goods requiring a long period of time and tremendous investments for their production." (According to Kondratieff, "these include such capital goods as big construction projects, the building of major railroads, the construction of canals, big land-improvement projects, etc."). *"The replacement and expansion of the fund of these goods does not take place smoothly but in spurts, and the long waves in economic conditions are another expression of that"* (Kondratieff, 1984, pp. 92-93, emphasis in original).

Kondratieff went on to argue "that the dynamics of the long cycles possess an inner regularity. Therefore, strictly speaking, we cannot regard this or that link of the cycle as the cause of the whole cycle. We can only say that the rhythm of the long cycles reflects the rhythm in the process of the expansion of society's basic capitalist goods" (Kondratieff, 1984, p. 99).

Thus Kondratieff offered an explanation of the "rhythm of the long cycles" which traced its source to major capital projects such as railroads—those very projects which Hyde Clarke had sought to show were only passively involved because the rhythm of long cycles came from exogenous physical factors. It follows from this that Schumpeter's attribution to Hyde Clarke of "a striking anticipation of the major cycles or spans of later days, especially of Kondratieff's long waves" has to be interpreted with caution. So far as the concept of the long wave and its dating are concerned, Hyde Clarke did indeed anticipate Kondratieff; so far as its causation is concerned, he did not.

However, if we extend comparison beyond the work of Kondratieff himself to the many other research studies of the long wave phenomenon which have been made more recently, the case appears somewhat differently. On the basis of such research, J.J. van Duijn has recently suggested that "Two different long cycles...appear to exist: one, a Kondratieff price cycle whose course is determined by discontinuities in the expansion of productive capacity in agriculture and raw material production; the other, a long wave in industrial production, which results from fluctuations in innovations over time and the way in which these innovations give rise to the establishment of growth sectors" (van Duijn, 1983, p 91). If we accept this view, it would seem possible to regard Hyde Clarke's work (although based on product yields rather than productive capacity in agriculture) as anticipating the idea of the first of these two types of long cycle, if not also the second.

ACKNOWLEDGMENT

The author is Emeritus Professor of Economics, Queen's University of Belfast. He is indebted to Mrs. J. Wright for valuable research assistance in connection with an earlier unpublished version of this paper, prepared in 1979-80. He would like also to thank Professor James P. Henderson for many useful suggestions and for allowing him to see an advance copy of his paper on Hyde Clarke; Dr. Nigel F. Allington and Dr. J.W. Taylor of the University of Wales Institute of Science and Technology, Cardiff, for advice and assistance in regard to John Rooke and to early English railway development; his colleague, Dr. Alun Davies, of Queen's University, Belfast, for bringing to his attention the interest in periodicity among horologists and astronomers in England in the 1830's; Dr. Joyce Brown, of Imperial College, London, for assistance on the question of Hyde Clarke's Indian career; and participants in the discussion when this paper was read at the History of Economic Thought Conference in Manchester, England in September 1987, whose comments prompted several improvements in it. He also gratefully acknowledges the helpful comments of three anonymous referees for this volume.

NOTES

1.   For an example of semi-popular literature on the subject, see Shuman and Rosenau (1972), and for a Marxist interpretation, Mandel (1975 and 1980). Perhaps the most comprehensive recent treatment is van Duijn (1983).

2.   The article was reprinted in Jevons (1884, pp. 221-243). Hyde Clarke had been known to Jevons since at least 1871, but their first exchange of views was on a very different topic, the geographical distribution of intellectual qualities (cf. Black, 1977, Vol. III, p. 243).

Although Hyde Clarke objected to being called "Doctor" by Jevons, he frequently appended the letters D.C.L. to his name. However, he is not included as a Doctor of Civil Law in the alumni lists of any of the British universities of his time, nor have I been able to discover any evidence that he held the rank of Colonel in any army.

3.   The notice in the *Annual Register* refers to "Hyde Clarke Nyndeen" but it has not proved possible to find any explanation for or corroboration of this curious additional name.

4.   Boase (1892/1965, Vol. I, p. 676) describes Hyde Clarke as "son of H. Clarke of Sandford House." This may well have been the same Sandford Manor House which Baedeker listed among "famous old houses of Chelsea," noting that Addison occasionally resided there (Baedeker, 1902, p. 380). This, like a number of other points in Hyde Clarke's biography, seems to suggest that his background was one of some affluence.

5.   I am indebted to the Assistant Curator of the Royal Engineers Museum, Brompton Barracks, Chatham, Kent, who checked through the Royal Engineers Lists on my behalf for Hyde Clarke's name and concluded "it is safe to say that he was not a Royal Engineer" (Letter dated 18 February 1980). See also Duncan (1877, pp. 41-51, 82).

6.   Lonsdale's actual words on the connection between Rooke and Hyde Clarke were: "For many years Rooke had been an observer; the railway interests made him an author on geology. Mr Hyde Clarke, the projector of a railway across Morecambe Bay, had induced Rooke to survey and report of the practicability of effecting that object: and this circumstance gave rise to a long discussion on the nature and influence of tidal action in sedimentary disposition" (Lonsdale, 1872, p. 256).

7.   I am indebted to the Archivist of the National Westminister Bank (into which the London and County Bank was ultimately absorbed), the Institute of Bankers, Professor R.S. Sayers and Dr. A.B. Cramp for having patiently dealt with my enquiries about Hyde Clarke's supposed connection with the London and County Bank; all agreed that there is no evidence for it. (See Gregory, 1936, Vol. I, pp. 322-91.)

8.   India Office Records, Railway and Telegraph Department 1847-1858, [2/ L/PWD/2/4]—Northern Bengal—Electric Telegraphs and Railways, Letters 133, 235, 345, 528. I am indebted to Mr. T. Thomas of the India Office Records section, Foreign and Commonwealth Office, London, for these references.

9.   Information kindly supplied by Mr. Peter W. Evans, Secretary of the Newspaper Press Fund, London.

10.   I am grateful to Professor James P. Henderson for drawing my attention to this reference.

11.   The chronology of Kondratieff's papers and their translations into German and English is fully set out in Garvy (1943).

REFERENCES

Ambirajan, S. 1978. *Classical Political Economy and British Policy in India.* Cambridge, England: Cambridge University Press.

The Annual Register: A Review of Public Events at Home and Abroad for the Year 1895. 1896. London: Longmans, Green & Co.

Baedeker, Karl. 1902. *London and its Environs.* Leipzig: Baedeker.

Bennett, J.A. 1980. "George Biddell Airy and Horology." *Annals of Science* 37: 269-85.

Black, R.D. Collison, ed. 1977. *Papers and Correspondence of William Stanley Jevons* Vol. III: Correspondence, 1863-1872; Vol. IV: Correspondence, 1873-1878; Vol. V: Correspondence, 1879-1882. London: Macmillan.

Boase, Henry. 1892/1965. *Modern English Biography.* 6 vol. London: Frank Cass. (Originally published 1892).

[Brewster, David]. 1818. "An Account of the System of the Weather of the British Islands, Discovered by Lieut. George Mackenzie." *Blackwood's Edinburgh Magazine* IV(October): 84-7.

Clarke, Hyde? 1838. "On the Mathematical Law of the Cycle." *The Railway Magazine and Annals of Science* V(November): 378-80.

Clarke, Hyde. 1838. "On the Political Economy and Capital of Joint-Stock Banks." *The Railway Magazine and Annals of Science,* IV, no. xxvii, 288-93, no. xxviii, 360-62.

Clarke, Hyde. 1846. *Theory of Investment in Railway Companies.* London: John Weale.

_____. 1847a. "Contribution to the Discussion on G.B. Wheeler Jackson's paper, "Description of the Great North Holland Canal," read February 9, 1847. *Minutes of Proceedings of the Institution of Civil Engineers* 6: 112, 118, 131.

_____. 1847b. *Physical Economy: A Preliminary Inquiry into the Physical Laws governing the periods of Famines and Panics.* NP.

_____. 1847c. *Practical and Theoretical Considerations on the Management of Railways in India.* London.

_____. 1865. "On a Form of Savings Banks among the Christians of Asia Minor." *Journal of the* [*Royal*] *Statistical Society* 28: 321-3.

_____. 1878. "On the Debts of Sovereign and Quasi-Sovereign States, owing to Foreign Countries." *Journal of the* [*Royal*] *Statistical Society* 41: 299-347.

_____. 1878-79. "Contribution to the Discussion on J. Purser Griffith's paper, 'The Improvement of the Bar of Dublin Harbour by Artificial Scour,' read May 20, 1879." *Minutes of Proceedings of the Institution of Civil Engineers* 58: 126-7.

_____. 1881. "The English Stations in the Hill Regions of India: their Value and Importance, with some Statistics of their Products and Trade." *Journal of the* [*Royal*] *Statistical Society* 44(September): 529-63.

_____. 1884. Discussion on J.H. Poynting's paper, "A Comparison of the Fluctuations in the Price of Wheat and in the Cotton and Silk Imports into Great Britain." *Journal of the* [*Royal*] *Statistical Society* 47(March): 65-68.

————. 1884b. *Morecambe Bay Railway and Reclamation in 1836 and 1883.* London: Lord and Gill.

Coats, A.W. 1968. "The Origins and Early Development of the Royal Economic Society." *Economic Journal* 78(June): 349-371.

de Foville, Alfred M. 1879. "Les Tâches du Soleil et les Crises Commerciales." *L'Economiste Français* (15 Fevrier): pp. 191-3.

Dubbey, J.M. 1978. *The Mathematical Work of Charles Babbage.* Cambridge: Cambridge University Press.

Duncan, F. 1877. *The English in Spain.* London: John Murray.

Ekelund, Robert B., and Hérbert, Robert F. 1975. *A History of Economic Theory and Method.* New York: McGraw Hill.

Garvy, George. 1943. "Kondratieff's Theory of Long Cycles." *Review of Economic Statistics* 25(November): 203-220.

Gregory, Theodore E. 1936. *The Westminster Bank through a Century.* London: Westminster Bank.

Hawke, Gary R. 1970. *Railways and Economic Growth in England and Wales 1840-1870.* Oxford: Clarendon Press.

Henderson, James P. 1992a. "Astronomy, Astrology and Business Cycles: Hyde Clarke's Contribution." *Research in the History of Economic Thought and Methodology*, 9.

————. 1992b. "Hyde Clarke's Publications...," *Research in the History of Economic Thought and Methodology*, 9.

Henderson, W.O. 1934. *The Lancashire Cotton Famine 1861-65.* Manchester: Manchester University Press.

Hudson, Derek, and Luckhurst, K.W.1954. *The Royal Society of Arts 1754-1954.* London: John Murray.

Jenks, Leland H. 1927/1963. *The Migration of British Capital to 1975.* London: Nelson. (First edition, 1927, New York: A Knopf).

Jevons, W. Stanley. 1884. *Investigations in Currency and Finance*, edited by H.S. Foxwell. London: Macmillan and Co.

————. 1977. *Papers and Correspondence of W.S. Jevons*, Vol. IV. London: Macmillan.

Kendall, Maurice George. 1948. *The Advanced Theory of Statistics* (2nd ed.). London: C. Griffin and Co.

Kondratieff, Nikolai D. 1925. "The Static and the Dynamic View of Economics." *Quarterly Journal of Economics* 39(August): 575-83.

————. 1935/1944. "The Long Waves in Economic Life." (Translated from the German by W.F. Stolper). *Review of Economic Statistics* 17(November): 105-115. (Reprinted in American Economic Association. *Readings in Business Cycle Theory.* Philadelphia: Blakiston, pp. 20-42.)

————. 1984. *The Long Wave Cycle.* (Translated by Guy Daniels.) New York: Richardson and Snyder.

Link, Raymond G. 1959. *English Theories of Economic Fluctuations, 1815-1848.* New York: Columbia University Press.

Lonsdale, Henry. 1872. *The Worthies of Cumberland: The Howards, Rev. R. Matthews, John Rooke, Captain Joseph Huddart.* London: Routledge.

Mackenzie, George. 1818. *The System of the Weather of the British Islands: discovered in 1816 and 1817 from a Journal commencing November 1802.* Edinburgh: W. Aitken.

———. 1829. *Manual of the Weather for the Year MDCCCXXX.* Edinburgh: W Blackwood.

Mandel, Ernest. 1975. *Late Capitalism.* London: New Left Books.

———. 1980. *Long Waves of Capitalist Development: the Marxist interpretation.* Cambridge: Cambridge University Press.

Mitchell, Wesley C. 1930. *Business Cycles, The Problem and its Setting.* New York: National Bureau of Economic Research.

Moon, G. Washington, ed. 1891. *Men and Women of the Time: A Dictionary of Contemporaries* (13th ed.). London: Routledge.

Ridley, Jasper G. 1970. *Lord Palmerston.* London: Constable.

Sanders, Lloyd C. (ed.). 1887. *Celebrities of the Century.* London: Cassell.

Schumpeter, Joseph A. 1939. *Business Cycles.* 2 vols. New York: McGraw Hill.

———. 1954. *A History of Economic Analysis.* London: G. Allen and Unwin.

Seligman, Edwin R. A. 1903. "On Some Neglected British Economists." *Economic Journal* 13: 335-63, 511-35.

Shuman, James B. and Rosenau, David. 1972. *The Kondratieff Wave.* New York: World Publishing Company.

Simmons, J. 1978. *The Railway in England and Wales, 1830-1914.* Leicester: Leicester University Press.

van Duijn, Jacob J. 1983. *The Long Wave in Economic Life.* London: G. Allen and Unwin.

Wright, William. 1884. *The Empire of the Hittites.* London: James Nisbet and Co.

[7]

RALPH GEORGE HAWTREY

1879–1975

I

THE increase in the number and importance of economists in
government since the beginning of the Second World War
is a fact which has been fully documented and widely discussed.
Many of these have been academics who forsook their university
posts temporarily or permanently to assist the work of various
Civil Service departments through their expertise as economic
advisers. This now familiar pattern was almost reversed in the
career of R. G. Hawtrey—a career in the Home Civil Service
lasting from 1903 to 1945 during which he used his spare
time to write and publish more learned articles and books on
economics than the majority of his academic contemporaries
and established an international reputation for his contributions
to the subject, mainly on the monetary side. As Claude Guillebaud wrote of him in 1944: 'An essentially academic economist,
[Mr. Hawtrey] is attached to no teaching university, but looks
out over the world from the Olympian heights of the Treasury.'

Like many distinguished servants of the Crown, Hawtrey
came into the Civil Service by way of Eton and Cambridge. The
family connection with Eton was an especially strong one; its
members have been associated with the college, both as pupils
and masters, for over four hundred years—the first Hawtrey
was recorded as a King's Scholar at Eton in 1565.

Ralph Hawtrey's grandfather, John William Hawtrey, was
Assistant Master of the Lower School at Eton from 1842 until
1869 and a second cousin of the famous Edward Craven
Hawtrey, Headmaster of Eton from 1834 to 1853 and Provost
from 1853 until his death in 1862. In 1869 John Hawtrey left
Eton to establish a preparatory school, St. Michael's, at Aldin
House, Slough, and later his son, George Procter Hawtrey,
became assistant master there. Hence it was at Slough
that Ralph was born on 22 November 1879, the third child of
George Procter Hawtrey and his first wife, the former Miss Eda
Strahan. The two other children of the marriage—Freda and
Phyllis predeceased their brother, but Freda lived with him in
his London house from the Second World War until her death in
1964.

It was not from Aldin House but from Mr. Brackenbury's school, Pinewoods, Farnborough, that Ralph Hawtrey came to Eton in 1893 as a King's Scholar, with Hugh Macnaghten, later Vice-Provost, as his classical tutor. Hawtrey's interests and abilities were not in classics but in mathematics; at that time, however, there were no mathematical specialists acting as modern tutors. A pupil of Dyer's in mathematics, Hawtrey won the Tomline Prize, Eton's highest mathematical award, in 1896. In the following year he gained a wider distinction, and even some notoriety, when his first article appeared in the *Fortnightly Review* for September 1897.[1] Entitled 'The Speed of Warships', it strongly criticized the then existing system of Admiralty steam trials as giving no accurate comparison of the capabilities of ships in the fleet, and concluded 'Certainly the present system seems anything but satisfactory and something ought to be done as soon as possible to make the trials more dependable'.

That the matter was 'one of great public interest and importance' was admitted by no less a person than Sir William Henry White, then Director of Naval Construction, in a rejoinder published in the next issue of the *Fortnightly* which amounted to an official examination and refutation of Hawtrey's charges. In the meantime it had become publicly known that the article was the work of an Eton boy and Hawtrey's father had been congratulated on his son's distinction by the aged Gladstone himself. In a somewhat ungracious postscript to his own article Sir William White declared 'Had I known the[se] facts I should have made no reply', but nevertheless conceded that 'in many ways the congratulation is deserved'.

From Eton Hawtrey went up to Cambridge in the autumn of 1898, gaining a Minor Scholarship to Trinity. There he read Mathematics and was twice a Prizeman—in his Freshman year and again in his third year. In 1901 he was nineteenth Wrangler —a result which, however creditable, disappointed his old Eton teacher, Dyer, and led another Eton mathematics master, Hurst, to hold Hawtrey up to another Eton pupil, Maynard Keynes, as 'a dreadful example of a person who has tried to do too many things'.[2]

Keynes, with whom Hawtrey's name and works were so often to be linked and contrasted in later years, could not bring himself to agree that Hawtrey had 'lost his soul in knowing something besides Mathematics'. With that judgement Hawtrey

---

[1] *Fortnightly Review*, 72 (New Series), 435–44.
[2] R. F. Harrod, *The Life of John Maynard Keynes* (1951), p. 41.

RALPH GEORGE HAWTREY   365

himself would surely have agreed; he might well have felt that he had not lost his soul but found it. As he himself wrote some seventy years later 'when I went up to Trinity, Cambridge, as an undergraduate I had the good fortune to come under the influence of G. E. Moore, who had just been elected a fellow'; and the influence of Moore's ethics upon him was profound and lasting.

Many of those who, like Keynes, came under the influence of that system of ethics at the beginning of this century later modified their views, but Hawtrey did not. The view which he learned from Moore, 'that the Good is a matter of direct judgment and is not to be explained away in terms of anything else' remained the core of his philosophy all through his long life.

With characteristic reticence, Hawtrey appears never to have written down any details of how he came to gain the interest and approval of Moore; but that he had it is unquestionable for as an undergraduate he was elected to the company of the Apostles, which then included E. M. Forster, Leonard Woolf, Desmond MacCarthy, Lytton Strachey, Roger Fry, and Saxon Sydney-Turner. Hawtrey was in fact one of the Apostles who elected Keynes to membership in 1903 and it was at this time that their long friendship began. Another friendship formed at Cambridge was with Bertrand Russell; here mathematical interests seem to have been the source and when Whitehead and Russell were writing *Principia Mathematica* in 1908, Russell was corresponding with Hawtrey concerning the proof of various theorems.

Many of Hawtrey's Cambridge friends and colleagues were later to form part of the Bloomsbury Group, and he continued his association with them when his career brought him back to London. Readers of the now extensive literature of and on Bloomsbury will thus encounter the name of Ralph Hawtrey frequently—staying in Cornwall with the young Stephens in the summer of 1905, spending Easter at Salisbury in 1908 with G. E. Moore, Lytton Strachey, Keynes, and Rupert Brooke, and from November 1914 joining the company at Lady Ottoline Morrell's Thursday evenings. That company often included the d'Aranyi sisters, all talented musicians, as befitted the great nieces of Joseph Joachim. The three sisters, of whom the youngest, Jelly d'Aranyi, was to become the best known, were then living with their mother at Beaufort Mansions, Chelsea, where Hawtrey also resided at this time. Hence it was that he met the girl who was to become his wife—Emilia d'Aranyi, second of the three. Like her sisters Emilia had exceptional musical ability but while Adila and Jelly were noted violinists, she enjoyed a considerable reputation as a pianist.

Emilia retired from the concert platform after she and Ralph Hawtrey were married in 1915. Their devotion to each other, remarked upon by Virginia Woolf when she encountered them as newly-weds, remained unaltered down the years, although shadowed by Emilia Hawtrey's long illness which lasted over fifteen years prior to her death in 1953.

Throughout the Bloomsbury years Hawtrey, like his fellow Apostle Sydney-Turner, was an established Civil Servant at the Treasury. He said in later years that his decision to work for the Civil Service examinations arose from the fact that while he was still at Eton he had been told that in the Civil Service one could be sure of an income of £1,000 a year by the age of forty, and of a pension too. At all events the prospects were sufficiently attractive in those days to produce intense competition and at least a year's preparation was considered essential for those who attempted the examinations. It seems to have been while engaged in this preparation at Cambridge that Hawtrey received such formal teaching in economics as he ever had—mainly from G. P. Moriarty, who was then acting as Director of Studies for those Cambridge men who intended to enter the open competition for the Home and Indian Civil Services. He also attended some of Clapham's lectures but was never a pupil of Marshall's—contrary to a widespread impression which seems to have developed from later attempts to categorize his theory of the demand for money as 'in the Marshallian tradition'.

A somewhat similar impression prevails that because Hawtrey spent so much of his career in the Treasury he also began it there. Yet in fact when he was successful in the open competition for the Civil Service in 1903 he went first to the Admiralty —perhaps because of his early interest in matters of naval policy. But in 1904 the Treasury's Upper Establishment of twenty-five was increased by the creation of one additional First Class Clerkship. As a result of the subsequent promotions, a new Junior Clerk was needed. One of the Joint Permanent Secretaries, Sir Edward Hamilton (who had begun his career as Gladstone's private secretary) proposed that the vacancy should be filled by 'the transfer from another office of one of the successful competitors at the last examination' and his choice fell on Hawtrey. Hence it was that the latter's long association with the Treasury began in January 1904, as a Second Class

Clerk in what was then the Third Division. In 1909 Hawtrey came into the First (Finance) Division as an acting First Class Clerk, but in 1910 Lloyd George, then Chancellor of the Exchequer, appointed Hawtrey to be his Principal Private Secretary and in that capacity he assisted in the work of preparing the Budget. He became an established First Class Clerk in the summer of 1911 and remained in that grade until appointed Director of Financial Enquiries in 1919.

The Financial Enquiries Branch had been established as a special branch of the Treasury in 1915 'to collect information upon all subjects of general financial interest and to prepare reports from time to time both on its own initiative and also upon any question which may be specially referred to it by the Chancellor of the Exchequer'. The post of Director of the branch was first held by Hartley Withers, but he relinquished it in July 1916, and the position was not filled until Hawtrey was promoted to it on 1 October 1919 with the rank of Assistant Secretary.

The rest of Hawtrey's career at the Treasury was spent in the Financial Enquiries Branch, apart from a period of nine months in 1928–9 when, unusually for a Civil Servant in those days, he was given leave of absence to take up a visiting Professorship at Harvard University. It had been intended that he should retire at the end of 1939, but with the outbreak of war he continued in post until his sixty-fifth birthday in November 1944. Even then his association with the Treasury was not at an end, for he was immediately re-employed to complete the chronicle of its wartime activities on which he had been working and only relinquished his appointment finally in October 1947.

It was in these years between 1919 and 1947 that Hawtrey made his most important published contributions to the development of economics, and between 1919 and 1939 he was the only established Civil Servant in the Treasury who could be considered a professional economist. An attempt to summarize and assess his achievement over these years in the twin spheres of monetary economics and economic policy cannot easily be combined with a narrative outline of his life, and is therefore attempted separately in sections II and III of this memoir.

Hawtrey's standing as a scholar in his chosen field, already recognized by his election to Fellowship of the British Academy in 1935, received further recognition in 1939 when London University conferred on him an honorary D.Sc. (Econ.). He was elected President of the Royal Economic Society for the years

1946–8 and in 1959 his old Cambridge college, Trinity, made him an Honorary Fellow. More significant perhaps was the fact that when the late Professor A. G. B. Fisher resigned the Price Chair of International Economics at the Royal Institute of International Affairs in 1946 the Advisory Committee set up to appoint a successor decided to offer the appointment to Ralph Hawtrey, and he took it up at the beginning of the academic year 1947–8, just after he finally left the Treasury.

Hawtrey served as Price Professor at Chatham House from 1947 until 1952. His position as the holder of a research chair gave him the opportunity to produce revised editions of some of his works—a fourth edition of his best-known book, *Currency and Credit*, and a second edition of his *Economic Aspects of Sovereignty*. He also began a new work, at that time provisionally entitled *Public Spirit, or the Ethics of Social and Political Motives*, an attempt to apply the ethical system of G. E. Moore to the problems of political judgements. His duties, however, required him to act as economic adviser on all aspects of the work of the R.I.I.A. and in consequence he became involved in work on Britain's balance of payments problem and early studies of the prospects and problem of Western European Union. Both of these studies resulted in publications—*The Balance of Payments and the Standard of Living* in 1950 and *Western European Union* in 1949; but the projected book on the ethics of politics did not appear.

After his retirement from the Price Professorship in 1952 Hawtrey seems to have considered that his first task was to use his knowledge of monetary economics to endeavour through public comment to change the course of what he considered to be the basically mistaken financial policies to which successive British governments committed themselves. This he continued to do in a series of books, pamphlets, articles, and newspaper comments right up to the time of his death in 1975. All these writings were dominated, some would have said and indeed did say, vitiated, by his unswerving belief that the devaluation of the pound in 1949 had been excessive and that its consequent under-valuation was the source of most if not all of Britain's international economic problems.

His work on philosophical problems was nevertheless continued; in the long tranquil evening of his life he went on thinking about that 'something else besides mathematics' which had first caught his interest at Cambridge some seventy years earlier, and he left behind at his death the completed typescripts of two books on ethics—*Right Policy: the Place of Value Judgments in Politics*, the final version of the study begun at Chatham House, and another more general work entitled *Thought and Things*.

Until the very end of his life Ralph Hawtrey remained active and interested in the world around him—a world which must have seemed to him almost incredibly different from the stable post-Gladstonian world of the Treasury of 1904, but which he yet looked on with more tolerance and understanding than many younger men could muster. At his Kensington home, 29 Argyll Road, W.8, where his domestic needs were well looked after by his faithful housekeeper Miss Ruse, he received hospitably many economists, making available to them his vast fund of recollections of the making of economic theory and economic policy in the first half of the twentieth century. Professor Richard Sayers who called on Sir Ralph (as he had become in 1956) to congratulate him on his ninety-fifth birthday in November 1974 noted afterwards 'I found him in most ways still the same charming and interesting man I first met some forty-two years ago'. It was Hawtrey's good fortune, perhaps not undeserved, to retain to the last that combination of great intellect and gentle character which impressed themselves on all who came into contact with him.

II

In the early 1960s a reviewer of one of the last in the long series of Hawtrey's books wrote that in it 'Sir Ralph Hawtrey does not disappoint the faithful who expect him to extol the importance first, of bank rate as an instrument of monetary policy and, secondly, of the alleged under-valuation of the pound sterling since it was devalued in 1949'. This neatly summarizes what may be said to be the current stereotype of Hawtrey's economics—dominated in the post-Second World War years by one King Charles's Head, the under-valuation of sterling, and in the inter-war years by another, the view that 'the trade cycle is a purely monetary phenomenon' which might be cured by appropriate adjustments of monetary policy in general and bank-rate policy in particular.

Like all stereotypes, this one contains an element of truth and an element of injustice. Certainly it draws attention to a central feature of Hawtrey's economics—that it was a monetary economics and monetary economics conceived in an international context. Yet that monetary economics was far more subtle and complex than the stereotype would suggest; and while it was certainly the major part of Hawtrey's economic thought it was not the whole; he also published ideas on the scope and method of economics and on the theory of production and distribution, the quality of which cannot fairly be judged by the neglect into which they have fallen.

A notable feature of Hawtrey's economics is its consistency. He was a contributor to the subject for a period of more than fifty-five years and many of the key ideas which he presented in his first book *Good and Bad Trade* (1913) are still to be found in his last, *Incomes and Money* (1967), as in many of the twenty other books which came between. As he himself wrote to Keynes in May 1937 'I have adhered consistently to my fundamental ideas since 1913 and in so far as they have developed and grown the process has been continuous since then. There has not been a departure followed by a relapse. I do not think this conservatism is a merit; indeed I should rather like to go in for something novel and extravagant if I could be convinced of it'.[1]

To some of his contemporaries Hawtrey's ideas appeared at times both novel and extravagant, but their development was undeniably continuous and based upon one fundamental and central idea—that of the wealth value of the monetary unit. Hawtrey, the Cambridge mathematician, came to this idea somewhat in the same way as Malthus, the first Cambridge economist, came to his central idea—through arguing with his father. In the political debates at the beginning of this century George Hawtrey was apparently convinced by the arguments of the tariff reformers while his son Ralph was equally firmly on the side of free trade. The latter was thus led to study with typical thoroughness the speeches of some of the leading politicians of the time and was particularly struck by a point made by Joseph Chamberlain in 1903, to the effect that British exports had not increased over the preceding thirty years. On looking into this he realized Chamberlain's figures related to the *value* of British exports in 1872 and 1902 and that the *volume* of those exports had actually increased substantially.[2] Hence the significance of changes in the general level of prices came home to Hawtrey and he began to study the forces affecting it—a study which was to become a life's work.

---

[1] Hawtrey to Keynes, May 1937; *Collected Writings of John Maynard Keynes*, xiv. 55.

[2] 'The Case for Tariff Reform', speech made in Glasgow by Joseph Chamberlain on 6 Oct. 1903, *Mr Chamberlain's Speeches*, edited by Charles Wood, 2 vols. (1914), ii. 145.

RALPH GEORGE HAWTREY

The basic ideas to which that study led him were outlined in *Good and Bad Trade* some ten years later and could be said to have emerged fully fledged in *Currency and Credit* (1919)—perhaps Hawtrey's most influential work and one which appeared just when he had first reached a senior level in the Treasury through his appointment as Director of Financial Enquiries.

Before examining the content of those ideas it may be useful to look briefly at their sources and the methods which Hawtrey employed in presenting them. It seems fair to say that Hawtrey arrived at the basic ideas of his system in almost complete independence from the work of other economists. In *Good and Bad Trade* there is a striking dearth of references to the contemporary literature of monetary economics—only Irving Fisher's work is actually mentioned by name. *Currency and Credit* has more references to current economic writings, but only from the rather obscure nineteenth-century work of H. D. Macleod on banking and credit does Hawtrey seem to have derived any of the ideas he put forward in the book. All of this is consistent with what Claude Guillebaud, writing with the authority of Sir Ralph himself, put on record in 1964—that 'he learnt his monetary economics as a Civil Servant in the Treasury, and cannot recollect having been influenced by Marshall; though he does acknowledge some indebtedness to Bagehot'.[1]

By what means exactly Hawtrey learnt his monetary economics in the Treasury can only be surmised; but it seems likely that he was considerably influenced by Sir John (afterwards Lord) Bradbury, who became Joint Permanent Secretary in 1913 and under whom Hawtrey had served in the Finance Division ('1D') from 1909. When, in his old age, Hawtrey reminisced about the Treasury he always described Bradbury as the ablest man he ever encountered in the Civil Service and stressed the intimate knowledge of City activities and the working of the monetary system which he possessed. Given the lack of close relations between the Treasury, the Bank of England, and the City before 1914, such knowledge was unusual and it seems likely that when the young Hawtrey began to look at the monetary system from the Treasury his view was largely formed with the aid of Bradbury's experience.

Although there seems no reason to question Hawtrey's disclaimer of any influence on him from Marshall, the method which he used in his economics was curiously similar to Marshall's. An able mathematician, as Marshall was, Hawtrey

[1] *Economic Journal*, 74 (June 1964), 475.

relegated any mathematics he used in his economic writings to footnotes and appendixes, and eschewed diagrams, as Marshall did. Clear, straightforward prose was the essential medium through which he conveyed his ideas. Many of those ideas were such as to admit of statistical testing and it must seem strange to modern economists that while Hawtrey sometimes discussed the possibilities of such testing he never attempted to carry it out; unlike Irving Fisher, that other leading theorist of the price level, he was not among the pioneers of econometrics. That cannot have been because of any lack of ability to command the necessary techniques; rather it may have been, as with Marshall, the result of a recognition of the qualitative complexity of reality. Certainly, like Marshall, Hawtrey had a great respect for the historical method; Keynes in 1920 remarked on the fact that 'so pure a theorist as Mr. Hawtrey should be so interested in economic history'. It was an interest which never waned and some of the historical studies which he made in search of evidence to support or disprove his theories are major works of scholarship in themselves; *A Century of Bank Rate* (1938) is the outstanding example.

Any attempt to outline the theories which Hawtrey developed with the aid of these methods must first set out the essentials of his monetary economics. Perhaps a summary can best begin from his own words in the Preface to the fourth (1950) edition of *Currency and Credit*:

The theme of the book in its original form was the underlying unity of certain economic happenings: inflation; the cyclical alternations of activity and depression; financial crises; disturbances of the balance of payments and rates of exchange. All these were to be traced to changes in the wealth-value or purchasing power of the money unit, and changes in the wealth value of the unit, as indicated by the price level, are symptoms of changes in the consumers' income and outlay.

The foundation of the whole theory is the function of the credit system as the source of money. The banks create the means of payment by lending, and thereby are in a position to regulate the flow of money.

Hawtrey conceived the economy which he sought to analyse as composed essentially of consumers and traders—a term which he used to include not only producers, but wholesalers, retailers, and dealers—to whom the interest cost of holding stocks is of special significance. 'Consumers' income' he defined simply as the total of incomes expressed in money, 'consumers' outlay' as the total spent *out of income*—whether on consumable goods and services or on the acquistion of capital assets. Any difference

RALPH GEORGE HAWTREY   373

between the income and outlay of an individual consumer over an interval of time is reflected in his cash balance; the total of consumers' and traders' balances—the total of money and bank credit—Hawtrey referred to as the 'unspent margin'.

For each individual consumer the appropriate money balance will bear a determinate proportion to his income, and for each trader it will bear a determinate proportion to his turnover. Consumers and traders can release or absorb cash by altering these proportions—or as a result of increases or decreases in the supply of credit made available by the monetary authorities. Hence, to quote Hawtrey again, 'an expansion of credit is a device for causing a release of cash and a contraction of credit a device for causing an absorption of cash'. A contraction of credit, for example, will produce an absorption of cash, and a reduction of consumers' outlay. Retail sales will be reduced in consequence; retailers and wholesalers find themselves holding increased stocks and cut orders to producers who in turn reduce output and employment. Traders will seek to stimulate sales by reducing prices, and the fall of prices tends to relieve the situation but 'the process of readjustment will not be complete till wages are reduced in proportion to prices and pending that stage there is likely to be unemployment'.

Through the machinery of credit, bankers thus possess the power of regulating consumers' income and outlay, and hence the level of prices and of employment. But, Hawtrey argued, there is an inherent instability in the creation of bank credit. In the opening chapters of *Currency and Credit* Hawtrey showed with great clarity that a pure credit system would not be self-righting, but could generate cumulative falls or rises in money demand, employment, and prices because 'an increase in the supply of credit itself stimulates the demand for credit, just as a restriction in the supply of credit leads to a decline in the demand for credit'.

Pointing out that 'the expansive tendencies of credit are in perpetual conflict with the maintenance of a fixed standard of value, and a great part of our subject is taken up with the problem of how best to reconcile this conflict', Hawtrey moved to consider the case of an economy with a central bank which adheres to a gold standard and hence must be guided in its credit policy by the foreign exchanges. In these circumstances he argued that there would be a tendency for the instability of credit to take the form of a cycle. A period of expanding credit leads to rising incomes, prices, and employment, but ultimately also to a drain on the gold reserves of the banking system;

bankers are then forced to protect their reserves by contracting credit and raising rates of interest. The resultant effects on consumers' income and outlay and on traders' holding of stocks is to produce a period of falling prices and employment. Reserves are restored and ultimately bankers will seek to extend credit again at rates of interest which being below even the reduced profit rates experienced by traders serve to create a fresh expansion.

It was on this analysis that Hawtrey based his famous dictum that 'the trade cycle is a purely monetary phenomenon'. As such it could be controlled and even prevented by the use of monetary weapons, primarily Bank Rate. To the objection that rises in Bank Rate served only to over-correct an over-expansion when it had already gone too far Hawtrey always replied that this was because the Bank of England and other central banks under the gold standard were 'guided by a very tardy signal' in the state of the gold reserves. To prevent a slump it was necessary sooner to control the previous boom, through the use of a credit policy designed to stabilize consumers' income and hence general demand and the price level. Clearly no single national central bank could operate such a policy individually while adhering to the rules of the gold standard. Hence it followed that if the international gold standard system was to be preserved some form of international action to prevent variations in the wealth-value of gold was essential.

From this outline it can be seen that the theory of the trade cycle which gained so much attention from Hawtrey's contemporaries in the inter-wars years was in fact only a particular case of the general monetary model which he evolved—and a case of limited interest to him for he always insisted that the trade cycle as such had ceased to exist after 1914—the post-1918 world economy, whatever its instabilities, did not seem to him to exhibit the same regular periodicity.

The general monetary model itself might now be characterized as a fairly simple aggregate demand macro-model with near-perfect markets and a minimum of structural rigidities in it. Its originality and pioneering significance only becomes evident when it is remembered that Hawtrey developed it during the war of 1914–18 and that it was published in 1919, four years before Keynes produced his *Tract on Monetary Reform*. It is not surprising then that Keynes regarded Hawtrey as his 'grandparent in the paths of errancy'.[1]

[1] J. M. Keynes, 'Alternative Theories of the Rate of Interest', *Economic*

The question of the relations between the ideas of Keynes and the ideas of Hawtrey is a fascinating one which has already been the subject of one detailed paper and may well provide material for more.[1] The two men had ample opportunities for discussion, both at Cambridge and in the Treasury, prior to 1919 and the extent and effect of those discussions can only be a matter for conjecture. Yet there seems no reason to reject the view suggested by the quotation given above, that the first influence was of Hawtrey on Keynes, rather than Keynes on Hawtrey. Here Hawtrey's lack of contact with Marshall is significant, for while Keynes had to emancipate himself from the 'classical economics' which he had learned from Marshall, Hawtrey was always independent of it. So he was able to lead the way in the transition from the quantity-theory approach to the short-period analysis of changes in income prices and employment which characterized the monetary economics of the inter-war years.

The character of the relationship between the thinking of Keynes and Hawtrey as it stood before the appearance of *A Treatise on Money* was well stated by Keynes himself in a discussion at the Royal Statistical Society in December 1929: 'There are very few writers on monetary subjects from whom one receives more stimulus and useful suggestion than from Mr. Hawtrey, and I think there are few writers on these subjects with whom I personally feel in more fundamental sympathy and agreement. The paradox is that in spite of that, I nearly always disagree in detail with what he says!'[2]

In the case of both the *Treatise* and the *General Theory* Keynes sent copies of the proofs to Hawtrey before publication. Hawtrey took immense pains to produce detailed criticisms, which he afterwards published,[3] but in spite of the most sincere efforts to understand each others' doctrines, the differences between the approaches of the two men seemed to grow as Keynes's ideas developed from the *Treatise* to the *General Theory*. Yet it may well be, as Professor E. G. Davis has suggested, that Hawtrey was influential in setting Keynes on the path which led from one book to the other, by drawing his attention to the

Journal, 47 (June 1937), reprinted in *Collected Writings of John Maynard Keynes*, xiv. 202.

[1] E. G. Davis, 'The Role of R. G. Hawtrey in Keynesian Economics and the Economics of Keynes', *Carleton Economic Papers*, No. 77-12.

[2] *Collected Writings of John Maynard Keynes*, xiii. 127.

[3] His critique of the *Treatise* appears in the *Art of Central Banking*, pp. 332–411, that of the *General Theory* in *Capital and Employment*, pp. 164–232.

importance of changes in output at a time when, as Sir Austin Robinson put it 'Keynes was still thinking primarily of the factors which made prices go up and down'.[1]

After the *General Theory* there developed what Sir John Hicks in 1939 described as 'the great dispute about the working of monetary control—a dispute which has made most English economists either Keynesians or Hawtreyans'.[2] Hawtrey, following out the implications of his basic model, stressed the key influence of Bank Rate on short-term interest rates generally and thus on the cost to traders of holding stocks.

Keynes did not believe in the effectiveness of this mechanism and argued that only in so far as a change in Bank Rate affected the terms on which long-term capital could be raised by industry would it affect economic activity. Hawtrey devoted a great deal of effort to a detailed examination of the historical evidence on the effects of Bank Rate on short- and long-term borrowing and it is now accepted that the case he made against Keynes's view in *A Century of Bank Rate* (1938) was conclusive.[3]

If Hawtrey's reaction to the *General Theory* was mainly to reaffirm his belief in the correctness of his own basic monetary model he did nevertheless introduce some modifications and innovations in his own ideas as a result of his studies not only of the work of Keynes but also of other monetary theorists such as Hayek and Harrod. Some of these changes are to be found in *Capital and Employment*, others in the fourth edition of *Currency and Credit* published in 1949. Perhaps the most notable feature of *Capital and Employment* was an analysis of the time structure of production and the physical processes of long-term investment along the lines of Jevons and Böhm-Bawerk—something which had been absent from the earlier books. It was in this context that Hawtrey introduced the useful distinction between the processes of 'capital widening' and 'capital deepening'. On it he based the argument that 'if the widening of capital equipment is insufficient to absorb the available flow of new savings, it is this favourable state of the investment market that ought to induce the deepening process and restore equilibrium'.

This conviction of the ability of the market to produce

[1] E. A. G. Robinson, 'John Maynard Keynes 1883–1946', *Economic Journal*, 57 (Mar. 1947), 39.

[2] J. R. Hicks, 'Mr. Hawtrey on Bank Rate and the Long-term Rate of Interest', *The Manchester School*, 10 (1939), 21.

[3] For a fuller discussion of this see Sir John Hicks, 'Hawtrey', *Economic Perspectives* (1977), pp. 118–33.

equilibrium between savings and investment was probably one of the main sources of difference between Hawtrey and Keynes. But Hawtrey did modify his position on it to some extent, and in the 1949 edition of *Currency and Credit* conceded that in his earlier writings he 'took for granted too readily that money saved would be invested and that money invested would be spent'. Among his unpublished papers a piece which he had intended to use in this edition but did not suggests further concessions towards the Keynesian viewpoint—notably in these words: 'But over longer periods the fluctuations of working capital become less significant; the increments of working capital due to growth are small compared to the increments of instrumental capital. And the growth of instrumental capital is itself susceptible of wide fluctuations.'[1]

It was always a corollary of Hawtrey's analysis that the economy, although lacking any automatic stabilizer, could nevertheless be effectively stabilized by the proper use of credit policy; it followed that fiscal policy in general and public works in particular constituted an unnecessary and inappropriate control mechanism. Yet Hawtrey was always prepared to admit that there could be circumstances in which no conceivable easing of credit would induce traders to borrow more and in such a case government expenditure might be the only means of increasing employment.

This possibility of such a 'credit deadlock' was admitted in all Hawtrey's writings from *Good and Bad Trade* onwards, but treated as a most unlikely exceptional case. In *Capital and Employment*, however, he admitted that 'unfortunately since 1930 it has come to plague the world, and has confronted us with problems which have threatened the fabric of civilisation with destruction'.

So indeed it had, and in the years that followed opinion, both academic and political, became increasingly convinced that the solution lay in the methods of stabilization by fiscal policy which followed from Keynes's theories rather that in those of stabilization by credit policy which followed from Hawtrey's.

To quote Sir John Hicks, 'Hawtrey would not admit that that is the end of the story';[2] nor is it, but it is the end of a central chapter. For during his years at the Treasury, when his official position involved him in matters of policy, Hawtrey appeared to the world primarily as a theorist. When he had left

[1] Hawtrey Papers, Churchill College, Cambridge, 6/5/17.
[2] Hicks, loc. cit, p. 123.

the Treasury he used his monetary theory mainly to criticize policy. Hence a discussion of his post-1949 writings, especially on the alleged under-valuation of the pound, will follow more naturally after a consideration of his role in policy during his Treasury career.

III

It was not until he was appointed Director of Financial Enquiries in 1919 that Hawtrey was sufficiently highly placed in the Treasury to be party to the inner processes of policy-making. He was already in the Treasury at the time of the financial crisis of 1907 and could recall Bradbury watching the drain of gold from the Bank of England and considering the possibility of a suspension of the Bank Act. The resolution of the crisis must have given him an early lesson in the efficacy of Bank Rate, even if only as a spectator of events. When he became private secretary to Lloyd George in 1910–11 this seems to have remained his role; although Hawtrey had been sent to America with an Inland Revenue official to collect information on United States local taxes in connection with Lloyd George's land-tax proposals he did not write a report on this and in later years he recalled how he 'sat in a corner' while Lloyd George dictated his 1911 budget speech.

After his promotion to First Class Clerk and move to '1D' in the summer of 1911 Hawtrey began to be assigned to work of greater significance; thus he assisted Basil Blackett in the preparation of the Memorandum on Gold Reserves in May 1914, which the Chancellor had called for following the bankers' request for a Royal Commission to examine the whole question of the size and control of gold reserves in London.[1] In the more famous crisis of August 1914 Hawtrey worked with Bradbury and admired his swift appreciation of the need for a special issue of currency notes; in the formulation of the necessary policy and its implementation '1D' played a significant part and Hawtrey gained valuable experience as a member of that small team. No doubt that experience grew as the Treasury's functions in economic management expanded during 1914–18, but in the story of those years Hawtrey's name does not figure prominently —certainly not as prominently as that of Keynes, for whom the special 'A Division' was carved out of the Finance Division in 1917.

[1] See R. S. Sayers, *The Bank of England 1891–1944*, i. 65 and iii. 3–30.

RALPH GEORGE HAWTREY   379

Nevertheless it was the First World War which led to the creation of the Financial Enquiries Branch and it was his appointment as Director of this branch which gave Hawtrey the opportunity to comment on and sometimes to participate in policy-making in the inter-war years. Under the very broad remit which was given to the branch Hawtrey drew up many and varied reports and memoranda on economic and financial matters which are now to be found among the papers of senior Treasury officials of that period, but the impression prevails that they did not often receive much attention, and that the Financial Enquiries Branch under Hawtrey was something of a backwater. Churchill's jocular demand that 'the learned man should be released from the dungeon in which we were said to have immured him, have his chains struck off and the straw brushed from his hair and clothes, and be admitted to the light and warmth of an argument in the Treasury Boardroom' has been more than once quoted.[1] Sir Warren Fisher's explanation to the Public Accounts Committee in 1936 of the work of the Financial Enquiries Branch was rather in the same genre: he felt that the Committee probably knew of Hawtrey, 'who works away on metaphysics and writes learned books and concerns himself primarily with the theory of higher finance . . . he is really continually examining into the theoretical side (at least as it seems to me the theoretical side), and we pull a stop out when we want something from him'.[2]

In the Treasury of the twenties and thirties Hawtrey was no doubt a rather unusual figure, perhaps almost the first of the 'back-room boys'. It would be a mistake to think that as such he was unimportant. Sir Warren Fisher did go on to tell the Public Accounts Committee that 'supposing some rather delicate exchange issue comes along to the Under-Secretary . . . he would get hold of Hawtrey and say "you ought to know all about this" and he would advise'; and Churchill's sally can be read as a criticism of his officials for not making sufficient use of the special expertise which Hawtrey could provide.

In fact the advice which Hawtrey gave always followed logically from his conviction that the central objective of policy, national and international, must be to stabilize the wealth-value of the monetary unit. Consequently the extent to which it was acceptable to his administrative and political superiors inevitably

[1] P. J. Grigg, *Prejudice and Judgment* (1948), p. 82.
[2] Minutes of Evidence taken before the Committee of Public Accounts, 30 Apr. 1936; *House of Commons Papers 1935/36*, 131–48, p. 399.

varied. When Hawtrey took up his position as Director of Financial Enquiries in the autumn of 1919 the movement towards a dearer money policy was beginning and that winter the Cabinet accepted the recommendations of the Cunliffe Committee favouring financial retrenchment in preparation for a return to the gold standard at the pre-war parity. On the whole Hawtrey agreed with these recommendations at this time and in March 1920 he advised the Chancellor (Austen Chamberlain) in favour of an increase in the Treasury bill rate which would allow a rise in Bank Rate to 7 per cent. This was in line with his credit theory, according to which the prospect of dear money should serve to change expectations of a further rise in the price level. But, unlike Keynes, who was disposed to advocate a prolonged period of dear money, Hawtrey felt that high rates of interest should continue only for a short time and by the beginning of 1921 he was advocating a reduction. In April 1921 he was writing to Blackett that 'the drastic deflation effected, here and in America, since last spring [is a] most remarkable confirmation of the theory of control of credit through the discount rate' and later he advocated a return to pre-war practice of frequent changes in Bank Rate.

The problem, however, was that a return to the gold standard at the old parity seemed to require continued deflation. Hawtrey accepted that 'the justification for struggling back through all the admitted difficulties to our pre-war pound of 113 gr. of fine gold is that this parity would command confidence in a way that no other could. . . . The risk of a crisis arises chiefly from a too rapid reduction of prices. The best safeguard against it is to make the deflation slow.' In addition, Hawtrey did not consider that struggling back to the old parity necessarily meant restoring all the other features of the pre-1914 gold standard. His preference, stated in a paper to Section F of the British Association in 1919, was for a gold exchange standard with international agreements on uncovered paper issues and control of credit, with a view to keeping the gold value of commodities (measured by an index number) more or less constant.

An opportunity to have this plan, or at least something approaching it, carried into effect seemed to offer when an International Economic Conference was called by the Supreme Council of the Allies at Genoa in April 1922. Hawtrey was a member of the British Delegation and his participation in framing the resolutions on monetary policy and central banking

adopted by the Conference was perhaps the highest point of
his influence in economic policy-making; certainly the Genoa
Resolutions always remained for him the most important
guidelines in international economic co-operation. This was
because they enshrined the principle of joint action by central
banks to regulate credit 'not only with a view to maintaining the
currencies at par with one another, but also with a view to pre-
venting undue fluctuations in the purchasing power of gold'.
To Hawtrey this was the key to stabilization not merely of
prices, but of incomes and employment: the wealth-value of the
money unit must be kept steady and there must be international
action to achieve it.

In preparing his proposals for Genoa Hawtrey had discussions with Montagu Norman, with whom he had begun to
build up contacts after his appointment as Director of Financial
Enquiries gave him greater freedom to act in this way. The
Board of Trade attempted to water down Hawtrey's proposals
but with Blackett's support he contrived to have the full version
brought forward at Genoa and adopted by the Conference.

Hawtrey himself recognized that 'in one respect the Genoa
Resolutions are really unsatisfactory. It is impossible to point to
any particular time at which effect can be given to them.' The
twelfth Resolution did indeed request the Bank of England to
call a meeting of central banks 'as soon as possible' and Norman
sent out invitations with a view to a meeting in September 1922.
Many felt that it should be postponed pending a political
settlement of war debts with the result that 'there was never
after 1922 any practical approach, and co-operation was left to
develop in concerted attacks on particular problems rather than
in general assembly round a single table'.[1]

At this time, however, Hawtrey still thought that a return to
gold would afford a basis for developing international price
stabilization along the lines of the Genoa Resolutions and that it
might be achieved without rapid or serious deflation. To this end
he pinned his hopes on a rise in the American price level and in
1923 he was writing memoranda in favour of an export of gold
to the United States, ostensibly as part of debt repayment, but
with the objective of provoking a rise in American prices. This
proposal 'emanated from the Bank' but it is not surprising that
Hawtrey gave it warm support at the Treasury for he had
advocated something of the kind as early as 1920. For a time it
was seriously discussed, but a fresh weakness of the pound in

[1] Sayers, *The Bank of England 1891–1944*, p. 162.

May 1923 put it out of court. Despite the opposition of Hawtrey and Niemeyer at the Treasury, who still favoured the gold shipment plan, Norman succeeded in having Bank Rate raised in July 1923 and the path to parity via orthodox deflation was resumed. Nevertheless even in March 1924 Hawtrey was arguing that 'it is still open to us to bring about an inflation of dollar prices and improve the exchange market without causing any set back to prices here'.

So in the debate which raged during 1924 concerning the priorities as between price stabilization and the return to gold there can be little doubt as to where Hawtrey's sympathies lay. Yet when the question of restoring the gold standard became practical politics in 1925 the answer which he gave to Churchill's well-known 'examination paper' was to the effect that it was 'both a British and world-wide interest that the pre-war system should be restored . . . exchange stability cannot be obtained at present by any other method than the gold standard'. However, he added that no active measures should be necessary before the end of the year; it was to be hoped that the exchange would come to par of itself and even if it did not credit contraction would still be undesirable.

Naturally Hawtrey was deeply disappointed and worried by the actual course of events which followed. Once he realized that the gambles on which the return to gold in 1925 had been based had not come off he moved into the position which he occupied at least until 1928, if not 1931, that of a persistent critic of British monetary policy and a persistent admirer of the American Federal Reserve. It was scarcely a popular stance for a Treasury official to take in those years; it placed Hawtrey in opposition to Norman and the Bank of England and sometimes to his own superiors as well, but he was fearless in his defence of it. When Bank Rate was raised to 5 per cent at the end of 1925 he characterized the move as 'nothing less than a national disaster' and he regarded its continuance as a major cause of falling prices not only in Britain but also in the United States. 'It is still true', he wrote in a Treasury memo at the end of 1927, 'that the Bank of England and the Federal Reserve Banks are pulling in opposite directions, the former contracting credit and the latter expanding. But whereas till last summer the Bank of England had prevailed and world prices had been falling now New York has the upper hand and world prices are either stationary or rising. From the point of view of this country that is a highly desirable state of affairs. . . .' Hawtrey had always a

high admiration for the way in which Benjamin Strong had
handled the credit policy of the Federal Reserve in the 1920s and
considered that Strong's death in 1928 was a major misfortune
for international monetary relations.

It could be said that Strong's task in these years was easy by
comparison with Norman's; if the $4.86 parity was to be main-
tained how could it be done without the pressure of a high Bank
Rate? One suggestion which Hawtrey put forward in 1927,
when the amalgamation of the Bank of England and Treasury
note issues was under consideration, was the abandonment of
the principle of fixed fiduciary issue and indeed of any legal
regulation of gold reserves—'there is no real need for the legislature to give any directions to the Bank of Issue except to
maintain convertibility into gold'. It was a far-sighted proposal,
but it drew from Niemeyer the comment, 'Far too theoretical,
and dangerous for the Bank', and no more was heard of it.[1]

In fact Hawtrey was always prepared to be unorthodox within
the terms of his own credit theory, but not beyond it. In 1929
the Liberal proposals for a major public works programme to
reduce unemployment, supported by Keynes and Henderson,
met with a bleak official response in the White Paper *Memoranda
on Certain Proposals relating to Unemployment*. It was widely believed
that Hawtrey had some responsibility for this 'Treasury view' of
the inefficacy of public works to generate employment; certainly
he saw no virtue in the public works proposals as such, but he
was as eager as Keynes to see the level of unemployment reduced.
The memoranda which he wrote on this subject in June 1929,
only weeks after his return from Harvard, show him translating
the Liberal proposals into his own terms:

> The virtue of Mr Keynes's plan, as advocated by the Liberal Party, is
> that the extensive schemes of capital outlay by the Government would
> affect the balance of payments by diverting part of the country's savings
> from external to internal investment. That would make possible an
> increase in the consumers' income, without which additional employment
> in one direction is bound to be offset by reduced employment in others
> . . . But there is another device which would likewise serve the
> purpose. Suppose the British government issues a loan on the London
> market and applies the proceeds to paying off Treasury Bills. . . . With
> fewer Treasury Bills the banks would seek other short-term commercial
> bills or advances. In so far as this occurs the government will have
> applied the resources diverted from external investment to provide
> additional working capital for industry and trade. . . . The fall of prices

[1] See ibid., p. 288.

and the unemployment are precisely the effects which ought theoretically to be expected from the policy of high discount rates which has prevailed since 1924. In so far as the funding of Treasury Bills stimulated short term lending . . . this disastrous tendency will be checked and, it is to be hoped, will be reversed.

Thus was Keynesian unorthodoxy translated into Hawtreyan unorthodoxy, but no hint of it appeared within the covers of the White Paper. As has been indicated above, Hawtrey's attitude towards the theoretical possibilities of increasing employment through public works underwent some modification in the thirties, but he nevertheless remained profoundly sceptical of their value in practice: in a 'Memorandum on Fiscal Policy during the Depression' prepared for the League of Nations in 1937 he compared British and American experience and concluded: 'The facts give no support to the theories of those experts who are inclined to assume that budget policy is the decisive factor in increasing or decreasing economic activity.'

These were not fashionable words even in 1937 and perhaps they give some indication of the reasons for the comparative decline of Hawtrey's influence in matters of policy which seems to have occurred in the thirties. For he held firmly to his basic monetary theories in a world where circumstances were changing rapidly and new advisers were growing up to interpret them in different ways.

In the evidence which he gave before the Macmillan Committee in 1930 Hawtrey was still arguing for international price stabilization along Genoa lines and urging that the Bank of England could and should give a lead in this respect by abandoning dear money. But by the spring of 1931 he had recognized that devaluation or depreciation of sterling was inevitable and was refusing to write memoranda in support of maintaining the $4.86 parity.[1]

After Britain had left the gold standard in September 1931 he was among those who produced memoranda on exchange-rate policy; his advice was to peg the pound at a new rate of £1 = $3.40, a 30 per cent devaluation, and subsequently to raise or lower the rate in line with movements of the world price level. Hawtrey's reasons for choosing a 30 per cent devaluation were typical—30 per cent was the extent of the fall in world prices since 1925, at which date he was prepared to assume that wages and prices had been in 'tolerable equilibrium'. At this time at

[1] Moggridge, *British Monetary Policy, 1924–1931*, p. 228.

RALPH GEORGE HAWTREY   385

least it seems that Hawtrey's views about the appropriate valuation of sterling and the concept of managing it in relation to world prices were in line with those of Keynes and of his Treasury superiors, although H. D. Henderson felt that the $3.40 valuation was too low.[1]

Henderson at this time was Joint Secretary of the Economic Advisory Council, of which Keynes was a member, and in 1932 its Committee on Economic Information gave its backing to what has come to be known as the 'Keynes–Henderson plan' for an international note issue, as part of the proposals to raise world prices and revive trade to be submitted to the World Economic Conference in 1933. Initially Hawtrey, when asked to comment, was decidedly sceptical; despite his growing anxieties about the 'credit deadlock' he still felt that central banks could if they chose do all that was necessary for revival through open market operations. Nevertheless he went on to concede that 'if it *did* become a practical proposition, I should say by all means press it for all it is worth. . . . It would require very careful handling to avoid landing the world in a fresh series of monetary fluctuations, and that careful handling would certainly not be forthcoming, but this danger seems to me less serious than a continuance of existing conditions.'

On the whole, however, the Treasury reaction to the Keynes–Henderson plan was that it was not a practical proposition to put forward to an international conference. In the search for a simpler and less ambitious plan Hawtrey was involved with Sir Frederick Phillips, Sir Otto Niemeyer (now at the Bank of England), and Sir Cecil Kisch, Secretary to the Financial Department of the India Office. The result, the 'Kisch plan', called for a redistribution of existing gold stocks through an International Credit Institute, probably controlled by the Bank for International Settlements. Although it seemed unlikely that this plan would ever secure American official support, the Treasury still hoped to bring it forward at the conference. In the event, before this could be done the World Economic Conference was effectively broken up by Roosevelt's 'bombshell' declaration that stabilization was not a matter for governments and that he could not obligate the United States to approve the export of gold.

Earlier in 1933 Hawtrey had predicted that Roosevelt 'will make a great effort to avoid devaluing the dollar'. In spite of

[1] See Howson and Winch, *The Economic Advisory Council 1930–1939*, pp. 102–5.

this and of the blow to international co-operation which Roosevelt's later actions involved, Hawtrey was inclined to be sympathetic when Roosevelt adopted the so-called 'Warren Plan' and raised the domestic price of gold in September of the same year. Despairing of seeing effective international co-operation to raise and stabilize the world price level, Hawtrey now envisaged exchange depreciation as the only way in which a country like the United States could 'break the credit deadlock by making some branches of economic activity remunerative'. Not unnaturally there were those, like Per Jacobsson of the Bank for International Settlements, who found it hard to reconcile this apparent enthusiasm for exchange depreciation with Hawtrey's previous support for international stabilization schemes. To them his reply was 'the difference between what I now advocate and the programme of monetary stability is the difference between measures for treating a disease and measures for maintaining health when re-established. It is no use trying to stabilise a price level which leaves industry under-employed and working at a loss and makes half the debtors bankrupt.' Here, as always, Hawtrey was faithful to the logic of his system, which implied that if international central bank co-operation could not be achieved, each individual central bank must be free to pursue its own credit policy, without the constraint of fixed exchange rates.

The lessons of the breakdown of international economic co-operation during the thirties had much to do with what Sir David Waley described as 'A curiosity of history', the fact that 'during a Total War in which unexampled efforts and sacrifices had to be made to avert defeat . . . a large proportion of the time and energy of the Treasury was devoted to the elaboration of post-war Utopias'.[1] Again, as in the First World War, Hawtrey was not involved in the major policy decisions to the extent which Keynes was—much of his time in the later years of the war was devoted to compiling his detailed chronicle of the evolving activities of the Treasury since 1939—but he saw and wrote comments on most of the plans for the post-war economy which circulated within government. Some of the papers in his files from this period show him, as so often before and afterwards, swimming against the tide of received opinion—for at a time when most economists were concerned with the problems of

[1] Waley, 'The Treasury during World War II', *Oxford Economic Papers*, Supplement to vol. v (1953), p. 47; quoted in Henderson, *The Inter-War Years* (ed. H. Clay), Introduction, p. xxvii.

maintaining full employment after the war and expressing fears of renewed deflation, Hawtrey was warning of the dangers of inflation which the post-war world would face.

In these papers can be seen the first hints of ideas which Hawtrey published and kept on developing and presenting in later years. When plans for international monetary co-operation had finally taken shape in the International Monetary Fund he gave them a very qualified welcome in *Bretton Woods for Better or Worse* (1946). 'It is no part of my purpose to find fault with the plan itself', he wrote. 'Given effective safeguards against undue variations in the wealth-value of the principal money units, whether upwards or downwards, the Bretton Woods plan might be a useful instrument of international co-operation. But without such safeguards it is likely only to complicate and aggravate the resulting troubles. Especially is the much-vaunted "expansionist" policy likely to end in disaster. If depression is to be staved off by uninterrupted monetary expansion, the time is bound to come when the continuance of expansion is found intolerable.'

In the years immediately after the end of the Second World War it seemed to Hawtrey that the lessons of deflation, which he had so often had to explain in the twenties, had now been too well learned. Not surprisingly, he was critical of the continuance of cheap money and the neglect of bank rate. 'The demand is for a vehicle without a brake', he wrote in the Preface to the fourth edition of *Currency and Credit*, dated June 1949. 'Due regulation of the flow of money requires means not only of expansion but of contraction. For contraction Bank Rate remains the indispensable instrument.'

By 1949 it seemed to Hawtrey that in Britain 'redundant money and easy credit' had created a state of over-employment through demand inflation, but not an inflation of wage costs. In this situation as he saw it the devaluation of the pound was a policy mistake of the same order of magnitude as the return to the pre-1914 parity had been in 1925. 'Whatever the illusions in Government circles in 1949 as to the state of costs in the export industries, there was never any pretence that the devaluation from $4.03 to $2.80 was not far greater than any supposed disparity of costs could have justified', he wrote in 1955. 'The idea that wages and costs could be prevented from adjusting themselves to the rate of exchange thus reduced was quite chimerical. The rate of exchange set a standard for wages and prices, which in course of time they were bound to reach. If five years have passed without their attaining it, this is because the standard itself has been continually receding: it has risen higher and higher, as American wages and prices have been raised.'[1]

This was the essence of the message which Hawtrey continued to preach in books, articles, and letters to the press all through the fifties and sixties. In those years, when 2 or 3 per cent per annum inflation seemed a very small price to pay for full employment, it was not a message which many people cared to hear. There were some economists, like Harry Johnson, who recognized 'the suggestive value of an independent approach to the problem of sterling, which attempts to view it from a broader angle than that of the immediate state of the international reserves'. But to the great majority of the profession Hawtrey seemed to be a venerable figure incorrigibly attempting to apply the ideas of the past to the problems of the present; and as he went on reiterating his message they tended to become embarrassed and inattentive.

Yet Hawtrey's thesis was not without foundation; the authors of a recent carefully researched account of inflation in Britain argue that it is 'quite plausible to assume that in 1954 sterling was still undervalued following the excessive devaluation of 1949' and indeed find evidence for the persistence of under-valuation into the mid 1960s.[2] The authors of this particular study make no reference to Hawtrey's theories, but other aspects of his work have gained fresh recognition in recent years. Thus modern exponents of the monetary approach to the balance of payments, who stress that an excess supply of money will be reflected in all the other accounts of the balance of payments, recognize that this theory is to be found in *Currency and Credit* and was applied by Hawtrey in many of his factual studies.[3]

It is not hard to see the reasons for such a revival of interest in Hawtrey's work, nor to predict how far it may go. The more economists are convinced that 'money does matter' the more they are likely to be impressed by Hawtrey's analysis. For some thirty years after the publication of the *General Theory* they became and remained on the whole convinced that it did not matter, or at least not much, and Hawtrey's reputation declined. In the last ten or twelve years more and more of them have

[1] *Cross-Purposes in Wage Policy*, p. 71.

[2] R. J. Ball and J. Burns, 'The Inflationary Mechanism in the U.K. Economy', *American Economic Review*, 66 (1976), 475–6.

[3] Cf. J. A. Frenkel and H. G. Johnson, *The Monetary Approach to the Balance of Payments*, pp. 34 and 37.

become convinced afresh that money does matter and while this continues Hawtrey's reputation may well rise again. Economics is a very fashion-ridden subject and Hawtrey made few concessions to fashion. To him what he had thought to be true in 1913 still seemed true in 1973—in a money economy changes in the wealth-value of the monetary unit have consequences, which can be understood, but not escaped.

IV

The contributions to monetary theory and policy which have been discussed in the two preceding sections are numerous and distinguished. Whatever Hawtrey's reputation may now be or become it has never been disputed that in its day his monetary work was on a par with that of Keynes, Robertson, and other leading thinkers in that field. Consequently this tends to be seen as the whole of his achievement; but the fact is that if every one of his publications on monetary economics were deleted from it the list of his writings would still exceed in quantity and quality that of many of his contemporaries. For it would include books such as *The Economic Problem, Economic Aspects of Sovereignty, Economic Destiny, Economic Rebirth, and* articles such as his Presidential Address to the Royal Economic Society on 'The Need for Faith' and his 1960 paper on 'Production Functions and Land—a New Approach'.

In *Economic Destiny* (1944) Hawtrey identified two 'vital matters' besides the monetary in which he held that economics 'has failed to base guidance on conviction—it offers no accepted theory of profit . . . and . . . it has not taken sufficient account of power as a continuing and dominant object of economic policy'. Much of his own thinking and writing in the books and papers already mentioned was devoted to these problems. On them he formulated ideas of his own which, typically, were both unorthodox and durable. They have attracted little attention, but Hawtrey would himself have regarded them as ultimately of more significance than his better-known monetary work and an understanding of them is fundamental to any complete appreciation of his economic thought.

It seems to have been as a result of his emphasis on the place of traders in the economy that Hawtrey arrived at his concept of profit. He stressed that profit must be seen not merely as a margin between selling price and costs but also as a proportion of turnover, to which profit income is proportional. Profits depend on selling power—the skill, efforts, and opportunities of traders—and not on uncertainty, for without uncertainty there could still be great inequality in the amounts which different traders sell. 'Free competition', Hawtrey argued, 'tends to establish a common standard between incomes derived on the one hand from salaries and on the other from profit on a very modest turnover. Beyond that free competition has *no* tendency to keep down the incomes derived from profit.' Hence profit is 'quite definitely an exception to the general principle of the equalisation of rates of remuneration through the labour market. There is here a congenital malformation of the individualist economic system.'

Profits thus appeared to Hawtrey as the principal source of inequality under what he called 'competitivism', but he recognized that they were essential to it both as an incentive to enterprise and a source of accumulation. Within an economy this implied that a division of the product of industry between wage-earners and profit-makers which preserved the incentive to enterprise on the one hand without exploiting the workers on the other was of the greatest importance, but Hawtrey was extremely doubtful of the capacity of the collective bargaining process to achieve this because 'there is no independent and generally recognised standard of what is fair in wage agreements. What the defects of the profit-making and wage-fixing systems together could lead to in a market economy he saw clearly enough: 'If the existence of a level of profits no more than sufficient to provide the requisite stimulus to enterprise for maintaining full employment, is seized upon as a signal for demands for higher wages, the result can only be chronic unemployment combined with a progressive depreciation of the wealth value of the monetary unit, the worst of both worlds.'

On the other hand, Hawtrey attached much importance to the links between accumulation out of profits and the pursuit of power, both by the individual and the state. Wealth gave power to 'men of substance' who would seek to use it to influence public policy in their own interests. At the same time it afforded a source of power on which the state could draw through taxation and borrowing especially in time of war. Hawtrey also emphasized the relationships between accumulation, the export of capital, and imperialism. He was under no illusions as to the persistence of mercantilism in practice if not in theory, and while he expounded the benefits of international investment he also showed how it could be used as an instrument of power.

RALPH GEORGE HAWTREY

The pursuit of power by nation states could involve war or the threat of war and so contribute to what he often described, in a phrase borrowed from Lowes Dickinson, as 'the International Anarchy'.

This exposition of the defects of the competitive system might seem to be powerful enough to amount to an indictment of it—an indictment which would lead on naturally, as it did for many, to an acceptance of collectivism as a preferable alternative. Hawtrey did indeed devote much space in several of his books to a careful appraisal of collectivism, but he never accorded it unqualified approval. His condemnation of totalitarianism, whether fascist or communist, was unreserved; but he considered that democratic socialism was a possibility. The major problem it would present would be the establishment of an effective economic discipline to take the place of the profit motive, and Hawtrey predicted that 'in fact the reconciliation of liberty with economic discipline may turn out to be the greatest problem of our economic destiny'. Neither in competitivism nor in collectivism did he envisage an easy solution of it.

The reasons for this seemingly ambivalent attitude must be sought in Hawtrey's view of the relation between economics and ethics. 'Economics', he wrote in 1928, '*cannot* be dissociated from ethics' and there is no evidence that he ever departed from this position. It was a position almost diametrically opposed to that which was adopted, or was coming to be adopted, by most economists at that period: they were increasingly becoming uncomfortable with the propositions about utility which formed the basis of welfare economics as presented by Pigou and endeavouring to give their subject a strictly positive character. Hawtrey had no desire, however, to bring back the utilitarian ethics into economics. In fact he specifically attacked Pigou's conception of economic welfare as consisting of such satisfactions as are amenable to the measuring-rod of money. Hawtrey contested this identification of welfare with satisfaction, arguing that 'the consumer's preferences have a very slight relation to the real good of the things he chooses'. Hence it followed that 'the aggregate of satisfactions is not an aggregate of welfare at all. It represents good satisfactions which are welfare and bad satisfactions which are the reverse.'

Now this clearly implies an ability to define and distinguish good and bad satisfactions which most economists would have denied that, *as economists*, they possessed. They sought to narrow the scope of the subject by excluding all ethical considerations from it: Hawtrey sought to widen it by specifically importing into it a non-utilitarian system of ethics—the ethics of G. E. Moore. As has already been stressed in section I, Moore's view of an inherently valid Good was always the core of Hawtrey's philosophy. Hence while to most economists what is good would be subjective, to Hawtrey it was objective.

It was thus, as he explained to his colleagues of the Royal Economic Society in his Presidential Address in 1946, that he accounted for economists' lack of authority in public affairs: 'The answer, I believe, is to be found in a dissociation of their reasoning from any accepted ethical background.' Hence they did indeed fail to base guidance on conviction: yet 'if the economists' conclusions are to command faith, they must be directed to right ends. And surely a fundamental condition of any faith is that there *are* right ends.'

Hawtrey himself had no doubt that there are right ends, and also false ends. 'By a false end', he wrote in *The Economic Problem*, 'we mean something which is so generally and almost certainly valuable as a means, that people seek it without considering for what end it is to be used.' The cult of money-making and the cult of national-power he characterized as the pursuit of false ends. Both communism and individualism, he considered, shared the view that wealth was '*the* part that matters' in welfare, and he did not share it with them.

Hawtrey's union of ethics with economics enabled him to bring within it many topics which those who treat the subject as a strictly positive science would regard as excluded from it. Hence today when positive economics is somewhat out of fashion and economists permit, and admit to making, value judgements Hawtrey's ideas in this field are also beginning to be noticed again[1] and may be more attended to in future.

Whatever may be thought of Moore's system of ethics, there can be no doubt of its profound influence on Hawtrey's thinking over seventy years. That influence can be seen indirectly in many of his economic writings, but it was only in the unpublished works *Right Policy: the Place of Value Judgments in Politics* and *Thought and Things*, left behind at his death, that he endeavoured to set out his philosophy fully and directly. In the first of these works he sought to apply 'the ultimate criterion of the Good' not merely to economic problems but to political issues, both national and international. Part of his argument was that the study of value judgements was not dependent on philosophy,

[1] See, for example, Scitovsky, *The Joyless Economy* (1976).

but in his last book, *Thought and Things*, he turned to philosophical speculation itself, seeking in particular to develop his 'theory
of Aspects', a theory of aesthetic perception which he had first
presented at a meeting of Virginia Woolf's Friday Club in 1910,
so that it could provide a means of reconciling the existence of
differences about ends and means with the concept of an
inherently valid Good.

V

Throughout this account of Hawtrey's life and work a certain
element of paradox has been evident. A mathematician and a
philosopher, he chose to spend his working life dealing with
practical problems. An adviser on economic policy, he made a
world reputation as an economic theorist. In debates on matters
of economic theory in the twenties and thirties his name was
most frequently linked with the name of Keynes and in a sense
his career was almost the inverse of that of Keynes: for although
it may be true, as Professor Patinkin has recently said, that 'the
major revolution effected by the *General Theory* was in the field of
theory, not of policy'[1] it is nevertheless the case that Keynes,
who operated from an academic base, had an enormous influence on policy, and notably on Treasury policy in the Second
World War. By comparison Hawtrey, who worked from an
official base, had more influence on academic thought than ever
he had on Treasury policy, although ultimately his influence
was less than that of Keynes in both areas.

It may be suggested that Keynes's ideas were better adapted
to the circumstances of his time than were Hawtrey's; the full
reasons for Keynes's comparative success and Hawtrey's comparative failure remain to be investigated and assessed by historians of economic thought and policy. In that assessment, some
part should be allowed to character and temperament. All those
who knew him concur in the view that Ralph Hawtrey was truly
a gentle man. He had the qualities of the pedagogue rather than
the propagandist and consequently it was natural that he should
have had more success in academic circles than in the corridors
of power.

Writing about C. P. Sanger in 1930, Lowes Dickinson
described him as belonging to 'a certain type' of Cambridge

[1] D. Patinkin, 'Keynes' Monetary Thought', *History of Political Economy*,
8 (1976), 19.

man: it seems fair to suggest that Hawtrey was another of that same type:

It is a type unworldly without being saintly, unambitious without being inactive, warm-hearted without being sentimental. Through good report and ill such men work on, following the light of truth as they see it; able to be sceptical without being paralysed; content to know what is knowable and to reserve judgement on what is not. The world could never be driven by such men, for the springs of action lie deep in ignorance and madness. But it is they who are the beacon in the tempest, and they are more, not less, needed now than ever before. May their succession never fail![1]

R. D. COLLISON BLACK

For help in compiling this memoir I am indebted to Mr. J. H. P. Hawtrey; Mrs. E. Panton, Sir Ralph Hawtrey's executrix; Professor R. S. Sayers; Sir Alec Cairncross; and Lord Robbins. I am also grateful to Professor D. E. Moggridge and Mrs. Patricia Bradford who gave me much assistance in connection with Sir Ralph's manuscripts and papers now in the Archives Centre, Churchill College, Cambridge; to Mr. J. W. Ford for access to files remaining in H.M. Treasury; to Ms Susan Howson, who allowed me to see an advance copy of her paper on Hawtrey presented at the International Economic History Congress, Edinburgh, 1978; and to Mr Patrick Strong, Keeper of Eton College Library, for details of Sir Ralph's career at Eton. Mrs J. Wright, Research Officer in the Department of Economics, Queen's University, Belfast assisted in finding many references and preparing the bibliography of Sir Ralph's writings.

BIBLIOGRAPHY

1897 'The Speed of Warships', *Fortnightly Review*, 72 (New Series) (Sept.), 435–44.
1913 *Good and Bad Trade. An inquiry into the causes of trade fluctuations* (Constable, London).
1917 'Note on Mr. Middleton's Pamphlet on German Agriculture', *Economic Journal*, 27 (Mar.), 143–5.
1918 'The Bank Restriction of 1797', ibid. 28 (Mar.), 52–65.
      'The Collapse of the French Assignats', ibid. (Sept.), 300–14.
1919 *Currency and Credit* (Longmans & Co., London).
      'The Gold Standard', *Economic Journal*, 29 (Dec.), 428–42.*

[1] G. Lowes Dickinson, *Nation and Athenaeum*, 22 Feb. 1930. Quoted in J. M. Keynes, *Essays in Biography, Collected Writings*, x. 325.

* Reprinted in *Monetary Reconstruction*.

RALPH GEORGE HAWTREY   395

1921   *The Exchequer and the Control of Expenditure* (World of Today, London).
        'The European Currency Situation', *Revue de metaphysique et de morale*
        (Armand Colin, Paris).*

1922   'The Federal Reserve System of the United States', *Journal of the Royal
        Statistical Society*, 85 (Mar.), 224–55.*
        'The Genoa Resolutions on Currency', *Economic Journal*, 32 (Sept.),
        290–304.*

1923   *Monetary Reconstruction* (Longmans & Co., London).

1924   'Discussion on Monetary Reform', *Economic Journal*, 34 (June), 155–76.
        'The Tenth Annual Report of the Federal Reserve Board', ibid.
        283–6.

1925   'Public Expenditure and the Demand for Labour', *Economica*, 5 (Mar.)
        38–45.†
        'Currency and Public Administration', *Journal of Public Administration*,
        3 (July), 232–45.†

1926   *The Economic Problem* (Longmans & Co., London).
        'The Trade Cycle', *De Economist*, 75 (Feb.), 169–85.†
        'The Gold Standard and the Balance of Payments', *Economic Journal*,
        36 (Mar.), 50–68.†
        'Mr. Robertson on Banking Policy', ibid. (Sept.), 417–33.

1927   *The Gold Standard in Theory and Practice* (Longmans & Co., London).
        'The Gold Standard', I–IV, *Journal of the Institute of Bankers*, 48 (Jan.–
        Apr.), 4–20, 53–67, 108–122, 176–90.
        'The Monetary Theory of the Trade Cycle and its Statistical Test',
        Quarterly Journal of Economics, 41 (May), 471–86.

1928   'What is Finance?', *The Accountant*, 78 (Jan.), 13–19.†
        Trade and Credit (Longmans & Co., London).

1929   'London and the Trade Cycle', *American Economic Association, Papers and
        Proceedings*, 19 (Mar.), 69–77.
        'The Monetary Theory of the Trade Cycle', *Economic Journal*, 39
        (Dec.), 636–42.

1930   *Economic Aspects of Sovereignty* (Longmans & Co., London).
        'Money and Index Numbers', *Journal of the Royal Statistical Society*, 93
        (Part I), 64–85.
        'Charles Percy Sanger', ibid. (Part II), 316.

1931   *Trade Depression and the Way Out* (Longmans & Co., London).
        'Consumers' Income and Outlay', *Manchester School*, 2, 45–64.

1932   *The Art of Central Banking* (Longmans & Co., London).
        'The Portuguese Bank Notes Case', *Economic Journal*, 42 (Sept.), 391–8.

1933   'Mr. Robertson on "Saving and Hoarding" II', ibid. 43 (Dec.), 701–8.
        'Public Expenditure and Trade Depression', *Journal of the Royal
        Statistical Society*, 96 (Part III), 438–58.

1934   '"The Theory of Unemployment" by Professor A. C. Pigou',
        Economica, 1 (New Series) (May), 147–66.
        'Australian Policy in the Depression', *Economic Record*, 10 (June), 1–10.
        'Monetary Analysis and the Investment Market', *Economic Journal*, 44
        (Dec.), 631–49.
        'Stabilisation of the Franc and French Foreign Trade: a Comment',
        ibid. 729–30.

* Reprinted in *Monetary Reconstruction*.   † Reprinted in *Trade and Credit*.

1935 'Sir Basil Blackett', *Journal of the Royal Statistical Society*, 98 (Part IV), 775-7.

1936 'French Monetary Policy', *Economica*, 3 (New Series) (Feb.), 61-71.

1937 *Capital and Employment* (Longmans & Co., London).
'Alternative Theories of the Rate of Interest: Three Rejoinders, III', *Economic Journal*, 47 (Sept.), 436-43.
' "Essays in the theory of employment" ', *Economica*, 4 (New Series) (Nov.), 455-60.
'The Credit Deadlock' in *The Lessons of Monetary Experience, essays in honour of Irving Fisher* . . . , edited by A. D. Gayer (Farrar and Rinehart, New York), pp. 129-45.

1938 *A Century of Bank Rate* (Longmans & Co., London).
'Professor Haberler on the trade cycle', *Economica*, 5 (New Series) (Feb.), 93-7.

1939 'Mr. Harrod's Essay in Dynamic Theory', *Economic Journal*, 49 (Sept.), 468-75.
'Interest and Bank Rate', *Manchester School*, 10, 144-56.

1940 'Money and Money of Account', *The Accountant*, 102 (Jan.), 11-14.
'The Trade Cycle and Capital Intensity', *Economica*, 7 (New Series) (Feb.), 1-15.
'Mr. Kaldor on the Forward Market', *Review of Economic Studies*, 7 (June), 202-5.

1941 'Professor Hayek's Pure Theory of Capital', *Economic Journal*, 51 (June-Sept.), 281-90.

1943 'Competition from Newcomers', *Economica*, 10 (New Series) (Aug.), 219-22.
'W. A. Shaw', *Economic Journal*, 53 (June-Sept.), 290.

1944 *Economic Destiny* (Longmans & Co., London).
'Livelihood and Full Employment', *Economic Journal*, 54 (Dec.), 417-22.

1946 *Economic Rebirth* (Longmans & Co., London).
Bretton Woods for Better or Worse (Longmans & Co., London).
'The Need for Faith', *Economic Journal*, 56 (Sept.), 351-65.
'Sir Charles Addis (1861-1945)', ibid. 507-10.
'Lord Keynes', *Journal of the Royal Statistical Society*, 109 (Part II), 169.

1947 'Irving Fisher', ibid. 110 (Part I), 85.

1948 'Monetary Aspects of the Economic Situation', *American Economic Review*, 38 (Apr.), 42-55.

1949 *Western European Union. Implications for the United Kingdom* (Royal Institute of International Affairs, London).
'The Function of Exchange Rates', *Oxford Economic Papers*, 1 (New Series) (June), 145-56.

1950 *The Balance of Payments and the Standard of Living* (Royal Institute of International Affairs, London).
'Multiplier Analysis and the Balance of Payments', *Economic Journal*, 60 (Mar.), 1-8.

1951 'The Nature of Profit', *Economic Journal*, 61 (Sept.), 489-504.

1954 *Towards the Rescue of Sterling* (Longmans & Co., London).
'Relative Strength of the Pound and the Dollar', *Bankers' Magazine*, 178 (July), 1-8.
'Keynes and Supply Functions', *Economic Journal*, 64 (Dec.), 834-9.

RALPH GEORGE HAWTREY

1955   *Cross-Purposes in Wage Policy* (Longmans & Co., London).
       'Bank Rate or Restriction of Credit?', *Bankers' Magazine*, 180 (Oct.), 265–72.
       'Basic Principles and the Credit Squeeze', ibid. (Dec.), 447–51.
1956   'Employment and Bank Rate', *Bankers' Magazine*, 181 (Mar.), 219–25.
       'Keynes and Supply Functions', *Economic Journal*, 66 (Sept.), 482–4.
       'Mr. Harrod on the British Boom', ibid. (Dec.), 610–20.
       'Approach to Convertibility', *Bankers' Magazine*, 182 (Dec.), 435–42.
1957   'Light on Montagu Norman's Policy', ibid. 183 (June), 505–9.
       'Questions for the Radcliffe Committee', *Oxford University Institute of Statistics Bulletin*, 19 (Nov.), 307–13.
       'Timing of Bank Rate', *Bankers' Magazine*, 184 (Dec.), 419–25.
1958   'Bank Rate: Progress and Prospects', ibid. 185 (Apr.), 285–91.
       'New Credit Measures and the Balance of Payments', ibid. 186 (Aug.), 90–6.
1959   'Implications of Convertibility', ibid. 187 (Apr.), 281–7.
1960   'Production Functions and Land: a new approach', *Economic Journal*, 70 (Mar.), 114–24.
1961   *The Pound at Home and Abroad* (Longmans & Co., London).
1962   'The Chancellor's Letter', *Bankers' Magazine*, 193 (Feb.), 99–107.
       'The Fourth Report of the Council on Prices, Productivity and Incomes', *Economic Journal*, 72 (Mar.), 251–4.
1964   'Diagnosis', *Bankers' Magazine*, 198 (Dec.), 341–5.
1966   'The Employment Tax and the Balance of Payments', ibid. 202 (July), 7–12.
1967   *Incomes and Money* (Longmans & Co., London).
       International Liquidity (University of Surrey, London).
1969   'The Case for a Floating Pound', *Bankers' Magazine*, 207 (June), 343–8.
       'The Return to Gold in 1925', ibid. 208 (Aug.), 61–7.
       'A Stable Floating Pound', ibid. (Dec.), 275–80.
1970   'Stopping Inflation, Nine Per Cent', ibid. 210 (Nov.), 201–6.

PART THREE

FROM POLITICAL ECONOMY TO ECONOMICS: THE WORK OF W.S. JEVONS

8

Transitions in Political Economy

I: Economic Analysis

I

The University of Manchester has been generous in its commemoration of the work of Jevons, having celebrated not only the centenary of his birth in 1835, but that of his first seminal papers to the British Association in 1862, that of the appearance of his *Theory of Political Economy* (hereafter referred to as *TPE*) in 1871, and the centenary of his death in 1882. It was my good fortune to be associated with the last three of these celebrations and when I came to think about what I should say on the occasion of the 1982 commemoration it was natural that I should start by considering what if anything, apart from the accidents of Jevons's own biography, links these three dates.

If one accepts the textbook conventions and sees Jevons as sharing with Menger and Walras in the striking intellectual coincidence usually labelled 'the Marginal Revolution', then it might seem that the 1971 celebration should stand by itself as the most significant one from the standpoint of the history of ideas. On the other hand, if one takes the view which I have always done (Black, 1972e, p.364) that the term 'Marginal Revolution' refers to a process rather than an event, then it can be argued that this process really occupied the whole of the 20 year period from 1862 to 1882 and perhaps longer. It was this idea that those years which comprised virtually the whole of Jevons's active life as an economist can be seen essentially as a period of transition in which classical economics was coexisting with and only gradually giving way to neo-classical economics which I decided to take as the theme to be developed in my Manchester Special Lectures.

The view of the years after 1870 as years of fairly slow transition is one which is well known and widely accepted among historians of economic thought. Professor D.P. O'Brien has very persuasively traced the way in which classical economics developed out of the *Wealth of Nations* and how its importance survived well beyond what we think of as the 'Marginal Revolution', and in doing so he identifies the characteristic of the post-1870 period 'as one of transition rather than of revolution' (O'Brien, 1983; in 1994, pp.34, 41). Essentially the same view is adopted by Professor Mark Blaug when, under the heading 'The Slow Uphill Struggle', he writes that 'the historical problem ... is to explain, not the point in time at which the marginal concept was applied to utility, but rather the delayed victory of marginal utility economics' (Blaug, 1985, p.307).

For the most part those who have accepted this view of the replacement of classical political economy by neo-classical economics as a fairly protracted process of transition have been looking at that process in a wider context and a longer perspective. Consequently they have generally described the transition itself in fairly broad terms, pointing out how in the last quarter of the 19th century some economists were pioneering in the development of new ideas, while others still employed the old ones. In such accounts the name of Jevons normally appears prominently among the pioneers of the new approach.

Now since I have no quarrel with this broad interpretation of the Marginal Revolution, it might seem that there is no more to be said, but I suggest that something fresh may be learnt by switching from the broad view to a narrower focus, from a long perspective to a shorter one. So I propose here to look more closely at the process of transition from the classical to the neo-classical research programme, rather than concentrating on its outcome. Let us try to look not, as we usually do, at the view from the present day but rather at the view from 1882. If we can place ourselves mentally at that vantage point I think we shall recognize that in England at least neo-classical economics was not fully established even by then, and if from then we look closely at the part which Jevons played in its establishment I believe we shall see more clearly the transition process taking place within the work of Jevons as much as between the work of, say, Cairnes and Jevons or Mill and Marshall.

In an excellent account of the 'remarkably sudden and rapid collapse of credibility and confidence' in the classical orthodoxy which occurred in Britain in the late 1860s and early 1870s, Professor T.W. Hutchison has stressed that this collapse 'seems to have been common to and more or less simultaneous among both the handful of competent contributors to economic theorizing and the wider "educated class" of the general reviews' and was 'concerned with policy and method as well as theory' (Hutchison, 1972, pp.442-3).

II

In the extensive debates produced by this crisis of confidence, methodology figured prominently, and it seems appropriate to consider it first here, since it affected not only theory but to some extent applied economic studies also. Moreover, it is a topic which loomed much larger when seen in the short perspective of the years from 1862 to 1882 than it does at the distance of a century and more.

One of the main criticisms levelled against classical political economy in those years was that it had come to rely too much on 'the abstract, *a priori* and deductive method', starting 'with the assumption of a "knowledge of ultimate causes" and deduces the phenomena from the causes so assumed' (Leslie, 1879b, p.241). Leslie argued for 'the deletion of the deductive method of Ricardo' and its replacement by an entirely inductive and historical approach and in this respect he was at the time the leading exponent of a methodology which had the support of a significant body of social and economic thinkers in England (*cf.* Koot, 1980). To many of the readers of the 'general reviews' in the 1860s and 1870s it must have seemed that the 'new political economy' which was going to supersede the old would use the historical method.

In a review of John Neville Keynes's *Scope and Method of Political Economy* in 1891, Edgeworth told how he 'once heard the question put to a lecturer: "Are you in favour of the Old or the New Political Economy?" "I am in favour of the true Political Economy," the person thus interrogated replied with sufficient readiness' (Edgeworth, 1891, p.420). The lecturer quoted might well have been Edgeworth's former friend and mentor W.S. Jevons, for in the methodological disputes of his time Jevons always took a balanced position. Despite his many criticisms of J.S. Mill, Jevons held him to be 'substantially correct in considering our science to be a case of what he calls the Physical or Concrete Deductive Method' and he refused to heed calls for that method to be abandoned: − 'as regards the fate of the deductive method, I disagree altogether with my friend Mr. Leslie; he is in favour of simple deletion; I am for thorough reform and reconstruction' (Jevons, 1879a, pp.18, xvi).

In the years between 1868 and 1874 when he devoted much time to the preparation and writing of his *Principles of Science* Jevons had made a more profound study of scientific method than perhaps any other economist before him (Schabas, 1990, p.78).   In the process he developed his view that 'Induction is an *inverse operation*, the inverse of Deduction, and can only be performed by the use of deduction.   Possessing certain facts of observation, we frame an hypothesis as to the laws governing those facts; we reason from the hypothesis deductively to the results to be expected; and we then examine these results in connection with the facts in question; coincidence confirms the whole reasoning; conflict obliges us either to seek for disturbing causes, or else to abandon our hypothesis' (Jevons, 1879a, p.19).[1]

Such was the method elsewhere described by Jevons as 'the complete inductive method', which 'combined deductive reasoning with empirical verification'.   He criticized those who fell into the 'fallacy of exclusiveness', 'speaking of inductive reasoning as if it were entirely distinct and opposite to deductive reasoning' (Jevons, 1876; in 1905, pp.192, 195).   Jevons saw no distinction between the natural and the social sciences so far as method was concerned; hence when this general methodology was applied to economics in particular it seemed evident to him that advocates of the historical and comparative approach such as Leslie 'may succeed in constituting a new science, but they will not utterly revolutionise and destroy the old one in the way they seem to suppose' (1876; in 1905, p.197).

It seemed equally evident to Jevons that 'Political Economy is in a chaotic state at present, because there is need of subdividing a too extensive sphere of knowledge'.   Consequently, he predicted 'there will be division into branches as regards the subject, and division according to the manner of treating the branch of the subject.   The manner may be theoretical, empirical, historical or practical' (Jevons, 1879a, pp.20, xvii).   Jevons envisaged one new branch of economic study, Economic Sociology, using the historical method,[2] but as regards the theoretical, empirical and practical branches he was emphatic that '*our science must be mathematical, simply because it deals with quantities*' (1879a, p.3).

This, to my mind, was the most novel, indeed revolutionary, aspect of Jevons's views on the method of economics.   In other respects his proposals were likely perhaps to give more encouragement to the advocates of the New Political Economy than the Old, but even these latter could hardly object to such a firm defender of the deductive method, although he did declare it to need reform and reconstruction. To declare unequivocally that the science *must* be mathematical was a different matter and neither the upholders of classical orthodoxy, nor the proponents of historical economics could bring themselves to endorse this idea with any enthusiasm.

Professor Schabas has argued persuasively that 'on many issues regarding method, the differences between Jevons, Cairnes and Mill were not as great as numerous remarks in the secondary literature suggest' and that 'while exonerating Mill, the proponents of the historical method tackled Cairnes rather than Jevons as the absolutist' so that 'in the various debates that ensued over the validity of the inductivist approach, Jevons emerged more or less unscathed' (Schabas, 1990, pp.109, 110). However she reminds her readers that while Cairnes allowed 'that some of the doctrines of political economy may be exhibited mathematically' in principle he regarded 'the practice with profound distrust', as indeed did Mill (*ibid.*, pp.101, 108).

Similarly, while the inductivists may not have attacked Jevons directly for his support of the deductive method, both Leslie and Ingram were openly critical of his use of mathematics.[3] (*Cf.* Leslie, 1879a, p.160; Ingram, 1888; 1915 ed., p.227). In the present context it is interesting that Ingram in 1888 described Jevons's prediction that economics would come to be divided into a number of branches, each studied by its appropriate method, as 'one of those eclectic views which have no permanent validity, but are useful in facilitating a transition. The two methods will doubtless for a time coexist, but the historical will inevitably supplant its rival.' The process of transition whereby Economics became a mathematical science was to prove a long one, but even in 1879 Jevons could tell Walras 'my impression is that the mathematical method is really making great progress though little is said about it' (21 February 1879: Black, 1972d-81c, hereafter referred to as *P & C*, V, p.22).

Although he displayed a considerable, and growing, respect for the historical method in Economics, on methodological issues there was no transition in Jevons's own ideas: they were carefully thought out and consistently applied. From the fact that *TPE* was abstract and mathematical while his later, unfinished *Principles of Economics* was institutional and literary in form, one might be tempted to accept the view put forward by Henry Higgs, who edited Jevons's manuscript of the *Principles*, that 'such economists as Cairnes had been unable to read the mathematical *Theory*, and Jevons, like Cournot before him, felt impelled to follow up his mathematical treatise by a volume written in plain language for the general reader' (Higgs, Preface to Jevons, 1905, p.v.) The evidence now available shows that this was not the case: Jevons regarded his *Principles* as complementing the earlier *TPE*, not superseding it, and practised what he preached by using what he saw as the appropriate method for each work (Black, 1992b, pp.126-7).

III

I turn now to consider that fundamental part of economic analysis which in 1882 (and indeed for some 60 years afterwards) was known as the Theory of Value and Distribution. Arguably it was in this branch of the subject that the transition from the classical to the neo-classical approach was most marked in England by 1882 and certainly this owed much to the influence of Jevons's work. It was in the theory of value that Jevons had deliberately sought to be a revolutionary, to provoke change. In seeking to gain for *TPE* in 1871 the attention which his 'Notice of a General Mathematical Theory of Political Economy' had failed to secure in 1862, Jevons deliberately overstressed the difference between his approach and that of his predecessors, putting at the opening of the first chapter the bold and bald assertion that 'value depends entirely upon utility' (1871, p.2).

It is this assertion, and his subsequent development of the concept of 'final degree of utility' which 'determines value' to which numerous commentators over the years have pointed as establishing Jevons as one of the founders of subjective value theory. Yet in *TPE* Jevons was not really attempting to present a theory of value and distribution in what later became the accepted neo-classical form at all.[4] What he was attempting to present he stated clearly in the Preface to the first edition: 'In this work I have attempted to treat Economy as a Calculus of Pleasure and Pain', and 'the great problem of Economy' he summed up at the close of the book as

'Given, a certain population, with various needs and powers of production, in possession of certain lands and other sources of material: required, the mode of employing their labour so as to maximise the utility of the produce' (Jevons, 1871, pp.vii, 255, emphasis in original).

Once the significance of these plain statements is grasped, the layout of *TPE* can be seen to follow logically from them. Having discussed method in his Introduction, Jevons next sets out the basic Theory of Pleasure and Pain, drawing directly on Bentham. There follows the Theory of Utility, showing how pleasure is derived from the consumption of commodities. This brings us to the centrepiece of the work, the Theory of Exchange, with its demonstration of how utility is increased by exchange, and how the parties to exchange can maximize utility. The ensuing Theory of Labour is then to be seen as the correlative of the Theory of Utility: 'Labour is the painful exertion which we undergo to ward off pains of greater amount, or to procure pleasures which leave a balance in our favour' (Jevons, 1871 p.162). This chapter provides a theory of cost of production in terms of disutility, not a theory of wages.

I have previously described the structure of *TPE* up to this point as 'perfectly symmetrical, and perfectly Benthamite' (Black, 1971b, p.19) and I see no reason to modify this description. But before Jevons's Concluding Remarks the book contains two further chapters – Theory of Rent and Theory of Capital. On the face of things, when taken along with the Theory of Labour these seem to be obviously the titles of chapters containing a typical tripartite theory of distribution or factor pricing and many commentators have interpreted their contents in just this way.

There is an alternative explanation, which I have long contended fits the circumstances of the case much better. The first five chapters of the book develop the theory of economy as a calculus of pleasures and pains – which can only be felt by human beings. Yet in the production of commodities to satisfy wants, humans must have the help of non-human agents – consequently a discussion of the role of land and capital is essential. A certain asymmetry comes into the treatment here – Jevons does not follow his Theory of Labour with a Theory of Land and a Theory of Capital, nor switch to a Theory of Rent and a Theory of Interest. Instead a Theory of Rent is followed by a Theory of Capital.

The explanation of this seems to me to be that Jevons's Theory of Rent was a corollary of the Theory of Labour designed to explain how, when labour is combined with land, a surplus over and above the 'necessary recompense' for the pain of labour can emerge. The Theory of Capital, however, is formally separate from the rest of the book because 'there is no close or necessary connection between the employment of capital and the processes of exchange. Both by the use of capital and by exchange we are enabled vastly to increase the sum of utility which we enjoy, but it is conceivable that we might have the advantages of capital without those of exchange' – for example, in the case of an isolated man. 'Political Economy, then, is not solely the science of Exchange or Value; it is also the science of Capital' (Jevons, 1871, pp.212-13).

As to 'the science of Exchange or Value' certain features of Jevons's treatment of it have particular relevance to my theme of transition. By claiming that 'value depends entirely upon utility' he undoubtedly made a sharp break with the accepted classical theory but equally he did not set out what later came to be the accepted form of value theory among neo-classicals who, as Dr Peach puts it, 'believed themselves well rid of Utilitarianism' (Peach, 1987, p.1014). Jevons, by contrast, 'appears to have shared with his classical predecessors the view that a theory of value must go beyond the phenomena of demand and supply to some more fundamental explanation which for him was to be found in utility, not labour' (Black, 1990b, p.12). The idea that utility was a concept of special significance to Jevons, notwithstanding the difficulties of its measurement, is one which has been increasingly recognized in recent studies. Professor Schabas has brought it out clearly, suggesting that for Jevons the problem of economics was 'to determine the laws of utility which give rise to relative price changes .... Ideally, then, an explanation in pure economic theory would consist of the reduction of the phenomena of the economy, the movement of the prices and quantities in the market, to individual mental states, to the mechanics of self-interest and utility' (Schabas, 1990, p.88; and *cf.* White, 1989, pp.441-3).

However, what Jevons called 'the theory of the equilibrium of utility' necessarily involved consideration of the quantities of commodities produced to satisfy wants and the disutility of the labour expended in their production. So when he asserted that 'value always depends upon degree of utility, and labour has no connection with the matter', he immediately added the qualification 'except through utility' (Jevons, 1874b, as reprinted in *P & C*, VII, p.83).

In the second half of his chapter on 'Theory of Labour' in *TPE* Jevons dealt with 'Relations of the Theories of Labour and Exchange' and the general result of this largely neglected part of his analysis is, as he put it, 'to confirm the prevailing doctrine that the values of commodities tend to become approximately equal to their cost of production' (*P & C*, VII, p.83). (For a fuller discussion of this analysis, *cf.* Black, 1971b, pp.24-5 and Peach, 1987, p.1016.) Now what did Jevons mean by 'cost of production'? I have argued elsewhere (1971b, pp.26-7) that 'it would be impossible to regard Jevons as accepting "foregone alternatives" as explaining the ultimate nature of costs', and many passages in his Theory of Labour chapter show that 'costs to him are in the last analysis painful efforts and sacrifices, real costs in the old classical sense'. So here – in the treatment of value where Jevons sought to be regarded, and came to be regarded, as at his most 'revolutionary' – the transitional character of his analysis comes out clearly, a novel and subtle theory of exchange between utility maximizers being coupled with a theory of production which, although presented mathematically, remains essentially classical.

As to the Theory of Distribution, this is perhaps the area in which the difference between the long view and the short is most evident. In many recent commentaries on the history of the theory classical distribution analysis has been presented as in essence a surplus theory whose exponents 'sought to explain all shares of income other than wages in terms of the residual or "surplus" left after the wage goods in the support of labourers and what is necessary for the replacement of the used-up means of production have been deducted from the annual output. Hence it is a characteristic feature of the classical theory of value and distribution that wages are taken to be given, *i.e.* determined in another part of the analysis.' On the other hand it is widely accepted 'that a characteristic feature of the marginalist or "neo-classical" approach consists in the fact that all kinds of incomes are explained *symmetrically*: wages, profits and rents are taken to be determined by the forces of supply and demand in regard to the services of the respective "factors of production", labour, "capital" and land' (Kurz and Salvadori, 1994, pp.36-7, emphasis in original).

In the short perspective of the years between 1862 and 1882 the state of the theory of distribution appeared very different from this. As Edwin Cannan showed in 1893, there had long been a tendency among the English classical economists to wander from the consideration of what he called 'Distribution Proper' – the division of the whole produce between aggregate wages, aggregate profits, and aggregate rents – into the discussion of 'Pseudo-Distribution' – wages per head, profits per cent and rent per acre (Cannan, 1893; 1903 ed., pp.229, 339).

Of the different theories which the classical economists had evolved to explain the determination of these rates, only the theory of rent had much sophistication and by the 1860s dissatisfaction with them, and especially with the wages-fund theory, was increasing. Yet although J.S. Mill's famous recantation of the wages-fund doctrine was published in 1869, effectively undermining the classical distribution analysis, no reasonably complete account of the marginalist theory of functional distribution appeared in English before 1882, or indeed before 1890.

Jevons has often been criticized for failing to fill this gap, or for filling it only incompletely. As I have argued briefly above and more fully elsewhere (Black 1971b, pp.17-19), such criticisms are to some extent beside the point, for in *TPE* Jevons did not really set out to present a theory of distribution at all. Nevertheless the book does incidentally contain considerable discussion of the forces determining wages per head, rent per acre and interest per cent, and in his 'Concluding Remarks' Jevons included a section on the 'Relation of Wages and Profit' as 'one of the branches of economic doctrine which have been passed over' in *TPE*. From an examination of these passages the transitional character of Jevons's thought again emerges.

It is now generally accepted that while Jevons's treatment of the 'Theory of Capital' is not without considerable flaws, yet it does contain a perceptive treatment of the linkage between capital and time, from which Jevons proceeded to develop a 'General Expression for the Rate of Interest', $\dfrac{f't}{ft}$, *'the rate of increase of the produce divided by the whole produce'* (1871, p.237, emphasis in original). As Dr Peach rightly says, 'here, if nowhere else, there was an explicit and substantive application of marginal productivity analysis' (Peach, 1987, p.1017) – although it related only to a special case in which the time element could be isolated clearly.

Jevons's presentation of the theory of rent follows classical lines, expressed in mathematical symbols. It is illustrated by a diagram (Jevons, 1871, p.209) which clearly shows labour's share of the product as determined by its marginal productivity, with the rent of land as the residual. 'Thus we are taken to the very brink of the idea that in a two-factor case the reward to both factors is determined by marginal productivity' (Black, 1971b, p.26), but unfortunately in the second edition of *TPE* Jevons marred the analysis by introducing the assumption 'that the increments of labour applied are equally assisted by capital' (Jevons, 1879a, p.234) so that his two-factor case became a three-factor case. Again in the section on the 'Relation of Wages and Profit' while he dismissed the wages-fund theory as 'a truism' and attacked the Ricardian idea that 'as wages rise, profits fall', Jevons only set out a produce-less-deductions view of wages (1871, p.259). This he conceded, involved 'the temporary application of the wage-fund theory' while in the long run 'the rate of wages of every species of labour will be reduced to the average proper to labour of that degree of skill' (*ibid.*, p.262) – which seems to bring him back towards classical 'natural wage' ideas.

Thus while in *TPE* there are revolutionary new features in the application of marginal analysis to utility and productivity, partly anticipating the neo-classical theory of value and distribution, the full 'symmetrical' presentation of it is not there, and quite a few features of classical cost and distribution analysis remain.

IV

In contrast to value and distribution, monetary theory was not a centre of controversy in the 20 years before 1882. As Professor Laidler has recently said, 'What Frank W. Fetter (1965) termed 'British monetary orthodoxy', a comprehensive body of doctrine about theory and policy which encapsulated the major achievements of classical economics in the monetary area, was then at the height of its influence' (Laidler, 1991, p.7). For the most part, Jevons accepted and expounded this body of doctrine in his monetary work, but his acceptance of it was by no means unthinking; it was in fact fully in line with his view of scientific method.

In his 1862 paper 'On the Study of Periodic Commercial Fluctuations' (first published in full in Jevons, 1884) Jevons proposed that 'every kind of periodic fluctuation, whether daily, weekly, monthly, quarterly or yearly' should be studied not only for its own sake but also in order to isolate 'those which are irregular or non-periodic, and probably of more interest and importance' (1884, p.4). A major part of the considerable volume of applied research into monetary questions which Jevons carried out in the ensuing 20 years can be seen as the execution of this programme. It was to the problem of 'correctly exhibiting' non-periodic fluctuations that Jevons first turned his attention – naturally enough, given his view of their importance.

That the work which Jevons did on this problem, first in demonstrating 'A Serious Fall in the Value of Gold' since 1845 and then extending his study of 'The Variation of Prices and the Value of the Currency' back to 1782 and subsequently down to 1869 (Jevons, 1884, papers II, III and IV) was of the highest quality and originality, setting new standards for research of this type, has been recognized since Keynes delivered his Centenary Allocution in 1936 (Keynes, 1972, p.120). Yet as I have said elsewhere, 'there was nothing revolutionary in its implications for monetary theory. Essentially it served to support the quantity theory, and although Jevons wrote little directly on that topic the implications of all his writings on money and price levels are that he accepted a version of the theory in which the supply of money was ultimately governed by the cost of production of the precious metals and the demand for it was a pure transactions demand' (Black, 1981b, p.19).

To quote Professor Laidler again, 'obviously, the great exponent of marginal utility as the determinant of value had no notion of the potential relevance of that analysis to the determination of the value of money, but that does not mean that his monetary economics was devoid of any idea of maximising behaviour' (Laidler, 1982, p.328). Jevons indeed wrote that 'money ... immensely facilitates and, so to speak, lubricates the operation of exchange' (1875, p.191) – through which utility is maximized, but he seems always to have worked on the assumption that 'Money is made to go' (1875, p.82). In this respect his analysis of the determination of the value of money does not go beyond what J.S. Mill had set out in his *Principles* (Mill, 1848, 1909 ed., Bk III, Chap VIII); indeed it hardly goes that far.

The explanation for this is perhaps not far to seek, when it is remembered that Jevons saw changes in the value of money as long-term phenomena and accepted that in the long-run 'value is proportional to cost of production' (Jevons, 1879a, p.202). Here again we should remember Jevons's view of the logical method of Economics, which I quoted above; the hypothesis of the Quantity Theory when examined against the facts, seemed to him to be verified; so there was no need 'to seek for disturbing causes, or else to abandon our hypothesis' (1879a, p.19).

When he came to deal with periodic commercial fluctuations, Jevons was in a different position. While to some extent he followed out his original advice, that 'every kind of periodic fluctuation, whether daily, weekly, monthly, quarterly or yearly' should be studied, in his *Two Diagrams* of 1862 (appended to Jevons, 1884), in his uncompleted *Statistical Atlas* (*P & C*, II, pp.459, 461-2), and in his 1866 paper 'On the Frequent Autumnal Pressure in the Money Market' (1884, pp.160-93), he later came to devote his attention more and more to 'great commercial fluctuations, completing their course in some ten years'. In *A Serious Fall in the Value of Gold* he had noted that the fact that such fluctuations 'diversify the progress of trade is familiar to all who attend to mercantile matters' but 'the remote cause of these commercial tides has not been so well ascertained' (1884, p.27).

Now something which could be called a classical theory of the cycle had been emerging from the late 1830s onwards, but 'classical monetary theory dealt with a "credit cycle" rather than a "business cycle", and stressed price fluctuations as its dominant endogenous characteristic' (Laidler, 1991, p.20). So when Jevons came to look for the 'remote cause' of decennial fluctuations existing analyses provided little help, although the treatment in Mill's *Principles* contained many shrewd insights (Mill, 1848; 1909 ed., Book III, Chaps XII and XIV).

Jevons's own first attempt to identify the cause of 'these commercial tides' was perceptive; as is well known, he suggested that 'it seems to lie in the *varying proportion which the capital devoted to permanent and remote investment bears to that which is but temporarily invested soon to reproduce itself'* (Jevons, 1884, p.28, emphasis in original). While this suggestion was the outcome of considerable empirical research on Jevons's part, there is no evidence that he framed any hypothesis to explain the cause of the variation at this stage in his work.

It seems to have been in 1866 that Jevons became acquainted with John Mills, the Manchester bank manager who was to succeed him as President of the Manchester Statistical Society in 1871, and in 1867 he prepared the diagrams for a paper which Mills contributed to that society, 'On Credit Cycles and the Origin of Commercial Panics'. In this Mills argued that commercial panics were demonstrably only one feature of a credit cycle with decennial periodicity, and 'not, in essence, a matter of the *purse* but of the *mind'* (Mills, 1867, p.17). In each phase of the cycle 'there appears to be a concurrent change in the mental mood of the trading public' (*ibid.,* p.29) and it was these changes in business expectations which Mills considered to be the underlying cause of the cycle itself.

Jevons had a high regard for the work of Mills, and referred to it approvingly both in his *Primer of Political Economy* and in his lectures to undergraduates at Owens College (Jevons, 1878, p.120; *P & C*, VI, p.132).[5] 'But', he wrote in 1875, 'it seems to me very probable that these moods of the commercial mind, while constituting the principal part of the phenomena, may be controlled by outward events, especially the condition of the harvests. Assuming that variations of commercial credit and enterprise are essentially mental in their nature, must there not be external events to excite hopefulness at one time or disappointment and despondency at another?' (Jevons, 1884, pp.203-204.)

These words are taken from the first paper in which Jevons suggested a connection between variations in sun-spot activity and fluctuations in economic activity. In 1863 he had suggested that these might be caused by periodic variations in fixed investment. What led him between 1863 and 1875 to switch his explanation from an endogenous to an exogenous cause? I have elsewhere suggested that it may have been due to his complete acceptance of the validity of Say's Law (Black, 1981b, p.20), but there are other significant pointers to be taken into account. From the record we have of what Jevons told his students when lecturing on 'Commercial Fluctuations since 1836' in 1876 it again appears that he had come to attach much importance to harvest variations – more than to changes in capital investment. He drew the attention of his class to 'a remarkable series of figures as to the number of *bricks* made' between 1843 and 1847, and the amount of timber used, linking the increases to the railway investment boom, but he went on to say that 'the main point which brings these speculations to a head is the price of corn' – without, however, mentioning the idea he had recently formed about a possible connection between this and the solar period (*P & C*, VI, p.123, emphasis in original).

That Jevons should make such a connection once he had come to regard corn prices as a key variable in commercial fluctuations is not surprising, given his training and experience in chemistry and meteorology together with his remarkably extensive knowledge of other natural sciences. (*Cf.* Black, 1972e, Sections II and III.) All of this, combined with his knowledge of logic, Jevons had deployed between 1868 and 1874 in writing his *Principles of Science.* In Book IV of this, entitled 'Inductive Investigation', he included a chapter on the 'Method of Variations'. This contains a section on 'Periodic Variations' which leads on to an explanation of Sir John Herschel's 'Principle of Forced Vibrations' (Jevons, 1874a; 1958 ed., pp.447-52).

In a paper on 'The Solar Influence on Commerce', written in 1878 or 1879 but not published until 1981, Jevons attempted 'to sketch out the course of inductive argument and enquiry which leads almost conclusively to a belief in the solar origin of commercial fluctuations'. 'In the first place,' he continued, 'we must look to the general principles of inductive logic by which our inquiries must necessarily be guided. The relation which we are attempting to establish is one of cause and effect, and both cause and effect are supposed to be periodic in character, and the one is supposed to produce the other. To this case there applies a general principle of mechanics called *the principle of forced vibrations.*' After re-stating Herschel's principle at some length, Jevons summarizes it thus: 'The direct simple effect of any periodic cause is likewise periodic, and in the absence of disturbing causes, the period of the effect will be exactly equal to that of the cause.'

Jevons's next step is to relate this to commercial fluctuations: 'When we perceive the existence of a periodic effect, such as commercial crises appear to be, how shall we proceed to discover its cause? We must proceed upon the great principle of inductive method, as laid down by Laplace and the several great mathematicians who created the theory of probability. This principle is to the effect that the most probable cause of an event which has happened is that cause which if it existed would most probably lead to that effect.' Jevons then argues that 'mere equality of period is a perfectly valid ground of inductive reasoning; but our results gain much in probability if we can analyse and explain the precise relation of cause and effect' (*P & C,* VII, pp.92-4).

Jevons at this stage in his work believed that he had statistical evidence which established virtual equality between 'the average period of recurrence of commercial crises' and the sun-spot period; his problem was to explain 'the precise relation of cause and effect' between the two. In seeking to solve this problem Jevons put forward first a theory of a direct relation between sun-spot activity, harvests and grain prices in England, and subsequently another in which the effect of increased solar radiation on British industry came indirectly through good harvests in India and China affecting their demand for British exports (*cf.* Black, 1981b, pp.21-2). In neither case did the available statistics adequately confirm his analysis but Jevons showed himself reluctant to practise what he preached and abandon his initial bold hypothesis. Nevertheless, as Professor Stephen Stigler has said, 'it is easy to understand that such a bold hypothesis as that of an economy driven by sunspots could exert a hypnotic influence' (Stigler, 1982, p.364), and in this case Jevons was working in almost uncharted territory.

For this reason, the transition in Jevons's thought on economic fluctuations was of a different order from that which I have suggested can be found in his work on the Theory of Value. In that case, Jevons departed radically from the classical orthodoxy but did not abandon it completely, so appearing as a transitional figure between the classical and neo-classical theorists. In this instance by 1862 the classical orthodoxy consisted of a general recognition of the significance of 'commercial panics', out of which had evolved a theory of a 'credit cycle'. Jevons, along with a few others like Mills, had observed the decennial cycle and recognized its importance. In 1876 Jevons told his students that these 'are not matters of currency. They involve the whole industry of the country' (*P & C,* VI, p.123). For such a business cycle there was no orthodoxy for him to adhere to or abandon, and only at this quite late stage in his short career did Jevons frame a hypothesis to explain its underlying causes.

The sun-spot theory which he advanced with characteristic boldness and enthusiasm was to be the subject of much criticism, and some ridicule, but at the stage when Jevons advanced it, it was unquestionably worth examination. Many other theories were to be put forward and rejected before even some degree of consensus as to the causes of the business cycle was established, and it is noteworthy that those historians of economic thought who have most recently published work on Jevons's sun-spot theory still find analytical merit in it (Laidler, 1982, pp.340-45; Peart, 1991, pp.261-4).

Taking a broader view, it can also be said that in the years from 1862 to 1882 important progress was made towards a general acceptance of the idea that 'commercial crises' were part of a decennial cycle which was not simply a credit cycle but a business cycle involving all sections of the economy, and to this process of transition Jevons was a significant contributor.

Notes

1. In a recent paper, Professor Sandra Peart has argued that Jevons's 'procedures of "inductive quantification" directed attention away from a problem that had much troubled J.S. Mill – that of explaining the difference between hypothesized and observed outcomes. The applied economist was to use techniques of approximation, which, assuming that unmodeled causes "balanced", would reveal the measured effect of the cause[s] of interest. Mill, by contrast, insisted that approximation was inappropriate in economics and assigned the difficult role of accounting for the difference between observed and predicted outcomes to the applied economist' (Peart, 1993, p.436). This would seem to afford another example of the differences between Mill's approach, grounded in moral philosophy and that of Jevons, grounded in experimental science. As Professor Schabas says, 'Jevons, like Herschel, was first and foremost the practical scientist with little patience for philosophical problems that might impede the task at hand (1990, p.55).

2. For a fuller discussion of this see Black, 1990a, p.13.

3. Professor Schabas (1990, p.110) differs from the judgement I made in 1962 that 'on the whole it seems correct to regard Jevons as assailed rather than supported by the writings of the "English Historical School" ' (Black, 1962, pp.214-15). But while in her book she deals with the reaction of Leslie and Ingram to Jevons's overall

methodology, my 1962 comment related specifically to his use of the mathematical approach.

4. In the ensuing explanation of this point I have drawn on material which first appeared in my 'Introduction' to the Pelican Classics edition of *The Theory of Political Economy* (Black, 1971b), pp.15-20.

5. The diagram taken from Mills's 1867 paper which Jevons showed to his students in 1876 was in fact the one which he had drawn for Mills in 1867 (*cf.* *P & C* VI, pp.130-31 and VII, p.126).

9

Transitions in Political Economy

II: Economic Policy

I

Was there a revolution in economic policy in Britain comparable with the 'Marginal Revolution' in economic analysis? No one would dispute that in this area there was a significant shift away from *laissez-faire* and free trade policies towards a more interventionist style of policy in the second half of the 19th century, but attempts to pinpoint a date from which this can be seen to commence have not produced a clear consensus comparable with that which has led to 1871 being recognized as a key date in the chronology of the 'Marginal Revolution'.[1]

However, if we adopt the short perspective once more, and try to look at developments since 1862 from the standpoint of 1882, or soon thereafter, it is clear that those who were then taking an interest in the subject recognized that in the previous 20 years a definite change had taken place in attitudes to economic policy. It is equally clear that this change had frequently manifested itself in the form of a crisis of confidence in 'orthodox political economy', not so much among the practitioners of the subject as among the reading public in general.

In 1867 it was still possible for Robert Lowe – who was to become Chancellor of the Exchequer in the following year – to write 'Political Economy is not exactly the law of the land, but it is the ground of that law. It is assumed as its basis and foundation' (Lowe, 1867, p.365). Yet it was little more than ten years later that Walter Bagehot made his well-known statement that the same Political Economy, the source of the doctrines of free trade and *laissez-faire*, 'lies rather dead in the public mind. Not only does it not excite the same interest as formerly, but there is not exactly the same confidence in it' (Bagehot, 1879, p.3). Seven years on Henry Sidgwick told members of Section F of the British Association that 'observers of the current drift of political thought and practice ... appear to be generally agreed upon one point – *viz.* that Socialism is flowing in upon us with a full tide. ... And a second point on which they appear to agree is that this socialistic movement – as it is often called – is altogether opposed to "orthodox political economy" (Sidgwick, 1886; in 1964, p.23).

Illustrations of this kind could be multiplied; indeed there is plentiful evidence that the process whereby classical economic analysis came to be challenged and ultimately replaced by new methods and theories was paralleled by another process as a result of which, over much the same time period, the policy doctrines which had been based on classical theory seemed to lose much of their hold on public opinion and were challenged by others. Professor Hutchison suggests that 'though either of these turning points could conceivably have occurred without the other, they are clearly interconnected in that they influenced and interacted on one another as regards the particular forms they took' (1978, p.94). Now this is indeed true, but it is also true that the influences and interactions were by no means simple or direct.   The inter-connections between economic theory and economic policy are never easy to track, and arguably this is particularly true of the period we are considering here.   It can be shown that the Smithian and Keynesian revolutions both led, in varying lengths of time, to the adoption of policy measures which owed their character in considerable measure to the new theories; the same cannot be said of the Jevonian revolution.   Nor can it be said that it was the enactment of new policies by government which led the economists to put forward new theories.

Historians and economists alike have on the whole tended to see problems of economic policy in the 19th century too simply in terms of state intervention and non-intervention, individualism and collectivism.   In fact they always involved a quite subtle balance between the individual, voluntary groups and associations, and local as well as central government (*cf.* Petrella, 1970, pp.152-3).   In the maintenance of this balance an important rôle was played by the prevailing social values – those very 'Victorian values' which have been so much discussed in the last 15 years.   If this debate has demonstrated anything, it is that these values are very difficult to define precisely or to summarize clearly, but in my judgement they are well captured in the words of Professor Geoffrey Best:

> Respectability and independence ran together because for the mid- and for the early Victorians, divinity and economics ran together; equal prescriptions of the divine/natural order of conduct. Respectability was a style of living understood to show a proper respect for morals and

morality; usually it meant some degree of formal Christianity, but you could be respectable and value your respectability without being Christian. Independence came to nearly the same thing in practice; it meant such an accommodation of expenditure to income as would make possible the respectable style of life; it proceeded from the premise that it was immoral (*viz*, for Christians, unchristian) to depend on any but your own resources unless you absolutely had to; it presumed that the voluntarily dependent were disreputable, and it expected the involuntarily dependent to forego, for at any rate the term of their dependence, the respect due to the properly respectable man. Respectability was the outcome of a vulgarisation and perhaps secularisation of established Christianity. Independence was the main social consequence of the vulgarisation of the creed of classical economics in a Protestant country. (Best, 1979, pp.279-80)

It was primarily the weakening of conviction in this hard doctrine which led to the rejection of the creed of classical economics and the change in the character of economic policy in the late Victorian years. The feeling was growing and spreading that not all of those who found themselves ill-housed, out of work or otherwise in poverty were necessarily the authors of their own misfortunes. Nor could the moral obligation of the respectable and independent towards their less fortunate fellow citizens always be relied upon to meet the needs of the deserving fully and efficiently – so 'there was a discernible tendency to prefer legal obligations which could be enforced to moral obligations which might or might not be discharged' (Burn, 1964, p.123).

Dicey's appraisal of the nature of the change which came over public opinion at this time still has validity:

Can the systematic extension of individual freedom and the removal of every kind of oppression so stimulate energy and self-help as to cure (in so far as they are curable by legislation) the evils which bring ruin on a commonwealth? To this inquiry the enlightened opinion of 1832 which for some thirty or forty years, if not for more, governed the action of Parliament, gave, in spite of protests from a small body of thinkers backed more or less by the sympathy of the working classes, an unhesitating and affirmative answer. To the same inquiry English legislative opinion has from about 1870 onwards given a doubtful, if not a negative, reply. (Dicey, 1905, p.216)

This brings us back to that aspect of public opinion which more particularly concerns us here – the attitude of the public towards political economy. In the circumstances which I have outlined it is scarcely to be wondered at that it 'lay somewhat dead in the public mind'. For the public in general did not make the fine distinctions which academic researchers can do. As W.L. Burn pointed out, it was easy for the well-to-do middle-class Victorian to overlook the fact that 'the liberty which he so happily enjoys is dependent to a large extent on the existence of coercive power, his own or that of the State' (Burn, 1964, p.135). It was equally easy for the less well-to-do to conclude that this same liberty and free trade which Political Economy sanctioned held out little or no prospects of benefit for them.   'When a working man is told that Political Economy "condemns" strikes, hesitates about co-operation, looks askance at proposals for limiting the hours of labour, but "approves" the accumulation of capital, and "sanctions" the market rate of wages, it seems not an unnatural response that "since Political Economy is against the working man, it behoves the working man to be against Political Economy" ' (Cairnes, 1873, p.261).

II

Now the picture of 'orthodox political economy' which was presented to 'the working man' both by its intellectual critics and its dogmatic supporters was often a crude caricature of the theory of economic policy which the classical school had developed. Not surprisingly, the reaction of the economists was to deny responsibility for it. It was Cairnes, often regarded as the last defender of classical orthodoxy, who urged that his subject should be seen as a neutral science: 'Political Economy is a science in the same sense in which Astronomy, Dynamics, Chemistry, Physiology are sciences.   Its subject matter is different; it deals with the phenomena of wealth while they deal with the phenomena of the physical universe; but its methods, its aims, the character of its conclusions, are the same as theirs.'   Hence, Cairnes argued, it followed that: 'Political Economy stands apart from all particular systems of social or industrial existence. It has nothing to do with *laissez-faire* any more than with communism; with freedom of contract any more than with paternal government, or with systems of *status*' (Cairnes, 1873, pp.255-6).

   Certainly the new theories which Jevons and his contemporaries were developing at the time when those words were written were in line with this conception of political economy as an abstract science.

They were not, I would contend, an outcome of contemporary conditions and were designed neither to assist with reform nor to justify the *status quo*. But of course that did not prevent the economists who framed them from taking an interest in economic policy, nor from being influenced in their approach to policy questions by the theories which they had developed.

Indeed notwithstanding their anxiety to be taken seriously as impartial objective scientists, neo-classical economists generally remained willing to provide guidance on economic policy. They found the solution to this dilemma in a growing emphasis on the distinction, first introduced into the subject by Nassau Senior, between the science and the art of political economy – which roughly corresponded to what later became the distinction between positive and normative economics. So while policy questions had been treated as an integral part of classical analysis, in neo-classical analysis they were moved into that separate division which came to be known as welfare economics.

According to a recent treatment of its historical background,

> ... refinements taking place in the post-classical era led to the emergence of welfare economics in its contemporary form. The great breakthrough was the specification and understanding of the significance of the concept of utility

and

> All post-classical and contemporary developments in welfare economics are therefore of two fundamental origins: (1) the development of subjective utility theory as the foundation of a theory of value, *including* the development of the marginal utility concept ... and (2) the refinement and application of Bentham's utilitarian precepts and his suggestion, mainly through philosophical premises, that competitive markets and free exchange might not lead to global welfare maximization in society. (Hébert and Ekelund, 1984, p.53)

A broadly similar account of the origins and characteristics of neo-classical welfare economics can be found in the earlier work of Professor Myint (1948, Chapter VIII), but it is notable that in both these histories the earliest exponents of this approach to receive mention are Sidgwick and Marshall. So there would appear to be a considerable gap between Mill's 1848 re-statement and refinement of the principles of classical welfare analysis and the emergence of the first hints of neo-classical welfare theory in Sidgwick's *Principles of Political Economy* in 1883. Yet if 'the great breakthrough was the specification and understanding of the significance of the concept of utility', it would seem that the work of Jevons should have an important place in the transition from the classical to the neo-classical treatment of economic welfare.

Undoubtedly, by his development of marginal analysis and the mathematical method, Jevons had pioneered the use of tools which were to be frequently employed in welfare economics at a later date, but he never devoted himself to trying to work out a *theory* of economic policy, as distinct from dealing with policy issues. There are suggestions in *TPE* that free exchange in competitive markets would in certain circumstances maximize utility for the whole population of an economy (Jevons, 1871, pp.132-4, 255) – suggestions which modern commentators have pointed out involved him in internal inconsistencies, of which he was not unaware but never really resolved (*cf.* Peach, 1987, pp.1015-16; Black, 1971b, p.23).

It is true that in 1876 Jevons did say, 'if such a thing is possible, we need a new branch of political and statistical science which shall carefully investigate the limits to the *laissez-faire* principle, and show where we want greater freedom and where less' (Jevons, 1876b; in 1905, p.204). This could be interpreted as a suggestion for a theory of economic policy, but its context indicates that Jevons did not see this 'new branch of political and statistical science' as part of the theory of economy. This is in line with the fact that his extensive work on economic policy really constituted a series of case studies – of cases in which the economic activities of individuals or groups might require regulation by central or local government, and cases where the provision of goods or services might be better undertaken by public rather than private enterprise. Since I have dealt elsewhere with Jevons's treatment of these specific cases (Black, 1981b, pp.23-8), I propose here to concentrate on a more detailed consideration of the philosophy which Jevons employed in that treatment.

III

Unquestionably the common factor in Jevons's work in economic analysis and in economic policy is Bentham's version of the utilitarian philosophy, but because the way in which he approached 'the mechanics of self-interest and utility' did not lead him to work out an analysis of market failure this common factor was never developed into a logical connection. In order properly to appreciate the character of Jevons's work in economic policy and its relation to his theoretical writings, I believe it is necessary to make use again of the short perspective – to try to look at matters from the standpoint of 1882 – and to do so bearing in mind the details of Jevons's biography.[2]

To start from the latter, the available records provide incontestable evidence of the sincerity of Jevons's commitment to social reform from an early age. In November 1857 he wrote to his sisters: 'To be *powerfully good*, that is to be good, not towards one or a dozen, or a hundred but towards a nation or the world, is what now absorbs me' (*P & C*, II, 307, emphasis in original). By the beginning of 1859 he had decided that his best hope of achieving this lay in the study of social science:

> ... just as in Physical Science there are general and profound principles deducible from a great number of apparent phenomena, so in treating Man or Society there must also be general principles and laws which underlie all the present discussions and partial arguments. ... All the investigations of Social Science must proceed on the assumption that there are causes to make people good and bad, happy and miserable, rich and poor, as well as strong and feeble ... Of course such is the infinite complexity of causes and of effect that we cannot treat them in detail. A few of the main features of Man and Society afford plenty of occupation. To attempt to define the foundations of our knowledge of man, is surely a work worth a lifetime, and one not excelled in usefulness or interest by any other. (*P & C*, II, 361-2)

To this work Jevons brought not only his training and experience in the physical sciences, together with all the studies in Political Economy and 'Mental Science' which he later completed at University College, London, but also a set of values derived from his upbringing in early Victorian Liverpool in a middle-class family in reduced circumstances, Liberal in politics, Unitarian in religion. A studious and earnest young man, he had been schooled from his earliest youth to accept those values of respectability and independence to which I have already referred. He had also known what it was to be at the risk of losing them and had made sacrifices to hold on to them for himself and for his brothers and sisters.

Given this background it is not surprising that Jevons's early writings on economic policy followed orthodox classical lines.

Thus, during his years in Australia, he wrote a vigorous letter to the editor of the Sydney *Empire* in 1857 'with view of shutting up writers about Protective Humbug' – which followed shortly after another in which he had unfavourably contrasted the government railway works in New South Wales with those undertaken by private speculators in the United States (*P & C*, II, 280, 262).

In the papers on policy matters which Jevons published in the 1860s, after his appointment to the Chair of Political Economy in Owens College, it is notable that the theme of independence and self-help is still strongly stated. Thus in 1869 he attacked medical charities as encouraging 'in the poorest classes a contented sense of dependence on the richer classes' and looked forward to the 'point at which the public or private charity of one class towards another can be dispensed with ... True progress will tend to render every class self-reliant and independent. Self-help is the truest kind of help, and you confer the greatest benefit upon a person or a class of persons when you enable and induce them to do without your aid for the future' (1869; in1883, p.191).

There was nothing here which would not have been received with approval by those believers in the 'truths of political economy' whose utterances were anathema to critics like John Ruskin and William Morris. Yet while Jevons continued to uphold the values of independence and self-reliance, his thinking on social and economic problems came to be more influenced by other philosophies during the 1860s. To the nodding acquaintance with 'the selfish theory of morals' which he had gained in Australia (*cf. P & C*, I, 27-8, 132-3) was added during his later studies at University College, London, a thorough knowledge of Bentham's utilitarian philosophy (Black, 1972b, pp.123-5) – which, as I have argued in the preceding paper, was the foundation of the analysis of economizing behaviour first set out in 1862.

In questions of economic policy some of the earliest papers written during his Manchester years show Jevons also applying Bentham's philosophy to the particular problems which he took up. This is well illustrated by a paragraph in a paper which he gave to the Manchester Statistical Society in 1867 on the question of public ownership of telegraphs and railways:

> Much difference of opinion arises, even in a purely economical point of
> view, upon the question of the limits of State interference. My own

strong opinion is that no abstract principle, and no absolute rule can guide us in determining what kinds of industrial enterprise the State should undertake, and what it should not .... Nothing but experience and argument from experience can in most cases determine whether the community will be best served by its collective state action, or by trusting to private self-interest. (Jevons 1867; in 1883, p.278)

Here Jevons showed himself at once a typical Benthamite in rejecting the idea of any 'absolute rule' that private interest would always lead to public benefit, and a typical scientist in advocating 'argument from experience', which he later developed into his idea of experimental legislation.

It seems to have been only after 1867, during his work on *The Principles of Science*, that another influence developed which was to affect Jevons's ideas on economic policy significantly; this was the evolutionary philosophy of Herbert Spencer. Jevons had been in correspondence with Spencer in 1865/6, having sent him a copy of his *Pure Logic*, and used Spencer's reply in support of his application for the Chair of Logic and Mental and Moral Philosophy at Owens College (*P & C*, III, 117), but while he must have been well acquainted with Spencer's writings before this, there is no reference to them in any of his earlier journals, diaries, or letters. This is curious for the two men came from very similar backgrounds, and the views which Spencer had published in his *Social Statics* (1850) and in his collected *Essays* (first series 1857, second series, 1863), 'advocating an extreme individualism' as the *Dictionary of National Biography* put it, would have been congenial to the young Jevons. Whatever the reason, it is only in the early 1870s that evidences of the influence of Spencer's theory of evolution as applied to societies can be found in Jevons's publications. Professor R.S. Bowman, who neatly sums up Jevons's social philosophy as 'a compound of evolution theory, utilitarianism and Baconian experimental method' quotes passages from *The Coal Question* (1865) and Jevons's Presidential Address to Section F of the British Association (1870; in 1883, pp.194-216) on the state of the working classes as evidencing 'the bad tendencies produced by evolution' (Bowman, 1989, pp.1124-5). Examined in context, these passages contain no specific references to evolution or to Spencer and are such as might have been written by any mid-Victorian deploring the social consequences of the Industrial Revolution.

In 1874 *The Principles of Science* was published, with a section in the final chapter devoted to 'The Theory of Evolution' as developed by Darwin and Spencer, whose theories Jevons had described the year before – in a letter to the editor of *Nature* – as 'among the most important additions ever made to human knowledge' (*P & C*, IV, 4). Subsequent to this, references, explicit or implied, to Spencer and his ideas on evolution in society begin to appear in Jevons's writings on economic policy. A few months after the publication of *The Principles of Science*, Jevons began working on *Money and the Mechanism of Exchange*. In this Spencer's name is mentioned with, interestingly, a reference to *Social Statics*. In that work:

> ... Mr Herbert Spencer advanced the doctrine that, ... as we trust the grocer to furnish us with pounds of tea ... so we might trust ... some of the ... enterprising firms of Birmingham to supply us with sovereigns and shillings at their own risk and profit ... Though I must always deeply respect the opinions of so profound a thinker as Mr Spencer, I hold that in this instance he has pushed a general principle into an exceptional case, where it quite fails. He has overlooked the important law of Gresham, that better money cannot drive out worse. (Jevons, 1875, p.64)

That supplying coinage was an activity which, for this very reason, the State must reserve to itself was a point virtually taken for granted by even the most ardent advocates of *laissez-faire* among the classical economists and Jevons was merely reasserting monetary orthodoxy here. In other areas of economic policy, however, the positions he had taken up in the 1860s might well have led his contemporaries to expect him to follow Spencer in the latter's championship of what T.H. Huxley called 'astynomocracy', the night-watchman state (Huxley, 1871, quoted Bibby, 1967, p.186).

Such did not prove to be the case; as Professor Hutchison says of Jevons, 'as the 1870s wore on, more cases occurred to him which seemed to call for government action, or at least for detailed empirical examination, and which were no longer to be disposed of by a sweeping application of *laissez-faire* principles' (Hutchison, 1978, p.97). So for Jevons, it would seem, increasing faith in the validity of Spencer's theory of evolution was combined with decreasing faith in the validity of *laissez-faire* as a guide for economic policy – which is wholly at odds with the view which Spencer himself took.

To resolve this apparent paradox it is necessary to follow out the further references to Spencer which occur in Jevons's writings from 1876 to 1882. In a paper on the regulation of the sale of alcohol, read to the Manchester Statistical Society in March 1876, Jevons referred to:

> principles which should guide a wise reforming legislator in the selection of the laws he should advocate. Solon, when asked whether he had given the Athenians the best laws he could devise, replied: 'Ay, the best laws that they could receive.' He has often been blamed, but the progress of Sociology is establishing his wisdom. We now know that laws are not good or bad with respect to any invariable standard, but in reference to the changing character of society and man. The successful reformer is one who sees for what legislative change the people are ripe, and concentrates the popular energy upon it. (Jevons, 1876a; in 1883, p.249).

Whether, with the changing character of society, legislative change would involve less regulation or more, Jevons did not specify at this stage.

Later in 1876, in his Introductory Lecture at University College, London, he did set out his views on this question. He declared that 'it is impossible to doubt that the *laissez-faire* principle properly applied is the wholesome and true one' but went on to ask 'does it follow that because we repeal old pieces of legislation we shall need no new ones? On the contrary, as it seems to me, while population grows more numerous and dense, while industry becomes more complex and interdependent, as we travel faster and make use of more intense forces, we shall necessarily need more legislative supervision.' (Jevons 1876b; in 1905, pp.203-4)

Again, Jevons did not attempt to reconcile what he said here about exceptions to *laissez-faire* with Spencer's well-known views on that topic, although earlier in the lecture he had referred to Spencer by name and asserted that 'the present economical state of society cannot be explained by theory alone. We must take into account the long past out of which we are constantly emerging. Whether we call it sociology or not, we must have some scientific treatment of the principles of evolution as manifested in every branch of social existence' (Jevons, 1876b; in 1905, pp.195, 197). By 1879, when the second edition of *TPE* appeared in June, Jevons's conviction on this subject seems to have grown stronger. In the new Preface he wrote that '*there must arise a science of the development of economic forms and relations*' and included 'economic sociology' specifically among the 'various sciences' into which he expected Economics to subdivide (Jevons, 1879a, pp.xvi-xvii, emphasis in original).

In December of the same year, Jevons's fourth article in his series 'John Stuart Mill's Philosophy Tested' was published (Jevons 1879b; in 1890, pp.268-94), an article devoted entirely to a critique of Mill's *Utilitarianism*. In this he attacked Mill's attempt to give 'a more free and genial character to the utilitarian speculations' by adopting the position 'that some *kinds* of pleasure are more desirable and more valuable than others'. Jevons would have none of this – 'Mill proposed to give "geniality" to the Utilitarian philosophy by throwing into confusion what it was the very merit of Bentham to have distinguished and arranged scientifically. We must hold to the dry old Jeremy, if we are to have any chance of progress in Ethics' (Jevons, 1879b; in 1890, pp.278, 286).

As in Economics, so in Ethics – Jevons refused to diverge from the idea that pleasures and pains could be brought to a common denominator and ultimately a 'hedonic balance-sheet' be drawn up. From this position he goes on to consider how Mill treats 'other moral elements, such as the Social or Altruistic Feelings', contending that Mill admits the existence of such feelings but is reluctant to allow that they are innate in human nature. 'Mill's idea of human nature was that we came into the world like lumps of soft clay, to be shaped by the accidents of life, or the care of those who educate us' but for Jevons 'Human nature is one of the last things which can be called "pliable". ... we start always with inherent hereditary powers of growth. The non-recognition of this fact is the great defect in the moral system of Bentham' (Jevons, 1879b; in 1890, p.290).

The problem of reconciling 'moral sense' doctrines with utilitarian philosophy had, according to Jevons, been solved by 'the establishment of the Spencerian Theory of Morals, which has made a new era in philosophy .... The moral sense doctrine, so rudely treated by Bentham, is no longer incapable of reconciliation with the greatest happiness principle, only it now becomes a moving and developable moral sense' (1879b; in 1890, pp.289, 291).

The concept of 'the natural evolution of conduct' towards an 'ideal goal' (Spencer, 1879, p.44) is one which seems to have impressed Jevons greatly at this time. It was in line with the prevailing Victorian desire for the improvement of 'character' (*cf.* Collini, 1991, pp.91-118) – in which Mill had shared, but in his discussion of Mill's logical reasoning Jevons did not refer to the passages in his *System of Logic* where Mill had asserted that the general science of society must be founded on 'ethology', a science of human character. Mill's idea that 'political ethology' might develop a 'theory of the causes which determine the type of character belonging to a people or an age' was not the same as Spencer's, but it was worthy of discussion and comparison with it. (*cf.* Black, 1990a, p.13).[3]

Although Jevons did not take up this point, he was aware of the criticisms of Spencer's philosophy being made by Sidgwick and others (*cf. P & C*, V, 24). In addition, between 1878 and 1881 he was working on the series of papers on 'Methods of Social Reform' in which he followed up a point which he had made in his 1876 lecture on 'The Future of Political Economy' – 'that the utmost benefits may be, and, in fact, are secured to us by extensions of government action of a kind quite unsanctioned by the *laissez-faire* principle. I allude to the provision of public institutions of various sorts – libraries, museums, parks, free bridges' (Jevons, 1876b; in 1905, p.205). It must have occurred to him that such 'extensions of government action' were in sharp contrast to the reduction of the role of government which Spencer thought social evolution would bring about. In December 1881, Jevons wrote to his brother Tom – 'I am getting towards the end of my book on the State in relation to Labour, but it involves a great deal of reading and thinking' (*P & C*, V, 154). Much of that thinking evidently related to the application of the social philosophy of Spencer to the problems of economic policy and Jevons gave the result of it in the book:

> ... the evolutionists aim, not so much at directly maximising happiness, as at maximising liberty of action, which they conceive to be equivalent to the means of greatest happiness. The principle of equal freedom is therefore put forth as an all-extensive and sure guide in social matters. It would lead me too far to attempt in this place to inquire whether the present course of industrial legislation, and the remarks to be made upon it in the present volume, are really reconcilable with this principle. I am inclined to think that the reconciliation is not impossible; but that, when applied to the vast communities of modern society, the principle fails to give a sure guiding light. So intricate are the ways, industrial, sanitary or political, in which one class or section of the people affect other

classes or sections, that there is hardly any limit to the interference of the legislator.

In 'a great modern manufacturing community', Jevons suggests 'evolution is doubtless at work' but it may need help from legislation. 'Based, at any rate, upon trial and experience, it is but the multiplying of the good tendencies, and the quick elimination of the bad. It is an attempt to save needless suffering by making the few teach the many, so as to bring individuals into conformity with their environment without the blind striving of individual action' (Jevons, 1882; 1894 ed., pp.14, 16). So Spencer's evolutionary ethics may be invoked in support of Benthamite utilitarianism, but it is still the greatest happiness principle which must be used to decide whether *laissez-faire* or state action is appropriate in each case. In 1882 Jevons not only restated but enlarged upon the position which he had stated to the Manchester Statistical Society in 1867:

> ... the first step must be to rid our minds of the idea that there are any such things in social matters as abstract rights ...
>
> As then in philosophy the first step is to begin by doubting everything, so in social philosophy, or rather in practical legislation, the first step is to throw aside all supposed absolute rights or inflexible principles ... No laws, no customs, no rights of property are so sacred that they may not be made away with, if it can be clearly shown that they stand in the way of the greatest happiness. (1882; 1894 ed., pp.6, 9, 12)

As might be expected, this view did not find favour with Spencer who quoted the first part of it disapprovingly when attacking Bentham's doctrine on natural rights in *The Man versus the State* (Spencer, 1884;1969 ed., p.161). Indeed, if Jevons's words here are taken at their face value this appears to be an extreme position from which Bentham himself would surely have drawn back, for of nothing was Bentham more convinced than the need to maintain the security of society, and by nothing was that security more likely to be undermined, in his view, than by interference with the rights of property. Yet eventually Jevons was not an extremist, and he goes on to say:

> But it ought to be evident that before we venture upon a great leap in the dark, we may well ask for cogent evidence as to the character of the landing place .... What are the means of proving inductively or deductively that a certain change will conduce to the greater sum of happiness? ... In the case of any novel and considerable change direct experience must be wanting ... A heavy burden of proof, therefore, lies

upon him who would advocate any social change which has not or cannot be tested previously on a small scale. (1882; 1894 ed., p.12)

Hence it emerges that Jevons was actually advocating what Professor Frank Petrella has called 'the incremental method' in social legislation, but as Petrella points out while that method is conservative 'incrementalism not only reinforces but accelerates reliance on the state in the resolution of problems' (1977, p.232).

Reliance on the state in the resolution of economic problems was not something to which Jevons was opposed in principle, and the closing pages of *The State in relation to Labour* make clear that for him in such matters Bentham's utilitarianism was ultimately more important than Spencer's evolutionism:

... where upon the grounds of clear experience interpreted by logical reasoning we can see our way to a definite improvement in some classes of people without injuring others, we are under the obligation of endeavouring to promote that improvement .... We must neither maximise the functions of government at the beck of quasi-military officials, nor minimise them according to the theories of the very best philosophers. We must learn to judge each case upon its merits, interpreting with painful care all experience which can be brought to bear upon the matter. (Jevons, 1882; 1894 ed., pp.170-71)

In a recent survey of 'Jevons's Applications of Utilitarian Theory to Economic Policy' Professor Peart lays special emphasis on 'the close continuity in the policy analysis of Mill and Jevons' and also stresses that 'there are many instances of continuity in Jevons's thought' (Peart, 1990, pp.304, 305). This latter point I would not deny, and I have myself said that 'Jevons's position on questions of economic and social policy was closer to Mill's than he probably would have cared to admit' (Black 1981b, p.24). Nevertheless, on what Professor Peart calls 'a much debated issue' – 'whether a "transition", a movement towards intervention, occurred in Jevons's own thought', it is my view that it did occur. In support of that view I submit one further piece of evidence. In April 1882 Foxwell wrote to Jevons: 'I have been expecting and recommending your "State in relation to Labour" ever since Xmas .... I hope to find that you have taken up – well I won't say a Socialistic position, because some dislike the word, but at all events a position from which you recognize the obligation of the individual to society, and the necessity for some control, in the public interest, of his endeavours to secure his private gain ....' To this Jevons replied, 'Judging from what you say I fancy the new book will almost exactly meet your views. It seems impossible to reconcile the needs of modern society with the ideas of the Individual Rights people' (*P & C*, V, pp.186, 187). He would not, I believe, have written in that vein in 1862.

IV

When I gave the Manchester Special lectures in 1982 my purpose was to present the idea that the period from 1862 to 1882 could be seen as a period of transition in ideas on both economic analysis and economic policy and to highlight the developing ideas of W.S. Jevons and their place in that process. Reviewing my lectures in 1994, I have found it necessary to make many changes in the light of work done on the subject, by others and by myself, in the intervening years, but I have not thought it necessary to change their central theme.

It still seems to me that the replacement of the classical system of economic analysis by the neo-classical one was a fairly protracted process rather than any sudden revolution. Using the terminology of Lakatos, the period from 1862 to 1882 can be regarded as one in which the classical and the neo-classical research programmes coexisted, the one declining, the other growing. In 1871 Jevons played a key role in initiating the process whereby the classical was to be replaced by the neo-classical, but this was only a part of his own personal research programme. It is scarcely surprising – although some commentators seem to find it so – that in carrying out his work Jevons sometimes took up and used tools developed in the classical system when these seemed appropriate for his purpose, so that his work can be seen as blending classical and neo-classical elements.

Yet to say that there was no *sudden* revolution is not to say that there was no revolution at all. The process of transition which led to the replacement of classical Political Economy by neo-classical Economics may have taken all the years from 1862 to 1882 and more, but it happened and ultimately its outcome was a fundamental change.

Turning to the side of policy, I have suggested that it is difficult to match the idea of a 'Marginal Revolution' in 1871 with a turning point at or about the same date in the orientation of British economic policy. But if we extend our view over the years from

1862 to 1882 we can much more clearly perceive a process of transition from a more individualist to a more collectivist approach to be taking place, with public opinion coming to question the established Victorian values of self-help and independence. And this very same process of transition can be traced out in the work of Jevons himself on economic policy.

Nowadays it is not by policy-makers but by the economics profession that Jevons is, and will continue to be, remembered. For both theoretical and applied economics he changed the agenda and the implications of his ideas are still being worked out by professional economists (see, for example, Creedy, 1992). To have achieved this, and more, amply merits the recognition which the University of Manchester has accorded Jevons.

Notes

1. Social, political and intellectual historians have all suggested dates from which a 'revolution in economic policy' in the third quarter of the 19th century could be said to commence. Professor T.W. Hutchison chooses 1870 as 'in round figures ... the most generally suitable starting date' (1978, p.94), and in this is followed by Professor J.F.C. Harrison (1990). Checkland dated the process from the end of Gladstone's first ministry in 1874 (1983, p.124); G. Kitson Clark selected 1865, 'an arbitrary date' but 'the year of a general election and the death of Palmerston' (1973, p.227), although in an earlier book he had held 'that the "period of *laissez-faire*" and the "period of collectivism" run concurrently like prison sentences, and cover most of the nineteenth century' (1967, p.163).

2. In this my approach and the results I derive from it differ substantially from those of Professor Rhead S. Bowman (1989). He contends that 'in his work on economic theory Jevons's purpose was to establish new theories in the principal areas treated by the science, value and distribution, which would, if my interpretation is correct, complement his social philosophy and provide a theoretical basis for a program of social reform' (Bowman, 1989, p.1134). While I find much to agree with in Professor Bowman's paper I cannot accept his contention that Jevons had first worked out his social philosophy and then developed his economic theory as a basis for his social reforms. The main grounds for this appear to be that 'Jevons apparently rejected the classical productive labour doctrine with its minimal public sector implications, several years *before* he formulated his own system of economic theory'. His evidence for this is that in the work on *Social Statistics, or the Science of Towns* which Jevons began in Sydney in 1856 (Black, 1981b, pp.12, 31) he did not include government and intellectual workers under the heading 'Unproductive Population', as a classical economist would have done. But Jevons was not, by his own account, using an economist's classification, but that developed by the

statistician William Farr for the English Census (Jevons, 1905, pp.106-107).   If
indeed Jevons had developed his ideas in this manner it would have been decidedly
out of character for him not to have published those ideas or referred to them, either
in *TPE* or in earlier writings.   The idea that a thinker of Jevons's stature should
have worked out his whole programme of social reform and then developed the
theories necessary to underpin them is naturally attractive; my own account here is
more untidy, but I hope it is closer to the historical facts.

3.   On the place of the idea of 'character' in Jevons's thinking, see also White 1994,
especially pp. 441-2.

References

Bagehot, Walter (1879), *Economic Studies*, London: Longmans, Green & Co.

Best, Geoffrey (1979), *Mid-Victorian Britain 1851-70*, London:
Fontana/Collins.

Bibby, C. (ed.) (1967), *The Essence of T.H. Huxley: Selections from his
writings*, London: Macmillan.

Black, R.D. Collison (1962), 'W.S. Jevons and the economists of his time', *The
Manchester School* **30** (3), September, 203-22.

— (ed.), (1971b) *The Theory of Political Economy by W.S. Jevons*, Pelican
Classics edition, Harmondsworth: Penguin Books.

— (1972b), 'Jevons, Bentham and De Morgan', *Economica*, **39** (153), 119-34.

— (ed.), (1972d-81c), *Papers and Correspondence of William Stanley Jevons*,
Vols I-VII, London: Macmillan for the Royal Economic Society.

— (1972e), 'W.S. Jevons and the Foundation of Modern Economics', *History of
Political Economy*, **4** (2), 364-78.

— (1981b), 'W.S. Jevons' in D.P. O'Brien and J.R. Presley (eds), *Pioneers of
Modern Economics*, London: Macmillan, pp.1-35.

— (1990a), 'Jevons, Marshall and the Utilitarian Tradition', *Scottish Journal of
Political Economy*, **37** (1), 5-17.

— (1990b), 'W.S. Jevons and the development of marginal utility analysis in
British economics', *Schriften des Vereins für Social-politik*, Neue Folge,
Band 115/IX: Studien zur Entwicklung der Ökonomischen Theorie, **IX**, 9-
18.

— (1992b), 'Attempts by Jevons and Walras to publicise each other's work',
Revue européenne des sciences sociales, **30** (92), 109-29.

Blaug, Mark (1985), *Economic Theory in Retrospect*, Fourth Edition,
Cambridge, England: Cambridge University Press.

Bowman, Rhead S. (1989), 'Jevons's Economic Theory in relation to Social
Change and Public Policy', *Journal of Economic Issues*, **23** (4), 1123-47.

Burn, W.L. (1964), *The Age of Equipoise, A Study of the mid-Victorian
Generation*, London: George Allen and Unwin Ltd.

Cairnes, J.E. (1873), *Essays in Political Economy, theoretical and applied*,
London: Macmillan & Co.

Cannan, Edwin (1893:1903), *A History of the Theories of Production and Distribution in English Political Economy from 1776 to 1848*, First ed., 1893; Second ed., London: P.S. King & Sons, 1903.

Checkland, S.G. (1983), *British public policy 1776-1939*, Cambridge, England: Cambridge University Press.

Clark, G. Kitson (1967), *An Expanding Society: Britain 1830-1900*, Cambridge, England: Cambridge University Press.

— (1973), *Churchmen and the Condition of England, 1832-1885*, London: Methuen & Co. Ltd.

Collini, Stefan (1991), *Public Moralists: Political Thought and Intellectual Life in Britain 1850-1930*, Oxford: Clarendon Press.

Creedy, John (1992), 'Jevons's Complex Cases in the Theory of Exchange', *Journal of the History of Economic Thought*, **14** (1), 55-69.

Dicey, A.V. (1905), *Lectures on the relation between Law and Public Opinion in England during the nineteenth century*, London: Macmillan & Co.

Edgeworth, F.Y. (1891), Review of *The Scope and Method of Political Economy* by J.N. Keynes, *Economic Journal* **I** (2), 420-23.

Fetter, Frank W. (1965), *Development of British Monetary Orthodoxy, 1797-1875*, Cambridge, MA: Harvard University Press.

Harrison, J.F.C. (1990), *Late Victorian Britain, 1870-1901*, London and New York: Routledge.

Hébert, R.F. and R.B. Ekelund (1984), 'Welfare Economics', in J. Creedy and D.P. O'Brien (eds), *Economic Analysis in Historical Perspective*, London: Butterworths, pp.46-83.

Hutchison, T.W. (1972), 'The "Marginal Revolution" and the Decline and Fall of English Classical Political Economy', *History of Political Economy*, **4** (2), 442-68.

— (1978), *On Revolutions and Progress in Economic Knowledge*, Cambridge, England: Cambridge University Press.

Ingram, J.K. (1888;1915), *A History of Political Economy*, London, A. & C. Black, First ed., 1888; New and enlarged ed., 1915.

Jevons, William Stanley (1865), *The Coal Question*, London: Macmillan & Co.

— (1867), 'On the Analogy between the Post Office, Telegraphs, and other Systems of Conveyance of the United Kingdom, as regards Government Control', *Transactions of the Manchester Statistical Society*, Session 1866-67, 89-104, reprinted in Jevons, 1883.

— (1869), 'On the Work of the Society in Connection with the Questions of the Day', *Transactions of the Manchester Statistical Society*, Session 1869-70, 1-14, reprinted in Jevons, 1883.

— (1870), 'Opening Address of the President of Section F (Economic Science and Statistics) of the British Association for the Advancement of Science, at the Fortieth Meeting, at Liverpool', *Journal of the Statistical Society of London*, **33**, 309-26.

— (1871), *The Theory of Political Economy*, London, First ed.: Macmillan & Co.

— (1874a), *The Principles of Science: A Treatise on Logic and Scientific Method*, London: Macmillan & Co.; Second ed., 1877: reprinted New York: Dover Publications Inc. 1958.

— (1874b), 'The Progress of the Mathematical Theory of Political Economy', *Journal of the [Royal] Statistical Society*, **37**, 478-88. (Reprinted in *P & C*, VII, pp.75-85).

— (1875), *Money and the Mechanism of Exchange*, London: C. Kegan Paul & Co.

— (1876a) 'On the United Kingdom Alliance, and its Prospects of Success', *Transactions of the Manchester Statistical Society*, Session 1875-76, 127-42, reprinted in Jevons 1883.

— (1876b) 'The Future of Political Economy', *Fortnightly Review*, **20** (n.s.) 617-31, reprinted in Jevons 1905.

— (1878), *Science Primers: Political Economy*, London: Macmillan & Co.

— (1879a), *The Theory of Political Economy*, Second ed., London: Macmillan & Co.

— (1879b) 'John Stuart Mill's Philosophy Tested, IV, Utilitarianism', *Contemporary Review*, **36**, 521-38, reprinted in Jevons 1890.

— (1882), *The State in relation to Labour*, London: Macmillan & Co., Third ed., 1894.

— (1883), *Methods of Social Reform and other papers*, London: Macmillan & Co.

— (1884), *Investigations in Currency and Finance*. Edited, with an Introduction by H.S. Foxwell, London: Macmillan & Co.

— (1890), *Pure Logic and Other Minor Works*, edited by Robert Adamson and Harriet A. Jevons, London: Macmillan & Co.

— (1905), *The Principles of Economics*, A Fragment of a Treatise on the Industrial Mechanism of Society and other Papers, with a Preface by Henry Higgs, London: Macmillan & Co. Ltd.

Keynes, J.M. (1972), 'William Stanley Jevons 1835-1882. A Centenary Allocution on his Life and Work as Economist and Statistician', *Essays in Biography, Collected Writings*, London: Macmillan for the Royal Economic Society, **X**, 109-60.

Koot, Gerard M. (1980), 'English historical economics and the emergence of economic history in England', *History of Political Economy*, **12** (2), 174-205.

Kurz, Heinz D. and N. Salvadori (1994), 'Competition and Long-Period Positions in Classical and Neo-Classical Economics', in C. Perrotta and V. Gioia (eds), *Where is Economics Going? Historical Viewpoints*. Lecce, Centro di Studi Economici, Università di Lecce.

Laidler, David (1982), 'Jevons on Money', *The Manchester School*, **50** (4), 326-53.

— (1991), *The Golden Age of the Quantity Theory*, Hemel Hempstead: Philip Allan.

Leslie, T.E. Cliffe (1879a), Untitled Review of Jevons's *Theory of Political Economy, The Academy*, no. 377, n.s., 26 July, 59-60. Reprinted in *P & C*, VII, 157-62.

— (1879b), *Essays in Political and Moral Philosophy*, Dublin: Hodges, Foster & Figgis.

Lowe, Robert (1867), 'Trades Unions', *Quarterly Review*, **123**, 351-83.

Mill, John Stuart (1848;1909), *Principles of Political Economy with some of their applications to Social Philosophy*, London: Parker & Co. New edition, edited by W.J. Ashley, London: Longmans Green & Co. 1909.

Mills, John (1867), 'On Credit Cycles and the Origin of Commercial Panics', *Transactions of the Manchester Statistical Society*, Session 1867-68, 6-40.

Myint, H. (1948), *Theories of Welfare Economics*, London: Longmans, Green & Co. in association with the London School of Economics.

O'Brien, D.P. (1983; 1994), 'Theories of the History of Science: A Test Case' in A.W. Coats, (ed.), *Methodological Controversy in Economics*, Greenwich, Conn. and London: JAI Press, pp.89-124. Reprinted in *Methodology Money and the Firm*, Aldershot: Edward Elgar 1994, Vol. I, pp.33-68.

Peach, Terry (1987), 'Jevons as an economic theorist', in John Eatwell, Murray Milgate and Peter Newman, (eds), *The New Palgrave. A Dictionary of Economics*, London: Macmillan Press, **III**, 1014-19.

Peart, Sandra J. (1990), 'Jevons's Applications of Utilitarian Theory to Economic Policy', *Utilitas*, **2** (2), 281-306.

— (1991), 'Sunspots and Expectations: W.S. Jevons's Theory of Economic Fluctuations', *Journal of the History of Economic Thought*, **13** (2), 243-65.

— (1993), 'W.S. Jevons's Methodology of Economics: Some Implications of the Procedures for "Inductive Quantification" ', *History of Political Economy*, **25** (3), 435-60.

Petrella, Frank (1970), 'Individual, Group or Government? Smith, Mill and Sidgwick', *History of Political Economy*, **2** (1), 152-76.

— (1977), 'Benthamism and the demise of Classical economic *Ordnungspolitik*', *History of Political Economy,* **9** (2), 215-36.

Schabas, Margaret (1990), *A World Ruled by Number: William Stanley Jevons and the Rise of Mathematical Economics*, Princeton, N.J.: Princeton University Press.

Sidgwick, Henry (1886;1964), 'On the Economic Exceptions to Laissez Faire'. Presidential Address to Section F of the British Association for the Advancement of Science. Reprinted under the title 'Economic Socialism' in R.L. Smyth (ed.), *Essays in the Economics of Socialism and Capitalism*, London: G. Duckworth & Co. Ltd., 1964.

Spencer, Herbert (1879), *The Data of Ethics*, London: Williams & Norgate.

— (1884;1969), *The Man versus the State*, First ed., London: Williams & Norgate, 1884; Pelican Classics ed.: Harmondsworth, Penguin Books, 1969.

Stigler, Stephen M. (1982), 'Jevons as Statistician', *The Manchester School*, **50** (4), 354-65.

White, Michael V. (1989), 'Why are there no supply and demand curves in Jevons?', *History of Political Economy*, **21** (3), 425-56.

— (1994), 'Bridging the Natural and the Social: Science and Character in Jevons's Political Economy', *Economic Inquiry*, **32** (July) 429-44.

[10]

W. S. Jevons and the Foundation of Modern Economics

R. D. Collison Black

We hope to go to Bellagio on Monday and stay about three nights there, then to Lugano . . .

Mrs. HARRIET JEVONS to her sister, Sarah Taylor,
Milan, 28 March 1874

I

IT WOULD have added to the aptness of this occasion if I had been able to record that 1871 had seen not only the publication of Jevons' *Theory of Political Economy* but also a visit by its author to Bellagio. Yet the fact that there was an untidy gap of some three years between those two events may serve to bring out the point of view on which I base this paper. The centenary of Jevons' first statement of his theory to the British Association was duly commemorated in 1962;[1] we are meeting now to commemorate another centenary, but one could perhaps justify a commemoration in 1979, the centenary of the publication of the second edition of Jevons' *Theory of Political Economy* (in some respects more definitive and significant than the first)—or at almost any other date through the seventies.

In other words, while 1971 may form a convenient focal point at which to celebrate the advent of marginalism, in my view it is not correct to think of 1871 as "the year of the marginal revolution." The phrase "marginal revolution" is attractive, and useful if employed with due caution, but so interpreted, it relates to a process and not to an event comparable with, say, the establishment of the Paris Commune. That process was neither begun nor ended in 1871, though it was certainly significantly forwarded. All this is familiar,

R. D. COLLISON BLACK *is Professor of Economics at The Queen's University of Belfast.*
1. Cf. *Manchester School* 30 (Sept. 1962): 203–73.

and I think hardly controversial, but the popular use of the term "revolution" tends to confine it so much to striking and violent events that it is perhaps worth emphasizing that the dictionary definition includes "fundamental reconstruction," which can be a lengthy process; and it is this with which we are concerned in the history of economic ideas of a century ago.

That process of fundamental reconstruction which transformed political economy into economics had many facets, but in one sense it could be seen as involving a shift from mainly macroeconomic to mainly microeconomic studies. So while we are surveying the whole process broadly, it may also be appropriate to come down to the micro level and to try to see it from the point of view of one of the main participants, W. S. Jevons.

We do not lack assessments of the life and work of Jevons and of his place in the history of economic thought, and these assessments have been made by some of the most eminent economists of our time,[2] so that for me to go over the ground again might result in that negative utility which, according to Jevons himself, "consists in the production of pain."[3] Instead I propose in this paper to attempt three more specific and limited tasks:

(i) An examination of the special qualities which Jevons brought to the study of political economy;

(ii) A consideration of the effect which they may have had in shaping his approach to the subject and the character of his contribution to it, especially the contribution which he made in 1871;

(iii) A comparison of Jevons' expectations concerning the future development of economics with the development which has in fact taken place in the intervening century.

II

"I think there is some fear of the too great influence of authoritative writers in political economy. I protest against deference for any man, whether John Stuart Mill, or Adam Smith, or Aristotle,

2. J. M. Keynes, "William Stanley Jevons, 1835–1882: A Centenary Allocution on His Life and Work as Economist and Statistician," *Journal of the Royal Statistical Society* 99 (1936): 516–48; reprinted in his *Essays in Biography* (1951 ed.), pp. 255–309; L. C. Robbins, "The Place of Jevons in the History of Economic Thought," *Manchester School* 7 (1936): 1–17.

3. Jevons, *The Theory of Political Economy*, ed. R. D. Collison Black, Pelican classics (Harmondsworth, 1970), p. 114; all page references are to this edition.

being allowed to check inquiry'' wrote Jevons.[4] This well-known passage, especially when taken in conjunction with the statement which precedes it, that ''in the republic of the sciences sedition and even anarchy are beneficial in the long run to the greatest happiness of the greatest number,'' has given rise to the impression that one of the qualities which Jevons brought to the study of political economy was the quality of being an outsider and a revolutionary—the man with a chip on his shoulder because he found it hard to get his ideas accepted.

The corollary of this proposition is that there were, at the time when Jevons was developing his ideas, insiders; or to put the matter more formally and precisely in the now familiar terminology of Professor T. S. Kuhn[5] that in British political economy there was a scientific community, its center in J. S. Mill, which had established a paradigm (in the shape of the classical theory of value and distribution) which governed their view of the economic world and enabled them to cope with its problems by the puzzle-solving techniques of normal science. However, awareness of anomalies was creating a state of crisis in the subject, giving opportunity for the emergence of revolutionary theories, preparatory to the occurrence of a radical paradigm shift.

How far does the experience of Jevons accord with this interpretation of the situation? In parts it accords with it quite well, in parts rather badly. In fact it seems to me to demonstrate that Kuhn's theory of scientific revolutions is itself a paradigm which is inadequate to explain all the facts.

In the first place, Kuhn's concepts relate to a scientific community whose field of research is not generally accessible to the layman, and whose members essentially report to one another.[6] Yet, as Professors Spengler and Eagly have argued,[7] economics did not attain

---

4. Jevons, *Theory*, p. 261.
5. Kuhn, *The Structure of Scientific Revolutions* (Chicago, 1962). Cf. A. W. Coats, ''Is There a 'Structure of Scientific Revolutions' in Economics?'' *Kyklos* 22 (1969): 289–96; M. Bronfenbrenner, ''The 'Structure of Revolutions' in Economic Thought,'' *History of Political Economy* 3, no. 1 (Spring 1971): 136–51.
6. Kuhn, pp. 20–21.
7. J. J. Spengler, ''Exogenous and Endogenous Influences in the Formation of Post-1870 Economic Thought,'' in *Events, Ideology and Economic Theory*, ed. R. V. Eagly (Detroit, 1968); cf. pp. 159–60, 189–90.

to this stage of professionalization until the post-1870 period. According to Kuhn, this would place the subject in a "pre-paradigm" phase; yet most of us would feel inclined to accept that classical political economy had established a paradigm.

In fact the state of economic thought in England from about 1850 to 1870 suggests that a discipline may very well have reached the stage of establishing a paradigm without being fully professionalized. Now an outsider who seeks to introduce new ideas, ultimately leading to a paradigm shift, has two problems—that of getting his ideas published in a reputable form, and that of getting them accepted. It would seem that when a subject is not professionalized, the first of these tasks at least ought to be easier; it is therefore interesting to find that one of the outsider economists of the period held precisely the opposite view.

In his *Recent Political Economy* published in 1867, William Lucas Sargant complained of the fact that England possessed no professional economic journal comparable with the *Journal des Economistes* in France:

> The natural result is an entire discouragement of individual inquiry, for who will work out a new theory, when he has no means of securing public attention? The more original is an author, the less will he be relished by the reading world; unable to appreciate him, and shrinking from the trouble of unlearning the lessons it has acquired; the more dependent therefore is such an author, on the good offices of those who profess to weigh the merits of new publications.
>
> So low has England sunk in an ignorant contempt of innovation in Political Economy, that new principles are not merely condemned: they are even refused a hearing, unless they are put forth by a friend of the reviewer: personal partialities and antipathies have taken the place of discriminating justice. An author, the cut of whose beard is disliked, may publish at his own expense and will not have the poor satisfaction of being abused.[8]

8. W. L. Sargant, *Recent Political Economy* (1867), Introduction, p. v. Sargant (1809–89) was a Birmingham small-arms manufacturer. He wrote a number of economic works which show independence of mind, if not great originality.

Was Jevons one of those who suffered from this state of affairs?
The evidence on this point is mixed, but it is noteworthy that his
first successes came, not with his *Notice of a General Mathematical
Theory of Political Economy*, but with his empirical works—his
Statistical Diagrams and *A Serious Fall in the Value of Gold*.
This fits interestingly with Sargant's argument, for the *General
Mathematical Theory* was a piece which could only be addressed to
and understood by an audience of professional economists, whereas
the other works were such as could be appreciated by laymen and
particularly by businessmen.

It is true that in the case of his statistical diagrams and *A
Serious Fall* Jevons had to resort to publication at his own expense,
and that he was at first depressed and discouraged by the lack of interest in them;[9] it is true also that one of the first notices which his
diagrams received in the *Economist* could be put down to "personal
partialities," for it was the work of Richard Holt Hutton, who was
related to Jevons by marriage.[10] Nevertheless some of the best notices
of Jevons' work came unsolicited, and it was not long until he had
achieved recognition beyond his expectations.[11]

So it would appear that it was not only "the cut of an author's
beard" which mattered in the literary London of the 1860's; editors
and reviewers were not necessarily hostile to a young unknown who
had something worthwhile to say. However if the initial difficulties of
getting his work published in a reputable form did not prove too
serious for Jevons, to have the content of his theories accepted by
his peers was another matter. I shall refer to this question again

9. Jevons, *Letters and Journal of W. Stanley Jevons* (1886), pp. 162, 175;
and cf. Rosamond Könekamp, "William Stanley Jevons (1835–1882): Some
Biographical Notes," *Manchester School* 30 (Sept. 1962): 262–63.

10. This review appeared in the *Economist* 19, no. 1267, 15 Nov. 1862. Richard
Holt Hutton (1826–97) was married to a granddaughter of William Roscoe,
Jevons' maternal grandfather. Hutton was best known as editor of the *Spectator*
and at this time had just begun his long association with Meredith Townsend on
that paper. However, he still retained a connection with the *Economist*, of which
he had been nominally editor from 1858 until 1861 under the direction first of
James Wilson and then of Walter Bagehot. Cf. A. Buchan, *The Spare Chancellor*
(London, 1959), p. 127.

11. E.g., the review of the Statistical Diagrams in the *Exchange Magazine*
referred to in *Letters and Journal*, p. 178. Cf. also the attention and public
praise given to *A Serious Fall* by Cairnes and Fawcett. R. D. Collison Black,
"Jevons and Cairnes," *Economica* 27 (Aug. 1960): 214–32.

later in this paper;[12] here I am concerned only to underline the point that there is a distinction between being accepted as a reputable author on a subject and having all one's theories accepted. Some of Jevons' own comments, and some of the interpretations placed on them by others, have tended to obscure this.

There is another attribute which Jevons brought to the study of economics which has not received anything like as much attention, but which I suggest is of considerably greater importance. Jevons was, as Keynes put it, "the first theoretical economist to survey his material with the prying eyes and fertile, controlled imagination of the natural scientist."[13] In this respect he was genuinely one of the "new men"—coming from an intellectual background markedly different to that of the established figures in political economy—and his approach to the subject might therefore be expected to be novel and challenging.

I suggest that it may be more relevant and valuable to look at Jevons, not in relation to the scientific community of economics (an entity whose existence *circa* 1860–70 I presume to question), but in relation to more recognized and recognizable communities in the natural sciences, particularly of chemists, astronomers, and meteorologists. It was in 1858 that Jevons reached the conclusion that "there are plenty of people engaged with physical science, and practical science and arts may be left to look after themselves, but thoroughly to understand the principles of society appears to me now the most cogent business."[14] At this time his training and experience were mainly in applied chemistry, although his personal research had led him into meteorology, "a sort of difficult *scientific exercise* rather than a science itself."[15] In chemistry Jevons had distinguished connections; he had been recommended for his post as assayer in Sydney by his teacher Thomas Graham, professor of chemistry at University College, London, and afterwards master of the Mint. On his return from Australia Jevons was told by Graham that he would have been prepared to recommend him for a post at the Kew Observatory, and

12. Below, end of Sec. III.
13. Keynes, *Essays in Biography*, p. 268.
14. *Letters and Journal*, p. 101.
15. *Ibid.*, p. 89. Cf. Keynes's contention that Jevons "approached the complex economic facts of the real world, both literally and metaphorically, as meteorologist." *Essays in Biography*, p. 267.

in 1862 Graham again offered to place Jevons in a lectureship in natural philosophy at the Andersonian Institution in Glasgow.[16]

Jevons was also strongly influenced by his cousin Harry Roscoe,[17] who was one of Bunsen's research students at Heidelberg and became professor of chemistry at Owens College, Manchester. It was the example of Roscoe which led Jevons towards scientific studies, Roscoe who arranged the reading and publication of his early papers, and Roscoe who was disappointed by his cousin's decision to become a political economist.

These early papers of Jevons were concerned with such problems as the forms of clouds; when Jevons sent copies of them to the great astronomer Sir John F. W. Herschel in 1861, they were favorably received and correspondence between the two men continued over the ensuing decade.[18] So it seems clear that Jevons could have made at the least a respectable career as a practitioner of "normal science" in chemistry or meteorology. He never lost his interest in the natural sciences, and indeed one of the very last papers which he published was on a meteorological topic—"Reflected Rainbows."[19]

On the foundation of this basic training in experimental science Jevons deliberately built a further training in logic and mathematics so that he ultimately acquired a knowledge of scientific method which was both broad and deep. This is abundantly demonstrated in his massive *Principles of Science* (1874), which has largely been ignored by economists, no doubt, as Professor Ernest Nagel has suggested, because it lacks any specific treatment of the methods of social science.[20] However Dr. Wolfe Mays has argued that "there is a close relationship between Jevons' philosophy of the natural sciences and his methodology of the social sciences," and I think it must be accepted that he has made out his case.[21]

16. W. S. Jevons to F. B. Miller, 5 Oct. 1859; Jevons to Henrietta Jevons, 3 March 1862, in unpublished letters in the Jevons Papers.

17. Sir Henry Enfield Roscoe (1833–1915), professor of chemistry at Owens College, Manchester, 1857–85; vice-chancellor of the University of London, 1896–1902; M.P. for Manchester (Southern Division), 1885; privy councillor, 1909.

18. W. S. Jevons to Sir John Herschel, 21 July 1861, in Herschel Papers, Royal Society, London.

19. *Field Naturalist*, Aug. 1882.

20. Nagel, Introduction to the Dover ed. of Jevons, *The Principles of Science* (New York, 1957), pp. lii–liii.

21. W. Mays, "Jevons's Conception of Scientific Method," *Manchester School* 30 (Sept. 1962): 223.

Two particular points made by Mays seem to me of special significance in relation to Jevons' economic work. The first is that "following Boole and De Morgan, he believed that any rational system of ideas could be put into symbolic form. The system could then be operated on according to the laws of logic to produce a chain of deductions. In discussing the logical method to be used in economics, Jevons therefore emphasized its deductive character." Mays goes on to emphasize that the familiar criticism of Jevons as a mathematical economist who knew very little mathematics misses the point that "as far as his formal studies were concerned Jevons was essentially a logician trying to base mathematics on logic." The second point is that "Jevons no doubt under the influence of his meteorological work . . . put considerable emphasis on the study of statistical data in economics."[22]

Both of these points can be explained by the nature of Jevons' early training and interests as a man of science; both have considerable importance in explaining the character of his contribution to economics in general and to economic theory in particular.

III

"The keystone of the whole Theory of Exchange," said Jevons, "and of the principal problems of Economics, lies in this proposition— *The ratio of exchange of any two commodities will be the reciprocal of the ratio of the final degrees of utility of the quantities of commodity available for consumption after the exchange is completed.*"[23]

Now this certainly represented a pathbreaking change in economic theory; and it may be instructive, as Professor Spengler has said, to ask "of the path-breaker, why he elected to break a particular path."[24] Professor Spengler adds that to answer such questions we need adequate biographical information, and in attempting to answer them for Jevons I think we shall realize again the truth of Professor Jaffé's statement: "If we consider carefully a truly original concept, even one couched in austere mathematical symbols, we find that it is inevitably composed of an intricate combination of elements which are derived not only from the discoverer's social, intellectual, and physical

22. Mays, pp. 233, 236, 228.
23. Jevons, *Theory*, p. 139.
24. Spengler, p. 179.

environment, but also from his own personal traits, attitudes and endowments.''[25]

In dealing with the question posed above, the distinction, which again we owe to Professor Spengler,[26] between the *core* and the *shell* of economics makes a useful point of departure. Few economists today would question that the concept of economizing behavior is an essential part of the core of their subject, but with the classical economists this was not so. Now, as I have argued elsewhere,[27] what Jevons was attempting to do from 1860 onwards was to formulate and present the ''true theory of economy'' as ''a very contracted science''—and this he himself states clearly as the objective of the *Theory of Political Economy*: ''But as all the physical sciences have their basis more or less obviously in the general principles of mechanics, so all branches and divisions of economic science must be pervaded by certain general principles. It is to the investigation of such principles—to the tracing out of the mechanics of self-interest and utility, that this essay has been devoted.''[28]

So my contention is that Jevons was really setting out to establish the core of our subject as a science of economizing behavior, and the reasons for his so doing can be found in his intellectual environment and in his personal circumstances. First of all, this is clearly the approach of a man trained in the natural sciences, the element in Jevons' intellectual background which I have stressed. Yet, secondly, it is an approach which grew out of Jevons' solitary years in Australia. Examination of his personal journal and correspondence, particularly during 1858–59, shows that he then thought long and deeply about his own position and prospects in terms of ''using life with true economy and effect'';[29] his conception of political economy as ''a sort of vague mathematics which calculates the causes and effects of man's industry, and shows how it may best be applied'' dates from that time also.

Many writers have felt that, as Professor Blaug says, ''A change

25. W. Jaffé, ''Biography and Economic Analysis,'' *Western Economic Journal* 3 (Summer 1965): 224.

26. Spengler, p. 187.

27. Black, Introduction to the Pelican Classics Edition of Jevons, *Theory*, pp. 12–13.

28. Jevons, *Theory*, p. 50.

29. W. S. Jevons to Lucy Jevons, 11 Jan. 1858; *Letters and Journal*, p. 99.

of emphasis as drastic as the marginal revolution . . . must surely have been associated with changes in the institutional structure of society and with the emergence of new practical problems.''[30] Nothing of this kind can be readily traced in the circumstances under which Jevons lived while preparing his theory; but if the interpretation put forward here is correct, it is unnecessary to look for it. For, as Professor Spengler has argued, a thought system which is based upon concepts by postulation is much more likely to be impervious to extraneous influences than one which is based on concepts by intuition— and this is precisely the type of logical thought system which Jevons was constructing.[31]

If Jevons was attempting to set out the core of economic behavior (as a process of maximizing utility) then it would seem that the mathematical logic of the process should have been more important to him than the psychological assumptions of hedonism, and I think that Jevons' own statements are consistent with this view. On any occasion when he expounded his conception of the changes which were taking place in economic studies, and his own contributions to them, he laid primary stress on the mathematical aspects of the utility concept as involving a functional relationship between variables.[32]

Ross Robertson has indeed suggested that ''the Benthamite approach was thoroughly understood by Jevons and subtly rejected,'' and Wolfe Mays has gone on from this to argue that ''Jevons's statement that economics deals with pleasures and pains would then seem little else but a *façon de parler.* . . . Jevons is . . . giving an operational definition of pleasure and pain in terms of our economic transactions.''[33] It would tend to strengthen and complete my own line of

30. Mark Blaug, *Economic Theory in Retrospect,* 2d ed. (1968), p. 5.

31. Spengler, p. 165. Spengler defines concepts by postulation as ''concepts by intellection, imagination, perception, the meaning of any one of which 'in whole or in part is designated by the postulates of some specific deductively formulated theory in which it occurs,' and the use of which in scientific and philosophic analysis entails the use of formal logical reasoning, deduction and mathematics.'' Cf. F. S. C. Northrop, *The Logic of the Sciences and the Humanities,* chaps. 5 and 13.

32. Cf. ''The Mathematical Theory of Political Economy,'' *Journal of the Royal Statistical Society* 37 (1874): 478–88, and especially p. 487.

33. Ross M. Robertson, ''Jevons and His Precursors,'' *Econometrica,* July 1951, pp. 233–34; Mays, 240–41. Compare Northrop's firm assertion that ''Jevons'

argument here if I could accept these views; but I do not think that Jevons in the *Theory of Political Economy* ''subtly rejected'' the Benthamite approach. His economics would have been better if he had —he could, for example, have come much closer to realizing his ideal of a quantitative science of economics if he had dealt simply with the ''laws of demand'' instead of trying to determine the ''laws of utility.''[34]

Adherence to Benthamism may well have been a main reason for Jevons' oft-remarked failure to construct a complete and consistent marginal theory of value and distribution. However, there were other reasons for this also. When Jevons was preparing the second edition of his *Theory*, he told Walras: ''My idea now is to produce a considerable volume with full references, descriptions and quotations from works on the math-method, also including translations of Cournot's and your works, and with the best abstract I can get of Gossen.'' He did not carry out this program, and Walras made no attempt to conceal his disappointment at the failure.[35]

Earlier, in 1875, Jevons had promised Walras that in that year he would give papers on mathematical economics to the Political Economy Club and to Section F of the British Association. He gave addresses to both bodies in 1875, but the first was on railway administration and the second on the coal question. This suggests a reason for the failure to live up to the expectations of Walras—Jevons simply was not a one-subject man. Having worked out and published his ideas on the basic ''mechanics of utility and self-interest,'' he was anxious to move on and contribute to some of the many other subdivisions into which he conceived economics must be separated.

It is not the purpose of this article to discuss or evaluate the contributions which Jevons made to subdivisions of economics outside the theory of value and distribution. Yet it is impossible to place his

---

economic theory presupposes a specific philosophical theory'' (i.e., Bentham's). Northrop, p. 350.

34. Cf. my note 41 to p. 174 of Jevons, *Theory*. I have attempted to explore the relationships between Jevons' economics and Bentham's utilitarianism somewhat further in the Jevons Centenary Lecture delivered at University College, London, ''Jevons, Bentham and De Morgan,'' *Economica* 39 (May 1972): 119–34.

35. Jaffé, *Correspondence of Léon Walras and Related Papers* (Amsterdam, 1965), 1:599, 645. Walras wrote: ''Je vous avouerai franchement que je n'ai pas trouvé que vous ayez fait de cette publication ce qu'il était possible d'en faire. . . .''

contribution to the development of marginalism in proper perspective without referring to them. So it should be remembered that after his first statement of the "true theory of economy" had failed to gain attention, Jevons turned to prosecute his studies in the statistical analysis of monetary problems with considerable success, even while he was devoting much time to the development of his system of logic.

By 1871 Jevons was well established in his chosen profession of social scientist—the Manchester professor traveling to London to read his papers to the [Royal] Statistical Society, to give evidence before parliamentary committees, to be consulted by the chancellor of the Exchequer.[36] It was, then, as an applied economist that his contemporaries knew and respected him, rather than as a theorist; "je vous connaissais de réputation, mais seulement comme auteur de travaux estimés sur la question de la variation des prix et de la dépréciation de la monnaie," wrote Walras to Jevons at the outset of their correspondence. "Je vous savais mathématicien, mais je me figurais que vos applications mathématiques étaient plûtot statistiques qu'économiques."[37] This comment suggests a view of Jevons which may in itself account to some extent for the failure of the *Theory of Political Economy* to gain rapid acceptance. Not only were its contents radically new, but they also came from an unexpected quarter. As the ideas of the marginalists gained ground, Jevons' reputation as a theorist grew; but although he did his share in propagating those ideas, he could not devote the whole of his restless energy and fertile mind to them. Already in 1875 he had begun to investigate "the Solar Period and the Price of Corn," and he had still to write many of the papers which were later collected into *Methods of Social Reform* and *Investigations in Currency and Finance*.

Jevons might well have returned to the core of theory if time had been given him. In the time that was given him, it may be asked, did he maximize the returns from his efforts by spreading them as widely as he did? Perhaps marginalism might have advanced more quickly had he concentrated more narrowly upon it; yet in the last analysis such speculation is surely, in every sense of the word, an impertinence. The history of every science is molded in part by the character of those who advance it, and it was not in the character of Jevons to advance

36. Cf. *Letters and Journal*, pp. 241, 245, 246.
37. Walras to Jevons, 23 mai 1874, in Jaffé, 1:397.

economics otherwise than as he did—by successive attacks on a number of fronts. To be one of the founders of marginalism was only one of his achievements, and in judging those achievements it must be remembered that the span from the time when Jevons presented his first paper to the British Association as a young unknown to the time of his death was just under twenty years. Few economists, indeed few scientists of any sort, can have accomplished so much in so short a lifetime.

IV

We are now perhaps in a position to see Jevons' *Theory of Political Economy* both in the wider perspective of his work in economics as a whole and in the longer perspective of a century of the development of economic thought since. As we look back over that century it may be instructive to consider what Jevons, as one of the participants in the "marginal revolution," thought the future development of economics should be and how far his expectations have been realized.

As is well known and documented, the 1870's were a period of heart searching and stock taking in economic thought,[38] and Jevons took his share in the process. His views on "The Future of Political Economy" are set out in his 1876 inaugural lecture of that title and in the Preface to the second (1879) edition of the *Theory*.[39] From these sources Jevons' specifications for the future shape of economics can readily be put together, and it is obvious that in his view it involved much more than simply the working out of the marginal principle.

Jevons frequently stated his belief in the "complete inductive method," which involved the combination of deductive reasoning with empirical verification. Hence, he was in no doubt that "the present economical state of society cannot possibly be explained by theory alone,"[40] but equally clear that empirical and historical studies alone

38. Cf. T. W. Hutchison, *A Review of Economic Doctrines, 1870–1929* (London, 1953), chap. 1.

39. Jevons, "The Future of Political Economy," Introductory Lecture at the opening of the session 1876–77 at University College, London, Faculty of Arts and Laws. *Fortnightly Review* 20 (Dec. 1876): 617–31, reprinted in *Principles of Economics* (1905), pp. 187–206.

40. *Ibid.*, p. 195.

would be valueless without the aid of deduction. From this followed his well-known prescription for "the present chaotic state of Economics": "Subdivision is the remedy. We must distinguish the empirical element from the abstract theory, from the applied theory, and from the more detailed art of finance and administration. Thus will arise various sciences, such as commercial statistics, the mathematical theory of economics, systematic and descriptive economics, economic sociology, and fiscal science."[41]

The basic theory of economy—all that was attempted in the *Theory of Political Economy*—must be essentially mathematical in character, while the empirical studies would involve the application of statistical method. Professor Spengler has pointed out that "the welding of statistical and mathematico-economic theory did not proceed apace until in or after the late nineteenth century,"[42] but it was certainly envisaged by Jevons in 1871, and he emphasized that "the future progress of economics as a strict science must greatly depend upon our acquiring more accurate notions of the variable quantities concerned in the theory."[43] So Jevons can be seen to have envisaged economics as developing into a strict science or complex of sciences, with a mathematical core and a statistical shell.

Looking back on the *Theory of Political Economy* after a century we may be tempted to echo Keynes's exclamation: "How disappointing are the fruits, now that we have them, of the bright idea of reducing Economics to a mathematical application of the hedonistic calculus of Bentham!"[44] We may reasonably point out the dangers inherent in Jevons' overenthusiastic identification of the theory of economy with elementary mechanics. Was not this sort of thing the cause of that sorry state of affairs now prevailing and recently described by Martin Shubik, in which "with the arrogance that characterizes our profession it is customary to refer to a set of moderately dull exercises on some constructs arising from mediocre, casual utilitarian psychological theorizing as 'the theory of consumer choice' "?[45]

Perhaps it was, but in justice to Jevons we should remember that

41. Jevons, *Theory*, Preface to 2d ed., pp. 49–50.
42. Spengler, p. 173.
43. Jevons, *Theory*, p. 174.
44. Keynes, *Essays in Biography*, p. 155.
45. Shubik, "A Curmudgeon's Guide to Microeconomics," *Journal of Economic Literature* 8 (June 1970): 410.

all he was attempting was a pioneer statement of one, certainly fundamental part of what he envisaged as a highly complex science. Whatever we may say about the marginal revolution, none of us would deny that we have lived through another revolution in economics in the last twenty years; and if we were asked to say in what that revolution consists, we would probably point to the increasing rigor of theory and to the stress on econometric testing of it. If Jevons could be called upon to give his opinion of the economics of 1971, I suspect that he would only express surprise that it has taken us so long to get so far; for are we not now applying those lessons of the need for logic and measurement which he taught? I would contend that these, more than any statement of marginal utility theory, are the true hallmarks of his originality and the true sources of the contribution which Jevons the scientist made to the foundation of modern economic science.[46]

46. In an interesting article reporting on the various commemorations of the centenary of the ''birth of Marginal Utility Economics'' held in 1971, Dr. P. J. Uitermark has pointed out that some of the main features of the assessment of Jevons presented here are anticipated in S. J. Chapman, *Outlines of Political Economy* (new ed., 1920), pp. 448–49. Chapman there noted that Jevons ''realized to the full the technical possibilities of Utilitarianism'' and ''assimilated research in positive economics to research in the natural sciences.'' This very concise and well-balanced account of Jevons' contribution to the development of economics does not appear in the original (1911) edition of Chapman's *Outlines* and was unknown to me until Dr. Uitermark sent me a copy of his paper, ''De Geschiedenis van de Economie, 1871–1971: Een Verslag,'' *De Economist* 119, no. 6 (Nov.-Dec. 1971): 719–39.

6

JEVONS'S CONTRIBUTION TO THE TEACHING OF POLITICAL ECONOMY IN MANCHESTER AND LONDON

R. D. Collison Black

At the beginning of the nineteenth century none of those thinkers in Britain who were advancing the study of political economy were doing so from academic chairs in the subject – with the sole exception of Malthus after 1805. At the beginning of the twentieth century almost all such British thinkers held chairs of economics or political economy. Understanding of the process by which this change came about may be helped by a study of the way in which one leading nineteenth-century economist came also to be an academic.

W. Stanley Jevons (1835–82) provides a good subject for such a study. He holds a well-defined and accepted place in the history of economic thought as one of the makers of the 'Marginal Revolution', and there is a strong case for regarding him as one of the pioneers of modern economics.[1] At the same time Jevons was one of the first English economists whose career was mainly centred upon academic appointments outside the ancient universities of the United Kingdom. In this chapter, the three main phases into which that career was divided will be examined in sequence. The first deals with his early years, detailing the process by which Jevons came to be first an economist and then an academic; the second covers the period of his appointments at what was then Owens College, Manchester, from 1863 until 1876; and the third examines the last period of his life in London, during most of which he held the Chair of Political Economy at University College, London.

---

1 R. D. Collison Black, 'W. S. Jevons, 1835–82', in D. P. O'Brien and J. R. Presley (eds), *Pioneers of Modern Economics*, London: Macmillan, 1981, p.1.

162

JEVONS'S CONTRIBUTION IN MANCHESTER AND LONDON

I

The facts of Jevons's biography are well known and documented and need not be repeated here,[2] but certain features need to be stressed if his development as an academic economist is to be fully understood.

Although generally 'not in academic bowers but oppressed by mercantile and senatorial cares',[3] the classical economists nevertheless contrived to be curiously detached from the Industrial Revolution which was going on all around them, although in that struggle the captains of industry appealed frequently to 'the principles of political economy'. London, Edinburgh, Oxford, and Cambridge formed the economists' personal milieu, and the background of their studies was moral philosophy, not the natural philosophy which was finding practical applications in the 'dark satanic mills'. By contrast, Jevons's whole background was that of the industrial north of England at the height of its development; he was born and reared in Liverpool, where his father's family were engaged in the iron trade. His mother was a daughter of William Roscoe, who had combined a career as a banker with distinguished contributions to botany and the history of the Renaissance. Jevons thus grew up in a family where the idea of obtaining a living by working in industry or commerce was taken for granted, but in which there was also a remarkable breadth of culture, both literary and scientific.

The Jevons and Roscoe families were Unitarians, and as such were part of the Nonconformist community of the north of England which played so large a part in the social and economic development of the country in the Victorian era. Their outlook was always liberal, sometimes almost radical, and they always preserved a sturdy independence of mind: 'we Unitarians don't pray by Command of any human authority', wrote Thomas Jevons to his son William Stanley, when a day of prayer for peace was decreed by Royal Proclamation in 1855.[4] Through a wide circle of Nonconformist relations and friends the Jevons family mixed with some of the leading intellectual families of the time, such as the Martineaus[5] – but only with those who shared their dissenting outlook.

---

2 R. Konekamp, 'Biographical introduction' in R. D. Collison Black (ed.), *Papers and Correspondence of William Stanley Jevons*, Vol.I, London: Macmillan, 1972, pp.1–52.
3 From Thomas de Quincey's comment on Ricardo in *Confessions of an English Opium Eater* (1821), quoted in M. Blaug, *Ricardian Economics*, New Haven: Yale University Press, 1958, p.v.
4 R. D. Collison Black (ed.), *Papers and Correspondence of William Stanley Jevons*, 7 Vols., London: Macmillan, 1972–81, Vol.II, p.132.
5 Konekamp, 'Biographical introduction', pp.2–3.

THE MARKET FOR POLITICAL ECONOMY

To people from such a background, the idea of sending their sons to public school and thence to Oxford or Cambridge simply did not occur at this time. Nonconformists were not allowed to graduate from Oxford until 1854, and from Cambridge until 1856, and all religious tests were not abolished at these universities until 1871. W. S. Jevons began his education at the Mechanics Institute High School in Liverpool, but in 1850 he was sent to University College School in London, founded in 1830 and 'remarkable for its originality . . . The aim throughout was mental discipline and as it contributed to that, so each subject was judged. There was no religious teaching, and the boys were of many creeds and denominations'.[6] Jevons left the school in 1851, at the age of sixteen, as was then normal, and entered University College, London.

During the two years which he spent there, 1851–3, Jevons's main interest was in chemistry, although he also took courses in botany, mathematics, classics, and history. In his spare time he took long walks through the commercial and manufacturing parts of the East End of London, and it seems to have been as a result of these that he became interested in what he called 'the industrial mechanism of society'.[7] Political economy in the formal sense formed no part of his studies, and indeed courses in it were not being offered at University College in those years.[8]

In the second term of the academic year 1852–3 Jevons had already 'firmly fixed not to enter a profession but rather to go into business of some kind'.[9] It appears to have been accepted without question by both Jevons and his family that he would not complete a third year at college, and the idea of leaving without a degree seems to have caused him no concern at this stage. His father suggested that he might use his interest and ability in chemistry to make a career as a manufacturing chemist, but that could not have been done in Liverpool, and at this time Jevons's preference was to live at home, working in some commercial concern and pursuing his scientific and literary interests in his spare time.[10] Neither the boy nor his family considered that any specific education for commerce would be necessary; that would all be a matter of learning on the job.

No sooner had these plans become settled in Jevons's mind than they were upset by an unexpected turn of events. His cousin, H. E. (Harry) Roscoe, with whom he lodged in London, was already a student at

---

6 H. Hale Bellot, *University College, London 1826–1926*, London: University of London Press, 1929, p.171.

7 W. S. Jevons, *The Principles of Economics and other Papers*, London: Macmillan, 1905, p.vii.

8 Bellot, *University College, London*, p.252.

9 Black, *Papers and Correspondence*, Vol.II, p.37.

10 Ibid., Vol.I, pp.78–9.

JEVONS'S CONTRIBUTION IN MANCHESTER AND LONDON

University College and determined to devote his life to the study of chemistry. According to Roscoe, Thomas Graham, the Professor of Chemistry at University College,

> sent for me one day and offered me the post of Assayer in the Mint at Sydney, which had just been established. It was worth £600–700 a year, and was a post which many young men would have jumped at. I felt, however, that I could not leave my mother and sister, as they did not wish to go to Australia, so I declined it with thanks, but told him that I knew a young man who was singularly well fitted for the position, and who I believed would accept it. This young man was Stanley Jevons.[11]

Jevons's first reaction to this proposal was that it was 'perfectly impossible'; nevertheless he consulted his father about it and was somewhat dismayed when the latter advised him to accept the post. It is not relevant to the subject of this chapter to examine why Thomas Jevons gave this advice and why Stanley followed it. For the latter, it might simply have meant that he traded the uncertain prospect of a business career in Liverpool for a lucrative but obscure post, or series of posts, as a gold assayer in Australia. Eventually though, Jevons had simply too much intellectual curiosity and originality to allow this to happen. Once he had settled in Sydney and established the Assay Department of the new Mint, his duties were light enough to enable him to devote a good deal of time to pursuing his own studies.

At first, these were mainly concerned with meteorology, culminating in a major study of *The Climate of Australia and New Zealand*,[12] but Jevons also published the results of his research into the geology of New South Wales. He recorded in his personal journals how his scientific interests had moved from chemistry to geology and then to meteorology,[13] but from late 1856 onwards, Jevons began to read widely in political economy, finding it, as he declared to his sister Henrietta, 'deeply interesting'.[14] By February 1858, the view of the relationship between economic theory and other social sciences to which he always adhered was clearly formulated in his mind, and he had firmly decided to devote himself to their study. 'You may feel assured', he told Henrietta,

> that to extend and perfect the abstract or the detailed and practical knowledge of man and society is perhaps the most useful and necessary work in which anyone can now engage. There are

11 H. E. Roscoe, *The Life and Experiences of Sir Henry Enfield Roscoe*, London: Macmillan, 1906, p.39.
12 Black, *Papers and Correspondence*, Vol.I, pp.22–5.
13 Ibid., p.114.
14 Ibid., Vol.II, p.292.

THE MARKET FOR POLITICAL ECONOMY

plenty of people engaged with physical science, and practical science and arts may be left to look after themselves, but thoroughly to understand the principles of society appears to me now the most cogent business.[15]

'I think that it is my mission to apply myself to such subjects', he told her, 'and it is my intention to do so.'

Once having formed that intention, Jevons was soon equally clear in his mind that to carry it into effect he must leave Australia, return to England, and extend his education. 'I do not know whether I have before explained why I desire at once to leave Sydney', he wrote to his sister Lucy in July 1858. 'It is because I believe my education is but now continuing, and that by staying here it is checked, and irretrievably deferred.'[16] At home in Liverpool, some of the older generation of his family were appalled by the folly of young Stanley's decision to leave a well-paid position with excellent prospects in order to come back to London as a student, condemning himself and his sisters to living in near penury on his savings without any assurance that his studies would lead to secure or profitable employment in the future. To himself and his immediate family, Jevons justified his decision in terms which have often been interpreted as foreshadowing the theory of capital which he later developed; 'You do not duly appreciate', he told Henrietta,

> the comparative importance of *preparation and performance*, or perhaps as I may illustrate it, of *Capital* and *labour.* You desire to begin and hammer away at once, instead of spending years in acquiring strength and skill and then striking a few blows of immensely greater effect than your unskilled ones, however numerous, could be. We enter here into one of those deeply laid and simple propositions of Economy which I hope someday to work out into a symmetrical and extensive manner hitherto unattempted even by Mills [sic] or Adam Smith. [17]

Six months earlier he had explained his position to Lucy with the words: 'Will the future be better than the present to one who makes no present sacrifices? Granting that a given position is good, may it not be wisely relinquished if a happier one may be attained, even after much trouble?'[18]

Harry Roscoe, who had been a student with Jevons at University College in 1851–2, had graduated in 1853 and gone on to carry out research for a doctorate in chemistry at Heidelberg under the great

15 Ibid., p.322.
16 Ibid., p.332.
17 Ibid., pp.359–60.
18 Ibid., p.331.

JEVONS'S CONTRIBUTION IN MANCHESTER AND LONDON

Robert Wilhelm Bunsen, who had just taken up his appointment as professor there. Returning to London in 1856, Roscoe had begun to practise as a consulting chemist, but when the Chair of Chemistry at the recently established Owens College in Manchester fell vacant, he applied for and was appointed to it in 1857.

Owens College, the forerunner of the present University of Manchester, had opened its doors to its first students in 1851. It had been founded as a result of a bequest by John Owens, a Manchester manufacturer, 'for the purpose of affording to youths of the age of fourteen years and upwards instruction in the branches of education taught at the English universities, free from the religious tests which limit the extension of university education'.[19] Since Roscoe came from the same Unitarian background as his cousin Stanley Jevons, Owens was one of the few colleges in England at which he was likely to obtain an appointment at this time. Roscoe was elated by his appointment and wrote to Jevons that he hoped 'in time to succeed in making this the school of Chemistry in the North',[20] but his initial prospects were uncertain enough, as the college had only thirty-five students and 'was at that time nearly in a state of collapse'.[21]

Nevertheless, Jevons saw Roscoe as a fortunate example of what could be achieved by study: 'I often think with pleasure of your agreeable position in England', he wrote to his cousin while still in Sydney,

> indeed if there is any man I envy it is a Professor. Still when I knew you in London, you devoted all your prospects to a pursuit of which the primary results are never very brilliant and often long deferred. Even well off as you now are, you may perhaps be considered to have better luck than many Scientific men. Do not blame me therefore, for abandoning a good salary because it interferes with other desirable things, even if I starve in consequence, as is not improbable.[22]

In spite of this, it seems clear that Jevons did not return to his studies at University College with any definite expectation that they would open the door to an academic career for him. At the start of the second term of his resumed studies, he wrote to his brother Herbert:

> I have no definite plan of earning money, but after my B.A. will try what can be done in the way of writing or teaching, so as to keep myself while working for my M.A. which I have a great desire to take

19 J. Thompson, *The Owens College: its Foundation and Growth*, Manchester 1886, pp.16–17.
20 Black, *Papers and Correspondence*, Vol.II, p.322.
21 Roscoe, *Life and Experiences*, p.102.
22 Black, *Papers and Correspondence*, Vol.II, p.347.

THE MARKET FOR POLITICAL ECONOMY

in the Political Economy and Mental Philosophy branch – as these are entirely the subjects I should follow in any case. Harry Roscoe whom I saw in London at Christmas is rather indignant that I am no longer a Chemist and wants to know how I shall get my bread, which perhaps is quite a pertinent question.[23]

Pertinent the question certainly was, and it gave Jevons a fair amount of anxiety, but in the years 1860 to 1862 it must have been forced to the back of his mind by the sheer volume of intellectual work he was undertaking. During this period Jevons was not only studying a wide range of subjects, some for the first time, to meet the course requirements of his BA and then of his MA, but he was also doing wholly original and pioneering work in both theoretical and applied economics.

In July 1860, in a letter to his brother Herbert, he set out the catalogue of work which he was about to 'attack in earnest' for the BA examination in October, in which he gained a first: 'Latin, Greek, Mathematics, Roman History, Greek History, English History, French, Animal Physiology, Logic, Natural Philosophy, Moral Philosophy, all of which require looking up seriously and many to be learnt from the beginning'.[24] He had already taken the college examinations in June in mental philosophy and political economy and was still smarting from the 'sad reverse' which he had suffered in the latter subject by being placed equal third with another student, when he had confidently expected first place. 'However', he consoled himself, 'I shall fully avenge myself when I bring out my "Theory of Economy" and re-establish the science on a sensible basis'.[25] For it was only in February of that year that Jevons had 'fortunately struck out what I have no doubt is *the true theory of Economy* so thorough-going and consistent, that I cannot now read other books on the subject without indignation'.[26]

Since he attributed his sad reverse 'to a difference of opinion which is perfectly allowable having prejudiced the Professor against my answers', Jevons feared that he would not succeed in winning the Ricardo Scholarship in Political Economy. But his fears were groundless, and he was awarded the scholarship in December 1860, adding a useful £60 to his income for the following year. By this time he was back to work at University College on mathematics and Greek, and attending James Martineau's lectures on mental philosophy.

Throughout 1861 Jevons went on with his studies for the MA degree and took the final examination in June 1862. He was awarded the

23 Ibid., p.406.
24 Ibid., p.415.
25 Ibid., p.416.
26 Ibid., p.410.

JEVONS'S CONTRIBUTION IN MANCHESTER AND LONDON

degree with honours and a gold medal. A letter which he wrote to his younger brother Tom, in December 1861, gives an indication of the range and depth of study which Jevons undertook to achieve this:

> Only lately the *additional* subjects for the M.A. were published – and are as follows:- 'On the nature and principles of Social order and Social progress, or of Civilization' and in the History of Philosophy, 'Greek Speculation – the Theaetetus and Gorgias of Plato and the Nicomachean Ethics of Aristotle'. Is not this a pretty prospect ... Then there is the whole of Mental and Moral Philosophy, Logic, Political Economy etc.[27]

In the spring and summer of 1861 Jevons had also been 'very busy at present with an apparently dry and laborious piece of work', the collection and compilation of data for his proposed Statistical Atlas. The Atlas itself was never fully completed, because Jevons could not find a publisher who would take it on, and could only afford to pay for the publication of two of the diagrams, which appeared in June 1862. This work formed the foundation of the paper 'On the Study of Periodic Commercial Fluctuations', which Jevons submitted to Section F of the British Association for the Advancement of Science in 1862, along with his 'Brief Account of a General Mathematical Theory of Political Economy'. It also led on to his classic work, *A Serious Fall in the Value of Gold Ascertained*, which was to appear in 1863. Thus, as one recent authority has put it, 'Jevons' statistical work was far-ranging, and in the early 1860's almost compulsive'.[28] What is really remarkable is that in 1862, he not only completed successfully the formidable programme of study required for his MA, but he also carried out what the same authority has rightly called 'his immense labour on banking and price statistics', and set out in his 'Brief Account' the essentials of the theory which has earned him a place in the history of economics as a pioneer of the Marginal Revolution.

Despite this prodigious effort and achievement, the autumn of 1862 saw Jevons in the same sad position as too many of our graduate students today – he was highly qualified, but he had no regular employment and little prospect of any. Beyond that superficial similarity, however, the comparison cannot be sustained; for one thing, the range of academic and other appointments open to Jevons was very small. The number of professorships of political economy in England at the time could still be counted on the fingers of one hand, and appointments below professorial level were almost unknown. It is not

27 Ibid., p.437.
28 S. M. Stigler, 'Jevons as statistician', *The Manchester School*, Vol.50 (1982), pp.354–65.

THE MARKET FOR POLITICAL ECONOMY

surprising, therefore, that Jevons did not at first think in terms of an academic post. His initial plan seems to have been to support himself by journalism, writing mainly for weekly reviews, and to carry on his research for publication in books and pamphlets which might gain him a reputation.

He had before him the example of another cousin, Richard Holt Hutton (1826–97), who had been associated with Walter Bagehot as joint editor of the *National Review* and assistant editor of *The Economist*. Hutton had left *The Economist* in 1861 to become editor of the *Spectator*. He helped Jevons by giving him the opportunity to write some articles for this periodical in the autumn of 1862; but Jevons, who had dashed off many pieces for the Sydney newspapers with apparent ease, now seemed to find 'hack writing . . . destructive of any true thinking',[29] and he made little progress with it. Since the opportunity to stay in London and work in the Reading Room of the British Museum was vital for his own research, Jevons hit on the plan of starting a form of literary agency, offering for a fee of three shillings an hour to look up material for 'Authors and others not at the moment within reach of works or objects to which they may need to refer'.[30]

The possibility of a university appointment first became a reality for Jevons in December 1862, when Harry Roscoe mentioned to him that there was an opening for a tutor at Owens College. It was a post which offered the prospect of hard work for small pay, for it 'involved tutoring students in difficulty from all the subjects taught in the college by the nine Professors who constituted the total teaching staff'.[31] Jevons was at first doubtful about the post itself, and about the wisdom of a move from London to Manchester. He decided to delay a final decision, but his scheme of a literary agency did not prosper, and in a few months Jevons had come round to the view that the tutorship 'will be a step in the right direction. After some experience in teaching, and by degrees in lecturing, I shall be more ready to offer myself for any professorship that may happen – perhaps one at Owens College itself. There is no doubt, I think, that the professorial line is the one for me to take'.[32]

So, late in April 1863, Jevons went up to Manchester 'to arrange or consider the tutorship affair'. Though still conscious of 'the dull nature of the town, and the regret in leaving London and the Museum', he was favourably impressed by the account of the tutor's duties given by the Principal, J. G. Greenwood (who had been one of his teachers at University College School), and by Owens College and its prospects. So

29 Black, *Papers and Correspondence*, Vol.III, p.6.
30 Ibid., Vol.I, p.190.
31 W. H. Chaloner, 'Jevons in Manchester, 1863–1876', *The Manchester School*, Vol.40 (1972), p.74.
32 Black, *Papers and Correspondence*, Vol.III, p.6.

JEVONS'S CONTRIBUTION IN MANCHESTER AND LONDON

it was agreed that he should go there 'if some 20 or 25 pupils offer to pay 3 guineas each for the Session'.[33] Presumably this condition was met, for Jevons wound up his affairs in London, spent the summer 'practising up my Mathematics, Greek and Latin for my tutoring work at Manchester but . . . chiefly working at my logical system',[34] and took up his duties at Owens College in October 1863.

II

The years which Jevons spent at Owens College, Manchester – from 1863 to 1876 – are perhaps the years of his career of most interest from the point of view of the institutionalization of political economy. For Jevons himself they were the years in which he devoted most time and effort to the teaching of the subject, and which witnessed his promotion from a very junior tutor to a full professor. For Owens College they were years of rapid growth and transition, away from the ailing state in which Harry Roscoe had found it, and towards becoming a major civic university.

In 1863 Owens College had 110 day and 312 evening students.[35] Day students could enter at the age of fourteen; evening students had to be at least sixteen; the only other entrance qualification required of them was an ability to read and write and a knowledge of 'the first four rules of Arithmetic'. With the day students Jevons's basic duties were to consist 'in teaching small classes of six or eight students for some two or three hours per day, as well as giving . . . general assistance',[36] but the number of students prepared to pay the three guinea fee for the tutor's services seems not to have come up to Principal Greenwood's forecast in the first year,[37] and so Jevons also undertook evening classes, for which there was an additional payment of £15 for a course of twenty lectures. His meticulously detailed reports to the Principal on each year's lectures still survive among his papers at the John Rylands Library in Manchester,[38] and show that in 1863–4 he gave a course on logic to twenty-two students, one on political economy to eleven students, and two others on 'Junior Geometry' and arithmetic to thirteen students. In the latter instance Jevons's comment that the attendance of the younger students was 'very uncertain, and their progress consequently could not be ensured', serves as a reminder of the wide range of age, ability, and application of the students he taught.

33 Ibid., p.14.
34 Ibid., p.29.
35 Thompson, *Owens College*, p.245.
36 Black, *Papers and Correspondence*, Vol.III, p.9.
37 Ibid., pp.9, 52.
38 John Rylands University Library of Manchester, Jevons Archives, 6/4/14.

THE MARKET FOR POLITICAL ECONOMY

Jevons had expected his first year's work as a tutor to be 'very novel and hard ... and most inadequately paid', and in none of these respects was he disappointed; his income from Owens College in 1863–4 was 'nearly £100'.[39] At the end of his first term of teaching he confessed himself, not surprisingly, 'slightly used up ... probably because my four evening lectures require considerable exertion after the day's work'.[40] Looking back on his first session as a college tutor in June 1864, Jevons admitted to himself that his work had often given him 'intense discouragement', but that he had also 'learned to speak with some composure in public'.[41]

Whatever problems and anxieties teaching may have brought for Jevons – and they were not slight – he did not allow them to interfere with the progress of his own research. At this time he was completing the work for his paper on 'The Variation of Prices and the Value of the Currency since 1782',[42] an important extension of the index number work he had done for *A Serious Fall.* The collection and collation of the data for it was, in Jevons's own opinion, 'a most long and tedious piece of work indeed',[43] but that did not deter him from spending the whole summer vacation of 1864 in London compiling material 'in connection with the question of the exhaustion of Coal, which I look upon as the coming question'.[44]

Jevons undoubtedly chose this because 'a good publication on the subject would draw a good deal of attention. I am convinced that it is necessary for the present at any rate to write on popular subjects', he told his brother Herbert.[45] Why should Jevons have taken this view? Keynes gave the generally accepted answer when he referred to Jevons's

> extreme anxiety that his ideas should not be overlooked. His highly original communications to the British Association (in 1862) had fallen flat. His diagrams for business forecasting ... had been published at his own expense and, barely mentioned in *The Times* and *The Economist*, lost him money. His pamphlet on Gold (in 1863) though it attracted attention a little later on, had sold 74 copies. Yet he had a passionate sense of vocation and of having something valuable to give the world.[46]

All this is true, and Keynes's interpretation of the facts is valid

39 Black, *Papers and Correspondence*, Vol.III, pp.34, 52.
40 Ibid., p.48.
41 Ibid., Vol.I, p.196.
42 *Journal of the* [*Royal*] *Statistical Society*, Vol.28, pp.394–420.
43 Black, *Papers and Correspondence*, Vol.I, p.197.
44 Ibid., Vol.III, p.58.
45 Ibid., p.52.
46 J. M. Keynes, 'William Stanley Jevons', in *Essays in Biography*, Vol. 10, *Collected Writings of John Maynard Keynes*, London: Macmillan, 1972, p.115.

JEVONS'S CONTRIBUTION IN MANCHESTER AND LONDON

enough, but there is a further point which he did not bring out. Jevons had deliberately sacrificed a good income and invested much of his savings in further education because of his passionate sense of vocation. But he still had his living to make, and after five years he had no secure source of adequate income. Had he been firmly established in academic life in 1864 he could have gone on in the knowledge that the works which did not sell widely were nevertheless gaining him recognition among his peers, and that his reputation would grow as his scholarly work progressed. At that time, however, he had no such place and could not be sure of gaining it; the only other way of giving his ideas to the world and making a living out of them was to become a nationally recognized author. Publishers and editors of weeklies, monthlies, and quarterlies would not then reject his productions, theoretical or applied, but, on the contrary, would be competing to pay for them.

So, Jevons spent the hot summer of 1864 researching the material for *The Coal Question* in London libraries. He gave the completed manuscript to Alexander Macmillan just after Christmas, but when the book appeared in April 1865 it was not the immediate success its author had hoped. By the end of the year, however, it was receiving wider attention, and when, in the spring of 1866, both Gladstone and J. S. Mill used it as an authoritative reference in the House of Commons, Jevons's status as a 'national name' was assured.

The price which he paid for this success, in terms of physical effort and mental strain, was considerable. 'I worked throughout one vacation at it', he wrote in his journal in December 1865, 'often writing for 5 or 6 hours at a stretch scarcely leaving my seat. No wonder I was somewhat the worse when college work came on in addition to the work of completing the book. I may well be glad it did not destroy my powers'.[47]

Pushing himself in this way, Jevons carried on with his tutoring at Owens during 1864–5. In January 1865 he applied for what he rightly called 'a small Professorship' in logic, mental and moral philosophy at Queen's College, Liverpool, which had been established in 1857 as an offshoot of the Mechanics Institute and 'was the first serious attempt actually to establish a college of higher education in Liverpool'.[48] Jevons was appointed Professor of Political Economy as well as Logic there in May 1865, but held office for only one year. For all its wide scope, the post was really a part-time one involving mainly evening teaching – for which the Council of the college took the unusual step of guaranteeing Jevons 'as to one lecture a week . . . a minimum payment of five shillings per lecture'. Despite the small pay, Jevons liked 'having such a place in the old town and the old Mechanics', and enjoyed the

47 Black, *Papers and Correspondence*, Vol.I, pp.200–1.
48 T. Kelly, *For Advancement of Learning: The University of Liverpool, 1881–1981*, Liverpool: Liverpool University Press, 1981, p.32.

THE MARKET FOR POLITICAL ECONOMY

weekly outing from Manchester which it gave him.[49]

In Manchester itself the academic year 1865–6 brought changes at Owens College which had an important effect on Jevons's position. At the same time as his appointment to Queen's College, Liverpool, Jevons had been asked to act as a substitute lecturer in political economy for R. C. Christie, who since 1855 had been Professor of Political Economy as well as holding the Chairs of History and Jurisprudence. In September 1865, A. J. Scott, who after resigning the post of Principal in 1857 had remained as Professor of English, and of Logic and Mental and Moral Philosophy, fell ill, and Principal Greenwood asked Jevons to take over his logic and philosophy classes. Jevons agreed, and at this point resigned his tutorship.[50]

Scott died on 12 January 1866, and two weeks later Christie, who had intended to resign his posts at the end of the session, brought forward his resignation to facilitate redistribution of the subjects hitherto taught by Scott and himself. The committee appointed to consider this question recommended the creation of a Chair of Logic, Mental and Moral Philosophy, and Political Economy.[51] Jevons was obviously a strong candidate for this, and, indeed, his appointment for one year only as a substitute for Christie had been made precisely because a reorganization of this kind was anticipated.[52] At first the trustees of the college wanted to offer the chair to Jevons straight away, but they then decided on principle that it should be advertised. This was done in April 1866, but the report which the trustees received from the appointing committee was that they had 'found the testimonials in favour of Mr. W. S. Jevons so decidedly superior to those of other candidates, that they [had] no hesitation in at once recommending him to the Trustees for election to the Professorship', and the trustees resolved to appoint him 'from the twenty-ninth day of September next at the yearly salary of two hundred and fifty pounds'.[53]

Thus Jevons finally attained the security of a chair, from which he could teach the subjects to which he had decided to devote his life some nine years previously. Principal Greenwood had 'hinted that in the course of a few years I might fairly look forward to a professorship in Owens College' when Jevons first went there 'to consider the tutorship affair',[54] and once Christie had resigned the Chair of Political

49 Black, *Papers and Correspondence*, Vol.III, pp.68, 76.
50 Ibid., pp.75–6.
51 Archives of the University of Manchester, Minutes of the Trustees of Owens College, 25 January and 22 March 1866.
52 Thompson, *Owens College*, p.254.
53 Minutes of the Trustees, 31 May 1866; for the testimonials, see Black, *Papers and Correspondence*, Vol.III, pp.106–20.
54 Black, *Papers and Correspondence*, Vol.III, p.9.

JEVONS'S CONTRIBUTION IN MANCHESTER AND LONDON

Economy 'there was never much reason to doubt that he [Jevons] would obtain the appointment', as his widow later wrote.[55] Nevertheless, Jevons was far from confident of the outcome until the final decision was announced – even though he had the support of most of the leading economists of the day – Bagehot, Newmarch, Thorold Rogers, Fawcett, Cairnes, and John Stuart Mill himself.

Jevons remained at Manchester for ten years – a decade which saw the peak of his achievements in both logic and political economy. The books and papers which he published during those years served to consolidate the place he had already begun to establish for himself in the development of both those disciplines. They have been extensively discussed in the history of ideas, and those discussions need not be repeated here. However, from the standpoint of the institutionalization of political economy, there is one aspect of Jevons's contribution to the subject in these years which deserves emphasis.

In *Portrait of a University*, written to commemorate the centenary of the foundation of Owens College, H. B. Charlton pointed out that it was largely through Jevons's cousin, H. E. Roscoe,

> that experimental science became the motive force by which the British idea of a university was revolutionised. Investigation by experiment was a general pattern of research which Roscoe had seen in operation in German universities. As a scientific technique, however, it was capable of adaptation to investigations occupied with problems in other fields of knowledge. To Roscoe's impetus on the scientific activities of Owens College, there was soon joined an ideally appropriate co-adjutator on the Arts side, A. W. Ward.

Ward, who succeeded A. J. Scott as Professor of English Language and Literature in 1866, had spent much of his youth in Germany and knew the German academic approach.

> So, whilst Roscoe was domiciling research as a major function in the academic pursuit of the physical sciences, Ward accepted a similar obligation to pass from a teacher's transmission to a researcher's extension of knowledge in the field of the humanities ... It was the Roscoe–Ward adoption of research as the directive and formative factor in academic development which took Owens College on its first big step forward towards university status.[56]

Jevons, who had begun his training in the same field as Roscoe, carried many of his ideas on research methodology from the physical

55 H. A. Jevons, *Letters and Journal of William Stanley Jevons*, London 1886, p.221.
56 H. B. Charlton, *Portrait of a University 1851–1951*, Manchester 1951, pp.54–5.

THE MARKET FOR POLITICAL ECONOMY

sciences into the social sciences, with striking results.[57] But for Owens College, the content of the work he did was perhaps of less significance than the simple fact that Jevons was intensely motivated towards research and contributed actively to the extension of knowledge in his field. In this respect Jevons made an important contribution to the 'new academic policy of research' which Roscoe and Ward were developing at Manchester, and helped to ensure that the growing college was more than simply a teaching institution.

As regards the transmission of ideas by teaching, Jevons's opportunities at Owens were fairly narrowly restricted. In his application for the chair he had written: 'I have long hoped to have an opportunity of extending the teaching of Economic Science. In addition to a course on Abstract Political Economy, I should desire to give courses of lectures on Commercial History, the Social Condition of the People, &c, in which the truths of Economy would be illustrated and enforced'.[58] These hopes were not realized; throughout his tenure of the Chair of Political Economy Jevons appears to have given only one course in the subject to day students, which was repeated in a somewhat condensed form for evening students. In addition, he gave one course of 'rudimentary instruction in political economy' to pupil teachers, because his professorship was partly endowed by the Cobden Memorial Committee, which had made it a condition of the endowment that all teachers in schools supported by public funds in Manchester and Salford should be admitted to such a course without paying a fee.

One student's notes of the course which Jevons gave to day students in his last year at Owens, 1875–6, have survived and have now been published.[59] They make clear that what Jevons himself said about this course was precisely correct: 'I have generally followed somewhat the order of subjects in Mill's Political Economy in perfect independence, however, of his views and methods when desirable'.[60] They do not, as Keynes claimed, show 'how his repression of his own theories had brought his own feeling against Mill to boiling point'.[61] By this time, in fact, Jevons was teaching his own ideas quite freely to his students, and advised them to read his own *Theory of Political Economy.*

In later years there were worthy Manchester bankers and merchants who had learned political economy in Jevons's lectures at Owens, but

57 R. D. Collison Black, 'W. S. Jevons and the Foundation of Modern Economics', in R. D. C. Black, A. W. Coats and C. D. W. Goodwin (eds), *The Marginal Revolution in Economics,* Durham N. C.: Duke University Press, 1971, pp.103–5.
58 Black, *Papers and Correspondence,* Vol.III, p.105.
59 Ibid., Vol.VI.
60 Ibid., p.23.
61 Keynes, 'William Stanley Jevons', p.138.

JEVONS'S CONTRIBUTION IN MANCHESTER AND LONDON

none of his students there themselves became academic economists. That in itself is hardly surprising; out of one course, covering virtually every aspect of the subject, theoretical and applied, Jevons had little or no opportunity to produce specialists. Yet, even if Jevons did not establish an oral tradition at Manchester as Marshall did at Cambridge, he still had more influence on the teaching of economics than is generally realized. In 1875 he produced what he termed a 'semi-popular' book, *Money and the Mechanism of Exchange*, and in 1878 followed the *Primer of Logic*, which he had written in 1876, with a *Primer of Political Economy*. All these texts had large sales, and 'for a period of half a century practically all elementary students both of Logic and of Political Economy in Great Britain and also in India and the Dominions were brought up on Jevons'.[62]

Reconciling the demands of teaching with those of his own research had been a serious problem for Jevons in his early years as a college tutor at Owens, but after his appointment to the chair he found his work 'much more easy, familiar and congenial'.[63] Even so, it was not long before the old dilemma recurred. After going to London to read his paper, 'On the Condition of the Gold Currency', to the Statistical Society in November 1868, he wrote to his brother Herbert: '. . . these journeys rather knock me up. I had three classes on Monday afternoon and evening, went to London on Tuesday morning, read the paper in the evening and back on Wednesday for two classes in the evening. Now, a thing of this sort knocks me up for the rest of the week'.[64] Nevertheless, Jevons 'was so scrupulous that other engagements should not interfere with his lectures at college that he would go through almost any amount of fatigue rather than fail to meet his class at the appointed time'.[65]

Matters came to a crisis early in 1872, after Jevons had written the *Theory of Political Economy* at great speed and had put immense efforts into the preparation of *The Principles of Science*. This time his health was seriously damaged; 'I have been rather more ill than I like to think of', he told his brother again; 'I seem to have exhausted my nervous system by over-work'.[66] He found evening lectures particularly tiring, and on medical advice he employed a substitute to give them in 1872–3, continuing the day lectures himself. Even with his duties reduced in this way, Jevons did not feel he had regained his strength sufficiently to resume all his classes in the following year, and in June 1873 he offered to resign.

62 Ibid., p.142.
63 Black, *Papers and Correspondence*, Vol.III, p.149.
64 Ibid., p.195.
65 H. A. Jevons, *Letters and Journal*, pp.250–1.
66 Black, *Papers and Correspondence*, Vol.III, pp.249.

THE MARKET FOR POLITICAL ECONOMY

As early as March 1872 Jevons and his wife had 'almost come to the conclusion, hastened by [his] present state, to leave Manchester and go and live quietly and economically in or near London'.[67] From 1873 until 1876 Jevons went through a long period of uncertainty about this matter. On the one hand, he felt a strong sense of obligation to the authorities of Owens College, and a great liking for the college and his colleagues there. On the other, he seemed to find the burden of teaching, especially evening teaching, almost insupportable, and he was attracted by the possibility of living near London libraries and being in touch with London institutions such as the Statistical Society and the Political Economy Club, of which he had been made an honorary member in 1874. The balance was further shifted in favour of London in 1875, when it became clear that Jevons could have first refusal of the then vacant Chair of Political Economy at University College.

The Council of Owens College was very reluctant to see Jevons resign in 1873 and readily agreed to the alternative which he proposed – that he should be reappointed for a further year but given leave of absence on condition of finding 'an efficient substitute'.[68] At this time the college had no other staff in political economy apart from the professor; the substitute whom Jevons found was W. H. B. Brewer, who had first completed his MA at London University in 1872 and had been helping Jevons with his bibliography of mathematical economics. This temporary appointment did not lead Brewer into a career of university teaching; he subsequently became an inspector of schools.

Jevons tendered his resignation for a second time in May 1874, but was persuaded to carry on, again on the condition that he could employ a deputy to give his evening lectures. So he continued at Owens for the year 1874–5, but in March 1875, John Robson, the Secretary of University College, London, wrote informing him that the Council was about to recommend him for appointment to the Chair of Political Economy there, 'his duties not to commence until next Session'.[69] Owens College then offered to increase Jevons' salary to £300 per annum.[70] Jevons was

---

67 H. A.Jevons, *Letters and Journal*, p.256.
68 Black, *Papers and Correspondence*, Vol.IV, pp.20–1.
69 Ibid., p.109.
70 His widow wrote: 'Mr. Jevons was very sorry that he did not know, before he withdrew his resignation at Owens College, that the professorship of political economy in University College, London, would become vacant in October' (H. A. Jevons, *Letters and Journal*, p.336). This appears to be inconsistent with the fact that Robson's letter to Jevons informing him that the Council of University College, London proposed to appoint him to the chair was dated 8 March 1875, whereas Principal Greenwood wrote to Jevons saying: 'I suppose the next formal step will be the withdrawal of your letters?' only on 7 May 1875 (Black, *Papers and Correspondence*, Vol.IV, pp.108–9, 112–13).

JEVONS'S CONTRIBUTION IN MANCHESTER AND LONDON

in a difficult position, not only because of his sense of obligation to Owens, but also because the loss of income involved in going to University College, where the professor's salary was only £100, was more than he could readily accept. He appealed to Robson for a delay of six months before matters were finalized, and later suggested that he might be appointed a temporary lecturer at University College, London for the session of 1875–6 so that he could continue to discharge his duties at Manchester for that year at least.[71] However, the Council of Owens College would not accept this, and Jevons had to look about for a substitute lecturer, this time to do the work in London. He told Robson that he had 'in his eye' Mr Alfred Marshall of Cambridge, but it was eventually Foxwell who agreed to take the temporary post. With this arrangement settled, Jevons finally submitted a formal application for the University College professorship in November 1875, and was appointed in December. The Senate of Owens College received this information 'with deep regret', but its members went on to record that 'they heartily wish you a long enjoyment of the honours your achievements have already secured for you, and all prosperity in your new Chair and home'.[72]

III

The circumstances surrounding Jevons's appointment to University College, London were indeed different from those involved in his appointment to the Manchester chair a decade earlier. Jevons was no longer the promising young man who had to respond to an advertisement and await the decision of the appointing committee, filled with uncertainty and anxiety. Now he was a Fellow of the Royal Society, a professor whom Owens College would go to considerable lengths to keep, one 'whose ability and energy have signally helped to advance its progress, and whose literary achievements have shed a lustre upon its reputation'.[73] After discussing the position with the Secretary of University College, he could tell his wife: 'it is quite evident that I have the refusal of it and they want me to apply', but the application itself was merely a formality.[74]

Nor was the chair at University College the only one which Jevons might have had in 1875. The same post which brought him confirmation of the London appointment also contained a letter from W. B. Hodgson, Professor of Political Economy at Edinburgh, saying that he was about to resign and hoping that Jevons might be his successor. The

71 Ibid., pp.123–4.
72 Ibid., p.164.
73 Ibid., p.163.
74 Ibid., p.118.

THE MARKET FOR POLITICAL ECONOMY

Edinburgh chair carried a salary of £600 per annum, but Jevons had made his decision and did not seriously consider altering it.[75]

This underlines the fact that, although Jevons was sought after as an academic at this time, his move from Manchester to London was not that of a man who, having secured his first chair at the age of thirty-one and fulfilled his earlier promise, was choosing at forty-one to move from a provincial university to a post of greater prestige and responsibility in the capital. Jevons was seeking less responsibility, not more, and reconciled himself to the loss of income involved because it seemed to him that in trying to accomplish what he had set out to do in political economy and logic, 'one labours under disadvantages in not living, like most of the political economists and literary men, in London'.[76]

This linking of political economists with 'literary men' is a recurrent theme in Jevons's correspondence. It serves to emphasize the point that to him an economist was first and foremost a writer, and it was therefore perfectly possible to function without an academic, or, indeed, an institutional base at all. What he deemed essential was access to libraries and 'literary circles' – editors, publishers, and fellow authors – which could best be had in London.

This is not to say that Jevons considered his position at University College, London to be of secondary importance, or that he took his responsibilities there lightly. There was at that time only one course in political economy there, usually consisting of about twenty-four lectures. In his formal application for the chair, Jevons announced his intention 'to extend the course of lectures considerably, giving from 40 to 50 in the session', and also 'to endeavour to make political economy and connected portions of the social sciences a more important feature in the curriculum of the college'. In the first year of his appointment, Jevons did double the number of lectures, but he then reverted to the previous plan of lecturing only once a week. It would seem that experience in London bore out what he wrote from Manchester: 'my own experience here, and that of other teachers in London and elsewhere, forbid me to be very sanguine as to the success of any extended courses of this kind'.[77] At the time of Jevons's appointment, the numbers taking political economy were disappointingly small; Foxwell had only four students in his class in 1875–6. When Jevons took over in 1876–7 this increased to twenty-three, and for the rest of his period of office he had between twenty-five and thirty students each year. The class lists, which still survive in the archives of University

75 Ibid., pp.150, 173.
76 Ibid., p.134.
77 Ibid., p.144.

JEVONS'S CONTRIBUTION IN MANCHESTER AND LONDON

College, do not reveal the names of any students who went on to become well known in English economics, but they do include a notable number of overseas students. Among these in 1878–9 was Maggiorino Ferraris, who edited the journal *Nuovo Antologia* from 1897 to 1926, and held ministerial portfolios in three Italian governments between 1893 and 1922. In every year, except 1877–8, Jevons's class included one or more Japanese student; these were among the earliest visitors to the West after the Meiji Restoration, and included members of the *samurai* and others who were to take senior offices in the Japanese government. Notable among them were Yoshitane Sannoniya (1843–1903), and Yoshio Kusaka (1851–1923). Sannoniya was a *samurai* who left Japan in 1870 as one of the attendants of Prince Higashi Fushimi, and stayed in England until 1877 when he was appointed Second Secretary in the Japanese Embassy in Berlin. Sannoniya returned to Japan in 1880 to serve first in the Ministry of Foreign Affairs, and later in the Ministry of the Imperial Household. Kusaka came to London in 1876 with Count Inoue to study economics and public finance. After his return to Japan in 1880 he introduced modern systems of registration of births, marriages, and deaths, and of official statistics, and reformed the postal system. He became a prefectural governor and a member of the Diet.

It would appear that through these and other pupils some of Jevons's ideas were carried back to Japan,[78] but from the standpoint of Western economic thought, perhaps the most important pupils Jevons had in London were those he met outside the classroom. He maintained a close friendship with H. S. Foxwell, who was to succeed him at University College, and   started him on his career as a book collector. Jevons was also a strong formative influence on F. Y. Edgeworth, whom he came to know when the latter was trying to develop his practice at the Bar.[79]

Hale Bellot, the historian of University College, London, pointed out that the Chair of Political Economy had three distinguished incumbents in the 1860s and 1870s: J. E. Cairnes, Leonard Courtney, and Jevons, 'yet none of them managed to put very much spirit into the Department'.[80] He did concede, though, that in those days 'the professors were little more than visiting lecturers', and in the circumstances Jevons could not reasonably have been expected to do much more in the college.

Even with the limited duties of his London professorship, it was not long before Jevons began to feel the old tension between the demands

78 I am indebted to Professors Hiroshi Mizuta and Takutoshi Inoue for providing me with information on the careers of Jevons's Japanese students.
79 Black, *Papers and Correspondence*, Vol.V, pp.98, 202.
80 Bellot, *University College*, p.331.

THE MARKET FOR POLITICAL ECONOMY

of the lecture room and those of his writing. In the spring of 1878 he was again in uncertain health as a result of overwork, and that autumn he confided to his brother Tom: 'I have, as usual, got a series of books and articles on hand, all of which want writing immediately, and I sometimes feel desperate about ever getting them done'.[81] His duties as an examiner for London University also interrupted his own writing; in September 1880 he wrote to Foxwell: 'You are quite right in thinking that I hate exams, but I hate lecturing even more'.[82] He had just returned from a seaside holiday with his family at Littlehampton, following a month's tour in Norway, but he had not derived much benefit to his health from either. He began his teaching as usual, but after a week or two he decided that he could not continue and resigned his professorship, after obtaining leave to appoint a substitute to carry on his lectures for the remainder of the academic year.[83]

To terminate his academic career so suddenly and finally was a drastic step which Jevons did not take lightly: 'It is impossible to relinquish the employment of eighteen years without some peturbation of spirits, and when I introduced my deputy to a well-filled classroom, I had some pangs of regret', he wrote. 'But I am nevertheless sure that the step was not only wise but indispensable. It is quite impossible for me to go on with trying fixed duties when I have so much literary work on my mind'.[84] So, for the few years of his life which remained, Jevons ceased to be an academic and became what he had originally intended to be when he was working for his MA – a London-based economist who was a freelance writer.

I have suggested elsewhere[85] that Jevons can be regarded as a transitional figure in both economic theory and economic policy, who broke with the classical approach, yet did not completely fit what has since come to be regarded as the neo-classical mould. Something similar might be said of him as regards the institutionalization of political economy. Jevons was very much in contrast to most of the older political economists – coming out of the Nonconformist middle class of the industrial north-west of England and bringing the methods of mathematics and experimental science to bear on the study of society in which his interest came to centre. He was one of the first economists to be trained outside the ancient universities and to make a living and a career out of teaching political economy in the new university colleges which were developing in nineteenth-century England.

81 Black, *Papers and Correspondence*, Vol.IV, p.291.
82 Ibid., Vol.V, p.106.
83 H. A. Jevons, *Letters and Journal*, p.419.
84 Black, *Papers and Correspondence*, Vol.V, p.110.
85 'Transitions in political economy', Manchester Special Lectures, 1982 (unpublished).

JEVONS'S CONTRIBUTION IN MANCHESTER AND LONDON

Like his cousin Harry Roscoe he proved that teaching a subject meant contributing to it as well as lecturing on it.

Yet Jevons was not the complete academic economist as the twentieth century would see it. He belonged to an era before economists became a scientific community with their own learned societies and journals. That he spent much, but not all of his career, in academic institutions, and that he finished as he began, a freelance writer, must in large part perhaps be attributed to his own physical and mental make-up, and to his preferences and priorities. Yet it seems also to be accountable in some degree to the fact that in Jevons's time the institutionalization of political economy was advancing, but was by no means complete.

[12]

JEVONS, MARSHALL AND THE UTILITARIAN TRADITION

R. D. COLLISON BLACK

Queen's University, Belfast

I

There are few, if any, thinkers who would quarrel with the view put forward by Professor John Rawls in his well known book *A Theory of Justice*, that 'the several variants of the utilitarian view have long dominated our philosophical tradition and continue to do so' (1972, p. 52). In one form or another, utilitarianism has been a major element in moral philosophy, in the English-speaking world at least, over the past two centuries; since in that same time political economy has developed from a branch of moral philosophy to the status of an independent social science, it would be surprising if the utiliarian element had not played a significant part in its development.

Not all the variants of utilitarianism which figure in the philosophical debates of the eighteenth and nineteenth centuries were of equal significance in classical political economy. Elements of the early utilitarianism of Hume and Hutcheson no doubt can be traced in the *Wealth of Nations*, but Adam Smith as moral philosopher cannot be simply classified as a utilitarian. That label might more easily be attached to Malthus, but it must be remembered that Malthus was 'a sincere Christian, committed both to natural theology and the truths of revealed religion' (Winch, 1987, p. 100). As such, his was a theological utilitarianism, akin to that of Paley and the earlier eighteenth-century moralist, Abraham Tucker (Bonar, 1924, p. 324).

However, undoubtedly the variant of utilitarian philosophy which came to assume the greatest importance and exert the greatest influence was the secular utilitarianism of Bentham, as originally expounded in 1789 in his *Introduction to the Principles of Morals and Legislation*. Perhaps only a minority of those political economists who wrote in English in the first half of the nineteenth century could be regarded as fully committed exponents of this philosophy, James Mill being the leading example. The influence which Bentham's version of utilitarianism exerted on economic thought through the work of the two Mills and Ricardo was unquestionably a major one, although even with these men, all to some extent Philosophic Radicals, that influence was greater in the field of economic policy than in the fundamentals of economic analysis. Looking beyond this influential minority

Date of receipt of final typescript: 11 October 1989.

5

one can still, in my view, say 'that while there were many classical economists who were not in a strict sense Philosophic Radicals or even more loosely Benthamites, there were none who opposed or would have opposed, the use of the greatest happiness principle as a touch-stone for economic policy' (Black, 1988, p. 30). In that limited sense a utilitarian tradition had been established in English political economy by the middle of the nineteenth century.

II

To any modern economist, or philosopher, familiar with the story of the close of the classical system of political economy and its ultimate replacement by neo-classical economics, it must seem that one effect of this change should have been to strengthen the utilitarian tradition in economic thought, for the neo-classical approach to the economic problem with its emphasis on rational maximizing fits very easily into a utilitarian mould. Certainly a good case can be made for the view that neo-classical economics was as much, if not more, permeated by utilitarianism than was classical economics; even modern radical critics of the subject can be found writing that 'positive economics supports an utilitarian view of the "status quo"' (Hollis and Nell, 1975, p. 48).

Such an outcome would scarcely have been expected by any contemporary philosopher or political economist in the mid-Victorian period. For at that time opposition to utilitarian doctrines, from laymen and philosophers alike, was strong and growing (Schneewind, 1977, pp. 166–74). On the other hand, new discoveries in the fields of geology and biology were creating fresh interest in the concepts of evolution and change and fresh thinking about their possible application to human society as well as to the natural world. 'The constants in the utilitarian system were turning into variables; and the natural result was a new interest in the other factors in the social situation, history and society' (Burrow, 1966, p. 66). Hence, a well-informed student of social thought in or about 1860 would probably have predicted, as some did, that the future of political economy would lie with the use of the historical method, informed perhaps by some version of idealist philosophy.

However, 'since the time of Mill, utilitarianism has proved to be a plant of most sturdy growth' (Warnock, 1962, p. 30) and it was in no small measure the publication of John Stuart Mill's *Utilitarianism* in 1863 which gave it fresh strength. 'He was convinced he could transform the party ideology of the Benthamites into a comprehensive theory and prove that it need not be merely a source of divisive newspaper slogans but could serve as the principle of a unifying social doctrine' (Schneewind, 1977, p. 166). Even if Mill did not succeed in these ambitious purposes, his reworking of utilitarian moral philosophy produced a considerable revival of interest in and acceptance of it, which was furthered by the careful endeavours of Sidgwick 'to transcend the commonly received antithesis between Intuitionists and Utilitarians' (Sidgwick, 1877, p. xi).

It is significant that in the Preface to the second edition of his *Methods of Ethics* Sidgwick also wrote: 'I have further been led, through study of the Theory of Evolution in its application to practice, to attach somewhat more importance to this theory than I had previously done' (1877, p. vii). Indeed, at this time the debate on evolution and its implications could not be ignored by either philosophers or economists. But it is a debate long concluded, and since its conclusion the tendency in the history of economic ideas has been to treat those thinkers who stressed the evolutionary and historical aspects of economics in the later nineteenth century in a separate chapter from the 'mainstream' neo-classical authors like Jevons and Marshall. This makes for a neat packaging of the material, but tends to obscure the simple obvious fact that in their time Jevons and Marshall did not live in a separate world from their contemporaries, whether historically or mathematically minded, utilitarian or non-utilitarian.

In fact, these various strands of thought are all intertwined and involved in the development of economic ideas in the latter half of the nineteenth century, and any attempt to locate Jevons and Marshall in relation to the utilitarian tradition must recognize this.

III

Anyone who wishes to know where Jevons and Marshall stood in relation to utilitarianism will find that recent commentaries provide what seems to be a clear and well-documented answer. That answer could be summed up in one brief sentence: Jevons was a thoroughgoing Benthamite, whereas Marshall was hardly a utilitarian at all.

The evidence in support of this clear-cut view appears strong. To take the case of Jevons first, his *Theory of Political Economy*—the work on which his enduring reputation primarily rests—can best be understood when it is recognized as founded on Bentham's 'Theory of Pleasure and Pain', as Jevons himself strove to make clear (Black, 1970, pp. 18–20). Similarly, in matters of economic policy, as Wicksteed put it, 'his determining principle was purely Benthamite. "Will a measure increase the sum of happiness?" was the only question which he would admit as ultimately relevant' (1933, p. 806). Many instances of Jevons's employment of this principle can be found in the papers which were collected under the title of *Methods of Social Reform* (1883) and in his last completed book, *The State in Relation to Labour* (1882).

Just how Jevons's political economy came to be so much imbued with Bentham's philosophy remains a matter for conjecture. In Sydney in 1856, after hearing a lecture on 'The Selfish Theory of Morals' by John Woolley, the Principal of Sydney University, Jevons sketched out in his Journal what could be described as a Utilitarian theory of morals (Black and Koenekamp,

1972, pp. 28, 133); but he could well have encountered such ideas even earlier in life, for his family were Unitarians and the tendency for Unitarians to accept Utilitarianism was always marked. Yet there is no mention of Bentham in any of Jevons's notes or diaries before his return to London in 1859 and it seems to have been during his studies at University College, London, in 1860 that Jevons encountered the Benthamite version of Utilitarianism and went on to incorporate it into his new 'Theory of Economy' (Black, 1972, pp. 122–7).

At ths time in his life Jevons also read other philosophers, among them Hobbes, Descartes, Spinoza, Leibniz and Berkeley. He 'tried a little of Kant's German' too, but with youthful certainty dismissed him as 'for the most part full of wordy nonsense' (Black, 1973–81, II, pp. 437–8). At all events none of these writers seem to have influenced his thinking to anything like the extent that Bentham did. In later years Jevons showed himself unwilling to follow John Stuart Mill in the latter's attempt 'to remove popular antipathy to and suspicion of the doctrine' of Utilitarianism (Schneewind, 1977, p. 178)—for example, by admitting that some kinds of pleasure are intrinsically more desirable and more valuable than others. Jevons would have non of this—because 'in all that Bentham says about pleasure and pain, there is not a word about the intrinsic superiority of one pleasure to another ... With Bentham morality became, as it were, a question of the ledger and the balance sheet; all feelings were reduced to the same denomination of value ...' And Jevons contended that 'we must hold to the dry old Jeremy, if we are to have any chance of progress in Ethics' (1890 [1879], p. 286).

Jevons held to the dry old Jeremy in his economics also, and perhaps it is not too difficult to understand why. It was Jevons who stated the problem of economics first as one of constrained maximization (1871, p. 255). Within this framework, rational behaviour can be readily explained as maximizing the net sum of pleasures and pains. One modern philosopher has suggested that nineteenth-century Utilitarians held that 'the plain man's morality could not simply be presumed to be rational. More likely it was in need of reform, and for this the utilitarian principle provided ... a rational method' (Schneewind, 1977, p. 8). In Jevons's time, political economy was in need of reform too, and to him it must have seemed that Bentham's Utilitarian principles were to hand to provide the rational methods. In this there was one crucial difficulty, as Jevons himself admitted: 'Greatly though I admire the clear and precise notions of Bentham, I know not where his numerical data are to be found' (1871, p. 12).

That difficulty did not deter Jevons from framing much of his analysis simply in terms of utility and disutility. For this he was justly criticized by Marshall, who charged him with having 'led many of his readers into a confusion between the provinces of Hedonics and Economics, by exaggerating the applications of his favourite phrases and speaking without qualification of the price of a thing as measuring its final utility not only to an individual, which it can do, but also to a "trading body", which it cannot do' (1961, I, p. 101). Moreover, Jevons also admitted that 'every mind is [as regards comparison of feelings] inscrutable to every other mind, and no common denominator of feeling seems possible' (1871, p. 21). This would appear to have excluded Jevons from dealing with social welfare considerations except in the most restricted manner: yet it certainly did not prevent him from using Bentham's greatest-happiness principle as his criterion of economic policy.

IV

In the light of such robust Benthamism Keynes would seem to have had good grounds for describing Marshall as 'at the opposite pole from Jevons' in the caution with which he handled all such matters (Keynes, 1925, p. 9). More recently, Professor Whitaker has described Marshall as 'so reluctant to endorse utilitarianism that the case seems weak for regarding him as a utilitarian at all' (1977, p. 195). Yet Keynes also deemed it 'true, I suppose, to say that Marshall never departed explicitly from the Utilitarian ideas which dominated the generation of economists who preceded him' (1925, p. 9), and Professor Whitaker in another passage in the article already quoted points out 'the paradox exposed by the comfortable coexistence in Marshall's thought of utilitarian modes of argument—verging at times on an almost crass Benthamism—with a recurring denigration of material ends and of leisure or consumption for their own sakes' (1977, p. 183).

In fact, Marshall's position on the relation of philosophy in general, and utilitarian philosophy in particular, to economics was characteristically reserved and subtle. A parallel may be suggested between his use of mathematics and his use of philosophy. Just as he was a highly-trained mathematician so also was Marshall a highly-trained philosopher, but he seems to have been as reluctant to parade his use of philosophical ideas in his economic writings as he was to parade his use of mathematical ideas. Undoubtedly Marshall, who came to economics through metaphysics and ethics (Keynes, 1925, p. 10), was far more widely versed in philosophy than Jevons. To quote Professor Whitaker again, in Marshall's early thought 'the chief formative influence appears to have been a heady but turgid mixture of German idealism, Spencerian evolutionism, and utilitarianism, the latter derived from a close reading of Bentham and Mill and from the personal influence of Sidgwick' (1977, p. 194). The German component in the mixture was strong: Keynes records how Marshall went to live in Dresden in 1868 in order to read Kant in the original. His reverence for Kant was again at the opposite pole to Jevons's easy dismissal of 'wordy nonsense', but the influence of Hegel's *Philosophy of History* on Marshall was also great.

It deserves to be remembered in this connection that Marshall's first Cambridge appointment was to a lectureship in Moral Science specially established for him at St John's College (Keynes, 1925, p. 11). Among the short courses he gave in it was one on Bentham in which—according to Mary Paley Marshall, as reported by Wesley Mitchell—he 'said that Bentham had more influence on economics than any other non-economist, his contribution being the stress laid on measurement' (Mitchell, 1969, p. 130).

Herein lies the essence of the similarity and the difference between Jevons and Marshall in their interpretation of the utilitarian tradition in relation to economic analysis. Both were convinced of the importance of measurement to the development of that subject: but while Jevons, as we have seen in Section III above, 'granted that we can hardly form the conception of a unit of pleasure or pain, so that the numerical expression of quantities of feeling seems to be out of the question' (1871, p. 19), that did not prevent him from framing his theories largely in terms of utility and disutility directly. Marshall, on the other hand, always insisted that the motives to economic activity must be measured indirectly in terms of money. Yet, as has been stressed by many commentators, that in turn did not prevent him from retaining the notion of utility maximization as the foundation of his demand theory at least—his objection was rather to any attempt to found the science of economics on so crude a basis as a psychology of hedonism.

Because of his strong awareness of the importance of historical and evolutionary trends in economic life, Marshall was not content to view the economic problem simply as one of maximizing the satisfaction of *given* wants. As Talcott Parsons pointed out almost sixty years ago, 'Marshall explicitly states that ... the subject matter of utility theory is only a part of economics, and the less important part. The more important is the influence of economic conditions on human character.' In Marshall's view, then, 'what raises civilised man above the animals and the state of savagery is his ... devotion to a particular set of activities and his development of a type of character. Wants not adjusted to such activities are not ultimate ends even for the purposes of economics, but are artificial. The real aims of life lie in the activities pursued as ends in themselves' (1931, pp. 106, 113).

Marshall, in the *Principles* and elsewhere, made very clear the type of character whose development he regarded as desirable (see, e.g., Marshall, 1961, VI, XIII, §13–15, pp. 716–22). It is abundantly clear from such passages as these that while in his anxiety to distance economics from hedonics Marshall may have been reluctant to appear to link it to Utilitarianism, or indeed to any specific ethical doctrine, he never sought to exclude all ethical elements from it. In comparison to Jevons, then, Marshall can be seen as seeking to develop a wider and more integrated type of economics, involving more complex motivations than mere pleasure and pain.

Remembering that Jevons spoke of his *Theory of Political Economy* as concerned with 'the mechanics of self-interest and utility' (1888, pp. xvi–xvii) while Marshall declared that 'economic biology rather than economic dynamics is the Mecca of the economist' (1898, p. 43), it is tempting to suggest that Jevons was chiselling out an economics along the lines of Newtonian physics, for which a simple form of Utilitarianism provided adequate behavioural assumptions, while Marshall was knitting up a much more complex pattern, involving processes of historical evolution deriving from Hegel, Darwin and Spencer.

V

What has been given in the preceding two sections is, and claims to be, no more than an outline of current views on its subject. As a general interpretation, they present nothing which is incorrect; and so it may seem that there is nothing more to be said. Yet one is left with a certain uneasiness; does this very tidy interpretation adequately fit the reported facts of the troubled intellectual scene in the latter half of the nineteenth century? After all, Darwin's *On The Origin of Species* had appeared in 1859 and Herbert Spencer's *First Principles* in 1862. Does it not seem strange that these works apparently had a great influence on Marshall's thinking, but apparently none at all on Jevons, despite the fact that his first interest and training was in scientific subjects, and that his largest work was *The Principles of Science* of 1874?

The treatment of this point by Wesley Mitchell is manifestly unsatisfactory. 'In a certain sense,' Mitchell wrote,

> Jevons fell between two stools and he had a further posthumous misfortune—not altogether posthumous, for the trouble was beginning in his lifetime. The Benthamite psychology on which he built his economics was being undermined in his own day and was progressively discredited by investigators who were trying to understand human behaviour. Perhaps the most powerful single force undermining the hedonistic psychology was the publication of Darwin's *On The Origin of Species* (1859) with its theory of natural selection and emphasis on instincts. Not unnaturally it was a considerable time before economists began to realise that this biological treatise had any direct bearing upon their problems. That realisation was prompted by Herbert Spencer... (1969, pp. 88–9)

The implication here seems to be that throughout his career Jevons remained unaware of the significance for social science of the work of Darwin and Spencer. Even a cursory examination of the writings of Jevons will show that this was not the case; but few historians of economic thought have looked into the question of the relations between Spencer and the economists of his day. One who has more recently done so, William L. Miller, acknowledges that 'at the height of his influence (1870–90) Spencer could not be ignored by economists', but sees Jevons as one of a group to whom there fell 'the task of battling Spencer and making the world of English economics completely safe for further application of marginalism to the welfare theory inherited from Bentham and Mill' (Miller, 1972, p. 227). Now it is true that Jevons did not share Spencer's unqualified faith in the virtues of *laissez-faire*, but to portray him as 'battling Spencer' risks getting the picture of his relationship to Spencer badly out of perspective.

Jevons was in fact personally acquainted with Spencer, and had a high regard both for the man and his work. 'I daresay', he wrote to his friend John Mills in 1873, 'that a great many of the details and illustrations of Spencer's philosophy will not stand examination,' but added 'nevertheless, I do not think that any criticism will shake the general truth and value of his fundamental ideas, which, especially as applied to mental and moral matters, are most fruitful' (Black, 1973–81, IV, p. 29). Six years later he told Sidgwick 'that in Herbert Spencer's case ... after striking off all errors there remains a new and true philosophy" (ibid., V, p. 24).

The contrast between this very favourable view of Spencer's system and Jevons's well known hostility to the philosophy of John Stuart Mill is remarkable. During the 1870s—the decade which saw the fullest flowering of all Jevons's ideas—he seems to have become more critical of Mill's attempted rehabilitation of Utilitarianism and more inclined to accept Spencer's attempted blending of Utilitarian and evolutionist ideas.

In 1879 Spencer published *The Data of Ethics*, the first application of his general evolutionist approach to moral questions. In the same year Jevons published the last of his four articles on 'John Stuart Mill's Philosophy Tested' in the *Contemporary Review*, under the title 'Utilitarianism'. In it he contended that 'since Mill's Essays appeared, Moral Philosophy has undergone a revolution. I do not so much allude to the reform effected by Mr Sidgwick's *Methods of Ethics*, though that is a great one, introducing as it does a precision of thought and nomenclature which was previously wanting. I allude, of course, to the establishment of the Spencerian Theory of Morals, which has made a new era in philosophy.' Describing Mill as 'the last great philosophic writer conspicuous for his ignorance of the principles of evolution', Jevons went on to argue that 'Mill discarded the admirable Benthamist analysis, but failed to introduced the true Evolutionist principles; thus he falls between the two. It is to Herbert Spencer we must look for a more truthful philosophy of morals than was possible before his time.' Referring specifically to Spencer's *Data of Ethics*, Jevons went so far as to suggest that 'a definite step has been made in a matter debated since the dawn of intellect. The moral sense doctrine, so rudely treated by Bentham, is no longer incapable of reconciliation with the greatest happiness principle, only it now becomes a moving and developable moral sense' (1890 [1879], pp. 289–91).

It is evident from some of his other writings around this time that Jevons was not failing to consider the application of evolutionist ideas to economic questions. In his Inaugural Lecture on 'The Future of Political Economy' in 1876 he had already said that 'the present economical state of society cannot possibly be explained by theory alone. We must take into account the long past out of which we are constantly emerging. Whether we call it sociology or not, we must have some scientific treatment of the principles of evolution as manifested in every branch of social existence' (1905 [1876],

p. 195). Consistently with this, in the 1879 Preface to the second edition of *The Theory of Political Economy*, Jevons declared: 'I hold that *there must arise a science of the development of economic forms and relations*', and among the 'various sciences' into which he forecast that the economics of the future would sub-divide was included 'economic sociology' (1888), pp. xv, xvi).

At this time Jevons had only three more years to live and although he filled them with research and writing, economic sociology was one branch of the subject to which he did not find time to make a contribution. The outline of contents which he had sketched for his *Principles of Economics* included one chapter on 'Progress', but how Jevons might have handled the topic can only be a matter for speculation (1905, p. xxvii). Nevertheless, the evidence exists to show that in his later years Jevons was disposed to blend evolutionism, along the lines indicated by Spencer, with the straightforward Benthamite Utilitarianism which had formed the basis for so much of his economic work. To that extent, Jevons's position was closer to that of Marshall than has been generally recognized, but still there remained important differences between the two.

In terms of sources of ideas, perhaps the most important of these differences lay in the relation of Jevons and Marshall to John Stuart Mill. The important influence of Mill's *Principles* in the formation of Marshall's ideas on value and distribution is well known and has been extensively discussed. On the philosophical side, Mill's restatement of the Benthamite doctrine in *Utilitarianism*, which Jevons found so unacceptable, seems to have been the one which appealed to Marshall as it did to many Cambridge men of his day. Less familiar perhaps is a point made by Shove, that

> in his *Logic* Mill had maintained that the general science of society must be founded on what he called 'ethology'—a science of human character—and in particular 'political ethology'—'the theory of the causes which determine the type of character belonging to a people or an age'. May we not find in this line of thought (which was characteristic of the epoch) a partial explanation of much that distinguishes Marshall's *Principles* from earlier and from later work? (1942, pp. 310–11)

It does indeed seem plausible to suggest that some of Marshall's ideas about the formation of character and its importance to economic progress could be traced back to Mill's conception of ethology, a science 'still to be created' (Mill, 1843, II, p. 527). Yet it seems even more likely that Jevons, who thought Mill's *Logic* 'a maze of self-contradictions' (Black, 1973–81, IV, p. 101) was not influenced even negatively by this conception, to which he made no reference in his articles on 'John Stuart Mill's Philosophy Tested'.

There were other sources too which appear to have influenced Marshall but not Jevons. The German Idealists have already been noticed in this context, but reference should also be made to their English followers, F. H.

Bradley and T. H. Green. These philosophers, as Professor Whitaker has pointed out (1977, p. 194) could not have influenced Marshall's early thought; but Marshall knew Green and his work from his Oxford years, and footnotes in various editions of the *Principles* (1961, I, p. 17; II, pp. 136–7) make clear that he had thoroughly read Green's *Prolegomena to Ethics*, a work in which Green was particularly concerned with how the individual forms his own character. None of this could have been known to Jevons, for Green died in the same year as Jevons, 1882, and his works were not published until after his death.

Jevons and Marshall may then have been more similar than the conventional wisdom suggests as late-Victorian social scientists blending the new evolutionism with the old Utilitarianism in the course of their efforts to reconstruct economic studies; but they used these two ingredients in different forms and at different strengths, while Marshall certainly added others to the blend.

Ultimately, though, the sources of ideas are less important than their uses, and it is in this latter respect that the differences between Jevons and Marshall show most clearly. It was not merely that they brought to their work different equipment in mathematics, in philosophy, even in economics itself; of more importance was the fact that they had differing conceptions of the shape which the reconstructed science would have. The point cannot be more clearly or concisely stated than it was by Shove: 'while Jevons fastened his hopes on a division of labour, a break-up of the science into separate branches or even separate sciences, Marshall's countermeasure was rather by way of a combination of methods—not only history permeated by theory but theory (as in the *Principles*) nourished, modified and illustrated by historical and contemporary fact' (1942, pp. 308–9).

In this respect it may seem that Jevons's approach derives from what Professor Sen has recently called 'the engineering-based origin of economics', while Marshall's comes within 'the ethics-related origin'. (See Sen, 1987, pp. 4–6). There is much that is attractive about using Sen's categories to help to deal with the question here being discussed, but again they prove not to fit the facts of our case quite so comfortably as may at first appear.

Jevons unquestionably did see some branches of economic theory in terms of mechanical analogies (see Jevons, 1888, pp. 102–6) and his method of sub-dividing the science left it open for those who, for example, found his espousal of Bentham's form of Utilitarianism unacceptable, to substitute for it something devoid of hedonist implications, such as a mere ranking of preferences, while leaving other parts of the science or sciences intact.

By comparison to this, Marshall certainly preferred to treat the subject matter of economics as an organism rather than a mechanism, providing material for the biologist rather than the engineer (Marshall, 1898, pp. 40–4). In itself such an approach is not necessarily ethics-related, but although with Marshall it was, it is arguable that the particular view of the relation between ethics and economics which he held contributed towards the tendency for later neo-classical economists to dispense with that relation altogether.

Marshall once spoke of ethics as being the mistress, to whom economics stood in the relation of servant (1893, p. 389). There is some truth in the comment of Clark Kerr that 'as Marshall grew older he became more interested in the "servant" and less in the "mistress"' (1969, p. 4). Marshall, unlike Sidgwick, had lost faith and interest in the development of moral philosophy as a discipline; he saw that economics had far greater possibilities for development in a scientific fashion, because it could set human motives against the measuring rod of money. 'The conception of *measurable* motives—that, and in the end that alone, is what Marshall carried over into economic theory from utilitarian philosophy' (Shove 1942, p. 306).

Yet for Marshall the new economics which he was seeking to develop was to be nothing less than a 'new, authoritative, applied social ethics' (Groenewegen, 1988, p. 628; cf. Skidelsky, 1983, p. 32). Marshall was prepared to argue that 'physical science is seeking her hidden unity in the forces that govern molecular movement; social science is seeking her unity in the forces of human character' (1925 [1897], p. 300). But what Mill had said about the science of human character in 1843 remained true in, and after, Marshall's time: 'Ethology is still to be created' (Mill, 1843, II, p. 527). Hence, as H. Scott Gordon convincingly argues, Marshall's 'line of thought in "biological economics" had led him to a dilemma, to all solutions of which he was temperamentally and philosophically averse,' for he 'was not one to lose hold of the solid methodological achievements of rationalism to follow the siren song of philosophical romanticism' (1982) [1973], p. 264).

VI

Professor John Creedy concludes his study of the work of Marshall's other great neo-classical contemporary, Edgeworth, 'with the thought that economics has generally become more "narrow" in its approach, not so much in a national sense but in terms of the perspective which is brought to the analysis of economic issues'. This is indeed true and if 'the difference between the outlook of the late Victorians and that of more recent generations of economists is brought into sharp focus by reading the work of Edgeworth' (Creedy, 1986, p. 132), that seems to be even more the case with the work of Marshall.

It may be contended that it was Edgeworth's mentor, Jevons, whose vision of the reconstructed science of economics in terms of sub-division and specialization contributed most, and most directly, to the narrowing of the subject. In contrast to this, Marshall's vision of an economic biology using a combination of methods and incorporating a social ethic as an integral feature would seem to have pointed towards making economics a much broader discipline. So indeed it did, but Marshall's reluctance to move outside the firm ground of measurable motives, combined with his characteristic habit of 'using as colourless and irenic terms as were available to express the ethical implications and presuppositions of his economics' (Viner, 1941, p. 230), made it possible for many later economists to disregard the fact that Marshallian economics was intended to be ethics-related.

The distancing of economics not merely from the Utilitarian tradition but from ethics generally which has since come about has resulted also, as Professor Sen has argued, in the impoverishment of both predictive economics and welfare economics (Sen, 1987, p. 57). Marshall, who would have deplored that, would surely have been glad to think that at the centenary of his *Principles* economists would be found turning towards a re-examination of the difficult but important subject of the relations between economics and ethics.

REFERENCES

BLACK, R. D. COLLISON (1970). Introduction to the Pelican Classics edition of Jevons, W. S., *The Theory of Political Economy*, pp. 7–38. Harmondsworth: Penguin.

BLACK, R. D. COLLISON and KOENEKAMP, R. (1972). *Papers and Correspondence of William Stanley Jevons*, Vol. I, Biography and Personal Journal. London: Macmillan in association with the Royal Economic Society.

BLACK, R. D. COLLISON (1972). Jevons, Bentham and De Morgan. *Economica*, 39 (May), pp. 119–34.

BLACK, R. D. COLLISON (1973–81). *Papers and Correspondence of William Stanley Jevons*, Vols II–VII. London: Macmillan in association with the Royal Economic Society.

BLACK, R. D. COLLISON (1988). Bentham and the Political Economists of the Nineteenth Century. *The Bentham Newsletter*, 12 (June), pp. 24–36.

BONAR, J. (1924). *Malthus and his Work*, second edition. London: Allen and Unwin.

BURROW, J. W. (1966). *Evolution and Society*. Cambridge: Cambridge University Press.

CREEDY, J. (1986). *Edgeworth and the development of neoclassical economics*. Oxford: Blackwell.

GORDON, H. S. (1982) [1973]. Alfred Marshall and the Development of Economics as a Science. In Wood, J. C., *Alfred Marshall, Critical Assessments*, Vol. IV, pp. 253–72. London, Croom Helm. Originally published in Giere, R. N. and Westfall, R. S. (eds), *Foundations of Scientific Method in the Nineteenth Century*, pp. 234–58. Indiana, Indiana University Press, 1973.

GROENEWEGEN, P. D. (1988). Alfred Marshall and the establishment of the Cambridge Economics Tripos. *History of Political Economy*, 20, 4 (Winter), pp. 627–68.

HOLLIS, M. and NELL, E. J. (1975). *Rational Economic Man*. Cambridge: Cambridge University Press.

JEVONS, W. S. (1871). *The Theory of Political Economy*, first edition, London, Macmillan.

JEVONS, W. S. (1888). *The Theory of Political Economy*, third edition. London, Macmillan.

JEVONS, W. S. (1890) [1879]. Utilitarianism. In: *Pure Logic and other Minor Works,* ed. Robert Adamson, pp. 268–94. London: Macmillan. Originally published in *The Contemporary Review,* XXXVI (November, 1879), pp. 521–38.

JEVONS, W. S. (1905) [1876]. The Future of Political Economy. In *The Principles of Economics and other papers.* London: Macmillan. First published in *The Fortnightly Review,* 20 (November), pp. 617–31.

KERR, Clark (1969). *Marshall, Marx and Modern Times.* Cambridge: Cambridge University Press.

KEYNES, J. M. (1925). Alfred Marshall 1842–1924. In *Memorials of Alfred Marshall,* ed. A. C. Pigou., pp. 1–65. London: Macmillan.

MARSHALL, Alfred (1893). Meeting of the British Economic Association: The President's Address. Speech on seconding the vote of thanks. *Economic Journal,* 3 (September) pp. 387–90.

MARSHALL, Alfred (1898). Distribution and exchange. *Economic Journal,* 8 (March) pp. 37–59.

MARSHALL, Alfred (1925) [1897]. The old generation of economists and the new. In *Memorials of Alfred Marshall,* ed. A. C. Pigou, pp. 295–311. London: Macmillan. Originally published in *Quarterly Journal of Economics,* January 1897.

MARSHALL, Alfred (1961). *Principles of Economics,* ninth (variorum) edition, ed. C. W. Guillebaud, 2 vols. London: Macmillan for the Royal Economic Society.

MILL, J. S. (1843). *A System of Logic,* 2 vols. London: John W. Parker.

MILLER, W. L. (1972). Herbert Spencer's Theory of Welfare and Public Policy. *History of Political Economy,* 4, 1 (Spring), pp. 207–31.

MITCHELL, W. C. (1969). *Types of Economic Theory,* Vol. II. New York: Augustus M. Kelley.

PARSONS, T. (1931). Wants and Activities in Marshall. *Quarterly Journal of Economics,* 46, pp. 101–40.

RAWLS, J. (1972). *A Theory of Justice.* Oxford: Clarendon Press.

SCHNEEWIND, J. B. (1977). *Sidgwick's Ethics and Victorian Moral Philosophy.* Oxford: Clarendon Press.

SEN, A. K. (1987). *On Ethics and Economics.* Oxford: Blackwell.

SHOVE, G. J. (1942). The Place of Marshall's 'Principles' in the Development of Economic Theory. *Economic Journal,* 52 (December), pp. 294–329.

SIDGWICK, H. (1877). *The Methods of Ethics,* second edition. London: Macmillan.

SKIDELSKY, R. (1983). *John Maynard Keynes,* Vol. I: Hopes Betrayed 1883–1920. London: Macmillan.

VINER, J. (1941). Marshall's economics, in relation to the man and to his times. *American Economic Review,* 31 (June), pp. 223–35.

WARNOCK, M. (1962). Introduction to the Fontana Library edition of Mill, J. S., *Utilitarianism.* London: Collins.

WHITAKER, J. K. (1977). Some neglected aspects of Alfred Marshall's economic and social thought. *History of Political Economy,* 9, 2 (Summer), pp. 161–97.

WICKSTEED, P. H. (1933). Stanley Jevons. In *The Common-Sense of Political Economy, and Selected Papers and Reviews on Economic Theory,* ed. Lionel Robbins, Vol. II, pp. 801–9. London: G. Routledge & Sons.

WINCH, D. (1987). *Malthus.* Oxford: Oxford University Press.

List of publications

1. (1945a), 'Trinity College, Dublin, and the Theory of Value, 1832–1863', *Economica*, **21**(47), 140–8.
2. (1945b), 'A Select Bibliography of Economic Writings by Members of Trinity College, Dublin', *Hermathena*, 66, 55–68.
3. (1947a), 'Economic Studies at Trinity College, Dublin', Part I, *Hermathena*, 70, 65–80.
4. (1947b), *Centenary History of the Statistical and Social Inquiry Society of Ireland 1847–1947*, Dublin: Eason & Son, pp. 160.
5. (1948), 'Economic Studies at Trinity College, Dublin', Part II, *Hermathena*, 71, 52–63.
6. (1950), 'Theory and Policy in Anglo-Irish Trade Relations 1775–1800', *Journal of the Statistical and Social Inquiry Society of Ireland*, **18**, 3–15.
7. (1953), 'The Classical Economists and the Irish Problem', *Oxford Economic Papers*, **5**(1), 26–40.
8. (1954), 'The Progress of Industrialization, 1850–1920' in T.W. Moody and J.C. Beckett (eds), *Ulster since 1800*, London: British Broadcasting Corporation, pp. 50–9.
9. (1960a), 'William Pirrie' in Conor Cruise O'Brien (ed.), *The Shaping of Modern Ireland*, London: Routledge & Kegan Paul Ltd, pp. 174–84.
10. (1960b), *Economic Thought and the Irish Question, 1817–1870*, Cambridge (England): at the University Press, pp. 313. Reprinted 1985, Westport, Conn.: Greenwood Press; 1993, Aldershot: Gregg Revivals.
11. (1960c), 'Jevons and Cairnes', *Economica*, **27**(107), 214–32.
12. (1962), 'W.S. Jevons and the Economists of his Time', *The Manchester School*, **30**(3), 203–22.
13. (1963), 'Economic Fashions'; An Inaugural Lecture delivered before the Queen's University of Belfast on 4 December 1963. Belfast, Queen's University, New Lecture Series, No. 15.
14. (1967), 'Parson Malthus, the General and the Captain', *Economic Journal*, **77**(305), 59–74.
15. (1968a), 'Cairnes, John Elliot', in David L. Sills (ed.), *International Encyclopedia of the Social Sciences*, New York and London, Collier-Macmillan, Vol. II, pp. 257–8.
16. (1968b), 'Economic Policy in Ireland and India in the Time of J.S. Mill', *Economic History Review*, **21**(2), 321–36.
    (Japanese translation by Kazuhiro Ikeda in *Seijo University Economic Papers*, 110 (Dec. 1990), 23–56.)
17. (1969a), *A Catalogue of Pamphlets on Economic Subjects published between 1750 and 1900 and now housed in Irish Libraries*, Belfast: Queen's University; New York: A.M. Kelley, 632 pp.

18. (1969b), 'Adam Smith's Library: A Note on the Volumes at Queen's University, Belfast', *History of Economic Thought Newsletter*, 3, 20–32.
19. (1971a), (ed.) *The Economic Writings of Mountifort Longfield*, with Introduction and Notes. New York, A.M. Kelley, 618 pp.
20. (1971b), (ed.) *The Theory of Political Economy*, by W.S. Jevons. Pelican Classics edition, Harmondsworth: Penguin Books, 272 pp.
21. (1971c), (ed.) *Readings in the Development of Economic Analysis 1776–1848*, Newton Abbot: David & Charles, Ltd; New York: Barnes & Noble, 282 pp. (Paperback edition, 1973).
22. (1971d), 'History of Economic Thought', Chapter 12 in J. Fletcher (ed.), *The Use of Economics Literature*, London: Butterworths, pp. 187–95.
23. (1972a), 'Jevons, Marginalism and Manchester', *The Manchester School*, **40**(1), 1–8.
24. (1972b), 'Jevons, Bentham and De Morgan', *Economica*, **39**(153), 119–34.
25. (1972c), 'The Irish Experience in relation to the Theory and Practice of Economic Development', in A.J. Youngson (ed.), *Economic Development in the Long Run*, London: Allen & Unwin, pp. 192–210.
26. (1972d) (ed. with Rosamond Könekamp), *Papers and Correspondence of William Stanley Jevons*, Volume I, Biography and Personal Journal. London: Macmillan in association with the Royal Economic Society, 282 pp.
27. (1972e), 'W.S. Jevons and the Foundation of Modern Economics', *History of Political Economy*, **4**(2), 364–78.
28. (1973a) (ed. with A.W. Coats and C.D. Goodwin), *The Marginal Revolution in Economics*, Durham, N.C.: Duke University Press, 368 pp.
    Japanese translation by K. Nakamura, *Keizaigaku to Genkai Kakumei* (Tokyo, 1975), 312 pp.
29. (1973b) (ed.), *Papers and Correspondence of William Stanley Jevons*, Volume II, Correspondence 1850–1862. London: Macmillan in association with the Royal Economic Society, 462 pp.
30. (1973c), 'Libero scambio e imperialismo nel pensiero e nella politica economica dei classici inglesi', *Rivista Internazionale di Scienze Economiche e Commerciali*, **20**(7), 640–50.
31. (1973d), 'Emigrazione e colonizzazione', *Rivista Internazionale di Scienze Economiche e Commerciali*, **20**(11), 1071–80.
32. (1976), 'Smith's Contribution in Historical Perspective', in A.S. Skinner and T. Wilson (eds), *The Market and the State*, Oxford: Clarendon Press, pp. 42–63.
    Japanese translation by H. Mizuta in *Keizai Seminar* 1977, 265(2), 63–72 and 266(3), 76–80.
33. (1977a) (ed.), *Papers and Correspondence of William Stanley Jevons*, Volume III, Correspondence 1863–1872. London, Macmillan in association with the Royal Economic Society, 257 pp.
34. (1977b) (ed.), *Papers and Correspondence of William Stanley Jevons*, Volume IV, Correspondence 1873–1878. London, Macmillan in association with the Royal Economic Society, 306 pp.
35. (1977c) (ed.), *Papers and Correspondence of William Stanley Jevons*, Volume

V, Correspondence 1879–1882. London, Macmillan in association with the Royal Economic Society, 202 pp.

36. (1977d) (ed.), *Papers and Correspondence of William Stanley Jevons*, Volume VI, Lectures on Political Economy, 1875–1876. London, Macmillan in association with the Royal Economic Society, 140 pp.

37. (1978), 'Ralph George Hawtrey, 1879–1975', *Proceedings of the British Academy*, **63**, 363–97.

38. (1979), 'The Jevons Papers – a note', *History of Economics Society Bulletin*, **1**(2), 22–4.

39. (1981a), 'W.S. Jevons – Shogai to Shiso' ('The life and work of W.S. Jevons' – translated into Japanese by H. Mizuta: not published in English), *Keizai Seminar*, 315(4), 98–106; 316(5), 92–97.

40. (1981b), 'W.S. Jevons', in D.P. O'Brien and J.R. Presley (eds), *Pioneers of Modern Economics*, London, Macmillan, 1981, pp. 1–35.

41. (1981c) (ed.), *Papers and Correspondence of William Stanley Jevons*, Volume VII, Papers on Political Economy. London, Macmillan in association with the Royal Economic Society, 357 pp.

42. (1982a), 'Political Economy and the Irish', *History of Economics Society Bulletin*, **4**(1), 33–47.

43. (1982b), 'W.S. Jevons's Correspondence with T.E. Jevons', *History of Economic Thought Newsletter*, 29, 1–11.

44. (1982c), 'Adamu Sumisu to Aiarando' ('Adam Smith and Ireland' – translated into Japanese by I. Ueno: not published in English). *Keizai-kenkyu Seijo Daigaku*, **77**, 475–494, and **79**, 71–83.

45. (1982d), 'The Papers and Correspondence of W.S. Jevons: a supplementary note', *The Manchester School*, **50**(4), 417–28.

46. (1983a), 'The Present Position and Prospects of Political Economy', in A.W. Coats (ed.), *Methodological Controversy in Economics: Historical Essays in Honour of T.W. Hutchison*, Greenwich, Conn., JAI Press Inc., 55–70.

47. (1983b), 'The Irish dissenters and nineteenth century political economy', *Hermathena*, 135, 120–37. Also published in A.E. Murphy (ed.), *Economists and the Irish Economy*, Dublin: Irish Academic Press, 120–37.

48. (1984), 'History of Economic Thought' in J. Fletcher (ed.), *Information Sources in Economics*, London: Butterworths, pp. 187–201.

49. (1985a), 'William Stanley Jevons' and 'Thomas Robert Malthus' in A. and J. Kuper (eds), *The Social Sciences Encyclopedia*, London, Routledge, pp. 418 and 481–2.

50. (1985b), 'Theories of Population in Britain and Ireland before Malthus', *Quaderni di storia dell' economia politica*, **4**, 3–19.

51. (1986a), 'Of Quantity and Quality', Presidential Address to the Society. *Journal of the Statistical and Social Inquiry Society of Ireland*, **25**(3), 209–21.

52. (1986b), 'Hawtrey, Ralph George', *in Dictionary of National Biography 1971–1980*, Oxford: Oxford University Press, pp. 391–2.

53. (1986c), 'Dentists and Preachers', Presidential Address to Section F, in R.D. Collison Black (ed.), *Ideas in Economics*, Proceedings of Section F (Economics) of the British Association for the Advancement of Science, Strathclyde, 1985,

London: Macmillan Press, pp. 1–15. Japanese translation by T. Tanaka, *Keizai Shiso to Gendai*, Tokyo: Nihon Keizai Hyoronsha, 1988.

54. (1987a), 'Banfield, Thomas Charles', Vol. I, p. 182.
        'Cairnes, John Elliot', Vol. I, p. 311.
        'Collet, Clara Elizabeth', Vol. I, pp. 481–2.
        'Ingram, John Kells', Vol. II, p. 851.
        'Jenkin, Henry Charles Fleeming', Vol. II, pp. 1007–8.
        'Jennings, Richard', Vol. II, p. 1008.
        'Jevons, William Stanley, Vol. II, pp. 1008–13.
        'Longfield, Mountifort', Vol. III, p. 237.
        'Utility', Vol. IV, pp. 776–9,
        'Whately, Richard', Vol. IV, p. 899.
in John Eatwell, Murray Milgate and Peter Newman (eds) *The New Palgrave: A Dictionary of Economics*, London: Macmillan Press.

55. (1987b), 'Le teorie della popolazione prima di Malthus in Inghilterra e in Irlanda', in G. Gioli (ed.), *Le teorie della popolazione prima di Malthus*, Milan, Franco Angeli, pp. 47–69.
Revised and extended version of (1985b), translated into Italian by G. Gioli.

56. (1988a), 'Comment on Chapter VI, Classical Re-Assessments, by D.P. O'Brien' in W.O. Thweatt (ed.), *Classical Political Economy*, Boston, Kluwer, pp. 221–5.

57. (1988b), 'Measurement, Measures and the Millennium: the Society's activities in the long perspective', *Journal of the Statistical and Social Inquiry Society of Ireland*, **25**(5), 163–84.

58. (1988c), 'Bentham and the Political Economists of the nineteenth century', *The Bentham Newsletter*, 12, 24–36.

59. (1988d), 'Editing the Papers of W.S. Jevons', in D.E. Moggridge (ed.), *Editing Modern Economists*, New York: AMS Press Inc., pp. 19–42.

60. (1989), 'William Stanley Jevons (1835–1882)' in J. Starbatty (ed.), *Klassiker des Oekonomischen Denkens*, Munich: Verlag C.H. Beck, Vol. II, pp. 76–96.

61. (1990a), 'Jevons, Marshall and the Utilitarian Tradition', *Scottish Journal of Political Economy*, **37**(1), 5–17.

62. (1990b), 'W.S. Jevons and the development of marginal utility analysis in British economics', *Schriften des Vereins für Socialpolitik*, Neue Folge Band 115/IX: *Studien zur Entwicklung der ökonomischen Theorie IX*, 9–18.

63. (1992a), 'Dr Kondratieff and Mr Hyde Clarke', *Research in the History of Economic Thought and Methodology*, **9**, 35–58.

64. (1992b), 'Attempts by Jevons and Walras to publicise each other's work', *Revue européenne des sciences sociales*, **30**(92), 109–29.

65. (1993), 'Jevons's contribution to the teaching of political economy in Manchester and London' in A. Kadish and K. Tribe (eds), *The Market for Political Economy; the Advent of Economics in British University Culture, 1850–1905*, London and New York, Routledge, pp. 162–84.

Name index

Ambirajan, S. 106
Artis, M. xxvi
Attwood, T. 98

Babbage, C. 110, 111
Bagehot, W. 64, 65, 68, 69, 74, 181,
  225, 230
Bailey, S. 59
Barkai, H. 77
Barucci, P. xxiv
Baumol, W.J. 37, 80
Bellot, H. 236
Bennett, J.A. 111
Bentham, J. xxx, 22, 26, 73, 188, 192,
  215, 239, 241, 242, 243, 245, 248
Berkeley, G. 242
Best, G. 182–3
Black, D. xiv, xv
Black, R.D.C. xiii, xiv, xv, xvi, xviii,
  xxvi, xxvii, xxviii, 10, 12, 13, 76,
  79, 83, 84, 85, 105, 112, 119, 163,
  167, 168, 169, 170, 171, 172, 174,
  177, 178, 186, 188, 195, 240, 241,
  242, 246, 247
Black, T.R.W. 51
Blackett, B. 141
Blaug, M. 35, 78, 96, 164, 210–11
Böhm-Bawerk, E. von 78, 139
Bonar, J. 239
Bowen, J. xxiii
Bowley, M. 35, 40, 44, 59
Bowman, R.S. 189
Bradbury, J. 134, 135
Bradley, F.H. 248
Brebner, J.B. xvii
Brewer, W.H.B. 233
Brewster, D. 113
Bright, J. 28
Buchanan, N.S. xv
Bunsen, R.W. 222
Burke, E. 76, 82
Burn, W.L. 183, 184
Burrow, J.W. 240
Butt, I. 12, 26, 35, 46, 48

Cairnes, J.E. xix, xx, 8, 9, 12, 64, 73,
  164, 167, 168, 184, 230, 236
Campbell, G. 22–3, 25

Cannan, E. 70, 71, 80, 84, 172
Canning, Lord 24
Carlyle, T. xvii
Carter, C.F. xx
Cassel, G. xii
Chalmers, T. 96
Chamberlain, A. 143
Chamberlain, J. 133
Charlton, H.B. 230
Christie, R.C. 229
Churchill, W. 145
Clarke, H. xxx, 103, 104–5, 106–7, 108,
  109, 110, 111, 112, 114, 115, 116,
  117, 118, 119, 120, 121
Coats, A.W. xxiii, 108
Cole, A.H. xvii
Comte, A. 13
Corry, B. 86
Cotton, A. 30
Courtney, L. 236
Creedy, J. 197, 249

Dalhousie, Lord 28, 30
Darwin, C. xx, 190, 245
Davis, E.G. 138
Davis, T. 13
Davitt, M. 11, 14
Dennison, S. xxi
Descartes, R. 242
Dicey, A.V. 183
Dickinson, L. 154, 156
Dobb, M.H. 38, 39, 40, 46
Domar, E.D. 91
Dorfman, J. xvii
Douglas, P.H. 70, 71, 85
Drummond, T. 29
Dubbey, J.M. 111
Duijn, J.J. van 103, 121
Duncan, G.A. xii, xiii
Dupuit, J. 109

Eagly, R.V. 204
Edgeworth, F.Y. 165, 236, 249
Edwards, R.D. 4
Ekelund, R.B. 109, 185
Ellett, C. 109
Engels, F. 6, 8, 10, 11

Economists of the Twentieth Century

Monetarism and Macroeconomic Policy
Thomas Mayer

Studies in Fiscal Federalism
Wallace E. Oates

The World Economy in Perspective
Essays in International Trade and European Integration
Herbert Giersch

Towards a New Economics
Critical Essays on Ecology, Distribution and Other Themes
Kenneth E. Boulding

Studies in Positive and Normative Economics
Martin J. Bailey

The Collected Essays of Richard E. Quandt (2 volumes)
Richard E. Quandt

International Trade Theory and Policy
Selected Essays of W. Max Corden
W. Max Corden

Organization and Technology in Capitalist Development
William Lazonick

Studies in Human Capital
Collected Essays of Jacob Mincer, Volume 1
Jacob Mincer

Studies in Labor Supply
Collected Essays of Jacob Mincer, Volume 2
Jacob Mincer

Macroeconomics and Economic Policy
The Selected Essays of Assar Lindbeck, Volume I
Assar Lindbeck

The Welfare State
The Selected Essays of Assar Lindbeck, Volume II
Assar Lindbeck

Classical Economics, Public Expenditure and Growth
Walter Eltis

Money, Interest Rates and Inflation
Frederic S. Mishkin

The Public Choice Approach to Politics
Dennis C. Mueller

The Liberal Economic Order
Volume I   Essays on International Economics
Volume II Money, Cycles and Related Themes
Gottfried Haberler
Edited by Anthony Y.C. Koo

Economic Growth and Business Cycles
Prices and the Process of Cyclical Development
Paolo Sylos Labini

International Adjustment, Money and Trade
Theory and Measurement for Economic Policy, Volume I
Herbert G. Grubel

International Capital and Service Flows
Theory and Measurement for Economic Policy, Volume II
Herbert G. Grubel

Unintended Effects of Government Policies
Theory and Measurement for Economic Policy, Volume III
Herbert G. Grubel

The Economics of Competitive Enterprise
Selected Essays of P.W.S. Andrews
Edited by Frederic S. Lee and Peter E. Earl

The Repressed Economy
Causes, Consequences, Reform
Deepak Lal

Economic Theory and Market Socialism
Selected Essays of Oskar Lange
Edited by Tadeusz Kowalik

Trade, Development and Political Economy
Selected Essays of Ronald Findlay
Ronald Findlay

General Equilibrium Theory
The Collected Essays of Takashi Negishi, Volume I
Takashi Negishi

The History of Economics
The Collected Essays of Takashi Negishi, Volume II
Takashi Negishi

Studies in Econometric Theory
The Collected Essays of Takeshi Amemiya
Takeshi Amemiya

Exchange Rates and the Monetary System
Selected Essays of Peter B. Kenen
Peter B. Kenen

Econometric Methods and Applications (2 volumes)
G.S. Maddala

National Accounting and Economic Theory
The Collected Papers of Dan Usher, Volume I
Dan Usher

Welfare Economics and Public Finance
The Collected Papers of Dan Usher, Volume II
Dan Usher

Economic Theory and Capitalist Society
The Selected Essays of Shigeto Tsuru, Volume I
Shigeto Tsuru

Methodology, Money and the Firm
The Collected Essays of D.P. O'Brien (2 volumes)
D.P. O'Brien

Economic Theory and Financial Policy
The Selected Essays of Jacques J. Polak (2 volumes)
Jacques J. Polak

Sturdy Econometrics
Edward E. Leamer

The Emergence of Economic Ideas
Essays in the History of Economics
Nathan Rosenberg

Productivity Change, Public Goods and Transaction Costs
Essays at the Boundaries of Microeconomics
Yoram Barzel

Reflections on Economic Development
The Selected Essays of Michael P. Todaro
Michael P. Todaro

The Economic Development of Modern Japan
The Selected Essays of Shigeto Tsuru, Volume II
Shigeto Tsuru

Money, Credit and Policy
Allan H. Meltzer

Macroeconomics and Monetary Theory
The Selected Essays of Meghnad Desai, Volume I
Meghnad Desai

Poverty, Famine and Economic Development
The Selected Essays of Meghnad Desai, Volume II
Meghnad Desai

Explaining the Economic Performance of Nations
Essays in Time and Space
Angus Maddison

Economic Doctrine and Method
Selected Papers of R.W. Clower
Robert W. Clower

Economic Theory and Reality
Selected Essays on their Disparity and Reconciliation
Tibor Scitovsky

Doing Economic Research
Essays on the Applied Methodology of Economics
Thomas Mayer

Institutions and Development Strategies
The Selected Essays of Irma Adelman, Volume I
Irma Adelman

Dynamics and Income Distribution
The Selected Essays of Irma Adelman, Volume II
Irma Adelman

The Economics of Growth and Development
Selected Essays of A.P. Thirlwall
A.P. Thirlwall

Theoretical and Applied Econometrics
The Selected Papers of Phoebus J. Dhrymes
Phoebus J. Dhrymes

Innovation, Technology and the Economy
The Selected Essays of Edwin Mansfield (2 volumes)
Edwin Mansfield

Economic Theory and Policy in Context
The Selected Essays of R.D. Collison Black
R.D. Collison Black

Location Economics
Theoretical Underpinnings and Applications
Melvin L. Greenhut

Spatial Microeconomics
Theoretical Underpinnings and Applications
Melvin L. Greenhut

Capitalism, Socialism and Post-Keynesianism
Selected Essays of G.C. Harcourt
G.C. Harcourt

Time Series Analysis and Macroeconometric Modelling
The Collected Papers of Kenneth F. Wallis
Kenneth F. Wallis

Foundations of Modern Econometrics
The Selected Essays of Ragnar Frisch (2 volumes)
Olav Bjerkholt

Growth, the Environment and the Distribution of Incomes
Essays by a Sceptical Optimist
Wilfred Beckerman